The Thought Adjusters
The Presence of God Within

The Thought Adjusters - The Presence of God Within

by Dr. Roger W. Paul

© 2025 Dr. Roger W. Paul. Dacula, Georgia USA, All rights reserved

Library of Congress Cataloging, in, Publication Data

Paul, Dr. Roger W.

Library of Congress Number:

ISBN: 979-8-9935479-8-5

Publisher Name is Dr. Roger W. Paul
Publisher Number For Title Management is: 2274327

Table of Contents

Thought Adjusters - The Presence of God Within 0

Forward 26
The Journey Within: Discovering God's Personal Presence 26
Why This Study Matters 26
The Source and Nature of This Material 27
Structure and Approach 27
Who Should Read This Book 28
A Word of Encouragement 29
The Practical Promise 30
Looking Ahead 30

Chapter 1: The Origin and Nature of Thought Adjusters 32
Introduction: The Divine Presence Within 32
The Universal Father's Dual Presence 32
The Essence of the Thought Adjuster 33
Divine Essence and Origin 33
The Divine Gift and Promise 33
The Imprisoned Fragment 34
Experiential Partnership with Deity 34
Mutual Experience 34
Consciousness of the Divine Presence 34
The Promise of Eternal Union 35
The Evolutionary Soul 35
The Three Stages of Adjuster Ministry 36
Thought Changers (Pre-Adult Years) 36
Thought Adjusters (Middle Years) 36
Thought Controllers (Mature Years) 36
The Mystery of Adjuster Origin 37
The Unfragmented Source 37
The Question of Number 38
Divinington: The Sacred Sphere 38

- The Classification of Adjusters 38
  - Virgin Adjusters 38
  - Experienced Adjusters 39
  - Advanced and Supreme Adjusters 39
- The Triune Destiny 39
- Spirit Fusion: An Alternative Path 40
- The Compensatory Equalization 40
- The Infallible Cosmic Compass 41
- Implications for Daily Living 41
  - The Sanctity of the Individual 41
  - The Nature of Prayer and Worship 42
  - Moral Decision-Making 42
  - The Purpose of Suffering 42
- Conclusion: The Foundation for Eternal Destiny 42

Chapter 2: Classification of Thought Adjusters 44
- Introduction 44
- The Three Destinies of Thought Adjusters 44
- The Seven Orders of Thought Adjusters 45
  - 1. Virgin Adjusters 45
  - 2. Advanced Adjusters 46
  - 3. Supreme Adjusters 47
  - 4. Vanished Adjusters 48
  - 5. Liberated Adjusters 49
  - 6. Fused Adjusters 50
  - 7. Personalized Adjusters 53
- The Unity of Divine Nature and Experiential Diversity 56
- Spiritual Implications for Ascending Mortals 56
- Conclusion: The Progressive Education of Divinity 57
- Introduction 59
- The Classification and Purpose of Thought Adjusters 59
  - Personalized Adjusters: A Unique Status 59

Divinington: The Sacred Home of the Adjusters 60
The Mystery of Divinington 60
The Divine Injunctions 61
Unrevealed Pre-Personal Entities 61
The Training of Thought Adjusters 62
The Paradox of Perfect Beings Receiving Training 62
The Necessity of Experiential Training 62
The Divine Nature of Thought Adjusters 63
Fragmented Divinity 63
Qualified Absolute Fragments 64
The Infallibility of Thought Adjusters 64
The Impossibility of Rebellion After Fusion 65
The Walking Dead 65
The Perception of Thought Adjusters 66
The Spirit Luminosity 66
Fear and the Hidden Light 66
The Significance of Adjuster Indwelling 67
The Eternal Revelation 67
God Consciousness: The Key Teaching of Jesus 68
The Search for God 68
The Balance of Spiritual Life 69
The Growing Light 69
The Return to Divinington 70
Conclusion: The Unlimited Partnership 71

Chapter 4: The Mindedness of Thought Adjusters 73
Understanding Divine Consciousness and the Absolute Level of Reality 73
Introduction 73
Section 1: The Challenge of Understanding Adjuster Mindedness 73
The Human Tendency Toward Mediation 73
The Absolute Level of Reality 74
Before Energy and Spirit Divergence 74

Section 2: The Experiential Mind of the Thought Adjuster 75
The Development of Adjuster Consciousness 75
Virgin and Non-Virgin Adjusters 75
The Communication Capacity of Adjusters 76
Section 3: The Nature of Adjuster Mindedness - Ancestral to the Conjoint Actor 76
The Trinity Pattern in Mind 77
Section 4: The Practical Implications of Adjuster Mindedness 77
The Independence of Adjuster Consciousness 77
The Question of Free Will and Divine Guidance 78
Virgin Adjusters and Human Evolution 78
The Communication of Revelation 79
Section 5: The Supreme Being and Experiential Deity 80
God's Creation of Experiential Divinity 80
The Purpose of Experiential Growth 80
Our Role in Supreme Growth 81
Conclusion: The Mystery and the Promise 81

Chapter 5: The Nature and Ministry of Thought Adjusters 83
Introduction: Understanding Divine Indwelling 83
The Universal Scope of Divine Fragments - Pre-Personal Entities and Adjuster Ministry 83
The Mystery of Mind Types 84
The Divine Partnership: Human and Adjuster - The Nature of Dual Minds 85
Contributing to the Supreme Being 85
The Essential Nature of Adjusters - Pure Spirit and Pure Spirit-Plus 86
The Implications of Pure Energy 87
Adjusters as Prisoners of Hope - The Divine Confinement 88
The Goal of Liberation 88
The Circuit of Divine Connection - Encircuited in Reality 89
The Reality of Spiritual Life 89
The Cosmic Scale of Adjuster Ministry - Beyond the Grand Universe 90
The Future of Finaliter Service 91

The Partnership Nature of Ascension - God-Knowing Mortals and God-Revealing Adjusters 92
The Stages of Spiritual Progress 92
Conclusion: The Living Reality of Divine Indwelling 93

Chapter 6: The Divine Gift Within - Understanding Thought Adjusters and Universal Reality 95
Introduction 95
The Antecedent Nature of Thought Adjusters - Beyond Material Gravity Circuits 95
The Nature of Divine Energy 96
The Imprisonment and Liberation of Divine Fragments 97
The Mystery of Pre-Personal Volition - The Paradox of Will Without Personality 98
The Distinction Between Divine and Human Will 99
The Selection Process 100
The Partnership of Human and Divine Will - The Supremacy of Mortal Choice 101
The Adjuster's Working Method 102
The Question of Partnership 103
The Reality of Spiritual Transformation - The Process of Fusion 104
The Journey After Fusion 105
The Continuity of Identity 106
The Universal Presence of Deity - The Fragments of God 107
The Cosmic Significance of Individual Souls 108
The Universality of Divine Ministry 109

Chapter 7: The Mission and Ministry of Thought Adjusters 112
Introduction 112
The Fundamental Mission of Thought Adjusters - Representing the Universal Father 112
Preparing the Soul for Paradise 113
A Unique Universal Technique 113
The Existential God and Experiential Reality - Understanding Existential Being 113
The Need for Experiential Reality 114
The Role of the Supreme Being 114

Election and Assignment of Thought Adjusters - Initial Equality and Experiential Diversity 115

    The Basis of Assignment 115

    The Volunteer Process 116

    Gender Neutrality in Assignment 116

The Commencement of Human Life - Life Begins at Conception 116

    Personality at Conception 117

    Birth and Separate Human Status 117

    The Arrival of the Thought Adjuster 118

The Seven Psychic Circles of Spiritual Attainment - Understanding the Circles 118

    Guardian Angel Assignment by Circle Level 118

    The Critical Third Circle 119

    Indicators of Third Circle Attainment 120

    Pre-Pentecost and Post-Pentecost Differences 120

    The Sleeping Survivors 121

The Emergence of Eternal Life - The Crucial Distinction 121

    Fusion: The Gateway to Eternity 121

    The Existential Transformation 122

    Memory and Identity Preservation 122

Practical Implications for Daily Living - Recognizing the Divine Within 122

    Making Moral Decisions 123

    The Practice of Stillness 123

    Responding to Divine Leading 123

    Building the Morontia Soul 124

Conclusion: The Partnership of Eternity 124

Chapter 8: The Divine Partnership - How Thought Adjusters Choose and Prepare Their Human Subjects 126

Introduction 126

The Comprehensive Nature of Spiritual Growth 126

    Foundational Principles of Spiritual Growth 127

    The Dynamic Nature of Spiritual Development 128

- The Apostles' Remarkable Growth 129
- Indicators of Genuine Spiritual Progress 129
- The Partnership Principle 130
- The Three Essential Qualifications 131
  - First Qualification: Intellectual Capacity 131
  - Second Qualification: Spiritual Perception 132
  - Third Qualification: Combined Intellectual and Spiritual Powers 133
  - The Significance of Gender Neutrality 134
  - The Volunteer Selection Process 135
- The Preparation Process: From Divinington to Human Mind 135
  - The Schools of Divinington 135
  - The Journey to Urantia 136
  - Prerequisites for Adjuster Indwelling 137
  - The First Moral Decision 139
  - The Significance of Early Life 139
- The Direct Relationship: God and Man 140
- Conclusion: The Cosmic Value of Individual Personality 141

Chapter 9: The Mission and Ministry of Thought Adjusters 144
- Part Three: Divine Presence in an Isolated World 144
  - Introduction 144
- The Arrival of Thought Adjusters Before the Spirit of Truth - The Historical Context 144
  - Six Factors Influencing Early Adjuster Arrival - 1. The Assignment of Personal Seraphic Guardians 145
- Organization and Administration of Thought Adjusters - Universal Scope and Unified Purpose 151
  - Serial Organization and Mysterious Tracking 151
  - Implications for Universal Mortal Population 152
- Records, Reports, and Cosmic Communication - The Reporting System 153
  - Human Identification and Universal Names 153
- Tabamantia's Tribute: Recognition of Adjuster Excellence - The Sovereign Inspector's Visit 154

- The Content of the Tribute 154
- Implications for Our Understanding 157

The Relationship Between Adjusters and Other Spiritual Influences - Independent Yet Coordinate Ministry 158
- Specialized Functions Within Unified Purpose 159
- The Unique Contribution of Thought Adjusters 160

Communication During Planetary Isolation - The Paradox of Quarantine 161
- Why Adjusters Remain Unaffected by Isolation 162
- Practical Implications of Unbroken Connection - Practical Implications of Uninterrupted Adjuster Ministry 162
- The Metaphor of Deep-Sea Diving 165
- Why Lucifer and Caligastia Lacked This Connection 165
- The Continuing Ministry to a Quarantined World 166

The Supreme Mystery: Divine Presence in Mortal Mind - Acknowledging the Limits of Understanding 166
- The Father's Reserved Right 167

The Eternal Significance of Adjuster Ministry - Beyond Temporal Circumstances 168
- The Mystery of Divine Indwelling 168
- Practical Application: Living with Divine Indwelling 169
- The Ultimate Purpose 170
- Coordinating with the Creator Sons' Drawing Power 171

Living with Divine Presence - Integration and Application 171
- The Path Forward 172

Conclusion: Advancing Toward Fusion 173
- Transition to the Next Chapter 174

Chapter 10: The Adjusters' Mission - Understanding Divine Indwelling 175
Introduction 175
The Diversity of Divine Fragments 175
- Personalized Monitors 175
- The Gravity Messengers and Mystery Monitors 176

The Nature of the Adjuster's Mission - Receiving and Translating Spiritual Messages 176

- Faithful Preservation Across the Circles 177
- The Psychic Circles and Spiritual Ascension 177
- What the Adjuster Is Not 178
  - Not Thought Helpers But Thought Adjusters 178
  - Not Providers of Selfish Consolation 178
  - Not Mechanical Operators 179
- Overcoming the Fetters of Fear 179
  - Fear of God Versus Love of God 179
  - The Friendly Universe 180
- The Adjuster in Moral Conflicts 180
- The Perfection of Adjuster Ministry - Angels May Err, But Adjusters Never Fail 180
  - The Guarantee of Perfection 181
- The Divine Condescension 181
  - The Probationary Nature of Mortal Existence 182
- The Adjuster's Torment 182
  - The Reality of Adjuster Suffering 182
  - The Contrast of Righteous Living 183
- The Destiny of Soul and Mind 183
  - The Preservation of Identity 183
  - When Fusion Occurs 184
  - The Fate of Non-Survivors 184
- Practical Implications for Daily Living 184
  - Worship as the Path to Fusion 184
  - Embracing Difficulty as Opportunity 185
  - Supplying the Psychic Fulcrum 185
- Conclusion 185

Chapter 11: The Relation of Thought Adjusters to Universe Creatures 187
- Introduction 187
- The Developmental Career of Thought Adjusters - The Training of Virgin Adjusters ... 187
  - The Retraining Process 188
  - The Nature of Experiential Growth 189

    The Process of Adjuster Development - The First Stage: Achieving Fusion 190

        Progressive Skill Acquisition 190

    The Classification of Self-Acting Adjusters - Defining Characteristics 191

        Prerequisites for Self-Acting Status - Prior Indwelling Experience 191

    The Capabilities of Self-Acting Adjusters - Autonomous Function 195

        Inter-Adjuster Communication 195

        Physical Independence 196

        The Ultimate Achievement 196

    The Significance for Mortal Destiny - The Mutual Partnership 197

        The Progressive Revelation 197

        The Assurance of Divine Investment 198

    Conclusion 198

Chapter 12: The Relation of Adjusters to Mortal Types 200

    Introduction 200

    The Uniformity of Adjuster Ministry 200

        Liaison Adjusters: Temporary Divine Companionship 201

    The Three Primary Classifications of Adjuster Service - Series One: Primitive Worlds and Virgin Adjusters 202

        The Nature of Primitive Humanity 203

        The Development of Worship and Wisdom 203

        Fusion Adjusters: The Partnership of Eternity 204

        The Role of Language in Spiritual Development 204

    Series Two: Worlds of Liaison Adjusters - Worlds of Non-Fusion Mortals 205

    Series Three: Urantia and the Betrothal Engagement 205

        The Significance of Betrothal 206

    The Impact of Bestowal Sons 206

        The Gift of Personality 207

        Post-Bestowal Changes 207

    The Evolutionary History of Urantia - Three Classes of Early Beings 207

    The Influence of Experienced Adjusters 208

        The Importance of Communication 209

    The Historical Transition 209

  The Role of Inheritance and Environment - Genetic Limitations 210

  The Mansion World Revelation 211

    The Universal Lesson 211

  Survival and Faith: The Essential Requirement 212

    The Universal Nature of Survival 212

    The Role of Children and the Mentally Impaired 212

    The Influence of Experienced Adjusters 213

  Universal Principles and Local Application - The Consistency of Adjuster Ministry ... 213

  The Cosmic Economy of the Ascension Plan 213

  The Brotherhood of Man and Social Progress 214

    Nothing of Value Is Ever Lost 214

  Conclusion 215

Chapter 13: The Persistence of Divine Values and the Triumph of Consecrated Will 217

  Introduction 217

  The Influence of Experienced Adjusters on Planetary Leadership 217

  The Cooperative Work of Adjusters in Civilizational Advancement 218

  Planetary Cross-Fertilization and Adjuster Experience 219

  Material Handicaps and Adjuster Ministry 220

  Hereditary Limitations and Spiritual Achievement 221

  The Persistence of True Values 222

  The Adjusters of Bestowal Sons 223

  The Triumph of Consecrated Will 224

  Conclusion 225

Chapter 14: The Destiny of Personalized Thought Adjusters 227

  Introduction 227

  The Heritage of Michael's Personalized Adjuster - A Legacy Spanning Millennia 227

    The Triumph of Divine-Human Partnership 228

    The Nature of Preserved Experience 229

  The Mechanism of Value Preservation - The Eternal Repository 229

    The Preservation Trinity 230

- The Nature of Personalized Adjusters - The Question of Personalizability 230
  - The Categories of Personalization 231
  - The Characteristics of Omnipersonality 232
- The Ministry of Personalized Adjusters - Administrators of Cosmic Purpose 233
  - Executives of the Architects 233
  - The Reserved Bestowal Type 234
- Personalized Adjusters in Universe Service - Rare Appearances and High Counsel 235
  - Emergency Service on Urantia 235
  - The Breadth of Ministry 236
- The Implications for Mortal Destiny - The True Passport to Divinity 237
  - The Preservation of Individual Achievement 237
  - The Unique Path of Each Mortal 238
- Conclusion: The Eternal Significance of Temporal Choices 238
- Introduction 240
- The Divine Cost of Free Will 240
- The Unique Nature of Divine Love 241
  - The Distinction Between Father and Mother Influences 241
- The Mind as the Dwelling Place of God - Beyond the Physical Brain 242
  - Communication Through the Superconscious 242
  - When the Mind is Damaged 243
- The Spiritual Work of the Thought Adjuster - The True Mission 244
  - Spiritual Significance in Daily Life 245
  - The Importance of Temporal Welfare 245
  - Mental Poisons 246
- The Courtship Period and Divine Predestination - A Divine Romance 247
  - The Divine Plan 247
  - Freedom to Accept or Reject 248
- Living in Partnership with the Divine, and Discovering Your Calling 248
  - Practical Cooperation 249
- The Vestibule of Eternal Life, This Life as Beginning 250
  - Building the Morontia Soul 250

    Your Real Life Begins 251

    Conclusion: The Divine Romance Continues 251

Chapter 16: Adjusters and the Human Will - The Divine Partnership 253

    Introduction: The Sacred Relationship Between Humanity and Divinity 253

    The Nature of Predestination and Free Will 253

    The Three Dimensions of Reality 254

    The Arrival and Purpose of the Thought Adjuster 255

    The Two Minds and the Superconscious 256

    The Mechanics of Divine-Human Cooperation 257

    The Morontia Mind and Spiritual Identity 258

    Practical Application: Discerning God's Will 259

    The Secret of Survival 261

    When Adjusters Succeed or Fail 262

    The Meaning of Life: A Summary 263

    Conclusion: The Divine Partnership 263

Chapter 17: Universal Circuits and Divine Communication 265

    Introduction 265

    The Nature of Spiritual Resistance and Survival - Understanding Confusion and Doubt
.... 265

        The Assurance of Survival 266

    Four Principles of Effective Cooperation, The Nature of Adjuster Communication 266

        The Four Pillars of Divine Cooperation 267

        The Teachings of Jesus 269

    The Superuniverse Circuits, The Nature of Cosmic Communication 270

        The Seven Master Circuits 270

        The Significance of Universal Connection 273

    The Local Universe Circuits - The Three Primary Local Circuits 273

        The Intelligence Ministry and Personal Records 274

        The Transition Beyond Local Universe Circuits 275

    The Universal Circuits of Paradise, The Foundation of All Reality 275

        The Pervasiveness of Paradise Circuits 276

    The Unity of All Circuit Systems 277

  The Challenge of Mortal Communication, The Difficulty of Adjuster Contact 277

    The Role of Subconscious Mental Activity 278

    The Superconscious Realm 278

    The Obstacles to Clear Communication 279

    The Danger of Misinterpretation 279

  The Crisis of Self-Acting Adjusters - A Disturbing Trend 280

    The Role of Self-Acting Adjusters in Revelation 281

    Proposed Solutions 281

  The Value of Struggle and Tribulation, The Necessity of Difficulty 282

    The Example of the Bestowal Sons 282

    The Value of Struggle in Universe Service 283

    The Spiritual Danger of Ease 283

  Conclusion 284

Chapter 18: Erroneous Concepts of Adjuster Guidance and the Seven Psychic Circles .. 286

  Introduction 286

  The Fundamental Distinction: Conscience Versus Divine Guidance, The Nature of
Human Conscience 286

    The Adjuster's True Function 287

    The Danger of Misattribution 287

  The Mystery of Dreams and Unconscious Sleep, The Incoherence of Dream Life 288

    When Dreams Do Carry Meaning 289

    The Adjuster's Work During Sleep 289

    The Problem of Interference 290

  Discernment and Individual Responsibility - The Challenge of Differentiation 290

    The Principle of Cautious Humility 291

    The Superconscious Reality 291

  The Seven Psychic Circles: The Framework of Spiritual Progress, Introduction to the
Circles 292

    The Seventh Circle: Beginning the Journey 292

    Progression Through the Circles 293

The Third Circle: A Critical Milestone 293
The First Circle: Relative Maturity 294
The Rare Case of Earthly Fusion 295
Balanced Development: The Danger of Imbalanced Growth, The Key to Circle Advancement 295
The Ideal of Triune Harmony 296
Practical Implications 297
The Adjuster and Circle Progression - The Adjuster's Independent Development 297
Personality Status and Soul Growth 298
The Whole Self Development 298
The Contact Personality: A Rare Case Study - An Example of Balanced Receptivity .. 299
The Virtue of Passive Cooperation 299
Implications for Receptivity 300
Practical Wisdom for the Spiritual Journey, Cultivating Realistic Expectations 300
The Role of Age and Experience 301
The Gift of Uncertainty 302
Conclusion: The Supreme Adventure 302

Chapter 19: The Seven Psychic Circles - Understanding Spiritual Attainment 304
Introduction: The Architecture of Spiritual Growth 304
The Nature of Divine Communication 304
The Power of Decision: Forging Spiritual Habits 305
Defining the Seven Circles: Framework and Limitations 306
1. Adjuster Attunement 306
2. Soul Evolution 306
3. Personality Reality 306
The Seventh Circle: Entrance into Potential Citizenship 307
The Third Circle: The Betrothal Stage 308
The First Circle: The Threshold of Direct Communication 309
The Morontia Soul: Beginning the Next Existence Now 309
Resurrection: Immediate or Dispensational 310
Practical Application: Living as Citizens of Two Worlds 311

    The Reality of Spiritual Support 312

    Conclusion: The Journey Continues 313

Chapter 20: The Psychic Circles of Mortal Progression 314

    Understanding Our Cosmic Journey Through the Seven Circles 314

    The Nature of the Circles: Quantity and Quality 314

    The Seven Circles: A Map of Spiritual Development 315

    The Blessing of Material Existence 317

    Common Questions About Circle Attainment 317

    The Role of the Thought Adjuster 319

    From Material to Morontia: The Great Transition 320

    The Supreme Being and Our Experience 320

    Practical Application: Living the Circles 321

    Looking Ahead 322

Chapter 21: The Seven Cosmic Circles and the Path to Adjuster Fusion 323

    Understanding Spiritual Progress in Mortal Life 323

    The Seven Cosmic Circles: From Animal to Morontia 323

        Mastery of the First Circle 324

    The Adjuster's Journey: From Ministry to Partnership 324

    The Mystery of Immortality and Fusion 325

    When Fusion Happens in the Flesh 326

    After Fusion: Becoming One 327

    The Challenge of Communication 328

    Hearing the Adjuster's Voice 330

    A Message from the Adjuster 330

    Conclusion: The Journey Continues 332

Chapter 22: The Adjuster and the Soul 334

    Introduction: The Divine Partnership Within 334

    The Historical Quest for Understanding 334

        Eastern Perspectives: The Atman and the Dual Nature 335

        Egyptian Wisdom: The Ka and the Ba 335

        Universal Intuitions Across Cultures 336

- The Mind: Arena of Choice 337
  - The Seven Mind-Spirits and Spiritual Development 337
  - The Material Foundation of Spiritual Growth 338
    - The Temporal Nature of Mortal Mind 339
    - Protecting the Temple of Consciousness 339
    - The Daily Practice of Spiritual Identification 340
  - The Integration of Science and Spirit 341
  - Conclusion: The Daily Path of Spiritual Growth 341
- **Chapter 23: The Nature of the Immortal Soul** 343
  - Understanding the Divine Partnership Within 343
  - The Sacred Partnership: Mind as the Captain's Ship 343
  - The Cosmic Loom: Weaving Eternal Fabric 344
  - The Three Essential Factors of Soul Creation 345
  - The Mid-Mind: Understanding Morontia Development 347
  - Laying Up Treasures in Heaven 348
  - The Supremacy of Human Will 350
  - The Transcendence of Temporal Limitations 351
  - The Cosmic Mind and Universal Unity 352
  - Making Choices That Echo Through Eternity 352
  - The Promise of Eternal Survival 353
  - Conclusion: The Beginning of Forever 354
- **Chapter 24: The Evolving Soul and the Divine Partnership** 356
  - Introduction: The Mystery of Soul Development 356
  - The Foundation: When Soul Development Begins 356
  - The Role of Human Will: Our Essential Contribution 357
  - The Soul's Unique Nature: Between Two Worlds 358
  - Meanings and Values: Two Pathways to God 359
  - The Mansion World Awakening: Becoming Your Soul 360
  - The Practical Question: What Survives? 361
  - The Role of Decisions: Building Eternity Day by Day 362
  - A Word of Caution: The Tension That Leads to Fusion 362

    Conclusion: The Embryo and the Butterfly 363

Chapter 25: The Inner Life - Recognition, Understanding, and the Soul's Creative Foundation 365

    Introduction: The Architecture of Spiritual Reality 365

    Recognition and Understanding: The Foundation of Experience 365

    The Problem of Material Reality 366

    The Morontia Mota: Where Material Meets Spirit 367

    Jesus and the Personalized Adjuster: A Profound Mystery 368

    The Soul as Spiritual Counterpart 369

    The Tragedy of Soul-less Survival 370

    The Creative Inner Life 371

    Uniqueness: The Cosmic Principle of Personality 372

    Happiness, Joy, and the Social Nature of Reality 373

    The Civilization Crisis: Youth and Material Values 374

    Controlling the Inner World 375

    The Stage of Consciousness 376

    The Mystery of Jesus' Soul and Future Role 377

    Practical Application: Living from the Inner Life 379

    Conclusion: The Inner Life and Eternal Adventure 380

Chapter 26: The Adjuster and the Soul - Ideas, Ideals, and the Human Paradox 382

    Introduction: The Inner World and Outer Reality 382

    Free Will: The Double-Edged Gift 383

    Inner Creativity and the Nobility of Character 384

    The Consecration of Choice 385

    The Human Paradox 387

    Sin, Evil, and the Misuse of the Finite 389

    Mind, Energy, and the Limits of Material Control 390

    Science, Facts, and the Foundation of Wisdom 391

    Conclusion: The Choice Before Us 392

Chapter 27: Personality Survival and the Divine Pattern 395

    Introduction 395

The Starting Point of Eternity 395
The Nature of Personality: Fifteen Defining Characteristics 396
    1. The Source of Personality 396
    2. Bestowal Upon Living Energy Systems 396
    3. Freedom from Antecedent Causation 397
    4. Spirit's Mastery Over Matter 397
    5. Unifying Identity 398
    6. Qualitative Response 398
    7. Changelessness 398
    8. The Only Gift to God 399
    9. Moral Consciousness 399
    10. Absolute Uniqueness 399
    11. Direct Response to Other Personalities 400
    12. The Primacy of the Father 401
    13. Survival Through the Soul 401
    14. Unique Consciousness of Time 401
    15. Summary: Personality as Unifying Gift 402
The Pattern: Human and Supreme 402
The Critical Role of Volition 403
The Path to Recognition 405
The Implications for Now 406
Conclusion: The Choice Before Us 406

Chapter 28: Personality and Survival - The Cosmic Dimensions of Identity 408
Introduction 408
The Foundation: What Is Personality? 409
Three Cosmic Planes of Function 410
The Critical Importance of the Supreme 411
Three Dimensions: Length, Depth, and Breadth 412
Seven Dimensions of Potential 414
Cosmic Reality and Unchallengeable Consciousness 415
The Morontia Enhancement 416

- Why We Struggle to Understand 417
- Life as Process 418
- The Uniqueness Problem 419
- Evolution and Environment 420
- The Attitude of the Whole Personality 421
- Looking Ahead 422

Chapter 29: Personality Survival - The Unity of Self and Cosmic Reality 424
- Introduction 424
- The Mind as Mediator Between Self and Environment 424
- The Social Nature of Personality 425
- From Relationships to Systems: Understanding Cosmic Organization 426
- The Cosmic Importance of Sharing Knowledge 427
- The Four Aspects of Selfhood 428
- Living First, Thinking Later: The Development of Cosmic Insight 430
- The Role of Personality in Unification 431
- What Makes a Soul Salvageable? 432
- Conclusion: Preparing for Cosmic Citizenship 433

Chapter 30: The Soul's Reality - Understanding Personality Survival and Spiritual Growth 435
- Introduction 435
- The Nature of Personality and Soul 435
- Jesus and the Greek Philosopher: A Pivotal Teaching 436
- The Moment of Soul Birth 437
- Survival Value and Moral Consciousness 438
- The Nature of Relationships and Soul Growth 438
- The Cosmic Gulf and the Reality of Love 439
- The Progressive Nature of Reality 440
- The Morontia Self Within 440
- Science, Philosophy, and Religion: An Integration 441
- The Supreme and the Preservation of Value 442
- Personality: The Divine Gift 443

    Practical Implications for Daily Life..444

    Conclusion: The Journey Ahead 444

Chapter 31: Personality Survival and the Three Types of Death 446

    Introduction...446

    The Cosmic Evolution Toward Spirit Dominance..446

    The Two Great Phases of Mortal Experience...447

        The Prefinaliter Experience: God-Seeking..447

        The Postfinaliter Experience: God-Revealing 447

        Descending Personalities and Their Mission 448

    The Foundation of Survival: Transferring Identity 449

    The Three Types of Death 450

        Type One: Spiritual (Soul) Death..450

        Type Two: Intellectual (Mind) Death...452

        Type Three: Physical (Body and Mind) Death 455

    What Happens After Death 455

    Conclusion 456

Chapter 32: The Reality of Death and Personality Survival...................................458

    The Moment of Death: What Actually Happens 458

    Why Communication with the Dead Is Impossible..459

    The Problem with Reincarnation 460

    What About Those "Ghost" Experiences?..461

    The Three Types of Death 462

    What Survives and What Doesn't..462

    The Process of Adjudication 463

    The Third Psychic Circle: What It Really Means 465

    What Happens to Non-Survivors?...465

    The Indestructibility of the World of the Cross 466

    Looking Forward 467

Chapter 33: The Survival Journey - Understanding Thought Adjusters and Resurrection 469

    Introduction: The Mystery of Divine Fragments 469

The Context: Death and Dispensational Resurrection 469

The Seven Assignments: A Persistent Mystery 470

The Experiential Nature of Divine Fragments 470

The Question of Evil and Reintegration 471

Guardian Angels and the Psychic Circles 472

The Certification Process: Checks and Double Checks 473

What the Adjuster Does Upon Approval 474

The Inevitability and the Exception 475

The Uniqueness of Personality and Adjuster 475

The Weight of Choice 476

Probation and Second Chances 477

Conclusion: The Narrow Door and the Broad Mercy 478

Chapter 34: The Survival of the Soul and Journey to the Mansion Worlds 479

Introduction 479

The Mercy of Transitional Classification 479

The Gift of Mercy Credits 481

The Final Choice: Conscious and Undoubted 481

Three Pathways to Resurrection 483

The Central Question: What About Jesus? 485

The Gospel Jesus Actually Taught 486

The Nature of the Soul 487

The Borderland of Life and Death 488

The One Exception: Adjuster Fusion 490

Practical Implications for Life Now 490

Conclusion 491

Chapter 35: The Mystery of Personality Survival and Resurrection 493

The Disruption of Consciousness 493

The Safeguarding of Identity 494

The Mystery They Don't Fully Understand 494

The Adjuster as Custodian 495

The Three Prerequisites for Resurrection 496

- The Morontia Energy Pattern 496
- The Return of the Adjuster 496
- The Delivery of the Soul 497

A Special Case: Fusion on Earth 497

The Seizure of Consciousness 498

The Unchanging Foundation 499

What Survives and What Doesn't 500

The Transformation Beyond Recognition 501

The Emerging Butterfly 501

Beauty Reflecting Reality 502

The Undifferentiated Mind 503

Closing Reflections 503

Chapter 36: The Morontia Mind and Soul Survival 505

Introduction: Understanding the Transition Beyond Mortal Life 505

The Morontia Mind: A Modified Cosmic Awareness 505

The Shocking Truth About Mortal Intellect 506

The Birth and Awakening of the Soul 508

The Exception: Pre-Fusion During Transit 509

The Challenge of Spirit-Fused and Son-Fused Mortals 509

Building Morontia Mota Now 510

The Role of Relationships and Communication 511

The Seven Psychic Circles 512

Creature Volition and the Will of God 513

The Continuity of Character 514

The Adjustment Period 515

The Persistence of Memory 516

Practical Implications for Our Lives Today 517

The Completion of Local Universe Progression 517

Conclusion: The Privilege of Conscious Cooperation 518

Chapter 37: The Divine Partnership - Understanding Thought Adjuster Fusion 520

The Transformation: From Potential to Actual 520

The Endowments of Fusion, Fixation of Divinity Quality	521
Past Eternity Experience and Memory	521
Immortality	522
A Phase of Qualified Potential Absoluteness	522
When Does Fusion Occur?	523
Fusion at Death	523
Delayed Fusion	524
The Mystery of Identity: Who Are We After Fusion?	524
The Habit of God	525
The Registry of Ascendington	526
The Journey Ahead: Standing Before Christ Michael	527
The At-onement Authorization	527
Our Destiny: Administrators of Outer Space	528
The Cosmic Significance: Children of the Supreme	528
From Dust to Divinity	529

Forward

The Journey Within: Discovering God's Personal Presence

For decades, I've taught *The Urantia Book* to seekers hungry for truth about our spiritual nature and cosmic destiny. Among the many profound revelations this text contains, none has captivated students quite like the teaching about Thought Adjusters, those mysterious fragments of God himself that dwell within human consciousness. This concept, while initially challenging to grasp, may well represent the most intimate and transformative truth we can encounter that the infinite Universal Father has chosen to experience mortal existence from within, sharing every moment of our lives through an actual fragment of his divine nature.

When I first began these studies in my teaching sessions, I quickly realized that understanding Thought Adjusters requires more than intellectual comprehension. It demands a fundamental shift in how we perceive ourselves, our relationship with God, and our eternal potential. The implications are staggering. We're not simply creatures being observed by a distant deity. We are, quite literally, housing God within our minds. Every thought, every choice, every struggle and triumph occurs in the direct presence of divinity itself.

This book represents years of careful study, reflection, and synthesis of Papers 107 through 112 of *The Urantia Book*, which contain the most comprehensive revelation about these "Mystery Monitors" ever given to humanity. I've attempted to make this complex material accessible without diminishing its profound depths. Whether you're encountering these concepts for the first time or deepening your existing knowledge, my hope is that this work illuminates the extraordinary gift we've received and the unlimited destiny that awaits those who choose to cooperate with their indwelling divine guides.

Why This Study Matters

You might reasonably wonder: Why dedicate an entire volume to this single aspect of spiritual reality? The answer appears straightforward when we consider what Thought Adjusters represent. They are not religious metaphors or abstract spiritual principles. According to *The Urantia Book*, they are actual, literal fragments of the Universal Father, portions of absolute deity that become individualized through association with evolutionary creatures like ourselves.

This teaching addresses humanity's deepest questions: Is God real? Does he care about individuals? Can we truly know him? Is there life beyond death? What is our ultimate destiny? The Thought Adjuster revelation provides concrete, detailed answers that honor both our capacity for reason and our hunger for spiritual meaning.

In an era when traditional religious authority faces justified scrutiny, when scientific materialism often dismisses spiritual experience, and when many seek authenticity beyond institutional dogma, understanding Thought Adjusters offers a framework that satisfies both intellect and soul. It presents a universe governed not by arbitrary divine decree but by loving administration rooted in actual experience and earned wisdom.

The Source and Nature of This Material

I should be clear about my sources from the outset. This book draws primarily from *The Urantia Book*, a 2,097-page text claiming revelation from celestial beings commissioned to expand and correct human understanding of spiritual reality. The book appeared in 1955, though its origins stretch back to the 1920s and 1930s, when a group in Chicago received communications through unusual circumstances that remain somewhat mysterious even today.

Whether you approach this material as divine revelation, inspired philosophy, or simply an alternative spiritual perspective, I believe the concepts presented offer profound insights that challenge conventional religious thinking while remaining internally consistent and remarkably comprehensive. I don't ask you to accept everything uncritically. Rather, I invite you to evaluate these teachings according to their fruits: Do they enlarge your conception of God? Do they illuminate spiritual reality with new clarity? Do they provide practical guidance for daily living? Do they resonate with truth as you understand it?

My role here is perhaps best described as translator and teacher rather than original author. I've spent years working with this material, teaching it to hundreds of students, and witnessing its transformative power in people's lives. What I offer in these pages is my understanding, developed through decades of study and reflection, of what *The Urantia Book* teaches about our divine indwelling.

Structure and Approach

This book follows a logical progression through the major themes presented in Papers 107-112, though I've reorganized and synthesized the material to create a more accessible narrative flow. We begin with foundational concepts about Thought Adjuster nature and origin, then progress through their classification, mission, and methods of operation. Later chapters explore the soul they help create, the fusion that ultimately unites mortal and divine, and the cosmic implications of this extraordinary partnership.

Each chapter builds on previous material, so I recommend reading sequentially rather than jumping around, at least on your first pass through the book. I've tried to maintain a balance between scholarly depth and readable prose. Where technical terms from *The Urantia Book* appear essential, I define them clearly. Where complex cosmological concepts require explanation, I break them down into digestible pieces, often using analogies from everyday experience. Each chapter contains a complete lesson within itself so many of the concepts are repeated throughout the lessons.

Throughout the text, you'll notice I write in first person and occasionally share personal reflections from my years of teaching this material. This isn't meant to center my own experience but rather to create connection and convey that these aren't merely abstract theological concepts. they represent lived spiritual reality that transforms how we approach each day.

I've also included what might be called "practical implications" sections in most chapters. The Thought Adjuster revelation isn't just theoretical or historical; it has immediate relevance for how we pray, make decisions, treat others, understand suffering, and approach spiritual growth. Understanding these divine guides changes everything about daily living, and I want readers to grasp not just the what but the so what of this material.

Who Should Read This Book

I've written with several audiences in mind, and I hope readers from diverse backgrounds will find value here.

Seekers of Spiritual Truth who sense that traditional religious explanations leave crucial questions unanswered will find a more complete understanding of spiritual reality. If you've felt there must be more to the God-human relationship than conventional theology describes, this material may resonate deeply.

Students of *The Urantia Book* familiar with the text but desiring comprehensive synthesis of the Thought Adjuster papers will find what amounts to a guided study through this crucial material. I've taught these papers for years and have learned which concepts require special attention, which connections often get missed, and which practical applications prove most helpful.

Christians Questioning Traditional Doctrine yet remaining committed to spiritual life will discover concepts that may challenge certain beliefs while deepening others. The Thought Adjuster teaching eliminates the need for blood atonement theology while magnifying the intimate, personal nature of God's love. It explains how prayer actually works, why Jesus's life and death matter, and what "being saved" really means.

Spiritual Philosophers interested in cosmology, the nature of deity, and the relationship between divine sovereignty and creature experience will find intellectually rigorous material that takes these questions seriously. *The Urantia Book* presents possibly the most detailed cosmology ever offered to humanity, and Thought Adjusters occupy a central place in that cosmic architecture.

Truth Explorers from Various Traditions who recognize that authentic spiritual understanding often transcends institutional boundaries will appreciate how this teaching builds bridges rather than walls. The Thought Adjuster concept doesn't require rejecting your current spiritual path; it may instead illuminate and deepen it.

A Word of Encouragement

I won't pretend this material is always easy to grasp. Some concepts, like the Adjuster existing at the absolute level of reality, pre-personal and prior to energy-spirit divergence, stretch our understanding to its limits. The seven classifications of Adjusters, their relationship to various orders of celestial beings, and the cosmic implications of fusion all require careful attention and reflection.

Don't be discouraged if certain passages seem opaque on first reading. I've been teaching this material for decades, and I still discover new insights each time I return to it. *The Urantia Book* has a remarkable quality of revealing itself in layers. What seems merely informational on first encounter often opens up into profound new territory when we approach it with expanded understanding.

Take your time. Reflect on what resonates. Don't worry about grasping everything immediately. The journey of understanding these teachings parallels the spiritual journey itself, gradual, progressive, and infinitely rewarding for those who persist.

Some readers may find certain teachings challenging or even disturbing, particularly regarding the nature of salvation, the character of God, and the relationship between divine guidance and human free will. I ask only that you give these ideas fair consideration before accepting or rejecting them. Truth has nothing to fear from honest examination, and the Thought Adjuster revelation stands up remarkably well to careful scrutiny.

The Practical Promise

This book is not merely theoretical or historical. Understanding that you house a fragment of God within your very consciousness has immediate practical implications. When you recognize that your Creator knows exactly what it means to be human because he experiences it directly through the indwelling Adjuster, prayer becomes conversation with one who genuinely understands. When you grasp that divine will isn't some arbitrary external command but rather the gentle leading of the God-fragment within you, spiritual growth becomes natural rather than forced.

When you comprehend that you're not a cosmic accident but a beloved child of a Father who cared enough to place his own essence within you, purpose replaces meaninglessness. Fear gives way to confidence. The struggle to "find God" ends when you realize he's been inside you all along, patiently waiting for recognition and cooperation.

These aren't empty religious platitudes. They represent the practical reality of how life changes when we understand and cooperate with our Thought Adjusters. I've watched this transformation in countless students over the years. People who felt spiritually lost discover profound direction. Those burdened by religious guilt find genuine freedom. Seekers exhausted from searching external sources for God experience the relief of discovering his internal presence.

Looking Ahead

The chapters that follow trace a journey from cosmic origins to intimate personal experience. We'll explore where Thought Adjusters come from, how they're trained, what they actually do within human consciousness, and the remarkable destiny that awaits those who achieve fusion with these divine gifts.

We'll examine practical questions: How can I recognize Adjuster guidance? What facilitates or hinders their work? Why does God sometimes seem silent? How do prayer and worship actually function? What happens at death? What does eternal life truly mean?

By the time you reach the final chapters, my hope is that you'll possess not just intellectual knowledge about Thought Adjusters but a transformed understanding of your own spiritual nature and potential. You'll see yourself differently, not as a struggling mortal trying to please a distant God, but as a divine-human partnership engaged in the greatest adventure possible: the journey from animal origins to Paradise perfection.

This journey has a guaranteed destination for all who choose to continue it. The Thought Adjuster within you represents God's absolute promise that perfection can and will be achieved. Your divine fragment works tirelessly to spiritualize your thinking, nurture your growing soul, and prepare you for fusion, that moment when two become eternally one, creating a new order of being that combines evolutionary experience with divine nature.

The path ahead is long. The adventure extends literally into eternity. But it begins right here, right now, with understanding and cooperation with the God-fragment dwelling within your own consciousness. That is what this book explores. That is the journey we now undertake together.

May this exploration deepen your appreciation for the magnificent scope of divine love and the eternal destiny that awaits all who choose the ascending path toward Paradise.

Dr. Roger W. Paul
Dacula, Georgia
2025

"The Universe is governed by love, administered through service, and measured by experience."

Chapter 1: The Origin and Nature of Thought Adjusters

Introduction: The Divine Presence Within

Among the most profound revelations contained within *The Urantia Book* is the teaching concerning Thought Adjusters, those mysterious fragments of divinity that dwell within the human mind. These divine presences, also known as Mystery Monitors or Father Fragments, represent the Universal Father's intimate and personal connection with each individual ascending mortal. Understanding the nature, origin, and function of Thought Adjusters provides the essential foundation for comprehending humanity's spiritual destiny and our relationship with God.

This chapter begins our comprehensive study of Papers 107 through 112 of *The Urantia Book*, exploring the remarkable truth that while the Universal Father resides on Paradise at the very center of all creation, He is simultaneously present within the minds of His mortal children throughout the vast universes of time and space. This paradox, that God is both infinitely distant and intimately near, finds its resolution in the reality of the Thought Adjuster.

The Universal Father's Dual Presence

The opening passage of Paper 107 establishes a fundamental paradox of divine reality: "Although the Universal Father is personally resident on Paradise, at the very center of the universes, he is also actually present on the worlds of space in the minds of his countless children of time, for he indwells them as the Mystery Monitors."

This remarkable statement reveals that the Eternal Father exists in two distinct yet complementary ways. On one hand, He maintains His absolute position at the center of all reality on Paradise. On the other hand, He achieves intimate personal contact with each mortal creature through the indwelling presence of Thought Adjusters. Thus, the Father is simultaneously the most removed from His planetary mortal sons and daughters in terms of physical distance, yet most intimately associated with them through spiritual presence.

For students of *The Urantia Book*, this teaching carries profound implications. When we seek God, we need not imagine Him as distant or inaccessible. Rather, a literal fragment of the Universal Father resides within our own minds, making God's presence as near as our own thoughts. The vast cosmic distance between our world and Paradise becomes irrelevant in light of this indwelling reality.

The Essence of the Thought Adjuster

The text describes Thought Adjusters as "the actuality of the Father's love incarnate in the souls of men." They represent far more than mere spiritual influences or abstract divine principles. Rather, they are actual fragments of God Himself, portions of His pre-personal deity that become individualized through their association with mortal creatures.

Several key characteristics define the nature of Thought Adjusters:

Divine Essence and Origin

Thought Adjusters are not created beings in the conventional sense. They are "fragmentized entities constituting the factual presence of the infinite God." Unlike other orders of celestial beings who are brought into existence through creative acts, Thought Adjusters proceed directly from the Universal Father as parts of His own divine nature. They are "undiluted and unmixed divinity, unqualified and unattenuated parts of Deity."

This means that the Thought Adjuster dwelling within each human mind possesses the same essential nature as God Himself. There is no diminishment of divinity, no dilution of the divine essence. As stated emphatically in the text: "They are of God and as far as we are able to discern, they are God."

The Divine Gift and Promise

The Thought Adjuster represents "the veritable promise of man's eternal career imprisoned within the mortal mind." This fragment of divinity serves as both guarantee and guide for humanity's spiritual future. The presence of a Thought Adjuster within a mortal being constitutes "the absolute and unqualified assurance that man can find the Universal Father."

Furthermore, the Adjuster embodies "the essence of man's perfected finaliter personality, which he can foretaste in time as he progressively masters the divine technique of achieving the living of the Father's will, step by step, through the ascension of universe upon universe until he actually attains the divine presence of his Paradise Father."

The Imprisoned Fragment

One of the most striking metaphors used throughout Paper 107 describes the Thought Adjuster as "imprisoned within the mortal mind." This imprisonment is not punitive but purposeful. The Adjuster commits itself fully to its mortal partner, unable to abandon its mission until either fusion occurs or the mortal makes a final decision against survival.

This imprisonment carries profound meaning. It signifies that God Himself has made an unbreakable commitment to each individual. The Universal Father, through His fragment, experiences every moment of mortal existence, every joy, every sorrow, every triumph, and every struggle. Nothing occurs in human life that escapes the Father's direct awareness.

Experiential Partnership with Deity

The relationship between mortal and Adjuster represents a unique form of divine-human cooperation. As the text states: "God, having commanded man to be perfect, even as he is perfect, has descended as the Adjuster to become man's experiential partner in the achievement of the supernal destiny which has been thus ordained."

This partnership operates on several levels: Mutual Experience

Through the indwelling presence of the Thought Adjuster, God gains direct experiential knowledge of mortal existence. Every sensation, thought, emotion, and experience that a human being undergoes is simultaneously experienced by the Father Fragment. This explains why God can have infinite numbers of mortal children, through their Thought Adjusters, He multiplies His experiential capacity infinitely.

This arrangement benefits both partners. Mortals receive divine guidance, wisdom, and spiritual power. God gains the rich diversity of countless individual experiences, each unique and unrepeatable. Neither partner could achieve their full potential without the other.

Consciousness of the Divine Presence

The text makes clear that "any mortal who is consciously or unconsciously following the leading of his indwelling Adjuster is living in accordance with the will of God." This means that discovering and following God's will need not be mysterious or complex. When we follow what we know consciously or unconsciously to be right, we align ourselves with divine guidance.

Moreover, "consciousness of Adjuster presence is consciousness of God's presence." Learning to recognize and respond to the subtle promptings of the Thought Adjuster constitutes the essence of spiritual growth. This consciousness can range from vague intuitions to clear spiritual perception, depending on the individual's receptivity and spiritual development.

The Promise of Eternal Union

The ultimate goal of the Adjuster-mortal partnership is fusion, "the factual experience of eternal union with God as a universe associate of Deity." When fusion occurs, the mortal personality and the divine Adjuster become one inseparable being, combining human experience with divine perfection. This represents not merely survival but actual transformation into a new order of being.

Significantly, no mortal who has ever achieved fusion with their Thought Adjuster has subsequently rebelled against God. This fact demonstrates that fusion eliminates any possibility of separation from the divine will. One cannot rebel against oneself, and the fused mortal-Adjuster being possesses such complete unity of purpose that rebellion becomes literally impossible.

The Evolutionary Soul

Central to understanding the Thought Adjuster's work is the concept of the evolving soul. The text refers to "the evolutionary soul of man" as the entity that eventually fuses with the Adjuster. This soul is not pre-existent but develops throughout mortal life through the interaction of human mind and divine spirit.

Each decision, each choice aligned with divine values, each moment of spiritual insight contributes to soul growth. The Thought Adjuster works constantly to spiritualize human thought, to elevate material concerns toward eternal values, and to transform mortal consciousness into something capable of surviving death and continuing the Paradise ascent.

When physical death occurs, it is this evolved soul that reunites with personality (a gift from the Universal Father) on the mansion worlds. The material body returns to dust, but the soul, that precious product of mortal-divine cooperation, continues its journey toward perfection.

The Three Stages of Adjuster Ministry

As mortals progress through life, their Thought Adjusters adapt their ministry to developmental stages. Paper 107 identifies three general phases:

Thought Changers (Pre-Adult Years)

From the arrival of the Adjuster (typically around age five or six) to approximately age twenty, the monitors function primarily as Thought Changers. During these formative years, young people face intense pressures and influences from their material environment. The Adjuster works to protect them from destructive choices and to redirect their thinking toward constructive patterns.

This period corresponds to youth's natural idealism and searching for meaning. The "unquenchable yearning and incessant longing to be like God" that characterizes adolescence, and young adulthood originates from the Adjuster's influence. When young people experience this spiritual hunger, they are responding, consciously or unconsciously, to the divine presence within.

Thought Adjusters (Middle Years)

From approximately age twenty to age forty, the Mystery Monitors function as Thought Adjusters in the truest sense. During these years, individuals typically establish their life patterns, career, family, values, and worldview. The Adjuster works to synchronize mortal thinking with divine ideals, to harmonize human will with the Father's purposes.

This phase often involves moving beyond the materialism and self-focus of youth toward broader concerns and deeper values. Individuals begin recognizing that temporary pleasures and material acquisitions cannot satisfy the soul's deepest needs. The Adjuster capitalizes on this growing awareness to foster genuine spiritual growth.

Thought Controllers (Mature Years)

From about age forty onward, Thought Adjusters increasingly function as Thought Controllers. By this stage of life, individuals have largely established their fundamental character and life direction. The Adjuster can now work more effectively to spiritualize thinking and prepare the soul for its eventual transition beyond mortal existence.

This period ideally sees the development of wisdom, the ability to discern meanings and values, to see beyond surface appearances, to prioritize eternal realities over temporal concerns. Those who cooperate with their Adjusters during these years make tremendous spiritual progress, building a soul of substantial quality and spiritual capacity.

The Mystery of Adjuster Origin

While much has been revealed about Thought Adjusters, significant mysteries remain. The text candidly acknowledges: "Since Thought Adjusters are of the essence of original Deity, no one may presume to discourse authoritatively upon their nature and origin."

What we do know comes from "the traditions of Salvington and the beliefs of Uversa", the accumulated wisdom of celestial beings who have long observed Adjuster ministry. Even these exalted personalities admit the limitations of their understanding, for Thought Adjusters proceed from a level of reality beyond full comprehension by created beings.

The Unfragmented Source

All sources agree that Thought Adjusters "proceed direct from the Universal Father, the First Source and Center." They are not produced through any creative process involving other Deities. The Eternal Son does not fragment himself in this manner, nor does the Infinite Spirit create Thought Adjusters. They come solely from the Father.

This direct origin from the First Source means that Thought Adjusters possess qualities that distinguish them from all other beings. They alone represent the actual presence of the Absolute within evolutionary creatures. They alone provide direct contact with the Source of all reality.

The Question of Number

An intriguing question concerns how many Thought Adjusters exist. The text presents two possibilities: "We presume that Adjusters are being constantly individualized as the universe enlarges, and as the candidates for Adjuster fusion increase in numbers. But it may be equally possible that we are in error in attempting to assign a numerical magnitude to the Adjusters; like God himself, these fragments of his unfathomable nature may be existentially infinite."

This uncertainty suggests that Thought Adjusters may not be countable in any conventional sense. Like their Source, they may transcend the categories of finite mathematics. Just as God has no beginning and no end, so the Adjusters flowing forth from Him may constitute an infinite reality that can never be exhausted or quantified.

Divinington: The Sacred Sphere

Thought Adjusters originate from or are associated with Divinington, one of the seven sacred spheres that circle Paradise. This world remains forever closed to non-Adjuster beings. Its secrets are "wholly concerned with the technique of origin" of Father Fragments and constitute knowledge reserved for the Father alone.

On Divinington, Adjusters receive preparation for their missions. Experienced Adjusters train newly individualized fragments. Here the mysteries of pre-personal deity fragmentization occur, processes that even exalted Paradise personalities cannot fully comprehend.

The Classification of Adjusters

Though all Adjusters are identical in divine nature when they emerge from the Father, they acquire experience through their service. The text alludes to various classifications based on this accumulated experience:

Virgin Adjusters

Some Adjusters serve first in mortals incapable of fusion, primitive human beings whose evolutionary status prevents the possibility of eternal survival. These Virgin Adjusters gain initial experience without the complexity of working toward fusion. After this preparatory service, they receive assignments to more advanced mortals on worlds like ours.

Experienced Adjusters

The Adjusters serving on contemporary Earth are all experienced, they have completed previous assignments. This means that every Thought Adjuster currently indwelling human minds possesses wisdom gained from prior mortal partnerships. They understand human nature from intimate personal experience and can apply that knowledge to their current assignments.

Advanced and Supreme Adjusters

Further classifications exist based on levels of achievement and experience, though these are not fully detailed in the introductory sections of Paper 107. The progressive nature of Adjuster development parallels the evolutionary growth of their mortal partners, both grow through experience and cooperation.

The Triune Destiny

The text mentions three possible destinies for Thought Adjusters:

1. **Fusion with a mortal ascender** — The ideal outcome wherein Adjuster and mortal become one eternal being.
2. **Personalization by fiat of the Universal Father** — Rare instances where Adjusters receive personality directly from the Father and become separate beings.
3. **Liberation from known assignments** — Release from service when a mortal makes a final decision against survival.

The most significant of these is personalization, particularly as illustrated by the case of Jesus of Nazareth. When Jesus was baptized by John in the Jordan River, the moment arrived when He would normally have fused with His Thought Adjuster. However, this Adjuster possessed unique characteristics that prevented standard fusion.

This particular Adjuster had previously indwelt Machiventa Melchizedek during his emergency bestowal on Earth over 2,000 years before Christ. Having served two beings of divine nature, both Melchizedek and Jesus, this Adjuster had acquired such exalted experience that returning to normal mortal service would have been inappropriate.

The only appropriate destiny for such an Adjuster was personalization. At the moment of Jesus's baptism, when the Spirit descended upon Him, the Thought

Adjuster that had faithfully served through His mortal years became personalized, receiving the personality pattern of Jesus Himself. This newly personalized Adjuster became, in effect, a duplicate of Jesus, possessing His character, His nature, and His earned spiritual status.

This personalized Adjuster received assignment as the future chief of all finaliters, those perfected beings who will serve in the outer space levels throughout eternity. Thus, all mortals who achieve the finaliter status will ultimately serve under the leadership of this personalized fragment who shared Jesus's mortal experience.

Spirit Fusion: An Alternative Path

While most mortals on Earth are destined for Adjuster fusion, the text acknowledges that "there exists no such differences concerning their origin" when discussing Spirit-fused mortals. These are individuals who cannot achieve Thought Adjuster fusion but instead fuse with a fragment of the local universe Creative Spirit.

Spirit fusion occurs primarily among primitive peoples whose evolutionary development has not yet enabled them to achieve the cosmic status necessary for Adjuster fusion. These mortals receive individualized portions of the Creative Spirit and ultimately fuse with those fragments, achieving eternal survival through a different path.

The eternal destiny of Spirit-fused mortals differs from that of Adjuster-fused beings. While Adjuster-fused mortals progress to Paradise and beyond, Spirit-fused individuals typically serve within their local universe, never achieving the Paradise status of their Adjuster-fused brethren. Nevertheless, they achieve genuine immortality and eternal service in God's vast universe.

The Compensatory Equalization

One of the more philosophical concepts presented in Paper 107 concerns what is called "the enormous universe tension which is created by the distance of man's removal from God and by the degree of his partiality in contrast with the universality of the eternal Father."

Simply stated, mortals exist at the extreme periphery of creation, separated from Paradise by inconceivable distances and vast differences in nature. We are partial, incomplete, imperfect beings, while God is infinite, complete, and perfect. This creates a kind of cosmic tension, a gap that seems impossible to bridge.

The Thought Adjuster provides "compensatory equalization" for this tension. By bringing the Father's actual presence into mortal minds, the Adjuster eliminates the effective distance between creature and Creator. The physical distance remains, but the spiritual separation vanishes. Through the Adjuster, finite mortals establish living contact with the Infinite, partial beings touch Absolute reality, and imperfect creatures commune with Perfection itself.

This equalization makes possible what would otherwise be impossible, the transformation of animal-origin beings into perfected spirits destined for eternal service in the presence of the Gods.

The Infallible Cosmic Compass

Among the many metaphors used to describe Thought Adjusters, one of the most evocative is found in this statement: "The Adjuster is man's infallible cosmic compass, always and unerringly pointing the soul Godward."

In an age before GPS navigation, the magnetic compass provided a reliable orientation that made long-distance travel possible. Even when lost in unfamiliar territory, one could trust the compass to indicate true direction. Similarly, regardless of how confused or disoriented mortals may become in life's journey, the Thought Adjuster provides unfailing guidance toward spiritual reality.

This guidance operates continuously, whether or not the mortal is conscious of it. The Adjuster never ceases in its ministry, never abandons its charge, never loses its orientation toward Paradise. Like a compass that always points north, the Adjuster always points toward God. The only question is whether the mortal will pay attention and follow that guidance.

Implications for Daily Living

Understanding Thought Adjuster reality transforms how we approach everyday life. Several practical implications emerge from these teachings:

The Sanctity of the Individual

If every human being houses a fragment of God Himself, then every person possesses infinite worth and deserves profound respect. The way we treat others reflects our recognition, or lack thereof, of the divine presence within them. Cruelty, exploitation, or dehumanization of any person constitutes an offense against the very presence of God.

The Nature of Prayer and Worship

Prayer takes on new meaning when understood as communion with the divine presence within. We need not imagine our prayers traveling vast cosmic distances to reach God's ears. The Father Fragment hears every sincere prayer in the very moment of its utterance. Worship becomes not merely outward religious practice but intimate fellowship with indwelling divinity.

Moral Decision-Making

When facing ethical choices, we can trust that the still, small voice of conscience often represents Adjuster guidance. The persistent sense that something is right or wrong, the discomfort with dishonesty, the attraction toward service and compassion, these may well be the Adjuster's influence upon our thinking. Learning to recognize and follow this inner guidance constitutes practical spirituality.

The Purpose of Suffering

Understanding that God shares every human experience through the Thought Adjuster provides new perspective on suffering. We do not suffer alone; God suffers with us. Every pain, every loss, every hardship is experienced by the Father Fragment within. This does not eliminate suffering, but it does mean that suffering need not be meaningless. Through the Adjuster, our struggles contribute to the experiential knowledge of God Himself and to the growth of our eternal souls.

Conclusion: The Foundation for Eternal Destiny

This opening exploration of Thought Adjuster nature and origin establishes the foundation for understanding humanity's spiritual potential. We are not abandoned creatures struggling alone in an indifferent universe. Rather, we are indwelt by fragments of the Universal Father Himself, divinely partnered in an eternal enterprise that will lead to Paradise and beyond.

The Thought Adjuster represents God's commitment to each individual, an unbreakable promise that perfection can and will be achieved by all who choose to cooperate with divine guidance. This fragment of Deity works tirelessly to spiritualize human thought, to nurture the growing soul, and to prepare each mortal for the tremendous adventure that lies ahead.

In the chapters that follow, we will explore more deeply the mission and ministry of Thought Adjusters, their relationship to other spiritual influences, the technique by which they work within human consciousness, and the ultimate destiny that awaits those who achieve fusion with these divine gifts. We will examine how Adjusters relate to the broader universe reality and how their presence within mortals connects to the vast Paradise plan for universe perfection.

Before we explore these further dimensions of Adjuster ministry, however, we must understand an event of supreme importance that preceded all Thought Adjuster bestowals in our local universe, the instructions given by Immanuel to Christ Michael before His seventh and final bestowal as Jesus of Nazareth. These instructions, recorded in Paper 120, provide essential context for understanding not only Jesus's life mission but also the enhanced spiritual ministry that became available to all mortals following His completion of that bestowal. It is to this momentous counsel that we now turn our attention.

This chapter is adapted from study sessions led by Dr. Roger Paul on Paper 107 of The Urantia Book. I have edited the text for clarity while maintaining fidelity to the original teachings.

Chapter 2: Classification of Thought Adjusters

Introduction

The Thought Adjuster represents one of the most profound mysteries in all of cosmic reality, a literal fragment of God the Father dwelling within the human mind. While Chapter 1 introduced us to the nature and origin of these divine monitors, this chapter explores their classification and the various orders through which they serve evolutionary mortals across the universe.

Understanding the classification of Thought Adjusters reveals not merely an organizational structure, but a divine progression of experience and purpose. Each classification represents a distinct phase in the eternal career of these mystery monitors, from their initial fragmentation from Divinity through their ultimate destiny as eternal partners with ascending mortals.

Paper 107 of *The Urantia Book*, which serves as our primary source for this study, acknowledges that while there are seven orders of Thought Adjusters, even the revelators do not altogether comprehend all aspects of these divisions. This honest admission reminds us that we are exploring territories of spiritual reality that transcend complete human comprehension yet remain accessible to sincere study and reflection.

The Three Destinies of Thought Adjusters

Before examining the seven orders in detail, we must understand the three primary destinies that await virgin Adjusters those serving for the first time. According to the revelation, all virgin Adjusters are destined to become one of the following:

Liberated Adjusters are those who have been eternally freed from assignment as indwelling monitors of individual mortals. These fragments of Deity are released to pursue other functions within the divine administration, though the specific nature of these functions remains largely unrevealed to us.

Fused Adjusters represent the most common destiny, union with an evolutionary mortal or another type of ascending being. Through this eternal fusion, the Adjuster and the mortal become one indissoluble being, creating a new order of universe personality that partakes of both human experience and divine nature.

Personalized Adjusters constitute a unique destiny, perhaps best exemplified by the Adjuster of Jesus Christ. These monitors, having served with incarnated

Paradise Sons or having achieved unusual distinction during mortal indwelling, are granted independent personality status while retaining their divine nature and accumulated experience.

These three destinies frame our understanding of Adjuster classification, reminding us that each fragment of the Father embarks upon an eternal adventure with its own unique outcome.

The Seven Orders of Thought Adjusters

1. Virgin Adjusters

Virgin Adjusters serve on their initial assignment in the minds of evolutionary candidates for eternal survival. The term "virgin" indicates inexperience, not imperfection. These mystery monitors are uniform in divine nature, each one a perfect fragment of God the Father, possessing identical spiritual potential and divine character.

However, this uniformity exists only at the moment of their emergence from Divinington, the dwelling place of the Father and the origin point of all Adjusters. The instant a virgin Adjuster departs Divinington and begins universe ministry, experiential differentiation begins. Though identical in divine essence, no two Adjusters will ever have precisely the same experiential history.

Virgin Adjusters typically receive assignment to beings who are not yet capable of eternal fusion with a Father fragment. These may include:

- Single-brained entities on primitive evolutionary worlds
- Early evolutionary mortals whose spiritual development remains nascent
- Beings who will later receive Spirit fusion or Son fusion rather than Father fusion

The critical point to understand is this: virgin Adjusters serve beings who cannot achieve fusion with them. This initial assignment serves as a training experience, allowing the Adjuster to gain familiarity with evolutionary mind patterns, mortal emotions, and the challenges of indwelling material beings. This experiential education proves invaluable for the Adjuster's subsequent assignments.

An important clarification concerns planetary reassignment: virgin Adjusters are never reassigned to the same planet where they served their initial ministry. Once a virgin Adjuster completes service on a particular world, that Adjuster will never return to serve another mortal on that same sphere. This fact has profound implications for understanding certain human phenomena, such as claims of "past life" memories purportedly derived from the Adjuster. Since Adjusters do not repeat planetary assignments, any authentic Adjuster-derived memories would necessarily originate from a different world entirely, not from previous lives on the same planet.

This restriction does not limit God's creative options, however. Should circumstance warrant, an Adjuster might conceivably transmit to their current subject impressions or insights from previous planetary service, though such experiences would be recognized as foreign to the current world rather than as "past life" memories of that world.

2. Advanced Adjusters

Advanced Adjusters have completed one or more assignments with "will" creatures on worlds where final fusion occurs between the mortal identity and an individualized portion of the spirit of the Third Source and Center (the Infinite Spirit) or with a fragment of the spirit of the Creator Son. Notably, these Adjusters have served on fusion worlds, planets where mortals can and do achieve eternal union with spirit fragments.

The designation "advanced" reflects experiential acquisition rather than any superiority of divine nature. An Advanced Adjuster possesses identical divinity to a virgin Adjuster but brings the wisdom of lived experience in mortal minds. This experiential knowledge enables Advanced Adjusters to accomplish things in the human mind that less experienced monitors could not achieve.

The text specifies that these Adjusters may have served "one or more seasons" with "will" creatures. This phrasing indicates that an Adjuster might experience multiple indwelling assignments before receiving classification as Advanced. The accumulation of varied experiences with different personality types, across different evolutionary stages, and in diverse cultural contexts contributes to the Adjuster's expanding repertoire of ministry techniques.

Advanced Adjusters represent the typical classification of monitors assigned to worlds like our own, spheres where evolutionary mortals possess sufficient spiritual development to achieve Father fusion. When we consider our own indwelling Adjusters, we should understand that each has previous experience on another world, having already guided at least one evolutionary being through mortal existence.

This experiential background provides our Adjusters with:

- Familiarity with evolutionary mind patterns and resistance mechanisms
- Understanding of the challenges posed by material existence
- Proven techniques for spiritual communication through the superconscious mind
- Patience developed through previous mortal service
- Wisdom regarding the long view of universe ascension

The revelation that all Adjusters serving on our world are Advanced rather than virgin monitors should inspire both humility and confidence. We receive the ministry of experienced guides who have already navigated the complexities of mortal indwelling.

3. Supreme Adjusters

Supreme Adjusters have served in the adventure of time on evolutionary worlds, but their human partners for various reasons declined eternal survival. Subsequently, these Adjusters have been reassigned to other adventures with other mortals on other evolving worlds.

The classification "Supreme" does not indicate greater divinity than virgin or Advanced Adjusters, all Adjusters share identical divine nature as fragments of the Universal Father. Rather, this designation reflects extensive experiential accumulation. A Supreme Adjuster has weathered the unique challenges of indwelling mortals who ultimately rejected survival, yet the Adjuster emerged from these experiences with enhanced understanding and capabilities.

The revelation explicitly states that a Supreme Adjuster, "though no more divine than a virgin monitor, has had more experience, can do things in the human mind which a less experienced Adjuster could not do." This increased functionality derives purely from experiential wisdom, the accumulated learning that comes from confronting the most difficult circumstances in mortal ministry.

Consider the profound implications: when a mortal chooses non-survival, the Adjuster must withdraw, carrying with it all the efforts, hopes, and preparations made during that indwelling. Yet rather than considering this a failure, the universe recognizes it as advanced education. The Adjuster has now experienced the full range of mortal rejection mechanisms, spiritual blindness, and willful resistance to divine guidance. This education proves invaluable in subsequent assignments.

We might reasonably speculate that Supreme Adjusters receive assignment to particularly challenging cases, mortals whose life circumstances, psychological makeup, or cultural conditioning present exceptional obstacles to spiritual development. The advanced experiential wisdom of these monitors equips them to persist where less experienced Adjusters might find the barriers insurmountable.

It's worth noting that some of history's greatest leaders, musicians, artists, and spiritual teachers may have received Supreme Adjusters. These accomplished individuals might have required the specialized ministry that only extensively experienced monitors could provide. The combination of exceptional human potential with Supreme Adjuster guidance could explain certain remarkable achievements in human history.

4. Vanished Adjusters

With the fourth classification, we encounter the first significant mystery in Adjuster orders. The revelators candidly admit: "Here occurs a break in our efforts to follow the careers of the mystery monitors. There is a fourth stage of service about which we are not sure."

The Melchizedeks, who provide much of the information in Paper 107, acknowledge uncertainty regarding the activities and status of Vanished Adjusters. However, the Solitary Messengers, another order of universe personalities, have formed a hypothesis regarding these mysterious monitors.

The Solitary Messengers believe that Vanished Adjusters are "at one with the First Source and Center, enjoying a period of refreshing association with the Father himself." This suggests that after extensive service, certain Adjusters are recalled to Divinington or to the Father's presence for what might be termed a spiritual sabbatical, a time of renewal, reflection, and direct communion with Deity.

The revelation adds to a remarkable possibility: "It is entirely possible that an Adjuster could be roaming the master universe simultaneously with being at one with the omnipresent Father." This statement challenges our linear concepts of time and space. An Adjuster, being a fragment of the eternal and omnipresent Father, might experience multiple states of existence concurrently, simultaneously enjoying Father-communion while also observing or experiencing universe events.

Who becomes a Vanished Adjuster? The text suggests these may be monitors who have served faithfully through multiple mortal assignments where the subjects chose non-survival. Rather than immediately receiving new assignment, these

Adjusters are granted respite, a return to direct Father-presence for refreshment and renewal.

The designation "Vanished" aptly describes these monitors from the perspective of universe administration. They have temporarily disappeared from the roster of active service, their location and activities known only to the Father himself. This classification reminds us that vast domains of spiritual reality remain beyond our current comprehension, humbling our attempts at complete understanding while inspiring wonder at the divine mysteries.

5. Liberated Adjusters

Liberated Adjusters are "those mystery monitors that have been eternally liberated from the service of time for the mortals of the evolving spheres." The revelation forthrightly admits: "What functions may be theirs, we do not know."

This classification represents Adjusters who have been permanently released from the duty of indwelling evolutionary mortals. Unlike Vanished Adjusters, whose status may be temporary, Liberated Adjusters have concluded their ministry to ascending beings and moved on to other forms of universe service.

Several pathways might lead to liberation:

Completion of Purpose: An Adjuster may have fulfilled some specific purpose or gained particular experiences that qualify it for specialized ministry unrelated to mortal indwelling.

Reassignment to Higher Service: Having accumulated vast experience through multiple mortal indwellings, the Adjuster may receive assignment to functions requiring such extensive evolutionary ministry background.

Universe Administrative Roles: Liberated Adjusters might serve in advisory capacities, sharing their experiential wisdom with other orders of spirit beings or contributing to universe planning and administration.

The frank acknowledgment of ignorance regarding Liberated Adjuster functions exemplifies the intellectual honesty of *The Urantia Book* revelation. Rather than inventing speculative details, the revelators clearly delineate the boundaries of revealed truth. This creates trust in the information that is provided while maintaining appropriate humility regarding cosmic mysteries beyond current human need or capacity to comprehend.

What we can know with certainty is this: liberation represents neither failure nor punishment but rather transition to new forms of divine service. These Adjusters carry within their experiential nature the accumulated wisdom of mortal ministry, qualifying them for specialized contributions to universe welfare.

6. Fused Adjusters

Fused Adjusters represent the ultimate destiny for the majority of Thought Adjusters, those who "have become one with the ascending creatures of the superuniverses, the eternity partners of the time ascenders of the Paradise Corps of Finality."

This classification merits extensive consideration, for it describes the destiny that awaits both our Adjusters and ourselves, should we choose survival and complete the long ascension to Paradise.

The Nature of Fusion

Thought Adjusters ordinarily become fused with ascending mortals of time. The revelation specifies that fusion typically occurs on the mansion worlds, the first stage of our post-mortal existence. Most mortals achieve fusion by mansion world number six, though some fuse earlier on mansion world five, and a few exceptional individuals achieve fusion even during mortal life on their native planets.

The moment of fusion marks the most significant transformation in the eternal career of both the mortal and the Adjuster. Two distinct beings, one evolutionary and experiential, the other divine and existential, become one indivisible entity. The revelation states that the Adjuster "becomes indissolubly linked with the ascending career of a surviving mortal."

The Ontological Transformation

At fusion, something profound occurs at the level of being itself. The revelation explains: "Upon fusion with the ascending evolutionary soul, it appears that the Adjuster translates from the absolute existential level of the universe to the finite experiential level of functional association with an ascending personality, while retaining all of the character of the existential divine nature."

Let us unpack this dense but crucial statement:

- **From Absolute to Finite**: The Adjuster, originally existing at the absolute level as a pure fragment of Deity, now functions at the finite level, the level of time-space reality where evolutionary experience occurs.
- **Existential to Experiential**: While retaining its existential divine nature (what it eternally *is*), the Adjuster now fully participates in experiential reality (what it is *becoming* through experience).
- **Retention of Divine Character**: Despite this transformation, the Adjuster loses none of its divine nature. The fusion-being partakes fully of both human evolutionary achievement and divine absolute character.

Registration and Residence

Prior to fusion, the Adjuster originates from and remains registered at Divinington, the dwelling place of the Father and the source of all Thought Adjusters. However, "upon fusion with the ascending evolutionary soul" the Adjuster becomes "registered in and out of Ascendington."

Ascendington is the Paradise sphere that serves as the receiving world for all ascending pilgrims who have achieved fusion with Father fragments. After fusion, neither the mortal nor the Adjuster returns to their origins, the mortal never returns to their evolutionary world as a permanent residence, and the Adjuster never returns to Divinington. Instead, both now call Ascendington their Paradise home, joining the vast company of ascending fusion-beings from throughout the seven superuniverses.

Implications for Human Destiny

The doctrine of Adjuster fusion carries staggering implications for human destiny:

1. **Becoming Divine**: Through fusion, we literally become part of Deity. We are not merely *with* God; we become partakers of the divine nature itself. The fragment of God the Father that indwells us merges with our evolving soul, creating a being that is truly a son or daughter of God, not metaphorically, but ontologically.
2. **Eternal Indissolubility**: The text emphasizes that fusion is "indissoluble", it can never be undone or reversed. From fusion onward through all eternity, we remain forever united with our Adjuster. This permanence provides absolute security for our eternal careers.
3. **Partnership in Finality**: Fused mortals become members of the Paradise Corps of Finality, joining the company of perfected beings who have traversed the entire ascension pathway from evolutionary origin to Paradise

achievement. This corps serves throughout the universes in capacities that will unfold throughout the eternal ages.
4. **Full Universe Citizenship**: As fused beings, we gain access to all levels of universe reality. The divine component of our nature serves as a universal passport, granting us entrance to spiritual realms that would otherwise remain inaccessible to purely evolutionary beings.
5. **Memory Integration**: Upon fusion, we begin to access the memory banks of our Adjuster. This means we gradually gain awareness of our Adjuster's previous experiences, including its ministry to other mortals on other worlds. Our memory expands both backward (through Adjuster memories) and forward (through enhanced spiritual foresight derived from our divine component).

The Mechanics of Fusion

While the revelators provide conceptual understanding of fusion, the actual mechanics remain mysterious. We know that fusion requires:

- **Spiritual Attainment**: The ascending mortal must achieve sufficient spiritual development and soul growth.
- **Adjuster Preparation**: The Adjuster must have successfully constructed a viable morontia soul from the mortal's worthy decisions and spiritual experiences.
- **Divine Timing**: Fusion occurs at the appointed moment when both mortal and Adjuster are ready, neither forcing the process nor delaying it unnecessarily.
- **Seraphic Collaboration**: Our guardian seraphim play crucial roles in facilitating the fusion event, though the details remain largely unrevealed.

Alternatives to Father Fusion

The revelation notes that some surviving mortals are "registered for exemption from Father fusion." These individuals will not fuse with Thought Adjusters but will instead achieve Spirit fusion (with a fragment of the Infinite Spirit) or Son fusion (with a fragment of the Creator Son of their local universe).

Spirit-fused mortals become permanent citizens of their superuniverse, serving throughout its sectors and never passing inward to Paradise as residential citizens. Son-fused mortals become permanent citizens of their local universe, rarely if ever progressing beyond its boundaries. These alternative fusions ensure that each level of universe organization maintains a permanent citizenship of ascending mortals who know its territories and peoples intimately.

However, Father fusion, Adjuster fusion, remains the most common destiny and the one that carries ascending mortals all the way to Paradise and beyond, into unrevealed destinies in the outer space levels currently undergoing physical organization.

7. Personalized Adjusters

The seventh and final classification of Thought Adjusters represents perhaps the most fascinating and mysterious order: "Those who have served with the incarnated Paradise Sons, together with many who have achieved unusual distinction during the mortal indwelling, but whose subjects rejected survival."

Personalized Adjusters differ fundamentally from all other classifications. While remaining divine fragments of the Father, they have been granted independent personality status, enabling them to function as distinct universe personalities rather than as indwelling monitors.

Pathways to Personalization

The revelation identifies two primary pathways by which Adjusters achieve personalization:

1. **Service with Incarnated Paradise Sons**: When Creator Sons (like Christ Michael of Nebadon, known to us as Jesus) or Magisterial Sons incarnate on evolutionary worlds, they receive Thought Adjusters despite already being divine Sons. These Paradise Sons cannot fuse with their Adjusters, they are already Sons of God and possess divine status. Therefore, when the bestowal mission concludes, these Adjusters are released from indwelling service and granted personalization as a reward for their unique ministry.
2. **Unusual Distinction During Mortal Indwelling**: Some Adjusters achieve exceptional accomplishment during their service with mortals who ultimately reject survival. Rather than viewing this as failure, the universe recognizes the Adjuster's extraordinary efforts and grants personalization as acknowledgment of distinguished service under difficult circumstances.

The Case of Jesus's Adjuster

The most significant example of a Personalized Adjuster is the monitor who indwelt Jesus of Nazareth. Understanding this Adjuster's career illuminates the nature of personalization itself.

Jesus's Adjuster had previously served with Machiventa Melchizedek during his emergency bestowal on our world nearly two thousand years before Jesus's birth. Melchizedek, though incarnated in human form, was already a high local universe Son and therefore incapable of Adjuster fusion. This initial assignment gave Jesus's future Adjuster extraordinary experience with divinity in human form.

When this highly advanced Adjuster later indwelt Jesus from his childhood, the Adjuster gained even more remarkable experience, serving within the mind of the Creator Son of our entire local universe, who had incarnated as a human being for his final bestowal. The Adjuster accumulated unprecedented experience observing and assisting Michael's human journey.

At Jesus's baptism, the moment when Michael of Nebadon fully assumed his bestowal role and began his public ministry, the Adjuster was personalized. Critically, this personalization did not mean the Adjuster departed from Jesus. Rather, the Personalized Adjuster remained with Jesus throughout the final three years of his bestowal, serving as companion, counselor, and divine liaison.

The Significance of Personalization for Jesus's Ministry

Understanding that Jesus's Adjuster was personalized at his baptism clarifies several aspects of his subsequent ministry:

Jesus's Full Humanity: From his baptism onward, Jesus conducted his ministry entirely as a human being, without the internal guidance of an indwelling Adjuster functioning in the normal capacity. This demonstrates that Jesus's teachings, his miracles, and his perfect life were accomplished through human will aligned with divine will, not through special internal divine presence unavailable to other mortals.

Divine Communication: When Jesus communed with "the Father," he often communed with his Personalized Adjuster, who served as the Father's representative. This explains the intimate, immediate quality of Jesus's prayer life, he spoke with a divine being who had shared his entire life experience and knew his human nature intimately.

The Wedding at Cana: The first miracle at the wedding in Cana illustrates the relationship between Jesus and his Personalized Adjuster. When Mary requested help with the wine shortage, Jesus initially responded humanly: "Woman, what have I to do with this?" But sensing his mother's faith in his ability to help, he said, "If it be my Father's will." At that moment, his Creator prerogatives, the divine powers inherent in his nature as Creator Son, activated in response to the Father's will transmitted through the Personalized Adjuster. The mechanical and physical controllers of the universe immediately transformed water into wine of surpassing quality. Jesus himself was somewhat surprised, having not willed the miracle directly but having submitted to the Father's will.

Parallel Personalization

We have reason to believe that all Creator Sons who complete their seventh and final bestowal receive Personalized Adjusters through similar process. Since there are seven hundred thousand Creator Sons in the grand universe, and each must complete seven bestowals to achieve full sovereignty over their local universe, potentially millions of Adjusters serve with incarnated Paradise Sons. Many of these are likely to achieve personalization, creating a corps of Personalized Adjusters with unique insights into divine incarnation and mortal experience.

Functions of Personalized Adjusters

The revelation provides limited information about the ongoing functions of Personalized Adjusters, stating: "We have reasons for believing that such Adjusters are personalized on the recommendations of the Ancients of Days of the superuniverse of their assignment."

The Ancients of Days, the triune rulers of the seven superuniverses, apparently nominate deserving Adjusters for personalization. Once personalized, these Adjusters presumably serve in advisory capacities, share their unique experiential wisdom with other orders of beings, or undertake special missions throughout the universes.

Jesus's Personalized Adjuster, for instance, continues to serve in capacities unrevealed to us, carrying within his experiential nature the complete memory of Jesus's human life and bestowal mission. This Adjuster constitutes a living record of the incarnation of a Creator Son, knowledge of incalculable value to universe administration.

The Unity of Divine Nature and Experiential Diversity

Having examined all seven classifications, we can now appreciate the elegant paradox that defines Thought Adjuster reality: absolute unity of divine nature combined with infinite diversity of experiential acquisition.

Every Adjuster, regardless of classification, is identical in divine nature. Each is a perfect fragment of God the Father, possessing the same absolute qualities, the same divine character, the same spiritual potential. In their essential being, Adjusters are utterly uniform, none is "better" or "more divine" than any other.

Yet simultaneously, no two Adjusters share identical experiential histories. From the moment an Adjuster departs Divinington, it begins accumulating unique experiences. Every mortal indwelt, every world served, every challenge encountered, every triumph achieved, all become part of that Adjuster's eternal memory and expanding wisdom.

This combination mirrors the human condition in profound ways. All humans share identical potential for Adjuster indwelling and eternal survival. None are divinely favored over others in their spiritual endowment. Yet each human develops a unique experiential history, personality expression, and character formation. The same principle applies to Adjusters, absolute equality of nature, infinite diversity of experience.

Spiritual Implications for Ascending Mortals

The classification system reveals the Father's infinite patience and long-term perspective. Adjusters are never considered failures, even when their human subjects reject survival. Instead, such experiences qualify them as Supreme Adjusters, more experienced and capable. The universe wastes nothing; every experience contributes to the eternal education of these divine fragments.

This perspective should profoundly encourage every sincere seeker. Your indwelling Adjuster is not discouraged by your struggles, mistakes, or slow progress. The Adjuster has all eternity and infinite patience. Every human confusion, every moral choice, every spiritual question becomes part of the Adjuster's expanding experiential repertoire.

Furthermore, knowing that our Adjusters are Advanced, having already served on another world, should inspire confidence. We are not the "practice run" for inexperienced monitors. Our Adjusters bring proven wisdom from previous mortal ministry. They know how to work with evolutionary minds, how to communicate through dreams and intuitions, how to gradually transform human thinking toward spiritual values.

The promise of fusion should electrify every sincere believer. We are not merely aided by God, we are destined to become part of God through eternal fusion with our Adjusters. This is not metaphorical language but literal truth. The same divine fragment that indwells you now will fuse with your soul on the mansion worlds, creating a new order of being that partakes of both evolutionary experience and divine nature.

You will become, literally and eternally, a son or daughter of God, not by adoption or courtesy, but by actual ontological transformation. Your nature will be divine, though you will never forget your mortal origin. You will possess divine prerogatives, serve in divine administration, and participate in universe destinies currently beyond our comprehension.

Conclusion: The Progressive Education of Divinity

The seven classifications of Thought Adjusters reveal a profound truth about the nature of the Father and his relationship with evolutionary creation: God educates himself through experience while simultaneously educating and transforming his evolutionary children.

Each Adjuster represents God the Father personally involved in evolutionary experience. Through the accumulated service of trillions of Adjusters across millions of worlds, God directly experiences every conceivable variation of mortal life, every possible combination of genetics and environment, every unique expression of emerging personality.

Yet this is not one-directional. While God experiences mortal life through Adjusters, mortals simultaneously experience divine presence through the same Adjusters. We are not merely objects of divine observation but active partners in mutual experience-sharing. The Adjuster introduces us to divine perspective, divine values, divine character. We introduce the Adjuster to time-space reality, to the challenges of material existence, to the triumph of faith in the absence of immediate evidence.

This partnership reaches its culmination in fusion, when two become one eternally. At that moment, the educational process achieves its first major goal: the creation of a new being who synthesizes evolutionary achievement with divine perfection, who knows both the human struggle and the divine perspective, who can forever serve as a bridge between material and spiritual realities.

The classifications we have studied represent way stations on this eternal journey. From virgin inexperience through advancing education to supreme wisdom, from mysterious vanishment through liberation to eternal fusion or personalization, each classification marks progression in the universe education of divine fragments and mortal beings.

In the next chapter, we will explore the mission and ministry of Thought Adjusters, how they actually function within human minds, what they can and cannot do, and how we can cooperate more effectively with their divine guidance. Understanding their classifications provides essential foundation for appreciating their ministry.

"The mystery of God's indwelling of the mortal mind is not merely the greatest of all universe mysteries; it is also the supreme challenge to human faith and divine courage. For in accepting the Father's presence, we accept both the gift of eternity and the responsibility of divine sonship."

— Dr. Roger Paul

Chapter 3: The Nature and Origin of Thought Adjusters

Introduction

In our continuing exploration of the Thought Adjuster, that divine fragment of God dwelling within the human mind, we now turn to examine the profound mysteries of their nature and origin. This chapter delves into Paper 107 of *The Urantia Book*, which reveals truths about these "mystery monitors" that even the highest spiritual beings in our universe only partially comprehend.

The questions we address here are fundamental to understanding our relationship with the divine: What is the true nature of these God fragments? Where do they originate? How are they trained and prepared for their mission within mortal minds? And perhaps most importantly, what does it mean for our destiny that an absolute fragment of the infinite Universal Father dwells within our finite mortal nature?

As we shall discover, the answers to these questions illuminate not only the extraordinary gift we have received but also the unlimited potential that lies before every human being who chooses to cooperate with this indwelling divine presence.

The Classification and Purpose of Thought Adjusters

Thought Adjusters may be classified in many ways: according to their universe assignment, by the measure of success in indwelling an individual mortal, or even by the racial ancestry of the mortal candidate for fusion. These classifications help us understand the vast diversity of experience these divine fragments accumulate in their service to ascending mortals.

Personalized Adjusters: A Unique Status

Among the most fascinating categories are the personalized Adjusters, those who have been granted independent personality status by the Universal Father. Most personalized Adjusters originate from the Paradise Sons during their bestowal missions. When a Creator Son completes his seventh and final bestowal upon the mortal races of his universe realm, his indwelling Adjuster becomes personalized, marking a significant milestone in cosmic history.

However, personalization can occur under other remarkable circumstances. Some Adjusters serve in regular mortals with such distinction, teaching, guiding, and nurturing their subjects through extraordinary challenges, only to have those mortals ultimately reject survival. When a mortal makes the final decision to reject eternal life, the Adjuster is typically released and would ordinarily be reassigned to another being.

Yet in certain cases, the Ancients of Days, recognizing the superlative service of these Adjusters, choose to personalize them despite their subjects' rejection of survival. By recommendation of the Ancients of Days, these Adjusters are transformed from pre-personal divine fragments into actual beings with independent personality status. They are then used for other types of specialized service throughout the universe.

This process underscores an important truth: The choice of survival, or its rejection, carries profound consequences not only for the mortal but also for the divine fragment that has invested itself so completely in that mortal's spiritual development. When someone commits suicide or makes a final, irrevocable decision to cease existence, they are not merely ending their own journey; they are also affecting the ministry of the God fragment that has labored within their mind, sometimes for decades.

The Ancients of Days must carefully adjudicate such cases, determining whether a suicide or other tragic end represented a final decision against survival or whether the individual might still be rehabilitated on the mansion worlds. This is why suicide is regarded in *The Urantia Book* as perhaps the most serious decision a mortal can make, it forces a cosmic judgment about the eternal destiny of the soul.

Divinington: The Sacred Home of the Adjusters

All universe activities related to the dispatch, management, direction, and return of the Thought Adjusters from service in the seven superuniverses appear to be centered on the sacred sphere of Divinington. This mysterious world, one of the seven sacred spheres of Paradise, serves as the headquarters for all mystery monitors and their related ministries.

The Mystery of Divinington

Divinington remains largely unknowable even to the highest spiritual beings in creation. A Solitary Messenger, a being of extraordinarily high spiritual order, wrote the material we study in Paper 107, yet even this exalted personality admitted significant limitations in understanding Divinington and its inhabitants.

The Solitary Messenger reflected: "I have often considered that it would be quite useless for me to go to Divinington. I probably should be unable to see any resident beings except such as the personalized Adjusters, and I have seen them elsewhere. I am very sure there is nothing on Divinington of real value or profit to me, nothing essential to my growth and development, or I should not have been forbidden to go there."

This admission reveals something profound about the nature of spiritual reality: Some truths are so sacred, so intimately connected to the Father's personal relationship with his creatures, that even beings of vast cosmic experience are excluded from their full comprehension. Divinington represents the Father's private domain, where he prepares these fragments of himself for their extraordinary mission within mortal minds.

The Divine Injunctions

Beings of high spiritual order who know about the seven sacred spheres of Paradise receive three divine injunctions regarding them:

1. **Always show adequate respect for the experience and endowments of their seniors and superiors.** This directive, while seemingly obvious, reminds even exalted beings to maintain humility before those of greater experience and wisdom.
2. **Be considerate of the limitations and inexperience of their juniors and subordinates.** Equally important is the instruction to exercise patience and understanding with those who are less developed, recognizing that all beings grow through experience.
3. **Never attempt a landing on the shores of Divinington.** This absolute prohibition preserves the sacred privacy of the Father's work in preparing these divine fragments for their mission.

These injunctions apply to all seven sacred spheres of the Paradise Father, but they hold special significance for Divinington, where the most intimate work of the Father's personal ministry is conducted.

Unrevealed Pre-Personal Entities

The Solitary Messenger who authored this section noted that numerous unrevealed pre-personal entities share Divinington as their home sphere with the Thought Adjusters. The Messenger conjectured that these fellow entities may in some manner be associated with the present and future ministry of the mystery monitors, though their exact nature and function remain undisclosed.

This acknowledgment of mystery, even at the highest levels of universe administration, should humble us and remind us that we are exploring truths that touch the very heart of infinity itself. The Universe is far more vast, far more complex, and far more wonderful than our finite minds can presently comprehend.

The Training of Thought Adjusters

One of the most intriguing revelations about Thought Adjusters concerns their training. At first consideration, this seems paradoxical: Why would perfect fragments of God require training of any kind?

The Paradox of Perfect Beings Receiving Training

The valor and wisdom exhibited by Thought Adjusters suggest that they have undergone a training of tremendous scope and range. Since they are not personalities in the technical sense, they are pre-personal, this training must be imparted in the educational institutions of Divinington.

The unique personalized Adjusters constitute the personnel of these Adjuster training schools. This central and supervising corps is presided over by the now-personalized Adjuster of the original Michael, the first Paradise Son of the Michael order, who completed his sevenfold bestowal upon the races and peoples of his universe realms.

But why would divine fragments, already perfect in their essence, require training? The answer lies in the distinction between perfection of being and perfection of experience.

The Necessity of Experiential Training

Though Thought Adjusters are fragments of God the Father and therefore possess inherent perfection, they lack experience with imperfection. They must learn to function within the chaotic, imperfect, and often resistant environment of the mortal mind. A barbarian living on an evolutionary world, driven by animal instincts and tribal prejudices, presents challenges that pure divinity has never encountered in the perfect realms of Paradise and Havona.

Consider the patience required of an Adjuster assigned to a primitive human being whose thoughts are consumed with survival, fear, superstition, and base desires. The Adjuster must learn to work within these constraints, gently guiding this creature toward higher thoughts while respecting the sacred gift of free will. This requires not theoretical knowledge but practical experience, or at least training based on the accumulated experience of other Adjusters who have gone before.

The personalized Adjuster of the original Michael possesses the most comprehensive experiential knowledge of all Adjusters, having indwelt a Creator Son throughout his seven bestowals, including his final bestowal as a mortal of the realm. This Adjuster is uniquely qualified to train other Adjusters in the delicate art of indwelling evolutionary creatures.

Furthermore, Adjusters may need training to recognize and respond appropriately to evil, something entirely foreign to their divine nature. In the perfection of Paradise, error, sin, and iniquity do not exist. Yet in the evolutionary worlds, these realities are part of the landscape through which mortals must navigate. The Adjuster must learn to distinguish between honest mistakes, willful sin, and embraced iniquity, responding to each with the appropriate guidance while never violating the mortal's free will.

The Divine Nature of Thought Adjusters

To say that a Thought Adjuster is divine is merely to recognize the nature of its origin. It is highly probable that such purity of divinity embraces the essence of the potential of all attributes of deity which can be contained within such a fragment of the absolute essence of the universal presence of the Eternal and Infinite Paradise Father.

Fragmented Divinity

This statement, while philosophically dense, conveys a stunning truth: Each Thought Adjuster, though a fragment, contains within itself the potential of all divine attributes. It is not a partial god or a limited deity; it is a complete expression of divinity, though focused and specialized for its unique mission.

Consider an analogy: When you strike a holographic plate with a laser and break it into fragments, each fragment contains the complete image, not just a portion of it. Similarly, each Thought Adjuster, though a fragment of the Father, contains the fullness of divine potential appropriate to its nature and function.

The actual source of the Adjuster must be infinite, and before fusion with the immortal soul of an evolving mortal, the reality of the Adjuster borders on absoluteness. Adjusters are not absolutes in the universal sense or in the deity sense, but they are probably true absolutes within the potentialities of their fragmented nature.

Qualified Absolute Fragments

This distinction is crucial to understanding the Adjuster's nature: They are qualified as to universality but not as to nature. They are limited in extensiveness but absolute in intensiveness of meaning, value, and fact. For this reason, the revelators sometimes denominate these divine gifts as the "qualified absolute fragments of the Father."

What does this mean in practical terms? It means that while a Thought Adjuster does not possess the infinite scope of the Universal Father, it cannot be everywhere at once or know all things simultaneously, it does possess the absolute quality of divinity in its essence. In terms of spiritual value, moral meaning, and divine reality, the Adjuster is genuinely absolute.

Before fusion with a mortal soul, the Adjuster already borders on absoluteness. After fusion, this absoluteness must grow experientially within the combined personality. The fused mortal-Adjuster entity must learn through billions of years of experience how to express and manifest this absoluteness in service throughout the grand universe and beyond.

In meanings and values, Adjusters are already absolute. But in experience and expression, they must grow toward absoluteness through the partnership with an ascending mortal. This is why the fusion of mortal and Adjuster creates such unlimited potential: It combines experiential growth with absolute divine potential in a union that can never reach a final limit.

The Infallibility of Thought Adjusters

One of the most reassuring truths about Thought Adjusters is their absolute loyalty to the Paradise Father. No Adjuster has ever been disloyal to the Paradise Father. The lower orders of personal creatures may sometimes have to contend with disloyal fellows, but never the Adjusters. They are supreme and infallible in their supernal sphere of creature ministry and universe function.

The Impossibility of Rebellion After Fusion

This infallibility has profound implications for the destiny of mortals who achieve fusion with their Adjusters. Once a mortal being fuses with their indwelling Adjuster, rebellion becomes impossible. Why? Because God the Father cannot rebel against himself.

The rebellions that have occurred in our universe, most notably the Lucifer Rebellion, involved beings who had not yet fused with their Adjusters or who were created as distinct personalities separate from Adjuster indwelling. Angels, Melchizedeks, and even Lanonandek Sons possess free will and can choose to rebel against divine authority.

But once a mortal fuses with their Adjuster, they become a new order of being, one that combines experiential personality with absolute divinity. To rebel at that point would require the being to tear itself apart, to separate divinity from personality. Such a separation is not merely difficult; it is ontologically impossible.

This is why, during the Lucifer Rebellion on our world and throughout our system, every ascending mortal had to make a definitive choice: Would they remain loyal to Michael, our Creator Son, or would they join the rebellion? This decision had to be made before fusion, while rebellion was still theoretically possible.

Those who chose loyalty and subsequently achieved fusion with their Adjusters can never rebel again. They have passed beyond the possibility of cosmic disloyalty. They have become, in essence, extensions of God's own will in the universe, not as mindless automatons but as perfected personalities who have freely chosen eternal alignment with divine purpose.

The Walking Dead

There is, however, a dark corollary to this truth about Adjuster infallibility. Just as the Adjuster cannot rebel against the Father, neither can divinity coexist with fully embraced iniquity. When a mortal being completely and finally embraces evil, choosing cosmic insanity over spiritual sanity, the Adjuster is released.

The Urantia Book refers to such individuals as "the walking dead." They continue to live physically, their bodies still functioning, but they are spiritually dead. Their Thought Adjusters have departed, and there is nothing salvageable about their souls. They have made a final, irrevocable decision against survival, and the cosmos respects that choice.

Such individuals are rare, but they do exist. Those who completely devote themselves to Satanic worship, who embrace iniquity with full knowledge and willful intent, who systematically cultivate evil in their souls, these beings are choosing cosmic extinction. Their physical death will be their final death; they will not awaken on the mansion worlds.

It is a sobering reality that even in this life of apparent freedom, eternal choices are being made. The gift of free will includes the terrible freedom to reject God finally and completely. The Thought Adjuster will not, indeed, cannot, remain in a mind that has fully embraced iniquity, for evil and divinity cannot occupy the same psychic space.

The Perception of Thought Adjusters

Non-personalized Adjusters are visible only to personalized Adjusters. The Solitary Messengers, together with Inspired Trinity Spirits, can detect the presence of Adjusters by means of spiritual reactive phenomena. Seraphim can sometimes discern the spirit luminosity of supposed association with the presence of monitors in the material minds of men. But none of these beings are able actually to discern the real presence of Adjusters unless they have been personalized.

The Spirit Luminosity

This spirit luminosity, sometimes called the "pilot light", is a characteristic spiritual glow that accompanies the divine presence. In the universe of Nebadon, this Paradise luminosity is widely known as the "pilot light." On Uversa, it is called the "light of life." On Urantia, this phenomenon has sometimes been referred to as "that true Light which lights every man who comes into the world."

Jesus spoke of this light when he taught his followers: "Let your light shine before men." He was referring to this spirit luminosity, this divine glow that emanates from every mortal who cooperates with their indwelling Adjuster. We are instructed not to hide our light under a bushel basket but to let it shine forth for all to see.

Fear and the Hidden Light

Why do so many people hide their spiritual light? The answer, sadly, is fear. They fear criticism from friends and family. They fear being labeled as religious fanatics or social misfits. They fear the responsibility that comes with acknowledging God's presence within them.

But here is a liberating truth: If people criticize you, reject you, or abandon you because you believe in God and seek to follow his will, they were never truly your friends. Genuine friendship supports spiritual growth; it does not discourage or mock it. Those who ridicule your faith in God are not companions worthy of your loyalty.

The pilot light within you, that fragment of God himself, deserves to be honored, acknowledged, and allowed to shine. When you cooperate with your Adjuster, when you make decisions in alignment with divine values, when you serve others with love and compassion, your spirit luminosity grows brighter. Others may not consciously recognize what they are seeing, but they will sense something different about you, something authentic and appealing.

The Significance of Adjuster Indwelling

Can you really realize the true significance of the Adjuster indwelling? Do you really fathom what it means to have an absolute fragment of the absolute and infinite Deity, the Universal Father, indwelling and fusing with your finite mortal nature?

When mortal man fuses with an actual fragment of the existential Cause of the total cosmos, no limit can ever be placed upon the destiny of such an unprecedented and unimaginable partnership. In eternity, man will be discovering not only the infinity of the objective Deity but also the unending potentiality of the subjective fragment of this same God.

The Eternal Revelation

Always will the Adjuster be revealing to the mortal personality the wonder of God and never can this supernal revelation come to an end, for the Adjuster is of God and as God to mortal man.

This promise should stagger the imagination. Your spiritual journey does not end when you reach the mansion worlds. It does not end when you traverse the local universe, the superuniverse, or even when you stand in the presence of the Universal Father on Paradise. The revelation of God continues forever, always deepening, always expanding, always revealing new dimensions of divine wonder.

You will spend eternity, literal, unending eternity, discovering the Father through the fragment of himself that dwells within you. And because God is infinite, this discovery will never reach completion. There will always be more to know, more to experience, more to become.

This is not tedious repetition or boring routine. Each new revelation brings fresh wonder, deeper understanding, and greater capacity for divine service. The Adjuster, being of God and as God to you, serves as your personal, eternal guide into the infinite depths of the Father's love and nature.

God Consciousness: The Key Teaching of Jesus

Jesus came to this world with one central mission: to reveal the Father to humanity and to reveal humanity to the Father. His core teaching was simple yet revolutionary: Become conscious that you are a son or daughter of God. Recognize the divine presence within you. Acknowledge the Father fragment that indwells your mind and seeks to guide you toward eternal perfection.

This God consciousness, this awareness of the Adjuster's presence and guidance, transforms everything. It turns every decision into a spiritual choice. It makes every human relationship an opportunity for divine love. It converts every challenge into a lesson in faith and every triumph into an occasion for gratitude.

Jesus taught us to be conscious of the indwelling Adjuster and to listen to its gentle guidance. This is what it means to "pray without ceasing", not to recite endless verbal prayers but to maintain constant awareness of God's presence within and to seek his will in all things.

The Search for God

People often speak of their search for God, as if the Almighty were hiding from them in some distant corner of the cosmos. But the truth is quite different: God is not hiding from us; we are hiding from him. God is constantly revealing himself to us from within our own minds. He has placed a fragment of his own infinite self within us, and this fragment is always seeking to guide us, teach us, and draw us toward himself.

The search for God need not take you to mountaintops or monasteries, though these may provide helpful environments for spiritual reflection. You need not travel to Mars or to the ends of the earth seeking divine truth. For God's sake, literally, he is inside you! The fragment of infinity dwells within your finite mind, patiently waiting for you to recognize his presence and cooperate with his leading.

This is the great secret, the supreme truth that religions often obscure with their elaborate rituals and complex theologies: The God you seek is nearer than your breath, closer than your thoughts. He is not distant or inaccessible. He has taken up residence within the very citadel of your selfhood, and from there he works tirelessly to transform you into his eternal child.

The Balance of Spiritual Life

As young people, we often struggle to find balance in our spiritual lives. The physical body has its demands, legitimate needs for food, rest, companionship, and pleasure. The social self has its requirements, the desire for friendship, romance, achievement, and recognition. These are not evil desires; they are part of normal human development.

The challenge lies in learning discernment: What is important, and what is merely urgent? What has eternal value, and what is temporary distraction? What builds spiritual character, and what erodes it?

This discernment does not develop overnight. It requires years of choices, mistakes, corrections, and growth. A decision made at twelve years of age to follow God, whether through baptism, confirmation, or personal dedication, is just the beginning. That commitment must be renewed, tested, refined, and deepened through decades of living.

Each stage of life brings new challenges to our spiritual commitments. Youth brings the challenge of hormones and peer pressure. Young adulthood brings the challenge of career and romance. Middle age brings the challenge of responsibility and ambition. Old age brings the challenge of decline and mortality. At each stage, we must choose again to follow the Adjuster's leading.

The Growing Light

Those who make and keep their commitment to follow God's will experience gradual but profound transformation. At age twelve, the spiritual light within might be dim and flickering. At age twenty-five years old, it burns somewhat brighter. At fifty, it shines with steady radiance. By the time we reach old age, if we have faithfully cooperated with our Adjusters, the light should be blazing with spiritual power and beauty.

This is not automatic. Many people reach old age with their lights barely glowing, having spent their lives pursuing purely material goals and pleasuring their animal nature while ignoring their spiritual destiny. Others, who chose God early and remained faithful, arrive at life's end with souls so illuminated that they seem to glow with inner light.

When such a person awakens on the first mansion world, they will be ready to continue their spiritual growth with minimal adjustment. They have already been living a spiritual life; death merely transfers them to a more congenial environment for continuing that life. But even there, the growth continues. Even in the mansion worlds, in the constellation spheres, in the superuniverse capitals, and beyond, the growth never stops.

If you think you will reach the mansion worlds and find that the struggle is over, that perfection has been achieved, that no further effort is required, you will be disappointed. The mansion worlds are merely the first step in removing the "mark of the beast," the animalistic and barbaric tendencies we inherited from our evolutionary origins. It takes seven mansion world experiences to fully eradicate these primitive tendencies and prepare us for higher service.

But even after completing the mansion worlds, the journey has barely begun. Before us lie the constellation worlds, the local universe capitals, the minor and major sectors of the superuniverse, the billion worlds of Havona, and finally Paradise itself. And reaching Paradise is not the end; it is merely the end of the beginning.

The Return to Divinington

Since we know very little about the non-personalized Adjusters, we can only contact and communicate with the personalized orders, we must rely on fragmentary information gathered from many sources. The personalized Adjusters are christened on Divinington; they are always known by name and not by number.

These names are significant. They represent the Adjuster's identity, accumulated experience, and unique character developed through service to ascending mortals. When a mortal finally fuses with their Adjuster, it is possible, even likely, that the new name received by the fused personality is actually the Adjuster's name, now shared by both the mortal and divine components of the unified being.

The personalized Adjusters are permanently domiciled on Divinington. That sacred sphere is their home. They go out from that abode only by the will of the Universal Father. Very few are found in the domains of the local universes, but large numbers are present in the central universe of Havona, where they serve in various capacities related to the perfecting of ascending pilgrims.

When Thought Adjusters return to Divinington, whether after completing service with a mortal or for periodic reporting, there is actual contact with the Father's Paradise personality as well as with the specialized manifestation of the Father's divinity which is reported to be situated on this secret sphere.

Think of it: Your Thought Adjuster, after laboring within your mind for decades, experiencing your struggles and triumphs, your doubts and faith, your failures and victories, returns periodically to Divinington to report directly to the Universal Father. Your life, your choices, your spiritual growth, all of this is known to the Father through the ministry of his indwelling fragment.

This should inspire both awe and accountability. We are not anonymous beings lost in a vast, impersonal universe. We are known, individually and intimately, by the Creator of all things. Every sincere prayer, every moral victory, every act of love and service, all of this is observed, cherished, and recorded in the eternal memories of both the Adjuster and the Father.

Conclusion: The Unlimited Partnership

The nature and origin of Thought Adjusters remain partially shrouded in divine mystery, yet what has been revealed should fill us with wonder and gratitude. These absolute fragments of the infinite Father, trained on the sacred sphere of Divinington, come to dwell within our imperfect minds not as a temporary arrangement but as eternal partners in an unprecedented cosmic adventure.

No limit can be placed upon the destiny of a partnership between an absolute divine fragment and an experiential mortal personality. In eternity, we will explore not only the objective infinity of God but also the subjective infinity of the God-fragment within us. The revelation of divine wonder never ends, for the Adjuster is of God and as God to us.

The key to unlocking this unlimited potential lies in one simple yet profound act: recognizing the divine presence within and choosing to cooperate with it. Jesus taught us to be conscious of our sonship with God, to acknowledge the Father fragment within, and to seek his will in all things. This God consciousness transforms ordinary human existence into the early stages of eternal divine partnership.

As we move forward in our study, we will explore in greater depth the actual working relationship between the Adjuster and the human mind, how these divine fragments communicate with us, how we can better cooperate with their leading, and what obstacles prevent or facilitate their work within us. The practical application of these profound truths awaits us in the chapters ahead, where theory gives way to practice and knowledge transforms into living experience.

Looking ahead

Chapter 4 will examine "The Work of the Thought Adjusters: Mission and Methods," exploring how these divine fragments actually function within the human mind and how we can better cooperate with their transforming ministry.

Chapter 4: The Mindedness of Thought Adjusters

Understanding Divine Consciousness and the Absolute Level of Reality

Introduction

In our continued exploration of Paper 107 of *The Urantia Book*, we arrive at one of the most profound and challenging concepts in the entire revelation: the nature of Thought Adjuster mindedness. This chapter addresses a mystery that has puzzled sincere students of divine truth throughout the ages, how does God's indwelling presence operate within human consciousness while maintaining its divine nature?

The concept of Thought Adjuster mindedness requires us to expand our understanding beyond conventional religious thought. We must grasp that these divine fragments possess their own consciousness, a mind that is distinctly divine, yet capable of experiential growth. This paradox lies at the heart of our spiritual evolution and illuminates the path toward eventual fusion with our indwelling divine presence.

As we examine this material, we will discover that the Thought Adjuster's mind operates on an entirely different level than human consciousness. Understanding this distinction is crucial for comprehending how divine guidance works within us and why achieving harmony with our Adjuster requires both patience and persistent spiritual effort.

Section 1: The Challenge of Understanding Adjuster Mindedness

The Human Tendency Toward Mediation

Evolutionary mortals naturally tend to perceive mind as a cosmic mediation between spirit and matter. This perspective makes intuitive sense from our human vantage point, for indeed, the principal ministry of mind discernible to us is precisely this mediating function. Our material minds constantly work to bridge the gap between our physical existence and our spiritual aspirations.

However, this framework, while accurate for understanding human consciousness, creates significant difficulty when we attempt to comprehend that Thought Adjusters possess minds of their own. The challenge arises because we instinctively try to fit divine consciousness into the same mediating pattern we experience in ourselves.

The Absolute Level of Reality

Thought Adjusters are fragmentations of God operating on an absolute level of reality. This bears careful consideration: they function at a level that is not only pre-personal but also exists prior to all energy and spirit divergence. To grasp this concept, we must understand that before God can be conceived as energy or as spirit, the absolute level of divinity already exists.

On this monistic level, antecedent to energy and spirit differentiation, there can be no mediating function of mind. Why? Because there are no divergences requiring mediation. The Thought Adjuster represents God in His undivided, absolute nature. Unlike human beings, who must constantly reconcile material and spiritual impulses, the Adjuster exists in perfect unity.

This is why the Thought Adjuster remains in perpetual, unbroken connection with God the Father. It is not merely connected to the Father; it *is* part of the Father. This fragmentation is literal, not metaphorical. When we speak of the Adjuster as a fragment of God, we mean that it is an actual portion of the Universal Father's divine essence, temporarily individualized for the purpose of indwelling an evolutionary creature.

Before Energy and Spirit Divergence

The revelation teaches us that the Thought Adjuster's existence precedes three fundamental aspects of created reality:

First, it is pre-personal. The Adjuster exists before personality is bestowed by the Universal Father. This explains why the Adjuster can indwell beings who have personality without becoming confused with or absorbed by that personality.

Second, it exists prior to the infusion of material energy that creates physical form. All material manifestation is essentially energy, organized and patterned according to divine plans. The Adjuster's reality transcends this level entirely.

Third, it precedes the spirit endowment that comes from the Eternal Son. Every spiritual impulse in creation ultimately derives from the Second Person of the Trinity. Yet the Adjuster operates at a level that existed before even this spiritual differentiation occurred.

Section 2: The Experiential Mind of the Thought Adjuster

The Development of Adjuster Consciousness

While Thought Adjusters exist on the absolute level of divinity, they nonetheless develop an experiential dimension to their consciousness. This represents one of the most fascinating aspects of the entire divine plan. When a Thought Adjuster departs from Divinington, the divine sphere from which all Adjusters originate, and begins its first assignment within a mortal being, something remarkable occurs: that Adjuster begins to acquire experience.

From that inaugural moment of indwelling, whether in a being with strong survival potential or in a primitive human with limited spiritual capacity, the Adjuster gains experiential knowledge. This experience becomes part of the Adjuster's consciousness, not replacing its divine nature, but adding an experiential dimension to its absolute consciousness.

We might conceptualize this as follows: The Adjuster possesses the mind of God the Father, absolute, perfect, and unchanging. Yet simultaneously, through its assignments in evolutionary creatures, it develops an experiential mind, a consciousness enriched by actual contact with imperfection, struggle, growth, and triumph. This experiential mind remains part of God, yet it is distinct in the sense that it carries the specific experiences of that particular Adjuster's journey.

Virgin and Non-Virgin Adjusters

The distinction between virgin and non-virgin Adjusters illuminates this experiential development. A virgin Adjuster undertakes its first assignment in a mortal being. During this initial mission, the Adjuster cannot communicate with other Adjusters in the same manner that experienced Adjusters can. The virgin Adjuster maintains its connection with God the Father, but it has not yet developed the experiential capacity for lateral communication with fellow Adjusters.

Once an Adjuster completes its first assignment, whether through the mortal's death, survival decision, or other circumstance, it returns to Divinington as a non-virgin Adjuster. This Adjuster now possesses experiential knowledge. It can communicate with other non-virgin Adjusters, sharing insights and coordinating efforts in ways that virgin Adjusters cannot.

The revelation informs us that virgin Adjusters are typically assigned to primitive humans or to beings with limited survival potential. This serves a dual purpose: it provides these early humans with divine indwelling (however they might respond to it), and it gives the virgin Adjuster valuable experience in the challenging environment of undeveloped human consciousness. Some of these early assignments do result in survival, though the percentage is comparatively small.

As humanity evolves spiritually and intellectually, more Adjusters assigned to human beings are experienced Adjusters. The book explicitly states that no virgin Adjusters are currently being assigned on our planet. Every Thought Adjuster now indwelling a human being on Earth has had previous experience.

The Communication Capacity of Adjusters

The revelation acknowledges that Thought Adjusters possess unlimited ability to communicate with each other, at least among all forms of Monitors above the first or virgin groups. However, the exact nature and purpose of these inter-Adjuster communications remain largely mysterious. The revelators candidly admit: "We do not know."

What we do know with certainty is that Adjusters must possess some form of mind, for "they must be minded in some manner else they can never be personalized." This statement carries profound implications. Personalization represents the ultimate destiny of those Adjusters who successfully fuse with their mortal subjects. Without mindedness, without the capacity for choice, preference, and independent thought, such personalization would be impossible.

Section 3: The Nature of Adjuster Mindedness - Ancestral to the Conjoint Actor

The mindedness of the Thought Adjuster is described as being "like the mindedness of the Universal Father and the Eternal Son, that which is ancestral to the mind of the Conjoint Actor." This description requires careful unpacking, for it reveals the cosmic origin of different types of mind.

The Conjoint Actor, the Third Person of the Trinity, also known as the Infinite Spirit, is the source of all mind in creation. When we human beings think, we participate in the universal mind circuit that emanates from the Infinite Spirit and is administered in our local universe by the Divine Minister, our Creative Mother Spirit.

However, the mindedness of the Universal Father and the Eternal Son is *ancestral* to this cosmic mind circuit. It preceded the emergence of the Conjoint Actor.

Therefore, when the revelation describes Adjuster mindedness as being "like" the mindedness of the Father and the Son, it is placing Adjuster consciousness in a category fundamentally different from human consciousness.

The Trinity Pattern in Mind

This leads us to a stunning realization about what happens when a human being fuses with their Thought Adjuster. Consider the elements involved:

The Thought Adjuster brings the mindedness of the Universal Father and the Eternal Son, the first two Persons of the Trinity.

The human being brings the mind derived from the Conjoint Actor, the Third Person of the Trinity, as mediated through the Divine Minister of our local universe.

When these two unite in fusion, we see another manifestation of the Trinity pattern. The fused being combines the mindedness of all three Persons of the Paradise Trinity. This represents far more than merely adding divine consciousness to human consciousness; it creates a new order of being that reflects the totality of Trinity mind.

This Trinity pattern appears repeatedly throughout the universe, at every level of reality. Its appearance in the fusion of mortal and Adjuster confirms the fundamental truth that the Trinity represents the ultimate pattern for all reality. Even at the most personal and intimate level, the fusion of an individual soul with its divine Adjuster, the Trinity template remains operative.

Section 4: The Practical Implications of Adjuster Mindedness

The Independence of Adjuster Consciousness

Understanding that the Thought Adjuster possesses its own mind, distinct from yet complementary to human mind, has profound practical implications for spiritual growth. Many sincere seekers assume that every uplifting thought or spiritual impulse originates directly from their Adjuster. While the Adjuster certainly works to spiritualize our thinking, we must recognize that our mind and the Adjuster's mind remain separate until fusion.

The Adjuster adjusts our thoughts toward spiritual concepts. This represents the Adjuster's primary technique for guidance: taking our human thoughts and subtly shifting them, elevating them, and directing them toward eternal values. However, this does not mean that every thought we identify as "spiritual" necessarily originates from our Adjuster or accurately reflects divine will.

Human beings possess genuine agency. We can think, choose, and act independently. The Adjuster respects this independence absolutely. Therefore, discernment becomes crucial in the spiritual life. We must learn to distinguish between our own spiritual aspirations (which may be noble but still human in origin) and the authentic leading of the Adjuster.

The Question of Free Will and Divine Guidance

This brings us to a critical question: Can external circumstances force a person to reject their Adjuster? The answer illuminates the inviolability of human free will.

Consider the example of individuals living under totalitarian regimes where worship of the state or its leader is mandatory. Does such coercion doom these individuals spiritually? Absolutely not. No external force can compel belief. A ruler may declare himself divine and demand worship, but he cannot force genuine belief in his divinity. Citizens may outwardly comply while inwardly maintaining their true convictions.

This principle held true throughout history. When Roman emperors demanded worship as gods, the Senate and populace often rendered the required honors without truly believing in the emperor's divinity. Similarly, in modern totalitarian states, people may mouth required doctrine while privately maintaining different beliefs.

The Thought Adjuster can work with genuine inner conviction regardless of outward circumstances. No political system, no matter how oppressive, can sever the connection between a sincere soul and its indwelling divine fragment. The only power that can terminate this relationship is the individual's own final, conscious, and complete rejection of God.

Virgin Adjusters and Human Evolution

The assignment of virgin Adjusters to early humans provides insight into both human spiritual evolution and the divine plan. For approximately the first 500,000 years of human existence on our planet, from the emergence of Andon and Fonta (the first true human beings) until the arrival of the Planetary Prince Caligastia, all Thought Adjusters assigned to humans were virgin Adjusters.

These early humans lived primarily at the survival level. Their consciousness centered on obtaining food, reproducing, and avoiding danger. They had not yet developed clear concepts of deity or moral law. Nevertheless, when the first humans made their first truly moral decision, the choice to leave their tribe and strike out independently, seeking self-improvement, they immediately received Thought Adjusters.

This reveals something crucial about what qualifies a being for Adjuster indwelling. Andon and Fonta did not receive Adjusters because they began worshiping God. They received Adjusters because they made a moral decision demonstrating self-awareness and the desire for personal growth. The concept of a force greater than themselves developed *after* they received their Adjusters, not before.

This pattern continued throughout early human history. Virgin Adjusters gained experience working with primitive consciousness, and a small percentage of these early humans did survive and continue their careers in the mansion worlds. After Caligastia's arrival with his staff (the Caligastia One Hundred), human spiritual capacity increased significantly, and more experienced Adjusters began to be assigned.

The default of Adam and Eve marked another crucial point in this evolution. Even these Material Sons and Daughters of God received Thought Adjusters after their default, demonstrating that no being is beyond the reach of divine mercy.

The Communication of Revelation

The communication capacity of experienced Adjusters played an essential role in the revelation of *The Urantia Book* itself. The entire text was transmitted through the Adjuster of a single human being, a self-acting Adjuster of the highest order. This Adjuster served as the communication channel through which numerous celestial authors transmitted their papers.

This method of revelation demonstrates both the capabilities of highly experienced Adjusters and the extraordinary difficulty of direct celestial communication with human minds. The normal channels for such communication are limited: guardian angels and secondary midwayers. Direct communication from higher celestial beings requires special circumstances and, typically, a specially prepared human mind with an unusually capable Adjuster.

This reality should give us pause when evaluating claims of angelic visitations or direct divine revelation. While we cannot categorically deny such experiences (for we know they occasionally occur), we should approach them with appropriate discernment. The pattern established in *The Urantia Book* represents the most extensive revelation in human history, yet even this required extraordinary arrangements and a unique human-Adjuster partnership. Claims of equally significant revelations through more casual means warrant careful scrutiny.

Section 5: The Supreme Being and Experiential Deity

God's Creation of Experiential Divinity

The development of experiential consciousness in Thought Adjusters connects to one of the grandest themes in *The Urantia Book*: the evolution of the Supreme Being. While God the Father exists as absolute, eternal, and unchanging divinity, He is in the process of eventuating (bringing into full existence) an experiential aspect of Himself, God the Supreme.

The Supreme Being represents the sum total of all evolutionary experience in the seven superuniverses. Every choice made by every evolutionary creature, every challenge overcome, every truth learned, all of this contributes to the growth of the Supreme. In this sense, God the Father is creating a new aspect of Himself that will embody all finite experience.

The parallel with Thought Adjusters is striking. Just as each Adjuster combines absolute divine nature with experiential consciousness, the Supreme Being will eventually combine absoluteness with the totality of finite experience. When the Supreme finally achieves full actualization, an event that will mark the completion of the present universe age, a new divine being will exist: one who knows experientially everything that has been lived, suffered, learned, and achieved throughout all time and space.

The Purpose of Experiential Growth

Why does God create experiential aspects of Himself? The answer relates to divine administration and the sharing of responsibility. Consider the analogy of Michael (Christ Jesus) creating Gabriel as the chief executive of our local universe. Michael did not create Gabriel out of weakness or inability to handle His responsibilities. Rather, He created Gabriel to share in the joys and duties of universe administration, to be a partner in the grand enterprise of universe building.

Similarly, God the Father eventuates the Supreme Being to assume ultimate responsibility for the evolutionary superuniverses. When the Supreme achieves full actualization, this being will possess both divine perfection and complete experiential knowledge of evolutionary imperfection and growth. The Supreme will be uniquely qualified to guide the completed superuniverses in their next phase of cosmic development.

This same pattern will continue as God moves beyond the present creation into the outer space levels. Each age brings new expressions of divinity, new partnerships between absolute and experiential deity, and new opportunities for creature participation in divine purposes.

Our Role in Supreme Growth

Every moral choice we make, every spiritual victory we achieve, every act of love or service we perform contributes directly to the growth of the Supreme Being. We are not merely improving ourselves; we are literally contributing to the evolution of deity. This realization should transform our understanding of the significance of our daily lives.

Even our Thought Adjusters participate in this process. As Adjusters gain experience through their assignments, they contribute their accumulated wisdom to the great reservoir of experiential knowledge that constitutes the growing Supreme. Nothing is wasted; every experience has cosmic significance.

Conclusion: The Mystery and the Promise

The mindedness of Thought Adjusters remains, in many respects, a profound mystery. We can grasp certain principles: that Adjusters possess divine consciousness operating on the absolute level; that they develop experiential minds through their missions; that they communicate with each other in ways we cannot fully comprehend; and that their mindedness reflects the primal consciousness of the Universal Father and the Eternal Son.

Yet much remains beyond our current capacity to understand. The revelators themselves acknowledge the limits of what they can explain about Adjuster inter-communication and many aspects of Adjuster function. This honest acknowledgment of mystery should encourage intellectual humility even as we pursue greater understanding.

What we can grasp with confidence is the practical reality: each of us hosts within our consciousness a fragment of absolute divinity that possesses its own mind, makes its own choices (within the parameters of divine nature), and works ceaselessly to spiritualize our thinking and guide us toward eternal survival. This indwelling presence respects our autonomy absolutely while offering us the opportunity for the most intimate partnership possible, eventual fusion into a single being that combines human experience with divine perfection.

The journey toward this fusion is the great adventure of mortal existence. As we learn to distinguish between our own thinking and the Adjuster's subtle influence, as we practice surrender to divine leading while exercising our own moral agency, as we gradually harmonize our will with the Adjuster's spiritual urging, we move step by step toward that ultimate unity.

In our next chapter, we will explore the practical aspects of Adjuster communication and guidance: how Adjusters actually work within human consciousness, the various techniques they employ, and the conditions that facilitate or hinder their ministry. Understanding these practical dynamics will help us become more effective partners with our indwelling divine guides as we continue our ascension toward Paradise.

Chapter Summary:

This chapter examines the profound mystery of Thought Adjuster mindedness, revealing that these divine fragments possess consciousness operating on an absolute level of reality, pre-personal and prior to all energy and spirit divergence. We explored how Adjusters develop experiential minds through their assignments while maintaining their divine connection to the Universal Father. The distinction between virgin and experienced Adjusters illuminated the evolution of both human spiritual capacity and Adjuster expertise. We discovered the Trinity pattern in fusion, where human mind (from the Conjoint Actor) combines with Adjuster mindedness (reflecting the Father and Son) to create a being embodying all three aspects of Paradise Trinity consciousness. Finally, we connected Adjuster experience to the grand cosmic process of Supreme Being evolution, recognizing our role in contributing to experiential deity. This foundation prepares us to explore, in subsequent chapters, the practical dynamics of Adjuster guidance and the techniques of divine-human cooperation.

Chapter 5: The Nature and Ministry of Thought Adjusters

Introduction: Understanding Divine Indwelling

The concept of divine indwelling represents one of the most profound and transformative teachings within The Urantia Book. In this chapter, we explore the nature, function, and eternal significance of Thought Adjusters, those mysterious fragments of God the Father that dwell within the human mind. These divine presences, also known as Mystery Monitors or Father Fragments, constitute the most direct and personal connection between mortal creatures and the Universal Father.

As we continue our examination of Paper 107, Section 5, we encounter revelations that challenge our conventional understanding of consciousness, reality, and spiritual potential. The material presented here builds upon foundational concepts introduced in earlier sections while unveiling new dimensions of the relationship between the human and the divine. Our study reveals not only what Thought Adjusters are, but also what they mean for our eternal destiny and our present spiritual lives.

This chapter addresses several critical questions: What is the true nature of these divine fragments? How do they function within both mortal and non-mortal beings? What does fusion with the Adjuster actually mean for our consciousness and identity? And perhaps most importantly, how does this partnership between the human and divine contribute to the evolution of the Supreme Being and the fulfillment of the cosmic plan?

The Universal Scope of Divine Fragments - Pre-Personal Entities and Adjuster Ministry

The Urantia Book reveals that human beings are not the only recipients of Thought Adjusters. The text explicitly states: "The type of mind postulated in an Adjuster must be similar to the mind endowment of numerous other orders of pre-personal entities which presumably likewise originate in the First Source and Center." This revelation expands our understanding of divine ministry far beyond the boundaries of mortal existence.

Pre-personal entities are beings who, like evolutionary mortals, exist in a state of incompleteness until the Universal Father bestows personality upon them. For human beings, this bestowal occurs at birth, or possibly even earlier, at the moment of conception. However, the precise timing remains among the mysteries not fully revealed. What we do know with certainty is that personality bestowal differs from Adjuster arrival, which typically occurs around the age of five to six years, following the child's first moral decision.

The existence of other pre-personal orders receiving Thought Adjusters indicates the universality of the Father's plan for experiential growth. These beings, though not explicitly described in detail within The Urantia Book, demonstrate that the divine indwelling strategy extends throughout creation. The revelation states: "It is also possible for these individualizations of original Deity to become unified with numerous evolving types of non-mortal beings and even with a limited number of non-evolutionary beings who have developed capacity for fusion with such Deity fragments."

This statement carries profound implications. Not only do evolutionary mortals, beings who ascend through experience, receive Adjusters, but certain non-evolutionary beings also qualify for this divine gift. These may include created beings of various orders who have demonstrated the capacity for spiritual growth and fusion. The universe teems with diverse orders of intelligent beings, most of whom are never mentioned in The Urantia Book due to space limitations. If the revelation attempted to catalog every order of being, the text would expand from its current 1,955 pages to countless volumes.

The Mystery of Mind Types

The passage indicates that the type of mind within an Adjuster resembles the mind endowment found in these other pre-personal entities. This suggests a universal pattern, a divine template, for consciousness that can interface with the Father's presence. While these other orders "have not been revealed on Urantia," they nonetheless "disclose minded qualities," meaning they possess consciousness, volition, and the capacity for spiritual relationship.

This universal scope of Adjuster ministry demonstrates several key principles. First, it reveals the Father's impartiality and infinite love, His desire to share Himself extends to all beings capable of spiritual response, regardless of their origin or nature. Second, it suggests that the experience-gathering function of Adjusters operates on a cosmic scale, contributing to the evolution of the Supreme Being through countless types of creatures across all creation. Third, it hints at the magnificent diversity of the universe, reminding us that mortal experience, while precious, represents only one pattern among many in the Father's eternal plan.

The Divine Partnership: Human and Adjuster - The Nature of Dual Minds

Until the moment of fusion, every indwelt mortal operates with what might be called a dual consciousness, the mortal mind and the divine mind of the Adjuster. The Urantia Book states: "When Thought Adjusters fuse with the evolving immortal morontia soul of the surviving human, the mind of the Adjuster can only be identified as persisting apart from the creature's mind until the ascending mortal attains spirit levels of universe progression."

This statement reveals a crucial truth about our present condition: we are, quite literally, of two minds. The mortal mind, evolved through biological and social development, perceives reality through material senses and conceptual frameworks limited by time and space. The Adjuster mind, by contrast, exists as a fragment of absolute deity, timeless, spaceless, and infinite in potential. These two minds coexist within the same being, the Adjuster working continuously to spiritualize mortal thinking while respecting the sacred sovereignty of human will.

The text continues: "Upon the attainment of the finaliter levels of ascendant experience, these spirits of the sixth stage appear to transmute some mind factor representing a union of certain phases of the mortal and Adjuster minds which had previously functioned as liaison between the divine and human phases of such ascending personalities."

This passage describes what happens at the culmination of the Paradise ascent. When an ascending mortal achieves sixth-stage spirit status, the level of Paradise finaliters, something profound occurs. The previously separate mortal and divine minds merge into a unified consciousness. The "liaison" function that characterized their relationship throughout the mortal and morontia careers transforms into complete integration. The ascending being becomes truly one in mind, purpose, and consciousness with the indwelling fragment of God.

Contributing to the Supreme Being

The revelation continues with a statement of cosmic significance: "This experiential mind quality probably 'Supreme evolves' and subsequently augments the experiential endowment of evolutionary Deity, the Supreme Being."

Here we discover the ultimate purpose of our experiential journey. Every decision, every struggle, every victory over selfishness and material limitation contributes data to the evolving Supreme Being. However, this contribution follows a specific pattern and timing. Throughout our ascension career, from mortal life through the morontia worlds and into the early spirit stages, our experiences are recorded and held in trust by the seventh Master Spirit, the Master Spirit who presides over our superuniverse and serves as the vice-gerent of the Supreme Being.

Only when we achieve finaliter status, when we become sixth-stage spirits having completed the Paradise ascent, does our accumulated experiential data transfer fully to the Supreme Being. At that moment, the totality of our struggles, insights, and spiritual victories becomes part of the experiential Deity whose evolution depends upon the completion of all such journeys by all ascending mortals throughout the grand universe.

This revelation answers a profound question: When will the Supreme Being achieve full actualization? The answer: only when all mortals across all seven superuniverses complete their ascension to finaliter status and when all evolutionary worlds achieve the status of Light and Life. At that moment, a moment that exists beyond our temporal comprehension, the cumulative experience of trillions upon trillions of ascending beings will pour into the Supreme Being, bringing about full actualization of evolutionary Deity.

Understanding this process helps us grasp the cosmic importance of even the smallest moral decision made on the most isolated evolutionary world. Every choice for truth, beauty, and goodness ripples through reality, eventually contributing to the Supreme Being's completion. We are not merely saving our individual souls; we are cosmic participants in the evolution of Deity itself.

The Essential Nature of Adjusters - Pure Spirit and Pure Spirit-Plus

The Urantia Book provides a carefully nuanced description of Adjuster nature: "Adjusters are pure spirits, presumably absolute spirits, but the Adjuster must also be something more than exclusive spirit reality. In addition to conjectured mindedness, factors of pure energy are also present."

This statement requires careful consideration. Adjusters are described as "pure spirits," but with an important qualification, they are "pure spirit-plus." The "plus" designation indicates that Adjusters transcend even our highest conception of spirit reality. They incorporate not only spirit essence but also "factors of pure energy." Since God the Father is "the source of pure energy and of pure spirit," His fragments naturally contain both elements.

This dual nature, spirit and energy, grants Adjusters capabilities that pure spirit alone could not provide. The text explains: "It is a fact that the Adjusters traverse space over the instantaneous and universal gravity circuits of the Paradise Isle." This statement reveals something extraordinary: Thought Adjusters can move through space instantaneously, unbound by time or distance. They utilize the absolute gravity circuits emanating from Paradise, circuits that connect all reality to the central dwelling place of God.

The Implications of Pure Energy

The revelation that Adjusters are composed of pure energy carries profound implications for our security and eternal survival. Consider a catastrophic scenario: suppose humanity, in a moment of unprecedented folly, unleashed weapons capable of destroying the entire planet instantaneously. What would happen to the billions of indwelt mortals?

Because Thought Adjusters are pure energy and can function instantaneously across space, God the Father possesses the capability to extract and transplant all human consciousness to a new realm in the same instant. The material bodies might perish, but the essential persons, the personality, soul, and Adjuster, would survive. We would awaken in morontia form, our mortal experience intact, our ascension careers continuing as if no interruption had occurred.

This capability explains why nothing can truly threaten the eternal survival of those who choose to continue. The Father's love and power combine to ensure that no cosmic accident, planetary catastrophe, or human foolishness can separate us from our divine destiny, provided we maintain our will to survive and our desire to know God.

The pure energy nature of Adjusters also reveals why artificial intelligence, regardless of how sophisticated it becomes, can never achieve true consciousness in the way humans experience it. Consciousness requires more than complex information processing; it requires the presence of mind circuits bestowed by the Infinite Spirit and, ultimately, the indwelling presence of the Father through the Thought Adjuster. Without this divine component, this encircuitment in pure energy and spirit, there can be sophisticated simulation but never genuine consciousness, true volition, or authentic spiritual capacity.

Adjusters as Prisoners of Hope - The Divine Confinement

One of the most poignant passages in The Urantia Book describes the Adjuster's situation: "The Adjusters are saturated with the beautiful and self-bestowing love of the Father of spirits. They truly and divinely love you; they are the prisoners of spirit hope confined within the minds of men. They long for the Deity attainment of your mortal minds that their loneliness may end, that they may be delivered with you from the limitations of material investiture and the habiliments of time."

The description of Adjusters as "prisoners" may seem jarring. How can a fragment of infinite God be imprisoned? The answer lies in understanding the nature of commitment. When a Thought Adjuster indwells a human being, that fragment becomes bound to that individual's choices and spiritual progress. The Adjuster cannot simply abandon the relationship, except in the rare cases where a person becomes spiritually insane, making final, irreversible decisions against survival and spiritual reality.

Throughout the mortal life, and even into the early stages of morontia existence, the Adjuster remains confined within the mortal or morontia mind, working tirelessly to spiritualize thinking, to present higher concepts, to illuminate truth. Yet the Adjuster must work within the limitations imposed by the creature's will, biological inheritance, and cultural conditioning. The divine fragment can suggest but never compel, can illuminate but never coerce.

The text speaks of the Adjuster's loneliness, a profound statement indicating that these divine fragments experience something akin to isolation while separated from the full consciousness of Deity. Confined within finite mind, surrounded by material thoughts and temporal concerns, the Adjuster longs for the moment when the mortal will finally choose wholehearted cooperation, when spiritual fusion becomes possible, when the limitations of material existence fall away.

The Goal of Liberation

The passage continues: "They long for the Deity attainment of your mortal minds that their loneliness may end, that they may be delivered with you from the limitations of material investiture and the habiliments of time." This statement reveals the mutuality of the salvation process. Fusion liberates not only the mortal but also the Adjuster. In fusion, both mortal and divine achieve something neither could accomplish alone, the creation of a new order of being, a finaliter, who combines authentic experiential growth with divine perfection.

Even after death and resurrection on the mansion worlds, when mortals receive morontia bodies and morontia minds, the Adjuster remains in a state of confinement until the moment of fusion. The morontia existence, while vastly superior to mortal life, still represents a transitional phase. The ascending mortal must progress through successive morontia levels, achieving increasingly spiritualized consciousness, until finally reaching the point where fusion becomes possible.

At the moment of fusion, the long partnership between human and divine consummates in eternal union. The two minds become one. The two wills become one. The finite and infinite unite in a being who will serve throughout eternity, first as a finaliter in the Corps of Mortal Finaliters, and eventually in capacities not yet revealed as the ages unfold toward ultimate destiny.

The Circuit of Divine Connection - Encircuited in Reality

The Thought Adjuster serves as our direct circuit connection to the cosmos, our grounding point in ultimate reality. Through the Adjuster, we connect not only to the Universal Father but also to the cosmic mind circuits, the spirit circuits, and the energy circuits that constitute the fabric of reality itself.

Without this connection, human existence would be merely a dream, a shadow play on the walls of material existence. The revelation states this clearly: without the Thought Adjuster making our experience real through divine participation, mortal life would constitute nothing more than a temporary phenomenon, significant only within its own limited context. But with the Adjuster present, recording every spiritually significant decision and experience, mortal life takes on cosmic meaning. Our choices matter eternally because they are captured and preserved by a fragment of eternal Deity.

Jesus, during his mortal life, understood this perfectly. When facing death, he could say with complete confidence: "What do I care what happens to this body? We're going on to the mansion worlds." This statement reflects the reality that our true identity, personality, soul, and Adjuster, transcends material existence. The body serves as a temporary vehicle, valuable for the experience it enables, but not to be confused with the actual person who inhabits it.

The Reality of Spiritual Life

The Urantia Book repeatedly emphasizes that spiritual life is real life, while material existence is preparatory and temporary. This teaching challenges conventional thinking, which tends to view material reality as solid and concrete while dismissing spiritual reality as abstract or metaphorical. The truth stands precisely opposite: spiritual reality is fundamental and eternal, while material existence is derivative and temporary.

Consider the nature of mortal life. We eat to maintain bodies that will eventually die. We sleep to restore energy in forms that will return to dust. We reproduce to continue a species trapped in time. All these activities serve necessary functions within the material phase of existence, but none of them represent ultimate reality. They are means to an end, not ends in themselves.

As mortals progress spiritually, even in this life, they begin to experience decreased attachment to purely material concerns. Spiritual communion provides sustenance that food cannot give. Divine presence provides rest that sleep cannot achieve. Cosmic family relationships provide fulfillment that biological family, precious as it is, cannot completely satisfy.

This principle accelerates in morontia existence. On the mansion worlds, ascending mortals gradually require less food and sleep as they progress. By the time an ascender reaches the higher spiritual levels, physical sustenance becomes unnecessary. The being draws all required energy directly from the spiritual circuits, becoming fully sustained by connection to divine reality.

The same principle applies to other material functions. Sexual reproduction, central to mortal life, becomes completely obsolete after death. Mansion world beings do not reproduce biologically because they are no longer biological. Yet the deep communion and unity that sexuality hints at does not disappear; rather, it transforms into something far more profound, a spiritual union of minds that surpasses anything possible in material existence.

The Cosmic Scale of Adjuster Ministry - Beyond the Grand Universe

The Urantia Book reveals that Adjusters operate not only within the seven superuniverses that constitute the grand universe but potentially beyond: "That the Mystery Monitors are thus associated with the material circuits of the universe of universes is indeed puzzling, but it remains a fact that they flash throughout the entire grand universe over the material-gravity circuits. It is entirely possible that they may even penetrate the outer space levels; they certainly could follow the gravity presence of Paradise into these regions."

This statement indicates the universal scope of Adjuster function. The material-gravity circuits mentioned here are the circuits that connect all material reality to Paradise, the central dwelling place of God. Adjusters utilize these circuits to traverse the grand universe instantaneously. Moreover, the text suggests they may even penetrate the outer space levels, the vast regions beyond the seven superuniverses where new orders of creation are currently being organized.

However, the revelation includes an important qualifier: "Though my order of personality can traverse the mind circuits of the Conjoint Actor also beyond the confines of the grand universe, we have never been sure of detecting the presence of Adjusters in the uncharted regions of outer space."

The speaker, presumably a Solitary Messenger or similar high personality, admits uncertainty about Adjuster presence in outer space. This uncertainty is reasonable because, at present, outer space contains no mortal inhabitants. The Adjusters would have no beings to indwell there. Yet the capability exists for Adjusters to function in those regions, and when the time comes for outer space to be inhabited, Adjusters will undoubtedly be there.

The Future of Finaliter Service

This leads to an important consideration about the eternal careers of Paradise finaliters. After achieving finaliter status, after completing the Paradise ascent and the training in Havona, what happens next? The finaliters do not retire to eternal leisure. Instead, they organize into finaliter corps, each group led by the Creator Son, Christ Michael in our case, who presided over their native local universe.

These finaliter corps will ultimately deploy to the outer space levels, serving in capacities not yet fully revealed. Some may function as administrators in emerging universes. Others may serve as ministers to new orders of beings. Still others may participate in creative activities appropriate to their combined mortal experience and Paradise training. The point is that the eternal adventure continues, always unfolding into new realms of service, experience, and growth.

Significantly, even while waiting for full deployment to outer space, finaliters will gain experience throughout all seven superuniverses. A finaliter from the seventh superuniverse, our own, will visit and serve in the other six, learning their cultures, meeting their inhabitants, and understanding the diverse ways the Father's love manifests across creation. This cross-pollination ensures that when finaliters eventually do serve in outer space, they bring comprehensive understanding of grand universe patterns and principles.

The Partnership Nature of Ascension - God-Knowing Mortals and God-Revealing Adjusters

The Urantia Book provides a succinct description of the Paradise ascent: "The Paradise ascent and the finality career are the partnership between the God-knowing, spiritualizing mortal and the spiritual ministry of the God-revealing Adjuster."

Note the precision of this language. The mortal is described as "God-knowing" and "spiritualizing." This is not a description of someone casually interested in religion or occasionally attending worship. Rather, it describes a mortal who actively seeks to know God, who makes progressive decisions to understand divine reality, and who willingly participates in the spiritualization process. Such a person recognizes that material existence is preparatory and actively cooperates with the divine plan for spiritual transformation.

The Adjuster, in turn, is described as providing "the spiritual ministry of the God-revealing" presence. The Adjuster does not merely observe or passively wait. The Adjuster actively ministers to the mortal, presenting concepts, illuminating truth, and revealing the nature of God through continuous subtle influence on mortal thinking.

The key word in this entire description is "partnership." Ascension is not something done to us, nor is it something we accomplish alone. It is a collaborative process requiring both human will and divine assistance. The mortal must choose, must act, must grow. The Adjuster provides guidance, inspiration, and gradually increasing spiritual capacity. Together, mortal and divine create something neither could create independently, a perfected ascending being who combines the authenticity of experiential growth with the reliability of divine nature.

The Stages of Spiritual Progress

The ascension career progresses through clearly defined stages, each representing a level of spiritual attainment:

Mortal Stage: The initial phase, lived in material body with material mind, represents the foundation of all subsequent growth. Here the personality makes its fundamental orientation toward or away from God. Here the soul begins forming through decisions that have spiritual significance.

Morontia Stage: Following death and resurrection, the ascending mortal receives a morontia body and mind, forms that blend material and spiritual qualities. Through 570 progressive changes, the morontia ascender advances from barely spiritualized forms toward increasingly pure spirit existence.

Spirit Stages: Upon graduation from the local universe and entrance into the superuniverse career, the ascender becomes a first-stage spirit. Subsequent progress leads through second, third, fourth, and fifth stages as the ascender traverses the superuniverse sectors and ultimately reaches Havona.

Sixth-Stage Spirit—Finaliter Status: Upon achieving Paradise and completing all required training, the ascender becomes a sixth-stage spirit, a Paradise finaliter. At this level, fusion of mortal and divine mind reaches completion. The experiential record transfers to the Supreme Being. The finaliter stands ready for eternal service.

Seventh-Stage Spirit: This ultimate stage awaits in the distant future, when finaliters take up their roles in outer space and subsequent ages of universe development. The nature of seventh-stage spirit existence remains largely unrevealed, reserved for those who attain it.

Conclusion: The Living Reality of Divine Indwelling

This chapter has explored the nature, function, and cosmic significance of Thought Adjusters, those mysterious fragments of God who make divine-human partnership possible. We have seen that Adjusters are pure spirit and pure energy, enabling instantaneous cosmic function. We have understood that Adjusters indwell not only mortals but also other orders of pre-personal beings throughout creation. We have grasped that fusion with the Adjuster represents the merging of two minds into one, creating a new order of being.

Most importantly, we have recognized that the Adjuster constitutes our circuit connection to ultimate reality. Without this divine presence, mortal life would be merely a dream, significant only within its own limited context. With the Adjuster present, our lives take on cosmic meaning. Every moral choice, every spiritual insight, every victory over material limitation becomes an eternal reality, preserved and ultimately contributed to the evolving Supreme Being.

The relationship between mortal and Adjuster is characterized by mutual commitment, progressive revelation, and ultimate fusion. The Adjuster comes as a "prisoner of spirit hope," confined within mortal limitations yet working tirelessly to illuminate truth and spiritualize thinking. The mortal, responding to this divine ministry, becomes increasingly God-knowing and spiritualized, participating consciously in the partnership that will eventually lead to Paradise.

As we close this chapter, we recognize that understanding Thought Adjusters is not merely an intellectual exercise. It is an invitation to conscious cooperation with the divine presence within. It is a call to become actively and deliberately what we are potentially, ascending sons and daughters of God, destined for eternal adventure in service to the Father and to all creation.

In Chapter 6, we will continue our exploration of Thought Adjusters, examining the practical aspects of Adjuster leading and the experiential reality of being guided by the divine presence within.

"The Adjusters are saturated with the beautiful and self-bestowing love of the Father of spirits. They truly and divinely love you; they are the prisoners of spirit hope confined within the minds of men."

Chapter 6: The Divine Gift Within - Understanding Thought Adjusters and Universal Reality

Introduction

In this continuation of our exploration of Paper 107 from *The Urantia Book*, we examine one of the most profound mysteries in all of cosmic revelation: the nature and function of Thought Adjusters. These divine fragments represent God the Father's direct, personal presence within each mortal being, a gift so extraordinary that even the most advanced celestial beings marvel at its implications.

This chapter delves into the intricate relationship between human free will and divine guidance, exploring how fragments of deity operate within the constraints of material reality while maintaining their connection to eternal perfection. We will examine the mechanics of spiritual fusion, the nature of pre-personal existence, and the cosmic significance of each individual's journey toward God-consciousness.

The material presented here addresses questions that have puzzled humanity throughout history: How does God communicate directly with His creatures? What is the relationship between divine will and human choice? What happens when a mortal being achieves complete spiritual unity with the divine presence within? These are not merely theological abstractions but practical realities that affect every decision, every thought, and every spiritual aspiration of mortal existence.

The Antecedent Nature of Thought Adjusters - Beyond Material Gravity Circuits

To understand the unique nature of Thought Adjusters, we must first grasp their relationship to the fundamental forces that govern the universe. While Thought Adjusters can utilize the material gravity circuits that organize and control physical reality, they are not subject to these forces in the way other beings are. This distinction is crucial to comprehending their true nature.

The Thought Adjusters are fragments of the ancestor of gravity, not the consequential of gravity. They have been segmentized on a universe level of existence that is hypothetically antecedent to gravity's appearance. This means that while gravity is fundamental to the organization of the physical universe, the essence from which Thought Adjusters derive predates even this universal constant.

To understand this concept, we must consider the sequence of divine emergence. God the Father and God the Son existed before the Infinite Spirit came into being. Most of the organizational systems of the universe, including material gravity circuits, mind circuits, and other fundamental energetic patterns, resulted from the creative work of the Infinite Spirit. However, God the Father existed prior to all these developments. Therefore, fragments of the Father possess attributes that transcend the later-developed systems of universal organization.

This pre-existence grants Thought Adjusters remarkable abilities. They can move instantaneously throughout all seven superuniverses, appearing wherever needed without delay. In contemporary terms, we might describe this as quantum-level existence, the ability to be present at any location through the power of thought alone. However, they can also choose to utilize the material gravity circuits when appropriate, demonstrating a flexibility that combines both transcendent and immanent modes of operation.

The central universe itself operates within gravity's influence, as gravity emanates from Paradise and extends outward throughout all creation. Yet this universal gravity does not constrain the Thought Adjusters in the way it affects other beings and forces. They represent a level of reality that underlies even the most fundamental physical laws.

The Nature of Divine Energy

A second profound characteristic of Thought Adjusters concerns their relationship to energy. Unlike virtually all other beings in the universe, Thought Adjusters require no energy intake. They do not rest, do not need sustenance, and do not experience the cycles of activity and repose that characterize even the most advanced spiritual beings.

The reason for this unique quality is foundational: Thought Adjusters *are* energy, energy of the highest and most divine order. Since all energy originates from the Father, and Thought Adjusters are actual fragments of the Father, they exist as pure divine energy in its most concentrated form. They do not draw upon energy; they embody it.

This characteristic distinguishes Thought Adjusters from other celestial beings who, while not requiring food or sleep as mortals understand these needs, do require periodic recharging through connection to universal energy circuits. The Guardian Angels, for example, work in pairs, with one active while the other enters a state of rest and recharging. The secondary midwayers similarly require periods of reduced activity to replenish their energy reserves. Even the more advanced seraphim and other ministering spirits must periodically connect with the spiritual energy circuits that sustain their existence.

But Thought Adjusters stand apart. From the moment of their bestowal within a mortal being until the day of their release, whether through natural death or through fusion, they maintain constant, unwavering presence and activity. They experience no respite, no pause, no diminishment of their essential nature.

There is one exception to this pattern: those rare individuals who achieve fusion with their Thought Adjusters during mortal life do not pass through the portals of natural death in the conventional sense. For these exceptional souls, the Thought Adjuster does not experience even the brief period of return to Divinington that normally occurs between the death of one mortal subject and assignment to the next. The moment of fusion creates an eternal, unbreakable bond, and the Adjuster remains continuously present with its mortal partner from that point forward.

The Imprisonment and Liberation of Divine Fragments

The language of *The Urantia Book* uses a striking metaphor when describing the Thought Adjuster's relationship to mortal life: it speaks of Adjusters being "imprisoned" within their human subjects from the time of bestowal until the time of release. This is not imprisonment in any punitive sense but rather describes the profound limitation that these infinite fragments of deity accept when they enter finite existence.

Consider the magnitude of this sacrifice: a fragment of the infinite, eternal, omnipresent Father voluntarily constrains itself within the limited consciousness of a material being, a creature bound by time, confined to space, subject to error, and prone to rebellion against the very divine guidance the Adjuster seeks to provide. The Adjuster must work within these constraints, never overriding the mortal will, always respecting the sovereignty of human choice, patiently waiting through years or decades for opportunities to influence the trajectory of the mortal life toward spiritual values.

When physical death occurs, the Thought Adjuster is released. It returns instantaneously to Divinington, the eternal home of the Thought Adjusters, where it reports on its mission and prepares for its next assignment. This process, though instantaneous from the Adjuster's perspective, represents a brief respite, the only rest these fragments of deity ever experience.

After this momentary return, the Adjuster departs again, this time to accompany its former mortal subject to the mansion worlds. The transition takes approximately three days from the mortal perspective, during which time the Guardian Angels carry the mortal's soul record and accumulated spiritual identity to the resurrection halls. When the mortal awakens on the first mansion world, the Thought Adjuster is there, ready to continue the eternal partnership.

However, for those who achieve fusion during mortal life, even this brief separation does not occur. The fusion itself is immediate and total. When a mortal being reaches the point of complete alignment with the divine will, when the human will and divine purpose become one, the result is instantaneous transformation. The material body cannot contain the glory and power of the divine presence once complete unity is achieved. The mortal form is consumed in what witnesses describe as a "celestial fire," and the newly fused being is immediately transported from material existence.

On planets advanced in light and life, where such fusions occur with greater frequency, this phenomenon is well known. Some worlds have constructed outdoor venues where people gather to witness these transformations, not as spectators of death, but as celebrants of transcendence. Instead of grieving a departure, the observers rejoice in the spiritual victory of one who has achieved the ultimate goal of mortal existence while still in the flesh.

The psychological and spiritual impact of witnessing such an event cannot be overstated. In our present world, we hear legends of Enoch and Elijah, said to have been taken up to heaven without experiencing death. We read of Jesus's transfiguration and ascension. But these events remain distant, shrouded in the mists of history and religious interpretation. Imagine, instead, living in a society where such transformations occur regularly enough that people gather specifically to witness them, where the reality of spiritual destiny is not a matter of faith alone, but an observable phenomenon that reinforces the reality of God's presence and the validity of the spiritual path.

The Mystery of Pre-Personal Volition - The Paradox of Will Without Personality

One of the most perplexing aspects of Thought Adjuster nature concerns their apparent possession of will, choice, and volition despite being pre-personal entities. This paradox challenges our understanding of consciousness, agency, and the nature of personality itself.

The facts are clear: Thought Adjusters volunteer to indwell specific human beings. They select their mortal subjects through a process of projection and evaluation. They make plans for the mortal's eternal career, adapting and modifying these plans as circumstances change. They respond to crisis situations with decisive action. They exhibit what can only be described as affection for their mortal partners. All of these behaviors suggest the presence of will, choice, and decision-making capacity, attributes we typically associate with personality.

Yet *The Urantia Book* explicitly states that Thought Adjusters are not personalities. They are pre-personal realities, entities that possess genuine individuality and real existence but lack personality in the technical sense that this term carries in cosmic philosophy. The question naturally arises: How can beings who lack personality exercise volition, make choices, and demonstrate preference?

The Solitary Messenger who authors this section of Paper 107 candidly admits that this mystery has never been fully explained. Even beings of his exalted order, personalities who have existed for eons and traveled throughout the grand universe, do not fully understand how the endowment of will, choice, and love can function in entities that are not personal.

The Distinction Between Divine and Human Will

The key to approaching this mystery lies in understanding the fundamental difference between divine volition and human free will. These are not simply different degrees of the same quality; they represent categorically different modes of willing.

Human free will operates at the personality level of universe reality. Personality, as bestowed by the Universal Father, carries with it genuine autonomy, the capacity for self-determination, moral choice, and creative decision-making that is not predetermined by prior causes. When a human being makes a choice, that choice is genuinely free, genuinely creative, and genuinely consequential. The human will stands as supreme within its own sphere of operation.

Divine volition, by contrast, exists at a pre-personal level. It represents not the autonomous choosing of a separate personality, but rather the unified purpose of deity itself. The Father's will is not a will among other wills; it is the foundation from which all other wills derive their capacity for willing. The Thought Adjuster's "volition" might better be understood as a reflection or manifestation of the Father's absolute purpose, adapted to the specific circumstances of individual mortal existence.

This distinction becomes crucial when we consider the relationship between Adjuster guidance and human choice. Throughout the cosmos, the impersonal, the non-personal, the sub-personal, and the pre-personal are ever responsive to the will and acts of existent personality. This represents a fundamental law of reality: personality is supreme within its own domain. No force, however powerful, and no will, however divine, can override the genuine free will of a personality-endowed being.

Therefore, while the Thought Adjuster possesses what might be called "absolute volition" in the sense of perfect alignment with divine purpose, this volition is always subservient to the mortal will during the period of mortal existence. The Adjuster's plans, adaptations, and modifications all occur within the framework of respect for human choice. The divine will never coerces; it only presents, suggests, and illuminates. The choice always remains with the mortal being.

This arrangement ensures the genuine reality of the mortal spiritual journey. If the Thought Adjuster could simply override human decision-making and impose divine will directly, the entire purpose of mortal existence would be nullified. The universe needs genuine experience, real choices made under conditions of uncertainty, real character forged through authentic struggle, real faith developed through the absence of coercive proof. The Thought Adjuster provides this possibility by respecting the absolute supremacy of human will while simultaneously offering unlimited access to divine wisdom and guidance.

The Selection Process

Despite their pre-personal nature, Thought Adjusters actively choose which mortal beings they will indwell. This selection occurs before the Adjuster departs from Divinington, based on a comprehensive analysis of the prospective subject's family history, genetic inheritance, environmental influences, and projected life trajectory.

The Adjusters examine the DNA of potential subjects, the character patterns of parents and grandparents, the cultural and social context into which the child will be born, and the range of probable life experiences that await. Through this analysis, they project the types of moral decisions the individual is likely to face, the challenges they will encounter, and the opportunities for spiritual growth that their life circumstances will provide.

This selection process demonstrates remarkable wisdom and foresight. The Adjuster chooses subjects with whom they can work most effectively, not necessarily those whose lives will be easiest or most conventionally successful, but those whose unique combination of heredity, environment, and potential creates the possibility for meaningful spiritual development. Each Adjuster brings particular experience and qualities that match well with the needs and potentials of their chosen subject.

This matching process reveals the deeply personal nature of God's relationship with each of His mortal children. The Father does not assign Adjusters randomly or mechanically. Each bestowal represents a thoughtful, deliberate decision based on perfect knowledge and infinite love. The Adjuster who comes to indwell a mortal being has specifically chosen that individual, has studied their background and potential, and has committed to a partnership that may last for eternity.

The Partnership of Human and Divine Will - The Supremacy of Mortal Choice

The relationship between human will and divine guidance represents one of the most delicate balances in all of cosmic reality. On one hand, the Thought Adjuster possesses perfect wisdom, unlimited patience, and complete alignment with the eternal purposes of deity. On the other hand, the mortal being possesses genuine autonomy, the right to make mistakes, and the freedom to reject even the most beneficial divine guidance.

The Urantia Book makes clear that human will functions at the personality level of universe reality, and at this level, the mortal's choice is supreme. No power in the universe, not the Thought Adjuster, not the angels, not even the Creator Son or the Infinite Spirit, can override this fundamental sovereignty. The gift of free will represents the Father's most precious bestowal, and He Himself refuses to violate what He has given.

This principle carries profound implications. It means that a human being can, through persistent rejection of spiritual guidance, effectively block the Thought Adjuster's influence entirely. The communication line between the divine fragment and the mortal consciousness can be severed, not by the Adjuster's choice, but by the mortal's. When a human being becomes completely immersed in iniquity, utterly devoted to self-serving purposes, and entirely resistant to higher values, the Adjuster's ability to function effectively diminishes to near zero.

In extreme cases, this separation can become permanent. While the Thought Adjuster never abandons its mortal subject prematurely, there comes a point, ratified by the highest spiritual authorities, when the human will has made its final choice against survival. At this point, the Adjuster is released, and the mortal being continues as what *The Urantia Book* calls "the walking dead", biologically alive but spiritually deceased, their cosmic career permanently terminated by their own irrevocable choice.

However, the opposite possibility exists as well. When a mortal being progressively aligns their will with divine guidance, when they make choices that reflect spiritual values and eternal purposes, the partnership between human and divine will becomes increasingly harmonious. The human will and the Adjuster's guidance begin to function in unity rather than in tension. The mortal begins to naturally desire what the Adjuster would have them do, not because their autonomy has been overridden, but because their values and purposes have evolved to align with eternal reality.

This progressive alignment represents the true meaning of "doing the Father's will." It does not mean the suppression of human personality or the abandonment of genuine choice. Rather, it means the transformation of desire, the elevation of purpose, and the voluntary submission of the finite will to infinite wisdom. When a mortal chooses God's will, they do not lose their freedom, they discover what freedom truly means.

The Adjuster's Working Method

Given the supremacy of human will, the Thought Adjuster must work with extraordinary subtlety and patience. The Adjuster cannot force decisions, cannot override choices, and cannot guarantee outcomes. Instead, the Adjuster works through influence, suggestion, and the gradual illumination of spiritual truth.

The Adjuster lays plans for the mortal's eternal career based on the projected trajectory of the human life. These plans include preparation for specific challenges, cultivation of particular virtues, and development of capacities that will be needed in future stages of the ascending career. However, these plans remain flexible, constantly adapted to the actual choices the mortal makes.

When circumstances change, whether through the mortal's decisions or through external events, the Adjuster modifies the approach. If one pathway toward spiritual growth becomes blocked, the Adjuster identifies alternative routes. If an expected opportunity fails to materialize, the Adjuster creates new possibilities from whatever circumstances actually exist. This constant adaptation demonstrates not weakness but the profound respect the divine fragment maintains for the reality of human choice and the unpredictability inherent in genuine free will.

The Adjuster functions in universal crises with decisive action, always within the boundaries of respect for mortal will. When danger threatens, when crucial decisions loom, when moments of supreme significance arrive, the Adjuster intensifies its efforts to communicate divine perspective without violating human autonomy. The quality of these communications depends heavily on the mortal's receptivity, their willingness to listen, their capacity to discern spiritual values, and their courage to act on divine leading even when doing so conflicts with immediate self-interest.

Throughout this process, the Adjuster exhibits what can only be described as affection for its mortal partner. This is not sentiment in the human sense, but rather a deep commitment to the mortal's welfare and success. The Adjuster desires not merely the survival of the mortal but their maximum possible growth, development, and eventual perfection. This divine affection persists regardless of how the mortal responds, whether with cooperation or resistance, with spiritual aspiration or material preoccupation, with steady progress or repeated failure.

The Question of Partnership

The relationship between mortal and Adjuster can be understood as a partnership, albeit an asymmetrical one. The human partner contributes free will, experiential reality, and the capacity for faith. The divine partner contributes wisdom, spiritual energy, and eternal perspective. Together, they create something that neither could produce alone: a unique, experiential fusion of finite and infinite, temporal and eternal, material and spiritual.

This partnership begins imperfectly. At the moment of Adjuster arrival, typically during the first moral decision of childhood, the human possesses only rudimentary spiritual capacity. The child cannot comprehend the significance of what has occurred. The Adjuster's communications register, if at all, only as vague intuitions or unnamed longings. The partnership exists in potential rather than in actuality.

As the mortal matures, the possibility for genuine partnership increases. Through repeated moral decisions, through exposure to spiritual truth, through experiences of worship and service, the mortal develops the capacity to consciously cooperate with divine guidance. What began as a one-sided relationship, the divine fragment working with an unconscious subject, gradually becomes a genuine collaboration between increasingly equal partners.

The ultimate expression of this partnership is fusion, the moment when mortal will and divine purpose become so perfectly aligned that they merge into eternal unity.

At this point, the partnership transcends itself. The distinction between human and divine will does not disappear, but it ceases to create tension or separation. The fused being possesses both the experiential wisdom gained through mortal existence and the spiritual power inherent in the divine fragment. The result is a new order of being, a finaliter, destined for service and adventure throughout the eternal ages.

The Reality of Spiritual Transformation - The Process of Fusion

Fusion represents the ultimate goal of mortal existence, the completion of the partnership between human and divine, and the beginning of an entirely new mode of existence. While most mortals achieve fusion in the later stages of their mansion world career, some exceptional individuals accomplish this supreme achievement during their mortal lives. Understanding what happens at the moment of fusion illuminates the nature of both human and divine reality.

When a mortal being reaches the point of complete alignment with the divine will, when every aspect of human desire, purpose, and choice harmonizes perfectly with the Adjuster's guidance, the conditions for fusion exist. At this moment, the barrier between finite and infinite, between material and spiritual, between temporal and eternal, dissolves. The mortal personality and the divine fragment unite in an embrace so complete that they become, in effect, a single being.

The material body cannot survive this transformation. Human flesh is not designed to contain the glory and power that results from conscious, complete union with deity. The physical form is consumed in what observers describe as a celestial fire, not a destructive burning, but rather a transfiguration in which the material is superseded by the spiritual. Where a moment before stood a human being of flesh and blood, there now exists a morontia being of light and life.

This transformation occurs instantaneously. There is no gradual process, no period of transition from one state to another. The moment fusion occurs, the mortal ceases to exist as a separate entity and becomes eternally one with the divine fragment. The personality survives, indeed, becomes more itself than ever before, but it now exists in a state of permanent union with deity.

On most worlds, particularly in the current age, fusion during mortal life occurs rarely enough to be nearly legendary. But on planets advanced in light and life, where spiritual understanding is more developed and where social conditions support rather than hinder spiritual growth, such fusions occur with greater frequency. The inhabitants of these advanced worlds recognize the signs that fusion is approaching. The midwayers, those permanent citizens who bridge material and spiritual realms, often arrange to transport the individual to an elevated location, ensuring that when the transformation occurs, the celestial fire will not inadvertently harm others nearby.

The psychological and spiritual significance of such events extends far beyond the individual who achieves fusion. Witnesses to these transformations experience a profound confirmation of spiritual reality. In our present age, we live by faith, believing in promises that seem distant and uncertain. But imagine watching a fellow human being—someone you know, someone like yourself, suddenly transfigured before your eyes, their material form replaced by spiritual glory. In that moment, faith becomes sight, hope becomes certainty, and the promises of eternal life become undeniably real.

This explains why some advanced worlds have constructed outdoor amphitheaters specifically for observing fusions. These gatherings serve a purpose similar to what we might imagine for worship services or religious festivals, but with the crucial difference that participants witness actual, observable demonstrations of spiritual reality. The community does not mourn a death but celebrates a graduation. They do not say goodbye to someone departing this life but congratulate someone entering the next stage of eternal existence while still retaining full memory and continuity of consciousness from their mortal experience.

The Journey After Fusion

For those who achieve fusion during mortal life, the journey to the mansion worlds follows a unique trajectory. Unlike those who die naturally and must await resurrection, the fused individual retains consciousness throughout the transition. Their awareness resides within the Thought Adjuster, or rather, they *are* now one with what was formerly their Thought Adjuster. The distinction between "my Adjuster" and "myself" no longer exists. They have become a unified being of a new order.

However, even fused individuals cannot bypass the established procedures that govern the mansion world experience. The Guardian Angels must still transport the soul records, the accumulated spiritual treasures of the mortal life, to the resurrection halls. The Archangels must still verify these records, ensuring that everything is in order for the beginning of mansion world education. This process requires approximately three days, the same period needed for those who experience natural death.

The difference is that the fused individual does not sleep during this interval. They exist in full, conscious awareness within their now-unified being. When they awaken on the first mansion world, they do not go through the initial stages of orientation and adjustment that others require. They have already achieved what others must work toward throughout the seven mansion worlds: complete fusion with their divine fragment.

This means they wake up with immediate knowledge of their new name, the name that reflects their new status as an eternal son or daughter of God. They possess full continuity of consciousness from their mortal life through the transformation and into their new existence. They have already completed the primary goal of mansion world experience and are ready to move forward into more advanced stages of universe education and service.

Yet they do not skip the mansion worlds entirely. Like all ascending mortals, they begin their post-mortal journey on the first mansion world, participating in the educational experiences provided there. The difference is that they approach these experiences from a position of already-achieved spiritual status rather than as seekers still working toward fusion. Their education focuses not on achieving fusion but on understanding and integrating the implications of what they have already achieved.

The Continuity of Identity

Throughout the process of death, resurrection, and even fusion, one element remains constant: personality. The personality bestowed by the Universal Father constitutes the unchanging core of individual identity, the thread of continuity that links the mortal life to the mansion world existence and beyond.

When natural death occurs, the material body returns to the elements from which it was formed. The brain, with its electrical and chemical patterns, ceases to function. Yet the individual does not cease to exist. The personality, along with all spiritually significant memories and accumulated character traits, survives in the keeping of the Guardian Angels and the Thought Adjuster. These treasures of identity await the moment of resurrection, when they will be reassembled into a new form on the mansion worlds.

The resurrected individual wakes up as themselves, recognizably the same person who fell asleep in death, yet now possessed of a morontia body suited to their new environment. They remember their mortal life, recognize loved ones who have preceded them, and resume the development of their character and personality from the point where physical death interrupted it. Death represents a pause, a transition, but not a rupture in the continuity of self.

For those with severe mental disabilities during mortal life, this continuity takes a unique form. If an individual lived for decades without ever achieving normal mental function, never making genuine moral decisions, never developing adult consciousness, their Thought Adjuster would have had little experiential content to record. When such an individual dies and awakens on the mansion worlds, they possess only the most basic identity: their personality and their relationships with those who loved them during their mortal life.

Everything else begins fresh. They have a clean slate, unencumbered by accumulated errors or moral failures, but also without the accumulated wisdom and character development that others bring from their mortal experience. They begin their mansion world education at the very beginning, learning and growing at the accelerated rate that characterizes morontia existence. Within a relatively brief period, perhaps weeks or months by mansion world reckoning, they can achieve the developmental progress that would have required decades of mortal life.

This arrangement demonstrates the fundamental fairness and mercy that characterize the divine administration of the universe. No one is ultimately disadvantaged by circumstances beyond their control. The child who dies in infancy, the individual whose mental development was impaired by genetic or environmental factors, the person whose life was cut short by accident or violence, all receive full opportunity to develop their potential on the mansion worlds. The playing field is leveled, and everyone begins their conscious spiritual career with genuine opportunity for eternal growth and service.

The Universal Presence of Deity - The Fragments of God

Thought Adjusters represent one of the most remarkable provisions in the entire divine plan for the universes. Through these fragments of Himself, the Universal Father achieves direct, personal, unmediated contact with each and every mortal being throughout the seven superuniverses. This represents a reservation by the Father, a direct intervention that exists apart from and in addition to all other forms of divine ministry.

Consider the magnitude of this gift. The Father might have relied exclusively on His Paradise Sons to represent Him to mortal creatures. He might have left mortal spiritual guidance entirely to the Infinite Spirit's ministering spirits. He might have established indirect systems of communication through the many levels of universe administration. But He chose instead to fragment Himself, to send actual pieces of His own divine nature to dwell within mortal minds.

This means that God is literally present within each person. Not present in some vague, metaphorical sense. Not present through intermediaries or representatives. Actually, directly, personally present as a living reality within the human consciousness. The implications of this truth cannot be overstated. Every human being, regardless of their knowledge or ignorance, their virtue or vice, their faith or skepticism, hosts within themselves an actual fragment of the infinite God.

This universal presence creates a fundamental unity underlying all human diversity. Beneath the surface differences of race, culture, religion, and philosophy, beneath the conflicts and divisions that characterize human society, there exists a deeper reality: every human being shares in the divine nature through the presence of the Thought Adjuster. We are not merely creations of God, not merely subjects of divine law, but actual living temples of the Most High, whether we recognize this truth or not.

The Cosmic Significance of Individual Souls

This universal presence of deity within mortal beings gives each individual cosmic significance. When one person dies, especially when death occurs through suicide or is otherwise premature, something irreplaceable is lost to the universe. The particular combination of personality, experience, and divine indwelling that constituted that unique individual will never exist again in exactly that form.

The Thought Adjuster returns to Divinington. The personality bestowal can be redirected to a new mortal being. But the specific fusion of those two elements, the unique experiential contribution that particular individual might have made to the evolving Supreme Being, is forever absent. Like a cell removed from a living organism, the potential represented by that individual soul is deleted from the cosmic whole.

This is why suicide represents such a tragedy in cosmic perspective. The individual who takes their own life may believe they are simply escaping unbearable suffering or ending an existence, they find meaningless. But in reality, they are destroying a unique opportunity for experience that took billions of years of cosmic evolution to create. They are removing from the universe a potential contribution to the growth of God the Supreme that can never be replaced.

This does not mean that those who succumb to such despair are condemned or judged harshly. Mental illness, unbearable suffering, and emotional anguish can overwhelm the capacity for rational choice. The universe administration understands this and deals with each case according to its actual circumstances and the true state of the individual's will. But from a cosmic perspective, such deaths represent genuine losses, not just to family and friends, but to the universal whole.

Conversely, every individual who survives mortal existence and continues the ascending career contributes something irreplaceable to cosmic reality. The experiences accumulated during mortal life, the character forged through struggle and choice, the unique perspective gained from that particular combination of heredity, environment, and circumstance, all of this becomes permanent treasure in the evolving universe. Each survivor adds a note to the cosmic symphony that could come from no other source.

This elevates human existence from insignificance to supreme importance. We are not cosmic accidents, not mere specks of consciousness briefly flickering in an indifferent universe. We are essential participants in the greatest enterprise in all creation: the evolution of experiential deity, the slow growth of God the Supreme toward completion. Our choices matter. Our experiences count. Our persistence or failure has genuine consequences that extend far beyond our individual lives.

The Universality of Divine Ministry

The Thought Adjusters represent the Father's direct ministry to mortal creatures, but they do not exhaust the scope of divine care. Each human being receives ministry from multiple sources: the Thought Adjuster from the Father, the Spirit of Truth from the Creator Son, the Holy Spirit from the local universe Mother Spirit, and the angels and other celestial beings who serve under the direction of these divine presences.

Even those rare individuals who, for reasons of neurological structure or other limitations, cannot receive Thought Adjusters, still receive divine ministry. Some are indwelt by fragments of the Eternal Son, others by fragments of the Infinite Spirit. No mortal being exists without some form of direct divine presence. God ensures that every one of His children has access to His guidance and love.

This universality of divine ministry reveals the fundamental character of God. He is not a distant monarch, ruling through intermediaries while remaining aloof from His subjects. He is not an impersonal force, operating through natural law without regard for individual welfare. He is a loving Father who gives Himself, literally fragments Himself, to maintain personal contact with each of His mortal children.

Even celestial beings who were created at higher levels of existence, who never needed to ascend from material origins, look upon this arrangement with wonder and longing. The Solitary Messenger who authors this section of *The Urantia Book* explicitly states that no created beings would not delight to be hosts to the Mystery Monitors. Yet only evolutionary will creatures of finality destiny receive this supreme gift. The very beings who might seem least worthy, material creatures, just beginning their eternal careers, prone to error and limited by their physical nature, receive what higher beings wish they could possess.

This paradox reveals a profound truth: God values experience above perfection, growth above static achievement, potentiality above established reality. The evolutionary journey from material origins to spiritual heights creates something that cannot be achieved any other way. The fusion of mortal experience with divine nature produces finaliters, beings who will serve throughout the eternal ages in capacities we can barely imagine, combining in themselves the wisdom of experiential growth with the power of divine indwelling.

Conclusion: The Divine Partnership

Chapter 6 has explored the profound mystery of Thought Adjusters: their pre-personal nature, their relationship to universal reality, their respect for human will, and their role in the divine plan for mortal ascension. We have examined how these fragments of the Universal Father work within the constraints of material reality while maintaining their essential divine nature, how they balance divine wisdom with human free will, and how they guide mortal beings toward the ultimate achievement of fusion.

Several key principles emerge from this exploration:

First, the Thought Adjuster represents God's direct, personal presence within each mortal being, not a mere influence or inspiration, but an actual fragment of deity dwelling within human consciousness.

Second, human free will remains supreme throughout mortal existence. The Thought Adjuster never coerces, never overrides genuine choice, but always respects the sovereignty of personality.

Third, the relationship between mortal and Adjuster constitutes a genuine partnership, evolving from an asymmetrical beginning toward eventual fusion and eternal unity.

Fourth, each individual possesses cosmic significance. Every human life represents a unique contribution to universal reality, and every survival carries implications far beyond individual destiny.

Fifth, the goal of mortal existence is not merely survival but transformation, the gradual alignment of human will with divine purpose, culminating in the supreme achievement of fusion.

As we move forward to Chapter 7, we will explore the mission and ministry of Thought Adjusters in greater detail, examining how these divine fragments actually function within human consciousness, how they communicate with their mortal partners, and how they guide the ascending career from its beginning in mortal life through the progressive stages of morontia and spiritual existence. We will discover that the partnership established during mortal life only begins a relationship destined to unfold throughout the eternal ages.

The understanding we have gained in this chapter provides the foundation for appreciating the practical operation of divine guidance in daily life. It prepares us to recognize the Adjuster's presence, to cooperate more effectively with divine leading, and to move with greater confidence toward the supreme goal of God-consciousness and eternal survival.

Chapter 7: The Mission and Ministry of Thought Adjusters

Introduction

Among the most profound revelations contained within *The Urantia Book* is the concept of the Thought Adjuster, a divine fragment of God the Universal Father that indwells the human mind. This chapter explores Paper 108, which details the mission and ministry of these extraordinary spiritual entities. Understanding the Thought Adjuster is essential to comprehending humanity's spiritual destiny and our intimate relationship with the Divine.

The Thought Adjuster represents God's most direct and personal gift to mortal creatures. Through this indwelling presence, the infinite and eternal Father connects with finite, temporal beings, bridging the vast chasm between divinity and humanity. This chapter examines the dual mission of Thought Adjusters, the process by which they are assigned to individual mortals, and the profound implications of their ministry for human spiritual evolution.

As we delve into this study, we will discover that the Thought Adjuster's presence within us serves not merely as a spiritual guide, but as the very mechanism through which eternal life becomes possible. The fusion of human will with divine purpose, facilitated by the Thought Adjuster, represents the ultimate destiny of every faith-motivated mortal who chooses to do the will of God.

The Fundamental Mission of Thought Adjusters - Representing the Universal Father

The primary mission of the Thought Adjuster is elegantly simple yet infinitely profound: to represent the Universal Father to mortal creatures of time and space. This is the fundamental work of these divine gifts. When we seek to commune with God the Father, we need not look beyond ourselves, for He dwells within us through His fragmentary presence. The Thought Adjuster makes the infinite accessible to the finite, bringing the Universal Father into immediate and continuous contact with each individual human being.

This indwelling presence cannot be separated from the human mind once it takes up residence, except in cases of complete moral bankruptcy or insanity, conditions in which the individual ceases to function as a normal, sanctioned human being. The Thought Adjuster remains constant, patient, and eternally committed to its mission of divine representation, regardless of the challenges presented by the mortal mind it indwells.

Preparing the Soul for Paradise

The secondary mission of the Thought Adjuster is equally vital: to elevate the mortal mind and translate the immortal soul upward to the divine heights and spiritual levels of Paradise perfection. This transformative work occurs continuously throughout mortal life. The Thought Adjuster spiritualizes human experiences, transmuting the temporal into the eternal, the material into the spiritual.

Through this process, the Thought Adjuster literally prepares the morontia soul, that emerging spiritual reality born from the union of material mind and divine spirit, for its long journey to Paradise. Every moral decision, every act of kindness, every moment of worship contributes to this soul-building enterprise. The Thought Adjuster records, interprets, and spiritualizes these experiences, weaving them into the fabric of an eternal identity.

A Unique Universal Technique

The relationship between a mortal creature and an indwelling Thought Adjuster produces a unique type of being, one that consists of the eternal union of a perfect Adjuster and a perfected creature. This union would be impossible to duplicate by any other technique in the universe. No other method exists by which the infinite God can so intimately participate in the finite experience of His creatures while simultaneously preparing them for eternal existence.

This divine-human partnership represents one of the universe's most magnificent mysteries. Through it, creatures of the lowest order of will-endowed beings can become, in time and through experience, perfected beings qualified for eternal service in the universes of time and space, and eventually for entry into the eternal Corps of the Finality.

The Existential God and Experiential Reality - Understanding Existential Being

To fully appreciate the significance of the Thought Adjuster ministry, we must understand the nature of God as an existential being. The term "existential" refers to that which always has been and always will be, reality without beginning or end, existing outside the constraints of time. God the Universal Father is existential; He has complete foreknowledge of all that will occur throughout eternity, for from His perspective, all time exists simultaneously.

However, this existential nature presents a profound limitation: God cannot, on His own level of infinite existence, experience the progressive, sequential reality that characterizes finite creature life. The existential God possesses complete pre-knowledge but lacks direct experiential knowledge of what finite beings encounter in their day-to-day existence.

The Need for Experiential Reality

Nothing in the entire universe can substitute for the fact of experience at non-existential levels. The infinite God is replete and complete, infinitely inclusive of all things except evil and creature experience. God cannot do wrong, He is infallible. Yet God cannot experientially know what He has never personally experienced. This represents not a deficiency but rather an inevitable distinction between the existential and the experiential levels of reality.

To bridge this gulf, the spirit of the Father descends from Paradise to participate with finite mortals in every bona fide experience of the ascending career. Only by this method can the existential God become, in truth and in fact, man's experiential Father. The infinity of the Eternal God encompasses the potential for all finite experience, and this potential becomes actual through the ministry of the Adjuster fragments that share the very life vicissitudes of human beings.

The Role of the Supreme Being

God the Father created the Supreme Being, an experiential deity separate from yet intimately connected to the Father, as another avenue for gathering creature experience. The Supreme is God's experiential aspect, evolving and growing through the collective experiences of all finite creatures across the seven superuniverses.

The Supreme Being represents the totality of all finite evolutionary experience. As every mortal makes choices and gains experience, these realities contribute to the growth and eventual completion of the Supreme. When all seven superuniverses achieve the status of light and life, a process requiring billions upon billions of years, the Supreme will emerge as a fully actualized deity, embodying the complete experiential reality of time and space.

This arrangement allows God to gather creature experience through two complementary mechanisms: individually through the Thought Adjusters who share personal mortal life, and collectively through the Supreme Being who synthesizes all finite experience into unified deity expression.

Election and Assignment of Thought Adjusters - Initial Equality and Experiential Diversity

When Thought Adjusters are dispatched for mortal service from Divinington, the Paradise sphere that serves as their headquarters, they are identical in their endowment of existential divinity. Each possesses the same divine nature and potential. However, they differ significantly in experiential qualities, proportional to their previous contact in and with evolutionary creatures.

This means that while all Thought Adjusters are equally divine, they are not equally experienced. Some Adjusters come to their mortal assignments as virgin Adjusters, having never before indwelt a mortal mind. Others bring extensive experience from previous indwellings, having served with other mortals on other worlds or even with previous mortals on Urantia (Earth) but never serving twice on the same planet in normal mortals.

The Basis of Assignment

The exact basis of Thought Adjuster assignment remains somewhat mysterious, even to the revelators of *The Urantia Book*. However, they conjecture that these divine gifts are bestowed in accordance with a wise and efficient policy of eternal fitness, matching the Adjuster's experiential background to the needs and potential of the individual to be indwelt.

Human inheritance proves to be a considerable factor in determining selection and assignment. The more experienced Adjusters typically indwell higher types of human minds with superior hereditary endowments. This does not mean that those with less experienced Adjusters are somehow inferior; rather, it reflects the matching of divine resources to mortal need and potential.

The Volunteer Process

Before any Thought Adjuster volunteers to indwell a specific mortal mind, it possesses full data respecting the candidate. Seraphic records of ancestry and projected patterns of life conduct are transmitted by reflectivity technique from the local universe capitals through the superuniverse headquarters to the Reserve Corps of Adjusters on Divinington.

This forecast covers not only hereditary antecedents but also estimates of probable intellectual endowment and spiritual capacity. The Adjusters volunteer to indwell minds whose intimate natures they have been fully apprised of in advance. They understand the probable challenges, opportunities, and ultimate potential of each mortal assignment before they undertake their mission.

This comprehensive foreknowledge demonstrates that your arrival on Urantia is no accident, and your spiritual journey is not unknown to Paradise. From the moment of conception, information about your ancestry, potential, and probable life trajectory has been transmitted all the way to Paradise. The universe expects you to grow, to choose, and eventually to arrive at the Paradise shores.

Gender Neutrality in Assignment

An important clarification regarding Thought Adjuster assignment concerns gender. The assignment of Adjusters makes no distinction between male and female mortals. Gender is a biological characteristic of material existence with no counterpart in spirit reality. Thought Adjusters minister equally to men and women, for in the spiritual realm, all mortals are equally sons and daughters of God.

What matters in Adjuster assignment is not the biological sex of the mortal but rather the quality of mind, the hereditary spiritual capacity, and the potential for moral decision-making and spiritual growth. These factors transcend gender and represent the true basis for the matching of Adjuster to mortal.

The Commencement of Human Life - Life Begins at Conception

One of the most significant clarifications provided in *The Urantia Book* concerns the beginning of human life. The text unambiguously establishes that life begins at conception. In the account of Jesus' birth, we are told that Gabriel's announcement to Mary was made the day following the conception of Jesus and was the only event of supernatural occurrence connected with her entire experience of carrying and bearing the child of promise.

This passage establishes a crucial principle: at conception, human life begins. The newly conceived embryo is not merely potential life or pre-life; it is actual, living human reality. From this moment, the conceived child becomes the ward of guardian angels operating in groups, ensuring that if death occurs before birth, the child's potential personality will be preserved and resurrected on the finaliter nursery world.

Personality at Conception

The gift of personality from the Universal Father appears to be bestowed at conception. Personality, that unique quality that unifies all aspects of individuality and provides identity, is God's direct gift to each human being. This personality endowment occurs at the very beginning of human life, establishing the conceived child as a cosmic reality with eternal potential.

However, this personality initially lacks the divine complement necessary for eternal fusion. The personality exists, the hereditary mind begins to develop, but the divine fragment, the Thought Adjuster, does not arrive until much later.

Birth and Separate Human Status

While life begins at conception, the child is not considered a separate, independent human being until birth. Throughout the gestation period, the developing child remains part of the mother's body, sharing her life systems. At birth, when the umbilical cord is severed and the child takes its first independent breath, separate human existence begins.

From conception through birth and until the arrival of the Thought Adjuster, the child remains under the care and protection of group guardian angels. These seraphic beings ensure that should the child die during this period, resurrection on the finaliter world nurseries is guaranteed. The child will sleep until the first parent, guardian, or suitable caretaker arrives in the morontia worlds, at which time the child will be awakened and given opportunity for continued growth and development.

The Arrival of the Thought Adjuster

The Thought Adjuster typically arrives shortly before the child's sixth birthday, marking a momentous transition in the child's spiritual status. This arrival usually follows the child's first moral decision, the first time the child chooses between right and wrong with genuine understanding of the moral implications.

With the Adjuster's arrival, the child becomes a potential candidate for eternal life. The indwelling divine fragment begins the work of soul-building, recording moral decisions and spiritual aspirations. From this point forward, the child is no longer merely a ward of group guardians but has become a child of the cosmos with destiny potential reaching all the way to Paradise.

It is crucial to understand, however, that the arrival of the Thought Adjuster does not automatically guarantee eternal life. Eternal life becomes actual only upon fusion with the Adjuster, an event that may occur during mortal life but more commonly takes place in the morontia worlds after death. Until fusion occurs, the personality with its accumulated experience remains dependent upon the resurrection mechanism for survival of death.

The Seven Psychic Circles of Spiritual Attainment - Understanding the Circles

Human spiritual progress can be understood in terms of seven psychic circles of attainment. These circles represent progressive levels of spiritual development, intellectual growth, and cosmic awareness. Paradoxically, they are numbered in reverse order: mortals begin in the seventh (lowest) circle and progress upward through the sixth, fifth, fourth, third, second, and finally to the first (highest) circle.

Attainment of these circles is not primarily intellectual, though intelligence plays a role. Rather, circle attainment represents the coordination of personality, mind, and spirit, the gradual unification of the human will with the divine will of the indwelling Adjuster.

Guardian Angel Assignment by Circle Level

The psychic circles directly correlate with guardian angel assignment and ministry:

Seventh Circle: One pair of guardian seraphim serves 1,000 mortals. At this lowest level of spiritual awareness, individuals show little interest in spiritual realities and make minimal moral progress. Guardian angels work with large groups, providing general guidance and protection.

Sixth Circle: One pair of guardian seraphim serves 500 mortals. Those who reach this level have begun to show some spiritual awareness and interest in religious or moral questions.

Fifth Circle: One pair of guardian seraphim serves 100 mortals. At this level, individuals demonstrate consistent moral behavior and growing spiritual consciousness.

Fourth Circle: One pair of guardian seraphim serves 10 mortals. These individuals have made significant spiritual progress and show dedication to religious or spiritual principles.

Third Circle: One pair of guardian seraphim (with cherubim and sanobim assistants) is assigned to each individual mortal. This circle marks a critical threshold in spiritual development. Upon reaching the third circle, the mortal receives personal seraphic guardianship, reflecting the enhanced potential for spiritual achievement.

Second and First Circles: Personal guardian angels continue their ministry, preparing the mortal for either mortal fusion with the Adjuster or for immediate resurrection should death intervene.

The Critical Third Circle

The third psychic circle represents the most significant threshold in mortal spiritual development. When an individual reaches this circle, several profound changes occur:

Personal Guardian Assignment: For the first time, the mortal receives the undivided attention of a guardian angel pair. These seraphim dedicate themselves exclusively to nurturing the spiritual development of this one individual.

Adjutant Mind Spirit Diminishment: The influence of the seven-adjutant mind-spirits (the seven mental circuits provided by the local universe Mother Spirit) begins to diminish. This occurs because the Thought Adjuster's influence has grown sufficiently strong to provide direct spiritual guidance, reducing the need for the preliminary ministry of the adjutants.

Guaranteed Survival: Perhaps most significantly, upon reaching the third circle, the mortal is guaranteed survival of death. Should such an individual die, they proceed immediately to the mansion worlds without waiting for the millennial (thousand-year) dispensational resurrections. They have become what is termed a "sleeping survivor", one who sleeps only for the brief period between death and repersonalization on the first mansion world.

Commitment to God's Will: The attainment of the third circle typically coincides with a sincere, sustained commitment to doing the will of God. The individual has progressed beyond merely acknowledging God's existence to actively seeking divine guidance in daily decisions and life choices.

Indicators of Third Circle Attainment

How can one know if they have reached this critical third circle? The primary indicator is a fundamental shift in motivation and decision-making. When you find yourself habitually asking, "What does God want me to do?" or "What is the Father's will in this situation?", when divine guidance becomes your primary reference point for life decisions, you have likely entered the third circle.

This does not mean perfection; far from it. Third circle attainment does not eliminate error, struggle, or even sin. What it signifies is a genuine reorientation of will, a sincere desire to align personal choice with divine purpose. The individual may still make mistakes, but the overarching direction of life has shifted from self-will to God-will.

Pre-Pentecost and Post-Pentecost Differences

Before the bestowal of the Spirit of Truth at Pentecost, Thought Adjusters typically arrived only after the individual had reached the third psychic circle. This meant that primitive humans and those living before Christ's bestowal received Adjusters much later in life, if at all. The bestowal of the Spirit of Truth changed this dramatically.

After Pentecost, every normal-minded individual receives a Thought Adjuster at approximately six years of age, regardless of their psychic circle status. The combined ministry of the Holy Spirit and the Spirit of Truth prepares the human mind for the Adjuster's early arrival. This represents an enormous spiritual advancement for the planet, exponentially increasing the number of mortals equipped with indwelling divine fragments and thus potential candidates for eternal life.

The Sleeping Survivors

Those who have reached the third psychic circle but die without achieving fusion with their Adjusters are known as "sleeping survivors." They sleep peacefully, unaware of the passage of time, until they are repersonalized on the first mansion world. This repersonalization may occur relatively quickly or may be delayed, depending on various factors including universe administrative considerations and the individual's specific needs.

In contrast, those who die in the lower circles (fourth through seventh) must await the periodic dispensational resurrections, which typically occur approximately every thousand years. These individuals sleep for much longer periods and, upon awakening, require more extensive remedial training to compensate for progress not made during mortal life.

The Emergence of Eternal Life - The Crucial Distinction

A profound truth must be clearly understood receiving a Thought Adjuster does not automatically confer eternal life, nor does survival of mortal death guarantee eternal existence. Many students of spirituality assume that death marks the passage into immortality, but *The Urantia Book* teaches a more nuanced reality.

Eternal life, true, unconditional, permanent existence, becomes actual only upon fusion with the Thought Adjuster. Until that moment of fusion, the personality remains conditionally immortal, dependent upon continued choice of survival and eventual fusion for permanent existence.

Fusion: The Gateway to Eternity

Fusion represents the eternal union of the perfected human will with the divine Adjuster. At the moment of fusion, the mortal becomes genuinely eternal, no longer subject to any possibility of extinction or cessation of existence. The fused being has achieved a status that ensures permanent continuance throughout all eternity.

This fusion may occur during mortal life, as it did with Enoch, Elijah, and a few others throughout human history. More commonly, fusion occurs on one of the mansion worlds after considerable morontia training and spiritual development. Some personalities do not achieve fusion until they reach higher morontia spheres or even the constellation worlds.

The Existential Transformation

When fusion occurs, the mortal becomes existential in a profound way. The experiential human personality merges with the existential divine fragment, creating a new order of being that partakes of both natures. The fused mortal gains access to the pre-existence memories of the Adjuster, not complete recall of all details, but an expanding awareness that grows progressively throughout the ascension career.

This principle works both backward and forward in time-consciousness. As the fused mortal gains increasing awareness of the Adjuster's pre-existence experience (backward in time), their capacity for existential foreknowledge (forward in time) expands proportionally. They begin to partake, in a limited but growing way, of the existential consciousness that characterizes Paradise Deity.

Memory and Identity Preservation

A virgin Adjuster brings no experiential memories from previous mortal indwellings because it has never before indwelt a mortal. However, non-virgin Adjusters carry the accumulated experiential wisdom from previous assignments. Upon fusion, these memories become available to the ascending mortal, though not immediately or completely.

The fused mortal gains access to this repository of experience gradually, as wisdom and spiritual capacity develop. This means that a mortal who fuses with an experienced Adjuster eventually benefits from the life lessons and spiritual insights gathered during the Adjuster's previous assignments, a magnificent inheritance of experiential wisdom.

Practical Implications for Daily Living - Recognizing the Divine Within

Understanding the Thought Adjuster ministry transforms daily life. Every quiet moment of reflection becomes an opportunity for divine communion. Every moral decision represents a choice with eternal significance. Every act of love or service contributes to the building of your morontia soul.

You need not seek God in distant heavens or ancient temples. The Universal Father dwells within you now, at this very moment, closer than breathing, nearer than hands and feet. The practice of the presence of God becomes not merely a religious technique but a recognition of existential fact.

Making Moral Decisions

The Thought Adjuster works ceaselessly to spiritualize your thought life and moral decisions. While the Adjuster cannot coerce your will, for free will is inviolate, it can and does influence your thinking, presenting spiritual alternatives, inspiring noble impulses, and illuminating moral choices.

Learning to recognize these gentle divine leadings requires practice, patience, and faith. Often, the Adjuster's guidance comes not as a voice or vision but as a subtle sense of rightness, an intuitive knowing of what is true, beautiful, and good. The more you practice seeking divine guidance, the more clearly you will recognize the Adjuster's ministry.

The Practice of Stillness

Regular periods of stillness, meditation, or worship provide optimal conditions for Adjuster ministry. In the quiet of reflective thought, freed from the clamor of daily demands, the human mind becomes receptive to spiritual influence. These moments of communion allow the Adjuster to present spiritual concepts, eternal perspectives, and divine values for your consideration.

This is not passive mysticism but active partnership. You bring your questions, concerns, and aspirations to these times of communion. The Adjuster responds not by solving all problems but by elevating your perspective, expanding your wisdom, and strengthening your spiritual resolve.

Responding to Divine Leading

The critical question in spiritual development is not "Does God speak to me?" but "Do I listen and respond when He does?" The Thought Adjuster ministers continuously, but human inattention, material preoccupation, and willful self-assertion often prevent recognition of divine leading.

Spiritual progress requires active cooperation with the indwelling Adjuster. This means cultivating habits of reflection, moral sensitivity, and willing obedience to recognized truth. It means asking regularly, "What does God want me to do in this situation?" and then having the courage to follow the answer received.

Building the Morontia Soul

Every experience of life provides raw material for soul-building. The Thought Adjuster observes all, records what is spiritually valuable, and weaves it into the developing morontia soul. Trials and difficulties, properly met, contribute as much to soul-growth as do success and joy. What matters is not the external circumstance but your internal response, whether you meet life's challenges with faith, courage, and trust in divine wisdom.

The morontia soul is not the physical body and not the material mind. It is a new reality born from the union of human will choosing to do God's will and the divine Adjuster responding to that choice. It is literally your developing eternal self, the you that will survive death and continue the Paradise ascent.

Conclusion: The Partnership of Eternity

The ministry of the Thought Adjuster represents God's most intimate gift to humanity, the gift of Himself. Through this indwelling presence, the infinite Father becomes the experiential companion of finite mortals. Through this partnership, human beings of animal origin become potential Paradise finaliters qualified for eternal service in universe administration.

This chapter explores the fundamental mission of Thought Adjusters: to represent the Universal Father and to prepare the mortal for Paradise. We have examined how existential Deity gains experiential reality through participation in mortal life. We have studied the selection and assignment process that matches each Adjuster to the mortal it will serve. We have clarified when human life begins and what it means to become a child of God in the fullest sense.

The seven psychic circles provide a roadmap for spiritual progress, with the third circle marking a critical threshold of achievement. The attainment of this circle brings personal seraphic guardianship, guaranteed survival, and clear indication that the individual has committed to doing the will of God. Yet even this attainment does not confer eternal life, which becomes actual only upon fusion with the Adjuster.

As we proceed in our study of the Thought Adjuster ministry, we will next explore the actual techniques employed by these divine fragments in their work of spiritualizing the human mind and perfecting the immortal soul. We will examine the various types of Adjusters, the nature of their ministry to different orders of human beings, and the factors that facilitate or hinder their transformative work.

The invitation stands before every person: to cooperate consciously with the indwelling divine fragment, to choose increasingly the will of the Father, and thereby to build an eternal soul destined for Paradise perfection. This is not merely religious idealism but the practical outworking of universe reality, the mission and ministry of Thought Adjusters in the lives of evolving mortals.

In the next chapter, we will continue our exploration of Paper 108, examining the specific techniques of Adjuster ministry and the various classifications of these divine fragments based on their experience and function.

Chapter 8: The Divine Partnership - How Thought Adjusters Choose and Prepare Their Human Subjects

Introduction

The study of Thought Adjusters represents one of the most profound and personally transformative aspects of The Urantia Book's revelation. In this chapter, we continue our exploration of Paper 108, examining the intricate and divinely orchestrated process by which these fragments of God select, prepare for, and ultimately indwell human minds. Understanding this process not only illuminates the mechanics of divine ministry but also reveals the extraordinary value that the Universe places upon each individual personality.

What makes this study particularly meaningful is its immediate relevance to our daily spiritual lives. The Thought Adjuster is not a distant theological concept but an ever-present divine reality working within each normal-minded person. By understanding how these divine fragments evaluate potential human subjects, prepare for their arrival, and begin their lifelong mission of spiritualization, we gain invaluable insight into our own spiritual development and the partnership we can consciously cultivate with this indwelling presence.

This chapter will examine three critical areas: first, the comprehensive nature of spiritual growth and how we can recognize it in our lives; second, the specific qualifications Thought Adjusters evaluate when volunteering for human assignment; and third, the remarkable preparation process that occurs before an Adjuster arrives in the mind of a child. Throughout this exploration, we will discover that every moment of our existence is known, valued, and recorded in the vast cosmic registry, a truth that should inspire both humility and profound gratitude.

The Comprehensive Nature of Spiritual Growth

Before examining how Thought Adjusters select and prepare for their human subjects, we must first understand what these divine fragments are seeking to accomplish: spiritual growth. The Urantia Book provides an extensive framework for understanding spiritual development, offering readers a comprehensive checklist against which they can evaluate their own progress toward God-consciousness.

Foundational Principles of Spiritual Growth

Spiritual growth manifests through numerous pathways, each representing a different aspect of our evolving relationship with the Divine. These pathways include:

The elimination of selfish qualities in love. True spiritual love transcends self-interest, focusing instead on the welfare and happiness of others. When we find ourselves naturally considering others' needs before our own desires, we demonstrate genuine spiritual progress.

Growth through faith and revelation. Salvation comes through faith, not merely intellectual assent but a living trust in divine reality. Revelation, both through The Urantia Book and through the daily insights our Thought Adjuster provides continually expands our understanding of truth and our capacity to live it.

Falling in love with truth itself. As we mature spiritually, we develop an intrinsic attraction to truth that transcends utility or personal advantage. We seek truth because we cannot help but love it, recognizing it as the foundation of all reality.

Father identification. This represents the progressive recognition of our true identity as children of God, increasingly aligning our will with the Father's will until the two become inseparable.

The integration of truth, beauty, and goodness. These three fundamental values of divine reality become the organizing principles of our thought life, informing our decisions and shaping our character. We learn to recognize truth intellectually, appreciate beauty aesthetically, and pursue goodness morally, understanding these as different expressions of the same divine reality.

Maintaining a living connection with Jesus. Our relationship with Christ Michael, the Creator Son of our local universe, provides both inspiration and practical guidance. This connection should be active and daily, not merely ceremonial or occasional.

Obedience to divine leadings. Spiritual maturity includes increasing sensitivity to the gentle promptings of the indwelling Adjuster and the courage to act upon those impressions, even when they lead us away from conventional paths.

Recognition of spiritual poverty. Paradoxically, spiritual growth requires honest acknowledgment of our spiritual neediness. Those who recognize their spiritual poverty are most open to divine ministry and transformation.

The Dynamic Nature of Spiritual Development

Spiritual growth is not a passive process but requires conscious effort and determination. Several key principles govern this development:

Spiritual transformation requires conscious participation. No one drifts accidentally into spiritual maturity. It demands intentional choices, sustained effort, and unwavering commitment. Growth cannot be accelerated through artificial situations or shortcuts; it unfolds according to divine timing and our genuine receptivity.

Thoughts, not merely feelings, lead us Godward. While emotions have their place in religious experience, authentic spiritual progress is guided by our thinking, by our moral decisions, our truth evaluations, and our will choices. Feelings may fluctuate, but the steadfast direction of our mind toward truth determines our ultimate trajectory.

The soul is made divine by what it strives to become, not merely by what it does. Divine approval rests upon our sincere intentions and persistent efforts rather than our specific achievements. God values the direction of our reach more than the height we have currently attained.

Spiritual growth is stimulated through intimate association with other religionists. We are not designed for solitary spiritual development. Fellowship with other truth-seekers provides mutual encouragement, accountability, diverse perspectives, and the practical expression of brotherly love. The very act of gathering for study and worship catalyzes spiritual growth in ways that solitary practice cannot duplicate.

Where man and God enter into partnership, no limitation can be placed upon future possibilities. This principle reveals the infinite potential inherent in our relationship with the Divine. Our limitations are not imposed by God but by our own receptivity and willingness to cooperate with divine purposes.

The Apostles' Remarkable Growth

One of the most striking examples of accelerated spiritual development appears in the experience of Jesus' apostles. The Urantia Book reveals that these men made more spiritual growth during one month alone, specifically, the month following Jesus' resurrection and before Pentecost, than they had achieved during all four years of their association with the Master.

This astonishing fact invites careful reflection. How could this be? During their years with Jesus, the apostles had enjoyed the incomparable advantage of daily personal instruction from the Creator Son himself. They witnessed his miracles, heard his parables, and observed his perfect life. Yet their growth during that period, while significant, paled in comparison to what they achieved in a single month without his physical presence.

The answer lies in the nature of dependence and independence in spiritual development. While Jesus walked among them, the apostles relied heavily upon his immediate guidance, his answers to their questions, and his intervention in difficult situations. They had not yet learned to make their own spiritual decisions or to rely directly upon their indwelling Adjusters and the Spirit of Truth for guidance.

When Jesus was no longer physically present, the apostles were compelled to turn inward, to seek divine guidance from the spiritual presences within and around them. They had to make their own decisions, take their own risks, and bear the full weight of spiritual responsibility. This necessity catalyzed profound growth. It forced them to activate their own spiritual resources and to forge direct, conscious partnerships with their Thought Adjusters.

This principle applies universally: spiritual growth accelerates when we cease depending upon external authorities and begin actively partnering with our internal divine guides. While teachers, fellowship, and study materials remain valuable, they cannot substitute for the direct personal experience of choosing God's will and following the leading of the indwelling Adjuster.

Indicators of Genuine Spiritual Progress

The Urantia Book provides specific indicators by which we can recognize authentic spiritual growth:

The ability to know God and the urge to be like Him. As we grow spiritually, our conception of God becomes clearer and our desire to emulate divine qualities intensifies. We move beyond merely knowing about God to actually knowing God as a personal presence.

Awakening to the needs of others. Spiritual maturity increases our sensitivity to the suffering, struggles, and spiritual hunger of those around us. We become less absorbed in our own concerns and more responsive to opportunities for service.

The discernment of meanings and the discovery of values. We develop enhanced capacity to perceive the deeper significance of our experiences and to recognize supreme values amid the confusion of competing claims.

The production of the fruits of divinity. Genuine spiritual growth manifests in observable qualities: love, joy, peace, patience, kindness, goodness, faithfulness, gentleness, and self-control. These fruits emerge naturally from a life increasingly dominated by spiritual values.

The human self-entering into new relationship with the divine self. We begin to experience our Thought Adjuster not as a foreign presence but as our truest, deepest self, the person we are becoming and, in a sense, already are in divine potential.

Increasing nearness to God and usefulness to our fellows. These two dimensions of growth are inseparable. We cannot draw closer to God without simultaneously becoming more loving toward our brothers and sisters, nor can we genuinely serve humanity without growing closer to our divine Source.

The progressive attunement to the Adjuster and increasing Father-likeness. Perhaps the most comprehensive indicator, this describes the gradual harmonization of human will with divine will until they beat in perfect synchrony.

The Partnership Principle

All authentic spiritual growth ultimately represents a partnership with God. It requires our active participation but recognizes that lasting transformation comes from divine indwelling. We supply the soil of willingness; God supplies the seed of eternal life. We make the decisions; God provides the power to execute them. We choose the direction; God provides the transforming presence that makes the journey possible.

This partnership principle illuminates an essential truth: spiritual growth is proportional to our spiritual content and signifies creative activity in the superconscious realm. It represents the conscious human personality cooperating with the indwelling divine presence to create something genuinely new, an immortal soul destined for eternal adventure.

Understanding these principles of spiritual growth provides the essential context for appreciating how Thought Adjusters evaluate potential human subjects. These divine fragments are not merely seeking intelligent creatures or emotionally responsive beings; they are searching for individuals with whom they can establish this transformative partnership, persons who possess the capacity and willingness to grow spiritually toward eventual fusion with the divine fragment itself.

The Three Essential Qualifications

When a Thought Adjuster volunteers for assignment to a human subject, that divine fragment must carefully evaluate three critical qualifications. These assessments are not arbitrary but reflect the necessary foundations for successful divine-human partnership. Understanding these qualifications helps us appreciate both the precision of divine ministry and the specific capacities that make spiritual growth possible.

First Qualification: Intellectual Capacity

The first question a volunteering Adjuster must answer is: **Is the mind normal? What is the intellectual potential and intelligence capacity? Can the individual develop into a bona fide will creature? Will wisdom have an opportunity to function?**

This evaluation focuses on the basic neurological and psychological capacity for rational thought, moral reasoning, and volitional choice. The Adjuster must determine whether the developing human brain will support normal mental function, the essential platform upon which all subsequent spiritual ministry depends.

The significance of mind normalcy cannot be overstated. Thought Adjusters cannot effectively minister to severely impaired minds. This is not a value judgment about human worth; every personality is equally precious to the Universal Father. Rather, it reflects a practical reality: the Adjuster's primary tool for spiritual ministry is the human mind itself. If that mind cannot function normally, the Adjuster cannot establish the necessary communication channels or create the spiritual counterpart that becomes the evolving soul.

For individuals whose minds do not develop normally, alternative provisions exist. These souls are not abandoned or disadvantaged in their eternal careers. They simply receive their spiritual ministry in a different sequence. Rather than receiving a Thought Adjuster during earthly life, they are assigned a fragment of either the Eternal Son or the Infinite Spirit when they awaken on the mansion worlds with newly constituted, perfectly functional minds. Their eternal potential remains completely intact; only the timing and method of spiritual ministry differ.

The assessment of intellectual potential extends beyond mere IQ measurements. The Adjusters evaluate whether wisdom will have opportunity to function, whether the individual can develop the capacity for sound judgment, mature reasoning, and the coordination of knowledge with experience. They assess whether this mind can eventually grasp abstract concepts, engage in moral reasoning, and make increasingly complex volitional choices.

This evaluation must be made before birth, based on genetic inheritance, parental history, and environmental factors that will shape early development. The precision required for this assessment staggers the imagination. From the combination of a single sperm and ovum, the supervising Adjuster orders must project the probable intellectual capacity of the resulting individual throughout an entire lifetime.

Second Qualification: Spiritual Perception

The second critical evaluation concerns spiritual receptivity: **What are the prospects of reverential development? Will the religious nature be born and grow? What is the potential of the soul? What is the probable spiritual capacity of receptivity?**

While intellectual capacity provides the platform for Adjuster ministry, spiritual perception determines its effectiveness. An individual might possess brilliant intellect but remain spiritually obtuse, capable of complex reasoning but blind to divine reality. Conversely, a person of modest intellectual gifts might demonstrate remarkable spiritual sensitivity and receptivity.

Spiritual perception involves several distinct capacities:

The ability to recognize and respond to beauty, both natural and spiritual. Beauty serves as a bridge between the material and spiritual realms, awakening the soul to realities beyond physical sensation.

The capacity for reverence, the ability to sense the sacred, to feel appropriate awe before ultimate reality, and to recognize one's true position in the cosmic family.

The development of the religious nature, an innate hunger for God, a yearning for righteousness, and a natural orientation toward worship and service.

The potential for soul growth, the likelihood that spiritual experiences will be preserved as eternal values, gradually building the morontia reality that will serve as the individual's resurrection vehicle.

The prospects for reverential development vary widely among individuals. Some persons demonstrate spiritual sensitivity from early childhood, exhibiting natural piety, spontaneous worship impulses, and keen moral consciousness. Others seem spiritually dormant for years before sudden awakening catalyzes rapid growth. The volunteering Adjuster must assess these prospects based on genetic inheritance, probable environmental influences, and the mysterious factor of personality itself.

This evaluation is particularly challenging because spiritual potential often lies hidden beneath layers of cultural conditioning, family dysfunction, or traumatic experience. The Adjuster must perceive not merely what is but what can become, the spiritual possibilities that might emerge under the right circumstances and with appropriate divine ministry.

Third Qualification: Combined Intellectual and Spiritual Powers

The third qualification represents the synthesis of the first two: **What is the degree to which intellectual and spiritual endowments may possibly be associated and combined so as to produce strength of human character and contribute to the certain evolution of an immortal soul of survival value?**

This evaluation recognizes that neither intellectual brilliance nor spiritual sensitivity alone guarantees successful partnership with the divine. What matters most is the potential for these two capacities to work together harmoniously, reinforcing and elevating each other.

The ideal human subject possesses:

A mind capable of grasping spiritual truth intellectually while a heart that responds to spiritual truth emotionally and volitionally.

The ability to coordinate knowledge with wisdom, to gather information efficiently while also evaluating it wisely and applying it appropriately.

Character strength, the moral courage to act upon spiritual convictions despite contrary social pressure, personal inconvenience, or temporal disadvantage.

Balanced development, neither purely intellectual nor merely emotional but integrating both dimensions into unified personality expression.

The certain evolution of an immortal soul is the ultimate criterion. The Adjuster evaluates whether this particular combination of intellectual and spiritual capacities can, under the likely circumstances of this individual's life, produce the minimum spiritual attainment necessary for survival. Will this person be able to make the faith choice for eternal life? Will sufficient spiritual progress occur to create a resurrectable soul?

This third qualification emphasizes that Thought Adjusters are not seeking perfect specimens but viable partners, individuals whose combined capacities provide a reasonable foundation for spiritual growth and eventual survival. The bar for assignment is not perfection but potential.

The Significance of Gender Neutrality

The text explicitly states that in the assignment and service of Adjusters, "the sex of the creature is of no consideration." This remarkable declaration deserves careful attention. In a universe of astonishing diversity, where virtually every imaginable variable affects function and relationship, the Adjusters regard gender as spiritually irrelevant to their ministry.

This principle reflects a profound truth: the essential person, the choosing, deciding, aspiring self that constitutes authentic identity, transcends biological sex. While gender significantly influences earthly experience and provides important contexts for growth, it does not determine spiritual capacity, limit divine ministry, or affect eternal potential. Before God, personalities stand equal in worth, opportunity, and destiny, regardless of whether they currently express themselves through male or female physiology.

The Volunteer Selection Process

With these three qualifications clearly evaluated, the actual assignment process can proceed. Multiple Adjusters typically volunteer for each human subject. This fact alone should inspire profound gratitude, multiple fragments of infinity consider you worthy of their eternal devotion, willing to invest themselves completely in your spiritual development.

From this group of volunteers, the supervising personalized orders select the Adjuster best suited for the task of spiritualizing and eternalizing the personality of the mortal candidate. This selection considers the previous experience of each volunteering Adjuster. Since our planet has no virgin Adjusters, all have served at least one previous subject, certain Adjusters possess experience that particularly qualifies them for specific types of human personalities.

Your Thought Adjuster was specifically chosen for you. This is not random assignment but divinely informed selection. The Adjuster you received had previous experiences that particularly prepared that divine fragment for effective ministry with your specific combination of intellectual capacity, spiritual potential, personality type, and life circumstances. You are not receiving generic divine ministry but personalized, expertly matched spiritual guidance.

This realization should transform our relationship with the indwelling Adjuster. We are not merely housing a divine fragment; we are partnered with a divine being who chose us, who was specifically selected for us, and who brings relevant experience to the challenges we will face. The partnership is not accidental but intentionally designed for maximum effectiveness.

The Preparation Process: From Divinington to Human Mind

Understanding the preparation that precedes an Adjuster's arrival deepens our appreciation for the care and precision characterizing divine ministry. The journey from the Father's bosom to a child's mind involves multiple stages, each revealing the extraordinary value the universe places upon individual human beings.

The Schools of Divinington

Divinington, the personal Paradise home of the Universal Father, serves as the departure point for all Thought Adjusters. This sacred sphere remains forever closed to all beings except those who have experienced divine fatherhood, a restriction that preserves the intimacy and mystery appropriate to the Father's personal domain.

When an Adjuster volunteers for human service and receives assignment, a brief but intensive preparation period follows. The waiting Adjuster is sent to the schools of Divinington, where the Adjuster receives specialized training for the specific subject to whom assignment has been made.

This training utilizes a working pattern of the waiting mortal mind. Consider the implications: before you were even conceived, the universe possessed a detailed projection of your mental and spiritual potential. This pattern, formulated through the superuniverse reflectivity service, provides your designated Adjuster with comprehensive information about your probable intellectual capacity, emotional temperament, personality type, and spiritual receptivity.

The reflectivity service, a cosmic intelligence network of astonishing sophistication, gathers data about your genetic inheritance, family history, cultural context, and probable life circumstances. This information is transmitted instantaneously to Divinington, where it is synthesized into a working model of your mind as it will likely develop from conception through early childhood.

Your Adjuster studies this model intensively, developing "the most effective plans for personality approach and mind spiritualization." The training is highly individualized, recognizing that effective ministry requires strategies specifically adapted to each unique personality. What works with one human subject might prove completely ineffective with another.

The personalized monitors who conduct this training are themselves experienced Adjusters who have successfully fused with mortal subjects and returned to Paradise for further service. They bring practical wisdom born of actual human partnership, understanding from experience the challenges, opportunities, and techniques that characterize successful Adjuster ministry. Your Adjuster's training is not theoretical but intensely practical, informed by the accumulated wisdom of countless previous Adjuster-human partnerships.

The Journey to Urantia

Once training is complete, the Adjuster is dispatched from Divinington. The journey itself provides insight into the priorities and efficiency of divine administration. The average transit time from Divinington to Urantia is precisely 117 hours, 42 minutes, and 7 seconds—approximately 4.8 days.

This specific timing reveals several important truths. First, Adjusters travel at extraordinary speeds, crossing vast cosmic distances in mere days. Second, virtually all of this time is occupied not with travel but with registration on Uversa, the superuniverse headquarters. The actual transit time is negligible; the administrative registration requires the days.

Registration on Uversa serves critical purposes. It formally records your existence in the superuniverse archives, establishing your cosmic identity in the administrative records of Orvonton. From the moment of this registration, you exist not merely as a biological organism on an isolated planet but as a recognized personality within the grand universe, a being whose every day is known, whose potential is recorded, and whose destiny matters to Paradise itself.

This registration process also ensures proper coordination among the various spiritual agencies that will minister to you throughout your life. The local universe Creative Spirit, the superuniverse Master Spirit, the Conjoint Actor, and ultimately the Universal Father himself maintain awareness of your existence and spiritual progress through the information networks established at this registration.

Prerequisites for Adjuster Indwelling

The Adjuster cannot enter the human mind at conception, birth, or even during early childhood. Several specific prerequisites must be satisfied before indwelling becomes possible:

First, the mind must be prepared by the indwelling ministry of the adjutant Mind Spirits. These seven mind-circuits, emanating from the local universe Creative Spirit, provide the foundational mental capacities that make human consciousness possible. All seven adjutants must achieve coordinate function before the Adjuster can arrive.

Animals possess the first five adjutants, intuition, understanding, courage, knowledge, and counsel. These circuits enable complex behavior, learning, social organization, and problem-solving. But animals lack the sixth and seventh adjutants: worship and wisdom. Without these higher circuits, neither moral consciousness nor reverential awareness can emerge. Consequently, animal behavior remains purely instinctual, guided by biological drives rather than moral choices.

The functioning of the sixth adjutant—worship—is particularly critical. This circuit enables the recognition of reality beyond the self, the capacity for reverence, and the impulse toward spiritual seeking. When worship begins to function, the creature transcends mere animal existence and enters the realm of potential spirituality.

The functioning of the seventh adjutant—wisdom—completes the preparation. Wisdom involves the ability to choose between emerging values of good and evil, to make genuine moral choices. This capacity for moral decision-making is absolutely essential for Adjuster indwelling because the entire purpose of Adjuster ministry is to spiritualize the moral choices of the human subject, creating from them the immortal soul.

Second, the Holy Spirit must prepare and encircuit the developing mind. The Holy Spirit, also emanating from the local universe Creative Spirit, represents the most foundational level of spiritual ministry. It has functioned on Urantia since the very first life forms appeared, preparing minds for the higher spiritual ministries that would eventually become available.

The Holy Spirit's role is preparatory and enabling. It sensitizes the mind to spiritual realities, creates initial spiritual receptivity, and establishes the basic circuits through which higher spiritual influences can later operate. Every creature, regardless of intellectual capacity or spiritual potential, receives this universal ministry.

Third, on bestowal worlds like Urantia, the Spirit of Truth must be present and functioning. The Spirit of Truth was poured out following Jesus' resurrection and ascension, fundamentally transforming spiritual conditions on our planet. Before Pentecost, Adjusters came only to individuals who had made significant moral and spiritual decisions, sometimes not arriving until individuals reached ages of 30, 40, or beyond.

After Pentecost, the Spirit of Truth began functioning as a spiritual coordinator of the various spiritual ministries. This coordination dramatically improved conditions for Adjuster indwelling. On post-bestowal worlds, Adjusters unfailingly come the instant the seventh adjutant mind-spirit begins to function, signaling the achievement of moral capacity.

The difference is profound. On pre-bestowal worlds, individuals must actively demonstrate spiritual seeking before receiving an Adjuster. On post-bestowal worlds, the mere capacity for moral choice triggers automatic Adjuster assignment. The Spirit of Truth creates spiritual conditions so favorable that divine indwelling can begin at the earliest possible moment.

The First Moral Decision

The actual trigger for Adjuster arrival is the child's first moral personality decision. This momentous event typically occurs around age five years, ten months, and four days, on average, the 2,134th day of terrestrial life.

What constitutes this first moral decision? It is the initial exercise of genuine moral choice, the first time the child consciously chooses between right and wrong, not based on fear of punishment or desire for reward, but based on an emerging sense that some things are inherently right and others inherently wrong.

This decision might seem insignificant to observers. Perhaps the child chooses to tell the truth despite knowing it will bring consequences. Perhaps the child shares a toy despite wanting to keep it. Perhaps the child shows kindness to another child despite social pressure to do otherwise. The specific content matters less than the essential fact: the child has made a choice based on moral perception rather than mere instinct or external conditioning.

This decision is automatically indicated in the seventh adjutant mind-spirit and registers instantly through an astonishing chain of communication. The information passes from the local universe Creative Spirit through the universal mind-gravity circuit of the Conjoint Actor (the Infinite Spirit) into the presence of the superuniverse Master Spirit, who immediately dispatches this intelligence to Divinington.

Within approximately four days, your designated Adjuster, already trained, already prepared, already intimately familiar with the projected pattern of your developing mind, arrives and takes up residence. The divine fragment that has volunteered for lifelong partnership with you, that has studied your projected mental and spiritual capacities, and that brings specific experience relevant to your needs, establishes presence in your mind, beginning the patient work of spiritual transformation.

The Significance of Early Life

One of the most striking revelations in this process concerns the period before Adjuster arrival. From conception through approximately age five years and ten months, every moment of your life is observed, recorded, and analyzed. The data gathered during these pre-Adjuster years provides the foundation for the Adjuster's subsequent ministry.

Your Adjuster arrives already familiar with your personality as it has expressed itself during these formative years. Every tantrum and every act of kindness, every moment of fear and every display of courage, every selfish choice and every generous impulse, all have been noted and incorporated into the Adjuster's understanding of who you are and how best to minister to you.

This reality places enormous significance on early childhood. The first five-plus years of life are not merely preparatory; they are definitional. The patterns established during these years, patterns of emotional response, social interaction, moral sensitivity, and spiritual receptivity, provide the raw material with which the Adjuster must work.

Parents and caregivers bear weighty responsibility during this critical period. While they cannot directly affect Adjuster assignment, they profoundly influence the personality pattern the Adjuster will inherit. Children raised with love, consistency, moral clarity, and spiritual awareness present more favorable conditions for Adjuster ministry than children raised in chaos, abuse, moral confusion, or spiritual vacuum.

Yet even under the most challenging circumstances, Adjusters work with what they receive. Divine ministry is infinitely patient, endlessly resourceful, and ultimately successful with all who make even the minimum faith choice for survival. The Adjuster that arrives in the mind of a traumatized child from a dysfunctional home is no less skilled, no less devoted, and no less capable of ultimate success than the Adjuster arriving in the mind of a beloved child from a spiritually mature family. The path may differ, but the destination remains equally attainable.

The Direct Relationship: God and Man

Perhaps the most revolutionary aspect of this entire process is its directness. Once the moral decision has been made and the Adjuster arrives, "there are no intermediaries or other intervening authorities or powers functioning between the divine Adjusters and their human subjects. God and man are directly related."

This principle cannot be overstated. You do not require a priest to mediate your relationship with God. You need no ecclesiastical authority to grant you access to divine presence. No religious institution controls your connection to the Father. The partnership is direct, immediate, and unmediated.

This does not diminish the value of religious community, wise spiritual counsel, or the accumulated wisdom of religious tradition. These resources provide invaluable support, guidance, and encouragement. But they cannot substitute for, control, or replace the direct relationship each individual enjoys with the divine fragment dwelling within.

When you are ready for divine guidance, nothing can prevent it from reaching you. No human authority can block your access to God. No personal unworthiness can disqualify you from divine ministry. No past failure can forfeit your opportunity for spiritual growth. The moment you genuinely turn toward the Father, seeking truth and desiring righteousness, the indwelling Adjuster responds immediately and completely.

This direct relationship revolutionizes religious life. It transfers spiritual authority from external institutions to internal experience, from hierarchical control to personal responsibility, from mediated religion to living faith. It places every believer on equal footing before God, regardless of education, social status, religious background, or personal history.

Yet this directness also imposes responsibility. We cannot blame failures on absent mediators or inadequate sacraments. We cannot excuse spiritual stagnation by citing lack of access to proper authorities. The divine presence dwells within, constantly available, eternally patient, and infinitely wise. Our spiritual progress depends not on external circumstances but on internal choices, our willingness to listen, our courage to obey, and our persistence in seeking.

Conclusion: The Cosmic Value of Individual Personality

This exploration of how Thought Adjusters choose and prepare for their human subjects reveals a truth of staggering proportions: each individual personality possesses cosmic significance. The universe does not regard you as one among billions of essentially interchangeable units. You are a unique, irreplaceable, eternally valuable being for whom specific divine provision has been made.

Before your birth, volunteer Adjusters expressed their willingness to devote themselves completely to your spiritual development. One was specifically selected as best suited for partnership with your unique personality. That Adjuster received specialized training focused specifically on the most effective strategies for spiritualizing your individual mind. Throughout your early childhood, every development was observed and recorded. And at the precise moment of your first moral choice, this prepared, trained, and devoted divine fragment arrived to begin lifelong ministry.

Every day of your life is known and recorded in the cosmic archives. Your growth matters not merely to you but to the vast array of spiritual personalities who minister to ascending mortals. Your choices affect not only your temporal welfare but your eternal destiny. Your partnership with the indwelling Adjuster contributes to the evolving Supreme Being and enriches the experiential dimension of deity itself.

This knowledge should transform our self-perception. We are not cosmic accidents, evolutionary flukes, or meaningless products of blind natural forces. We are intentionally created personalities of infinite potential, personally known to the Universal Father, individually valued by Paradise authorities, and specifically prepared for eternal adventure.

Neither should we take this for granted. The privilege of Adjuster indwelling brings corresponding responsibility. We have been given extraordinary spiritual resources; much will be expected in return. We have received personalized divine ministry; we should respond with wholehearted cooperation. We have been granted direct access to the Father; we should avail ourselves of this precious gift through daily communion and willing submission to divine leading.

As we continue our study of Paper 108 in subsequent chapters, we will explore the nature of Adjuster ministry throughout human life, the challenges these divine fragments face, and the techniques by which they seek to spiritualize mortal minds. We will examine the process of soul building, the possibility of Adjuster fusion, and the destiny awaiting those who successfully partner with their divine indwellers.

For now, let us rest in the profound realization that we are not alone. A fragment of infinity dwells within, knowing us completely, loving us unconditionally, and working tirelessly for our eternal welfare. Our part is simple yet profound: to believe, to trust, to choose, and to grow. As we do so, we fulfill the very purpose for which we were created and embark upon the greatest adventure in all reality, the eternal ascent from humanity to divinity, from Urantia to Paradise, from creature to creator.

Chapter Summary:

This chapter has examined the comprehensive nature of spiritual growth, the three essential qualifications Thought Adjusters evaluate when selecting human subjects, and the remarkable preparation process preceding Adjuster arrival. We have discovered that spiritual growth requires conscious effort, that multiple indicators reveal authentic progress, and that the apostles' experience demonstrates the power of personal spiritual responsibility. We have learned that Adjusters evaluate intellectual capacity, spiritual perception, and the potential for these to combine effectively. Finally, we have traced the Adjuster's journey from Divinington through specialized training to registration on Uversa and ultimate arrival at the moment of the child's first moral decision, establishing a direct and unmediated relationship between God and man.

In the next chapters, we will explore the ongoing nature of Adjuster ministry throughout human life, examining how these divine fragments work within our minds, the challenges they face, and the techniques they employ to spiritualize our thinking and build our immortal souls.

Chapter 9: The Mission and Ministry of Thought Adjusters

Part Three: Divine Presence in an Isolated World

Introduction

In this continuation of our exploration of Paper 108 from *The Urantia Book*, we delve into one of the most profound mysteries of divine ministry, the arrival, organization, and function of Thought Adjusters in the minds of evolutionary mortals. This chapter examines the intricate mechanisms by which fragments of God the Father come to indwell human consciousness, even on worlds isolated by rebellion.

The material presented here addresses fundamental questions that have puzzled spiritual seekers throughout the ages: How does God maintain personal contact with individual mortals? What determines when this divine presence arrives in human consciousness? How does spiritual isolation affect our connection to the Father? These questions become particularly poignant when we consider that our world, Urantia, has been in spiritual quarantine for over 200,000 years following the Lucifer rebellion.

As we examine the arrival of Thought Adjusters before the bestowal of the Spirit of Truth, we gain insight into the Father's unwavering commitment to maintaining direct, personal contact with His evolving children, regardless of planetary circumstances. This chapter reveals that even in the darkest periods of spiritual isolation, God's presence within the human mind remains constant, unaffected, and eternally accessible.

The Arrival of Thought Adjusters Before the Spirit of Truth - The Historical Context

Before examining the specific conditions that facilitate Thought Adjuster arrival, we must understand the distinction between two great dispensational epochs in planetary evolution. The first epoch encompasses the long ages before a bestowal Son appears on a world, a period that on most planets extends for hundreds of thousands or even millions of years. The second epoch begins with the bestowal mission and continues thereafter, fundamentally altering the spiritual landscape of the inhabited world.

On Urantia, the dividing line between these two epochs occurred approximately 2,000 years ago with the bestowal of Christ Michael as Jesus of Nazareth.

Following his resurrection and return to universe headquarters, the Spirit of Truth was poured out upon all flesh during the event known as Pentecost. This epochal event transformed the spiritual receptivity of every human being on the planet.

After Pentecost, all normal-minded individuals automatically receive Thought Adjusters upon making their first moral decision, typically occurring between the ages of five and six years. This represents the establishment of a new spiritual dispensation, one in which divine indwelling becomes universal rather than selective.

However, the period before such bestowal missions presents a markedly different situation. During these earlier ages, Thought Adjuster bestowal appears to be determined by a complex interplay of spiritual influences, personality attitudes, and cosmic factors. While we do not fully comprehend all the laws governing these earlier bestowals, *The Urantia Book* reveals six primary influences and conditions associated with Thought Adjuster arrival in pre-bestowal epochs.

Six Factors Influencing Early Adjuster Arrival - 1. The Assignment of Personal Seraphic Guardians

The first factor involves a profound but mysterious relationship between Thought Adjusters and seraphic guardians. If a mortal who has not previously been indwelled by an Adjuster receives the assignment of personal seraphic guardians, the Thought Adjuster arrives forthwith. This connection suggests a deep administrative coordination between these two orders of divine ministry.

It is important to distinguish between group seraphic guardianship and personal seraphic guardianship. All human beings at birth are assigned seraphic guardians who work in groups, typically overseeing dozens or even hundreds of individuals simultaneously. However, the assignment of *personal* seraphic guardians, a dedicated pair of seraphim devoted exclusively to one individual, represents a significant spiritual achievement.

This personal assignment typically occurs when a mortal reaches the third psychic circle of spiritual attainment. The psychic circles represent progressive levels of intellectual achievement and spiritual growth, ranging from the seventh (lowest) to the first (highest) circle. Attainment of the third circle signifies that an individual has achieved sufficient spiritual momentum to warrant personal angelic ministry.

The immediate arrival of a Thought Adjuster upon personal seraphic assignment reveals the Father's consistent pattern of providing increased spiritual resources to those who demonstrate spiritual receptivity and growth. It represents divine recognition of genuine spiritual progress and the allocation of enhanced ministry to support continued development.

2. The Attainment of the Third Psychic Circle

The second factor relates directly to intellectual and spiritual achievement. Thought Adjusters have been observed arriving in mortal minds upon the conquest of the third psychic circle, even before such accomplishment could be signaled to local universe personalities.

The third psychic circle represents a critical threshold in mortal development. It marks the point at which an individual becomes a full-fledged member of the cosmos, a recognized participant in the grand universe of intelligent, spiritually progressing beings. The significance of this achievement extends far beyond the local planet or even the local universe. Through the mechanism of universe reflectivity, the attainment of the third circle is instantly communicated throughout the superuniverse and ultimately to Paradise itself.

This cosmic recognition carries profound implications. When you achieve the third psychic circle, your existence and spiritual status become known to the Ancients of Days on the superuniverse headquarters world, to the administration of the local universe, and even to the eternal records maintained on Paradise. You have graduated from being merely a potentially surviving mortal to becoming an actively participating universe citizen.

The automatic arrival of a Thought Adjuster at this juncture, if one has not already been received, underscores the Father's personal interest in every mortal who achieves this level of cosmic consciousness and spiritual commitment. The third circle represents sufficient spiritual maturity to ensure productive collaboration between the human mind and the divine indweller.

Spiritual attainment, as revealed in *The Urantia Book*, encompasses far more than mere intellectual knowledge or religious observance. It involves the vigorous exercise of faith, the sincere pursuit of truth, the consistent practice of divine values, and the progressive transformation of character. The topical index of *The Urantia Book* provides an extensive list of indicators of genuine spiritual growth, including increased perception of truth, enhanced capacity for worship, growing love for fellow beings, strengthening moral character, and deepening commitment to doing the Father's will.

3. Supreme Decisions of Unusual Spiritual Import

The third factor involves personal crisis and momentous decision-making. Upon making a supreme decision of unusual spiritual import, such human behavior in a personal planetary crisis is usually attended by the immediate arrival of the waiting Thought Adjuster.

A supreme decision represents a choice that fundamentally alters the trajectory of one's life, a decision that places spiritual values above all other considerations, regardless of potential consequences. Such decisions often arise during periods of intense personal crisis, when external pressures would seem to justify compromise or expediency, yet the individual chooses the higher path.

The historical example of Andon and Fonta, the first two human beings on Urantia, perfectly illustrates this principle. Approximately one million years ago, these twin siblings made the epochal decision to leave their tribe and journey into unknown territory. This decision was not motivated by mere wanderlust or rebellion against their tribe. Rather, it represented a profound spiritual choice, a decision to seek something higher, to pursue an undefined but deeply felt spiritual aspiration.

This decision of unusual spiritual import immediately resulted in the arrival of Thought Adjusters for both Andon and Fonta, making them the first human beings on our planet to be indwelt by fragments of the Father. Their decision demonstrated the essential qualities that warrant divine indwelling: courage in the face of uncertainty, willingness to sacrifice security for principle, and commitment to spiritual ideals over material comfort.

Throughout human history, countless individuals have experienced similar moments of spiritual crisis and decision. The missionary who chooses to serve in dangerous territory rather than accept comfortable assignments, the whistleblower who exposes corruption despite personal risk, the individual who stands alone for truth when all others compromise, these represent modern examples of supreme decisions that attract immediate divine attention and support.

4. The Spirit of Brotherhood and Unselfish Ministry

The fourth factor reveals perhaps the most accessible pathway to Thought Adjuster arrival: the development of genuine love for one's fellows and consecration to unselfish ministry. Regardless of psychic circle attainment or personal guardian assignment, when an evolving mortal becomes dominated by love for their fellows and consecrated to unselfish ministry to their brethren in the flesh, the waiting

Thought Adjuster unhesitatingly descends to indwell the mind of such a mortal minister.

This factor deserves special emphasis because it demonstrates that the highest spiritual achievement, divine indwelling, remains accessible to individuals of ordinary intellectual capacity and limited educational opportunity. One need not be a philosopher, theologian, or scholar to attract a Thought Adjuster. The simple desire to serve others, coupled with genuine love for humanity, suffices to warrant this supreme divine gift.

The phrase "dominated by love" suggests more than occasional charitable impulses or periodic acts of kindness. It indicates a fundamental reorientation of personality around the principle of loving service. Such individuals think first of others' needs, find genuine satisfaction in serving, and organize their lives around opportunities to help their fellows. This love manifests not as sentimental emotion but as practical, consistent, self-forgetful ministry.

This pathway to divine indwelling embodies the profound truth Jesus taught: "Inasmuch as you have done it unto one of the least of these my brethren, you have done it unto me." The Father recognizes authentic love for His children as evidence of spiritual receptivity, regardless of the intellectual or philosophical sophistication accompanying such love.

The concept of "unselfish ministry" deserves careful consideration. Genuine service springs from authentic concern for others' welfare, not from desire for recognition, reward, or spiritual advancement. The moment service becomes calculated, performed primarily to achieve spiritual status or merit, it loses the quality that attracts divine recognition. The Father looks not merely at actions but at motivations, and He responds to the pure desire to bless and serve others.

This principle underlies the fundamental teaching often summarized as "the Fatherhood of God and the Brotherhood of Man." Recognition of God as Father naturally leads to recognition of all human beings as brothers and sisters. This family consciousness, when translated into active loving service, creates ideal conditions for divine indwelling and spiritual growth.

5. Declaration of Intention to Do the Will of God

The fifth factor involves perhaps the most direct pathway to Thought Adjuster arrival: the sincere declaration of intention to do the Father's will. Many mortals appear to be in readiness to receive Adjusters, yet the monitors do not arrive. Then, quietly and almost unconsciously, these individuals arrive at the decision to begin the pursuit of doing the will of the Father in heaven. This decision triggers the immediate dispatch of Thought Adjusters.

The decision to do God's will represents the supreme choice available to mortal creatures. It encompasses and transcends all other spiritual decisions because it involves the complete surrender of self-will to divine guidance. This decision acknowledges that the Father's wisdom surpasses human understanding, that His purposes merit complete trust, and that alignment with divine will represents the highest possible achievement for evolutionary beings.

Importantly, this decision need not be dramatic or publicly declared. Many individuals arrive at this commitment "quietly" and "almost unconsciously", through gradual spiritual growth rather than sudden conversion. What matters is not the external drama accompanying the decision but the internal reality of genuine commitment.

The immediate dispatch of Thought Adjusters following this decision reveals divine wisdom and perfect timing. Until an individual genuinely commits to doing the Father's will, a Thought Adjuster might find it difficult to provide effective guidance. The human will, exercised in opposition to or independence from divine leading, can effectively neutralize the Adjuster's ministry. However, once the mortal will aligns with the purpose of seeking and doing the Father's will, the Adjuster can begin effective collaboration toward spiritual transformation.

This commitment to doing God's will does not require perfect understanding of what that will might be in specific situations. Indeed, most individuals making this commitment have only the vaguest notion of how it will express itself in daily life. What matters is the sincere intention and the willingness to be led. The Thought Adjuster, once arrived, provides the guidance necessary to transform general commitment into specific action.

The need for guidance explains why the Thought Adjuster arrives immediately upon this decision. The individual has essentially said, "I want to do God's will, but I need help understanding what that means and how to accomplish it." The Father's response is to provide His personal presence, a fragment of Himself, to serve as guide, teacher, and companion throughout the eternal adventure of discovering and doing the divine will.

6. Supreme Being Influence and Cosmic Reflex Action

The sixth and final factor introduces an element of mystery that even the revelators acknowledge they do not fully understand. On worlds where Adjusters do not fuse with evolving souls, Adjusters are sometimes bestowed in response to influences wholly beyond the comprehension of the revelators themselves. They conjecture that such bestowals are determined by some cosmic reflex action originating in the Supreme Being.

The Supreme Being represents God the Supreme, the evolving, experiential deity of the grand universe. Unlike the existential Paradise Deities (the Universal Father, Eternal Son, and Infinite Spirit), the Supreme is not complete but growing, not infinite but finite, not perfect but perfecting. The Supreme grows through the experiences of all creatures throughout the seven superuniverses, and every creature's spiritual progress contributes to the Supreme's evolution.

The suggestion that the Supreme Being might trigger certain Thought Adjuster bestowals points toward profound cosmic interconnections we barely comprehend. It implies that the spiritual needs and potentials of individual mortals somehow register in the consciousness of evolving deity, triggering responses that facilitate both individual growth and the Supreme's evolution.

Particularly intriguing is the reference to worlds where Adjusters "do not fuse with the evolving souls of mortal inhabitants." *The Urantia Book* reveals that mortal beings fall into different categories based on their fusion potential. Most mortals, including those on Urantia, are Adjuster-fusion candidates, beings capable of eternally fusing with their Thought Adjusters to become immortal ascending sons and daughters of God.

However, other mortals are Son-fusion or Spirit-fusion candidates. These beings receive Thought Adjusters who serve as temporary indwellers, providing spiritual guidance and moral direction, but who ultimately return to Divinington while the mortal fuses with a fragment of the Creator Son or the Creative Mother Spirit. These Adjusters are called "virgin Adjusters", fragments gaining initial experience with mortal mind before moving on to potential fusion assignments with other mortals.

Why certain bestowals occur remains a mystery even to highly advanced celestial beings. This acknowledged limitation in understanding reminds us that we stand at the beginning of an eternal journey of discovery. The universe contains mysteries that will engage our interest and challenge our understanding throughout the ages of eternity. Even revelatory knowledge, while vastly expanding our comprehension, leaves room for continued exploration and discovery.

Organization and Administration of Thought Adjusters - Universal Scope and Unified Purpose

Having examined the conditions facilitating Thought Adjuster arrival, we now turn to their organization and administration throughout the universes. As far as the revelators know, Thought Adjusters are organized as an independent working unit in the universe of universes, administered directly from Divinington, the Paradise sphere serving as headquarters for the Father's ministry.

The independence of Thought Adjuster organization merits careful consideration. Unlike most celestial personalities who function within clearly defined administrative hierarchies, Thought Adjusters appear to operate with remarkable autonomy. They are not subject to local universe administrators, superuniverse authorities, or even the coordination of other Paradise personalities. Their administration flows directly from Divinington, suggesting that the Father Himself maintains immediate oversight of these fragments of His own being.

Despite this organizational independence, Thought Adjusters demonstrate perfect uniformity throughout all seven superuniverses. Every local universe receives identical types of Mystery Monitors. This universality reveals that Thought Adjusters embody a standardized expression of the Father's personal presence, adapted to function effectively with mortal minds regardless of the local universe in which those mortals evolve.

This uniformity carries profound implications. It means that mortal ascenders from the most distant parts of the grand universe share an identical experience of divine indwelling. The Father fragment dwelling in the mind of a mortal on Urantia in the superuniverse of Orvonton functions exactly like the Father fragment indwelling a mortal on a world in the far reaches of superuniverse seven. This universal consistency ensures that all mortals have equal access to divine guidance and equal opportunity for eternal survival and Paradise attainment.

Serial Organization and Mysterious Tracking

Observation reveals that numerous series of Adjusters exist, involving serial organization extending through races, over dispensations, and to worlds, systems, and universes. However, tracking these Divine gifts proves exceedingly difficult because they function interchangeably throughout the grand universe.

The concept of "series" suggests classification systems beyond our current comprehension. These series might relate to levels of experience, specialized training, particular mission focus, or other factors known only to the administrators on Divinington. What remains clear is that despite this complex organization, Adjusters can and do serve interchangeably, a virgin Adjuster can serve effectively on any world with any race during any dispensation.

This interchangeability demonstrates the universal adaptability of Thought Adjusters. Unlike most celestial ministers who develop specialized expertise through extended service in particular locations or with specific types of beings, Thought Adjusters come pre-equipped to function effectively in any mortal mind anywhere in the grand universe. This universal competence reflects their origin as direct fragments of the Universal Father, whose infinite nature encompasses all possible situations and circumstances.

Implications for Universal Mortal Population

The fact that identical types of Mystery Monitors serve all local universes throughout all seven superuniverses carries a stunning implication: mortal beings exist throughout the grand universe. Every local universe created by Creator Sons includes mortal populations receiving Thought Adjusters. The program of divine indwelling extends far beyond Urantia, beyond Nebadon, beyond Orvonton, encompassing countless trillions of evolving mortals across all organized space.

This universal scope transforms our understanding of humanity's place in creation. We are not unique experiments or isolated anomalies. Rather, we represent one instance of a universal pattern, the pattern of evolutionary mortals endowed with personality, gifted with relative free will, indwelt by Father fragments, and destined for eternal adventure in the ascending career.

However, we must also recognize that mortals are not the only order of beings receiving Father fragments. *The Urantia Book* reveals that other types of beings receive different types of divine gifts. The Father has fragmented Himself in various ways to minister to different orders of creation. Mortals receive what we call Thought Adjusters, but other beings receive Father fragments specifically adapted to their nature and needs.

Some mortal types cannot achieve fusion with their Thought Adjusters. These beings, possessing one-brain, two-brain, three-brain, or four-brain configurations, may receive virgin Adjusters for experiential purposes. While most cannot achieve

Adjuster fusion, they can achieve Son fusion or Spirit fusion, ultimately uniting with a fragment of the Creator Son or the Local Universe Mother Spirit.

Even these non-fusion mortals have survival potential. If they demonstrate any inclination toward recognizing deity and any desire to survive beyond material existence, they receive opportunity for mansion world resurrection and continued spiritual growth. They simply achieve immortality through union with a different type of divine fragment than do Adjuster-fusion mortals like ourselves.

Records, Reports, and Cosmic Communication - The Reporting System

The complete record of Thought Adjusters exists outside of Divinington only on the headquarters worlds of the seven superuniverses. Each superuniverse headquarters maintains detailed records of the number and order of every Adjuster indwelling every ascending creature within that superuniverse. These records are reported from Paradise authorities to superuniverse headquarters and then communicated to local universe headquarters and relayed to particular planets.

However, local universe records do not disclose the full number of Thought Adjusters. The Nebadon records contain only local universe assignment numbers as designated by representatives of the Ancients of Days. The real significance of complete Adjuster numbers remains known only on Divinington.

This limitation of information reveals the carefully structured nature of universe administration. Knowledge is distributed on a need-to-know basis, with complete information available only at the highest administrative levels. Local universe administrators require sufficient information to coordinate ministry to their own worlds but do not need comprehensive data about Adjuster populations throughout other universes.

One reason for this information limitation might involve security and appropriate confidentiality. If complete Adjuster numbers were universally known, one could calculate exactly how many living, potentially surviving creatures exist in any given universe. Such information might not serve the best interests of developing mortals or the smooth functioning of universe administration.

Human Identification and Universal Names

Prior to Adjuster fusion, mortal subjects are often known by the numbers of their Thought Adjusters rather than by personal names. This practice reflects the temporary nature of mortal existence before fusion. The Thought Adjuster represents the only truly eternal element in the pre-fusion mortal, making it the logical basis for identification in universe records.

Mortals do not receive true universe names until after Adjuster fusion. This union is signalized by the bestowal of a new name upon the creature by the destiny guardian, the seraphic guardian who has accompanied the mortal throughout their ascension career. This new name represents recognition of the birth of a truly eternal being, a perfected union of divine and human elements that will endure throughout all future eternity.

The practice of withholding permanent names until fusion emphasizes an important spiritual reality: until we fuse with our Adjusters, we remain incomplete, temporary, and unfinished. The Adjuster represents our potential for eternity, but that potential becomes actualized reality only through the fusion process. Once fused, we become genuinely eternal beings worthy of permanent identification in the cosmic records.

Tabamantia's Tribute: Recognition of Adjuster Excellence - The Sovereign Inspector's Visit

Paper 108 preserves one of the most moving passages in *The Urantia Book*, the tribute delivered by Tabamantia to the chief of Thought Adjusters serving on Urantia. Tabamantia serves as sovereign supervisor of all decimal or experimental planets in the universe of Nebadon. Every tenth world in Nebadon is designated as an experimental planet where life patterns receive special modifications and innovations, and Tabamantia maintains oversight of these special worlds.

His periodic inspection of Urantia included the customary delivery of charges and admonishments to various chiefs of superhuman personalities attached to world administration. However, he also delivered an extraordinary acknowledgment to the chief of Thought Adjusters. The records do not definitively indicate Tabamantia's location during this communication, he might have been on the planet, on Salvington (universe headquarters), on Edentia (constellation headquarters), or on Divinington itself. The message could have been relayed through the reflectivity system that allows instantaneous communication throughout the universes.

The Content of the Tribute

Speaking as one temporarily placed in authority over the experimental planetary series, Tabamantia expressed admiration and profound respect for the magnificent group of celestial ministers, the Mystery Monitors who have volunteered to serve on "this irregular sphere." His words deserve careful attention:

"Now to you, superiors far above me, I come as one placed in temporary authority over the experimental planetary series, and I come to express admiration and profound respect for this magnificent group of celestial ministers, the Mystery Monitors, who have volunteered to serve on this irregular sphere."

This opening acknowledgment establishes the proper perspective. Despite Tabamantia's high position as supervisor of all experimental worlds in Nebadon, he recognizes Thought Adjusters as "superiors far above" himself. This recognition of Adjuster supremacy reflects their origin as direct fragments of the Universal Father, making them representatives of deity in a sense that no created being, however high, can claim.

The description of Urantia as an "irregular sphere" carries significant meaning. Urantia's irregularity stems from multiple factors: its status as a decimal planet (subject to experimental life modifications), its victimization by rebellion (the Lucifer rebellion and its continuing effects), its experience of default (the Adamic default that deprived the world of planned biological uplift), and its selection as a bestowal world for Michael (creating both unique opportunities and particular challenges).

Tabamantia continued:

"No matter how trying the crises, you never falter. Not on the records of Nebadon, nor before the commissions of Orvonton, has there ever been offered an indictment of a Divine Adjuster."

This statement deserves extended reflection. In a universe where many orders of beings have failed their trusts, where Lucifer and a third of the Lanonandek Sons chose rebellion, where administrators have proven inadequate, where teachers have misled students, the Thought Adjusters maintain a perfect record. Not one Adjuster has ever failed their trust. Not one has proven unfaithful. Not one has been subject to indictment or correction by higher authorities.

This perfect record becomes even more remarkable when we consider the challenges Adjusters face. They work with imperfect, often resistant material minds. They must respect mortal free will even when that will chooses paths leading away from survival. They labor in isolation, unable to directly communicate with their subjects except through the subconscious mind. They serve on worlds like Urantia where rebellion has created conditions of extraordinary difficulty. Yet despite all these challenges, their record remains unblemished.

The tribute continues:

"You have been true to your trusts; you have been divinely faithful. You have helped to adjust the mistakes and to compensate for the shortcomings of all who labor on this confused planet."

The phrase "true to your trusts" echoes throughout *The Urantia Book* as the highest commendation any being can receive. Trust represents the foundation of all universe relationships. When we fail to be true to our trusts, when we betray confidence, abandon responsibility, or pursue selfish ends rather than assigned duties, we undermine the very fabric of cosmic cooperation.

The Thought Adjusters' faithfulness stands in stark contrast to the unfaithfulness of other beings who have served on Urantia. The Planetary Prince, Caligastia, betrayed his trust by joining the Lucifer rebellion. Adam and Eve, though well-intentioned, defaulted in their mission to biologically uplift the human race. Numerous other personalities have proven less than fully faithful to their assignments.

Yet through all these failures, the Thought Adjusters have maintained their ministry. They have "helped to adjust the mistakes and to compensate for the shortcomings of all who labor on this confused planet." When rebellion threw the world into chaos, the Adjusters continued their patient work. When default deprived humanity of planned advancement, the Adjusters redoubled their efforts to achieve spiritual progress through direct ministry to individual minds. When confusion and error multiplied, the Adjusters remained steady, true, and faithful.

Tabamantia's tribute reaches its climax:

"You are marvelous beings, guardians of the good in the souls of this backward realm. I pay you respect even while you are apparently under my jurisdiction as volunteer ministers. I bow before you in humble recognition of your exquisite unselfishness, your understanding ministry, and your impartial devotion. You deserve the name of the Godlike servers of the mortal inhabitants of this strife-torn, grief-stricken, and disease-afflicted world. I honor you; I all but worship you."

These words from a high universe administrator, a being far advanced beyond human comprehension, reveal the extraordinary status of Thought Adjusters in the cosmic hierarchy. Tabamantia bows before them. He "all but worships" them. He recognizes them as "Godlike servers" whose devotion transcends anything demonstrated by created beings.

The description of Urantia as "strife-torn, grief-stricken, and disease-afflicted" accurately characterizes our planetary condition. The strife stems from rebellion's legacy, the confusion of truth with error, the mixing of evolutionary progress with deliberate distortion, the perpetuation of systems and practices rooted in selfishness rather than brotherhood. The grief arises from broken relationships, disappointed hopes, tragic losses, and the suffering inherent in a world where love often seems defeated by hatred and cruelty.

The disease affliction encompasses both physical maladies and spiritual sicknesses. Physical disease, while partly inevitable in evolutionary worlds, has been exacerbated by millennia of poor practices, inadequate understanding, and the biological consequences of rebellion and default. Spiritual disease, the sicknesses of doubt, despair, cynicism, and faithlessness, perhaps proves even more debilitating than physical ailments.

Yet despite serving in these extraordinarily difficult conditions, the Thought Adjusters maintain their faithful ministry. They deserve honor, respect, and gratitude from every human being who has ever lived or ever will live on this troubled world. Their presence within our minds represents God's personal assurance that despite all appearances, despite all the evidence of evil and suffering, He has not abandoned us. He remains present, personally and intimately, within every willing human heart.

Implications for Our Understanding

This tribute by Tabamantia should profoundly affect how we understand our spiritual situation. First, it confirms that higher authorities fully recognize Urantia's abnormal condition. When we survey human history with its endless wars, injustices, cruelties, and suffering, we might wonder if celestial authorities understand how difficult life on this planet truly is. Tabamantia's words assure us that they do understand. They recognize this world as backward, strife-torn, grief-stricken, and disease-afflicted.

Second, the tribute reveals that the faithful ministry of Thought Adjusters provides compensatory blessing for our planet's deficiencies. We cannot restore what rebellion and default have taken from us. We cannot undo the biological damage from the Adamic default. We cannot erase the confusion introduced by Caligastia's betrayal. But the enhanced ministry of Thought Adjusters works to compensate for these losses, helping individuals achieve spiritual heights despite planetary handicaps.

Third, Tabamantia's words remind us that we are never alone in our struggles. However, isolated we might feel, however overwhelming our challenges might seem, we carry within us a divine fragment that has proven faithful across hundreds of thousands of years and billions of human minds. This fragment will never fail us, never abandon us, never prove untrue to its trust. If we listen to its leading and follow its guidance, we cannot ultimately fail.

Finally, the tribute calls us to reciprocate the Thought Adjusters' faithfulness with our own fidelity. These divine monitors have proven "true to their trusts." The question facing each of us is whether we will prove equally true to ours. We have been entrusted with free will, with personality, with the capacity for spiritual growth, and with the opportunity to contribute to the Supreme Being's evolution. Will we be true to these trusts? Will we honor the faithful ministry of our indwelling Adjusters by cooperating with their leading?

The Relationship Between Adjusters and Other Spiritual Influences - Independent Yet Coordinate Ministry

One of the most intriguing aspects of Thought Adjuster ministry involves their apparent independence from other spiritual influences while simultaneously functioning in perfect coordination with all other ministries. Paper 108 addresses this paradox directly, revealing both the autonomy and the interdependence characterizing divine spiritual ministry.

Thought Adjusters function "quite apart from those [laws] which govern and control the performances of all other spiritual influences." They appear to operate according to universal laws distinct from those directing the ministry of the Holy Spirit, the Spirit of Truth, seraphic guardians, and other celestial ministers. This independence allows Adjusters to maintain their ministry regardless of what happens to other spiritual circuits or agencies.

The practical significance of this independence becomes clear when we consider Urantia's experience. When Caligastia joined the Lucifer rebellion, numerous spiritual circuits were severed. The normal channels of communication between Urantia and universe headquarters were cut. Many spiritual ministries were curtailed or modified. Yet through all this disruption, the Thought Adjusters continued functioning exactly as they had before rebellion. Their ministry remained unaffected by the planetary isolation.

This independence from external spiritual circuits explains how Thought Adjusters can function effectively on completely isolated worlds, on primitive worlds lacking any revelation, and on worlds where rebellion has severed normal spiritual connections. The Adjuster's connection to the Father flows directly from Paradise through channels unaffected by local universe circumstances.

However, despite this functional independence, long-range observation "unquestionably discloses that they function in the human mind in perfect synchrony and coordination with all other spiritual ministries." This coordination occurs not through direct administrative oversight but through the natural harmony of purposes among all agencies working toward the same spiritual goals.

The Holy Spirit of the Local Universe Mother Spirit, the Spirit of Truth proceeding from both the Creator Son and the Creative Mother Spirit, the ministry of seraphic guardians, the influence of the adjutant mind-spirits, and the work of Thought Adjusters all converge on the same objective: fostering spiritual growth in mortal minds and facilitating eternal survival. Because they share this unified purpose and because they all ultimately represent expressions of divine love and wisdom, their ministries naturally harmonize despite their administrative independence.

Specialized Functions Within Unified Purpose

Each spiritual ministry contributes unique elements to the total spiritual environment surrounding and permeating mortal consciousness:

The Adjutant Mind-Spirits, emanating from the Local Universe Mother Spirit, provide the basic intellectual framework for conscious thought. The seven adjutants, intuition, understanding, courage, knowledge, counsel, worship, and wisdom, establish the mental foundation upon which all higher spiritual ministry builds.

The Holy Spirit, the direct personal circuit of the Local Universe Mother Spirit, creates spiritual receptivity, nurtures faith potential, and establishes the fundamental God-consciousness that makes religion possible. The Holy Spirit functions universally on all normal-minded mortals from birth, preparing minds for higher spiritual ministry.

The Spirit of Truth, bestowed following Creator Son bestowal missions, enhances spiritual perception, illuminates truth, and creates the spiritual environment in which faith can flourish. The Spirit of Truth particularly functions to reveal the character and nature of the Creator Son, making personal relationship with Michael more attainable for mortals.

Seraphic Guardians provide external spiritual ministry, protecting their charges from certain dangers, suggesting beneficial courses of action, and manipulating material environments (within carefully defined limits) to create conditions favorable for spiritual growth. Seraphim work from outside the mind, while Adjusters work from within.

Thought Adjusters represent the direct personal presence of the Universal Father. They provide moral guidance, spiritual direction, and the actual presence of divinity within human consciousness. Unlike other ministries that nurture spiritual capacity, Adjusters actually contain divine reality. Fusion with the Adjuster literally makes the mortal one with God.

This diversity of ministry creates a rich spiritual environment supporting mortal growth from multiple directions simultaneously. The coordination of these ministries produces effects far exceeding what any single agency could accomplish alone. Together, they weave a network of spiritual influence encompassing and permeating every aspect of human experience.

The Unique Contribution of Thought Adjusters

Within this network of spiritual ministry, Thought Adjusters make unique contributions impossible for any other agency:

Direct Personal Connection to the Universal Father: While other ministries represent the Father's love and will indirectly, Adjusters literally are fragments of the Father. They provide actual experiential contact with Paradise Deity.

Eternal Survival Potential: While other ministries nurture spiritual growth, only the Thought Adjuster provides the mechanism for actual eternal survival through fusion. The Adjuster becomes the foundation of eternal identity, preserving essential memory and character while enabling infinite future growth.

Moral Guidance from Infinite Perspective: The Adjuster's guidance springs from perfect knowledge of divine will and infinite wisdom regarding eternal consequences. No other ministry can provide guidance based on such complete understanding.

Pre-Personal to Personal Transformation: The Adjuster arrives as a pre-personal entity but through collaboration with the human will and personality, becomes increasingly personalized. This transformation represents a unique aspect of divine-mortal partnership found nowhere else in creation.

Independence from Planetary Circumstances: While other spiritual ministries can be affected by planetary isolation, rebellion, or default, Thought Adjusters function with complete independence. Their connection to Paradise remains unbroken regardless of local universe conditions.

This unique contribution explains why even evolved and perfected beings who have never experienced Adjuster indwelling regard such mortals with a mixture of envy and awe. To be indwelt by an actual fragment of the Universal Father, to have the potential for literal fusion with deity, to carry within oneself the eternal presence of the First Source and Center, these represent spiritual privileges of the highest order.

Communication During Planetary Isolation - The Paradox of Quarantine

Among the most remarkable revelations in Paper 108 is the assertion that planetary isolation, even quarantine resulting from rebellion, in no way affects Thought Adjusters or their ability to communicate with any part of the local universe, superuniverse, or central universe. This statement addresses one of the most troubling aspects of Urantia's spiritual situation: our isolation from normal universe circuits and communications.

When a planetary administration joins rebellion against universe authority, certain circuits are immediately severed to prevent the spread of rebellion and to protect loyal worlds from contamination by seditious philosophies. This quarantine affects numerous aspects of normal planetary function. Transportation circuits close, preventing physical travel to and from the isolated world. Communication circuits shut down, eliminating normal information exchange. Certain spiritual ministries are curtailed or modified.

Yet through all this isolation, through over 200,000 years of spiritual quarantine, Thought Adjusters have maintained uninterrupted connection with Paradise, with superuniverse headquarters, with local universe administration, and with each other. The quarantine that isolated Urantia from normal universe fellowship could not touch the communication channels used by these divine fragments.

This continuing connection reveals profound spiritual truth: regardless of external circumstances, regardless of rebellion or isolation, regardless of any material or spiritual barriers, the connection between a willing human soul and God the Father remains unbreakable. We are never, under any circumstances, cut off from the Father. His presence within us maintains an eternal lifeline connecting our troubled world directly to Paradise itself.

Why Adjusters Remain Unaffected by Isolation

First, Thought Adjusters maintain direct connection to Divinington and through Divinington to Paradise itself. This connection does not depend on local universe circuits, superuniverse administration, or any intermediate spiritual mechanisms. It flows directly from the Father and remains inviolate regardless of local circumstances.

Second, the Adjusters themselves embody divine reality that transcends and supersedes any rebellion or isolation. They are not created beings who might be affected by disruption of created mechanisms. They are actual fragments of eternal deity, and no rebellion of created beings can interfere with their essential nature or function.

Third, the Father's will that all His children have opportunity for eternal survival supersedes all other considerations. Rebellion cannot be allowed to permanently prevent survival opportunities for mortals who had no part in initiating or supporting that rebellion. The continuing ministry of Thought Adjusters ensures that even on quarantined worlds, every individual retains access to divine guidance and survival potential.

Practical Implications of Unbroken Connection - Practical Implications of Uninterrupted Adjuster Ministry

The continuing ministry of Thought Adjusters during Urantia's quarantine has profound practical implications. Most importantly, it means that despite our planetary isolation, we have never been cut off from God the Father. The most essential spiritual reality, personal contact with Paradise Deity, has continued uninterrupted throughout our world's darkest periods.

This reality transforms our understanding of what rebellion accomplished and what it failed to accomplish. Yes, rebellion caused enormous damage. It deprived our world of progressive revelation, disrupted normal evolutionary advancement, spawned confusion and error, and created conditions of unnecessary suffering. But rebellion utterly failed to separate us from the Father's love or to prevent direct divine ministry to individual human minds.

Every person who has ever lived on this planet since rebellion, regardless of how spiritually dark the times or how confused the religious environment, has had access to divine guidance through the indwelling Thought Adjuster (assuming normal mental capacity and age). Every individual who sincerely desired to know and do God's will could receive direct spiritual leading from a fragment of the Father Himself. Rebellion never prevented this most crucial spiritual reality.

The unbroken connection maintained by Thought Adjusters during planetary isolation enabled several crucial developments on Urantia:

Continued Spiritual Progress: Despite the confusion introduced by rebellion and the absence of normal teaching from universe personalities, spiritually motivated individuals continued making genuine progress. The Thought Adjusters within their minds compensated for missing external guidance through enhanced internal ministry.

Reserve Corps of Destiny: The formation and function of the Reserve Corps of Destiny, special individuals prepared for emergency service during crises, depended entirely on Thought Adjuster communication. These reservists, often unconscious of their status, received preparation and occasional activation through self-acting Adjusters capable of achieving unusual degrees of mind contact during crises.

The Urantia Papers Themselves: Perhaps most significantly, the very existence of *The Urantia Book* demonstrates the effectiveness of Thought Adjuster communication during quarantine. The revelation was transmitted to our world through methods that depended partly on unusual Thought Adjuster contact. Even in rebellion's midst, even under full quarantine, the Father's will for epochal revelation could not be thwarted.

The revelation specifically notes that "contacts with the supreme and self-acting Adjusters of the reserve corps of destiny are so frequently made on quarantined worlds" as a means of circumventing the handicaps of planetary isolation. When normal communication channels remain closed, enhanced Thought Adjuster contact provides alternative pathways for essential information and guidance.

The continuing function of Thought Adjusters during quarantine also enabled the formation and operation of the Reserve Corps of Destiny. This group consists of individuals recruited and trained for special planetary service, individuals prepared to act in emergencies, to fill crucial positions when needed, and to maintain spiritual progress despite rebellion's handicaps.

Paper 108 specifically mentions that contacts with the supreme, self-acting Adjusters of the Reserve Corps of Destiny provided one means of circumventing communication handicaps created by planetary isolation. While the archangels' circuit also functioned on Urantia (though limited largely to Archangel Corps transactions), the Adjusters of reserve corps members maintained fuller communication capacity.

This enhanced communication capacity explains how epochal revelation could reach Urantia despite quarantine. The Urantia Papers themselves represent a remarkable demonstration that rebellion, though severely damaging, cannot ultimately thwart the Father's purposes. In the midst of continued isolation, during a period when the rebel leaders still maintained some influence, the most comprehensive revelation of universe reality ever given to our world was successfully transmitted.

The mechanism involved Thought Adjusters communicating with Paradise authorities and coordinating with numerous celestial agencies to prepare, compile, and transmit the revelation. The contact commission, a small group of human beings serving in the Reserve Corps of Destiny, provided the necessary human linkage for this communication. Their Thought Adjusters, functioning in coordination with their seraphic guardians and numerous other celestial ministers, made possible what normal circuits could not accomplish.

This achievement demonstrates a crucial principle: God's will cannot ultimately be frustrated by rebellion. Rebellion can delay, distort, and damage, but it cannot permanently prevent divine purposes from achieving fulfillment. The continuing ministry of Thought Adjusters ensures that even on isolated, rebellious worlds, the Father's purposes eventually triumph.

The Metaphor of Deep-Sea Diving

One way to visualize this unbroken connection involves imagining a deep-sea diver descending into dangerous waters. The diver wears a heavy suit and depends entirely on the air hose connecting them to the surface. No matter how deep the diver descends, no matter how dangerous or isolated the environment becomes, that air hose maintains their life connection to the support team above.

Similarly, we on Urantia might compare ourselves to divers working in the deep, isolated from normal universe fellowship, surrounded by the dangerous environment of a rebellion-scarred world. Yet we maintain our lifeline, the Thought Adjuster connection that links us directly to the Father on Paradise. This connection provides not physical air but spiritual sustenance, guidance, and the assurance that we are never truly alone or abandoned.

When the time comes for us to ascend, to be "pulled up" to the mansion worlds, that same lifeline facilitates our resurrection and transition to higher spheres. The Adjuster that maintained connection during our earthly sojourn preserves our essential identity and ensures continuity of consciousness across the transition from material to morontia existence.

Why Lucifer and Caligastia Lacked This Connection

An important point deserves emphasis: Lucifer and Caligastia, the primary rebel leaders, did not possess Thought Adjusters. As perfected, created beings of high order, they never experienced Father-fragment indwelling. Their communication with higher authority flowed through administrative channels, precisely the channels that rebellion severed.

This difference helps explain how rebellion became possible and how it spread. Had Lucifer and Caligastia maintained direct Thought Adjuster connection to the Father, their rebellion might never have occurred. The constant presence of divine guidance, the immediate awareness of the Father's will, the direct experiential connection to Paradise reality, all these factors that protect Adjuster-indwelt mortals from ultimate spiritual disaster were absent in these high but created beings.

In contrast, we are supposedly inferior mortals possess a spiritual advantage denied to even perfect administrators. Our Thought Adjusters provide direct access to the Father unavailable through any administrative channel. We can bypass all intermediate authority and appeal directly to the Father's presence within us. This represents an extraordinary privilege, a divine gift compensating for our lowly origin and limited initial capacity.

The Continuing Ministry to a Quarantined World

The unbroken Thought Adjuster connection during Urantia's quarantine also reveals divine determination to maintain personal contact with His children regardless of circumstances. When rebellion occurred, the Father did not withdraw His fragments. When planetary administration betrayed their trust, the Father did not abandon His mortal children. When confusion and error multiplied, the Father intensified rather than reduced His personal ministry.

This divine faithfulness stands as our greatest assurance. If the Father maintained His presence and ministry throughout 200,000 years of rebellion, confusion, and isolation, we can trust Him to maintain that presence through whatever personal or planetary challenges the future might bring. The same divine fragments that guided our ancestors through the darkest ages of planetary history continue guiding us today and will continue guiding future generations until this world finally achieves light and life.

The Supreme Mystery: Divine Presence in Mortal Mind - Acknowledging the Limits of Understanding

Paper 108 concludes its discussion of Adjuster relations to other spiritual influences with a remarkable acknowledgment of mystery. Despite all the revelation provided in *The Urantia Book*, despite all the understanding granted to mortal minds regarding Thought Adjuster function and purpose, the revelators admit they "do not so fully comprehend the methods of the all-wise Father's functioning in and through these mystery monitors which live and work so valiantly within the human mind."

This honest acknowledgment of limited understanding serves multiple purposes. First, it reminds us that revelation, while vastly expanding our comprehension, never eliminates all mystery. The universe contains depths of meaning and reality that will engage our exploration throughout eternity. Complete understanding of all things belongs to God alone; creatures will always stand before aspects of reality that exceed their current comprehension.

Second, this acknowledgment guards against the presumption of complete understanding. When we receive revelation, we might be tempted to think we now comprehend everything. The revelators' admission that even they, beings far advanced beyond human capacity, do not fully understand Thought Adjuster ministry reminds us that much remains to be discovered.

Third, the statement preserves appropriate reverence before the mystery of divine indwelling. The fact that the infinite Father fragments Himself to dwell in finite mortal minds, the fact that this indwelling leads to eternal fusion and literal sonship with God, the fact that mortal will and divine will can collaborate to produce outcomes satisfying to both, these represent mysteries so profound that even extensive revelation cannot fully explain them.

The Father's Reserved Right

The passage emphasizes that "the Father has certainly reserved to himself the unchallengeable right to be present in the minds and souls of his evolving creatures." This reservation of divine prerogative carries significant implications.

While the Father has apparently delegated most direct personal ministry to the Eternal Son, the Infinite Spirit, and their various offspring and associates, while He seems to have "resigned the exercise of all direct personal power and authority throughout the grand universe", He has not completely withdrawn from personal contact with His creatures. Through Thought Adjusters, the Father maintains direct, intimate, personal relationship with billions upon billions of evolving mortals throughout the seven superuniverses.

This reserved right reveals the Father's priorities. Of all the ways He might exercise continuing personal presence in the universes, He chooses to do so within the minds of His humblest children, the imperfect, error-prone, struggling mortals just beginning their eternal careers. This choice speaks volumes about divine values and purposes.

The Father apparently considers personal relationship with evolving mortals important enough to warrant His direct, personal involvement. He does not leave our spiritual nurture entirely to created ministers, however capable. He Himself comes to dwell within us, to guide us personally, to fuse with us ultimately. This represents divine love and humility of the highest order, the infinite stooping to indwell the finite, the perfect dwelling within the imperfect, the eternal choosing relationship with the temporal.

The Eternal Significance of Adjuster Ministry - Beyond Temporal Circumstances

As we conclude this chapter's exploration of Thought Adjuster arrival, organization, and ministry, we must step back to consider the eternal significance of what has been revealed. The Thought Adjuster represents far more than a helpful spiritual influence or a source of moral guidance, though it certainly provides both. The Adjuster embodies the Father's personal investment in our eternal future and His guarantee that perfection attainment remains genuinely possible for every willing mortal.

The various factors triggering Adjuster arrival, seraphic guardian assignment, circle attainment, supreme decisions, brotherhood spirit, will consecration, and Supreme Being influence, all point toward a consistent divine principle: the Father responds immediately and personally to every indication of spiritual receptivity. He does not wait for perfection before offering His presence. He does not require comprehensive understanding before providing His guidance. He responds to the first flickering of authentic spiritual aspiration with the gift of His own divine presence.

This responsive divine generosity should profoundly affect how we understand our relationship with God. We need not achieve perfection to merit divine attention, such achievement lies eternally beyond our unaided capacity. We need not comprehend cosmic reality before God takes interest in us, such comprehension will require the entire Paradise ascent to even approach. What we need is simple: genuine desire for truth, authentic love for our fellows, sincere intention to do God's will, or any other expression of spiritual aspiration.

The Father's response to even elementary spiritual hunger demonstrates the fundamental nature of divine love. God loves us not because of what we have achieved but because of what we are, His children, created in His image, endowed with survival potential, capable of eternal growth. He loves us enough to fragment Himself, sending pieces of His own infinite being to indwell our imperfect minds, patiently working across decades of mortal life to prepare us for the eternal adventure ahead.

The Mystery of Divine Indwelling

Despite all that *The Urantia Book* reveals about Thought Adjusters, their ministry retains elements of profound mystery. The revelators themselves acknowledge not fully comprehending the methods by which "the all-wise Father functions in and through these Mystery Monitors that live and work so valiantly within the human mind."

This acknowledged mystery reminds us that even the most comprehensive revelation remains partial. We receive what we can understand and productively use at our current level of development. Much remains beyond our present comprehension, awaiting discovery during the long ascension ahead. The mystery surrounding Adjuster ministry ensures that we will never exhaust the possibilities for new understanding, fresh appreciation, and deeper worship of the Father's magnificent plans.

The mystery also serves important spiritual purposes. If we fully understood Adjuster mechanics and methodology, we might be tempted to manipulate or control the process rather than humbly cooperating with it. Mystery preserves the necessary relationship of trust, faith, and dependence that characterizes authentic spiritual growth. We learn to trust divine guidance not because we understand its mechanisms but because we recognize its source and experience its beneficial effects.

Furthermore, the mystery of Adjuster indwelling maintains appropriate worship orientation. If we fully comprehended how the Father fragments Himself to indwell mortal minds, we might lose something of the worshipful awe appropriate to contemplating such divine condescension. Mystery preserves reverence, ensuring that even as we grow in understanding, we never lose sight of the infinite gulf between created and Creator, between mortal and divine.

Practical Application: Living with Divine Indwelling

Understanding Thought Adjuster ministry should transform how we live daily life. Several practical implications deserve emphasis:

First, we should cultivate conscious awareness of the divine presence within. While the Adjuster normally works through the superconscious mind rather than conscious awareness, deliberately acknowledging this indwelling presence can enhance spiritual receptivity. Regular periods of worship, meditation, and prayer create optimal conditions for Adjuster influence.

Second, we should actively cooperate with Adjuster leading by consistently choosing the highest values we perceive. The Adjuster can only work with the materials provided by human decision. When we habitually choose truth over falsehood, beauty over ugliness, goodness over selfishness, and love over hatred, we provide the Adjuster optimal materials for spiritual development.

Third, we should maintain faith and confidence in divine guidance even when circumstances seem adverse. The Adjuster sees from eternal perspectives impossible for mortal mind. What appears as tragedy from temporal viewpoint may serve crucial spiritual purposes visible only from eternal perspective. Trusting the Adjuster's wisdom even when we cannot perceive the path ahead represents mature spiritual living.

Fourth, we should recognize that listening to Adjuster guidance requires spiritual receptivity rather than intellectual brilliance. The simple person sincerely seeking God's will may hear divine leading more clearly than the sophisticated philosopher preoccupied with theoretical speculation. Spiritual receptivity depends on humility, sincerity, and whole-hearted consecration to truth.

Fifth, we should remember that Adjuster indwelling places us in direct connection with the Universal Father, transcending all temporal circumstances. Whatever challenges we face, personal tragedy, social upheaval, economic hardship, health crisis, or any other difficulty, we remain connected to infinite divine resources adequate for every need.

The Ultimate Purpose

The passage also reveals the ultimate purpose behind Thought Adjuster ministry: "to the end that he may so act as to draw all creature creation to himself." Despite all the complex organization, despite all the specialized ministries, despite all the administrative machinery of the universes, the fundamental goal remains simple: bringing all willing creatures into eternal fellowship with the Father.

The Father draws us to Himself not through compulsion but through attraction. The Thought Adjuster within gradually transforms our values, slowly changes our desires, progressively aligns our will with divine will, all through patient, loving ministry that respects our freedom while consistently presenting higher alternatives. Over time, if we cooperate, we discover that what we want increasingly coincides with what the Father wills. Eventually, through fusion, our will and His will become one, and the drawing is complete.

This drawing power represents the spiritual gravity of Paradise, the magnetic attraction of perfect love, infinite wisdom, and eternal reality. Just as material gravity draws all physical matter toward material mass centers, spiritual gravity draws all spirit-responsive creatures toward the Paradise center of all spiritual reality. The Thought Adjuster serves as the immediate connection point for this spiritual gravity, making us responsive to the Father's drawing power from our earliest moral choices.

Coordinating with the Creator Sons' Drawing Power

The passage also addresses the relationship between the Father's drawing power (exercised through Thought Adjusters) and the Creator Sons' drawing power (exercised through their creative activities and spiritual ministry). When Jesus said, "If I be lifted up, I will draw all men unto me," he spoke of genuine spiritual drawing power inherent in Creator Sons.

The revelators acknowledge they "recognize and understand" the methods of the Paradise Sons' spiritual drawing power. This makes sense because Paradise Sons and their associates operate within the observable universe system, their methods following patterns accessible to study and comprehension.

However, the Father's methods remain more mysterious. The revelators honestly state they do not fully comprehend how the Father functions through Thought Adjusters. This distinction between comprehensible and mysterious levels of divine operation reminds us that the Father represents the ultimate source of all reality, the one being whose nature and methods will forever contain elements transcending creature comprehension.

Yet Creator Son drawing power and Father drawing power work in perfect harmony, never in competition. Michael's sovereignty over Nebadon and the Father's presence within individual Adjuster-indwelt mortals represent complementary aspects of one unified divine purpose. Both work toward the same goal: bringing evolving creatures to perfection and to Paradise. Both express the same divine love. Both manifest diverse aspects of the same essential Divinity.

Living with Divine Presence - Integration and Application

This exploration of Thought Adjuster mission and ministry on worlds before the bestowal of the Spirit of Truth, and particularly on our isolated, quarantined planet, yields numerous practical applications for daily living:

Recognition of Divine Presence: We must cultivate constant awareness that God the Father literally dwells within our minds. This is not metaphor or symbolism but objective reality. The presence within us deserves recognition, reverence, and cooperation.

Trust in Unbroken Connection: Regardless of how isolated or alone we might feel, regardless of personal crises or planetary difficulties, our connection to the Father through the indwelling Adjuster remains unbroken and unbreakable. This lifeline provides security beyond any earthly assurance.

Response to Faithful Ministry: The Thought Adjusters have proven absolutely faithful across hundreds of thousands of years and billions of human minds. They have maintained perfect ministry on our confused, strife-torn, rebellion-scarred world without faltering. This faithfulness deserves our reciprocal fidelity, being true to our trusts as they have been true to theirs.

Cooperation with Divine Leading: While the Adjuster respects our free will absolutely, refusing to coerce or override our choices, effective spiritual progress requires conscious cooperation. We must learn to recognize the Adjuster's leading, to distinguish divine guidance from mere human thinking, and to progressively align our will with the Father's will.

Appreciation for Compensatory Blessing: While we live on a world deprived of normal advantages through rebellion and default, we receive compensatory blessings through enhanced Thought Adjuster ministry. Rather than lamenting what we lack, we should appreciate what we have, direct, personal, unmediated access to the Universal Father.

Commitment to Spiritual Growth: The elaborate spiritual support system surrounding us, adjutant mind-spirits, Holy Spirit, Spirit of Truth, seraphic guardians, and Thought Adjusters, exists to facilitate our spiritual growth. This growth does not happen automatically but requires our active participation, consistent choices, and persistent effort.

The Path Forward

As we conclude this examination of Thought Adjuster mission and ministry, we stand better equipped to understand our place in the cosmic scheme. We are not accidents, not abandoned, not forgotten. We are personally attended by a fragment of God Himself, supported by a network of spiritual ministries, and destined, if we choose, for Paradise and eternal fellowship with the Father.

The journey ahead stretches across ages and encompasses experiences we cannot currently imagine. We will traverse the mansion worlds, progress through the constellation and local universe training spheres, advance through the superuniverse educational centers, and ultimately arrive at Paradise itself. Throughout this entire journey, the Thought Adjuster now indwelling our minds will remain our constant companion, guide, and, after fusion, our eternal identity foundation.

The immediate challenge facing us is not the distant future but the present moment. Will we recognize the divine presence within? Will we cooperate with the Adjuster's leading? Will we make the supreme decision to seek and do the Father's will? Will we prove true to our trusts as the Adjusters have proven true to theirs?

These questions define our current spiritual status and determine our eternal destiny. The answers lie not in intellectual acceptance but in living choices, daily decisions that either align with or diverge from the Father's will, that either nurture or neglect our spiritual natures, that either advance or retard our preparation for eternal adventure.

Conclusion: Advancing Toward Fusion

This chapter explored the arrival, organization, and ministry of Thought Adjusters, emphasizing particularly their function during planetary isolation and their relationship to other spiritual influences. We have seen that despite Urantia's rebellion-induced quarantine, the Thought Adjusters have maintained faithful ministry across hundreds of thousands of years, earning the profound respect of high universe administrators and providing essential compensatory blessing for our world's handicaps.

The foundation has been laid for understanding the ultimate goal of Adjuster ministry: the achievement of fusion, that sublime moment when mortal and divine unite eternally, creating a new order of universe being. The remaining sections of Paper 108 will explore this fusion process, examining its preparation, achievement, and eternal consequences.

As we move forward in our study, we should carry with us the profound reassurance this chapter provides. We are not alone in our spiritual struggles. We are not cut off from divine help by our planet's tragic history. We are not abandoned to face evolutionary challenges without supernatural assistance. Within each of us dwells a fragment of infinity itself, a divine monitor who has proven faithful across eons of time, who will never betray our trust, and who works unceasingly toward our eternal welfare.

The Father has not merely sent guidance from afar. He has not contented Himself with wise counsel and beneficial laws. He has actually come to dwell within us, sharing our every experience, feeling our every emotion, participating in our every decision. This indwelling presence represents divine love of the highest order, love willing to fragment infinity itself to ensure that even the humblest mortal has direct access to Paradise perfection.

In our next chapter, we will examine how this indwelling presence works to transform human consciousness, preparing mortal mind for that sublime achievement that represents the goal of Adjuster ministry and the destiny of all faithful mortals: the eternal fusion of human and divine into a perfected ascending son or daughter of God.

Transition to the Next Chapter

Having examined the arrival and organization of Thought Adjusters and having considered their faithful ministry during even the most difficult planetary circumstances, we now turn our attention to more detailed aspects of their nature and classification. In the next chapter, we will explore the different types and categories of Thought Adjusters, examining how their previous experience and particular characteristics influence their ministry. We discover that not all Adjusters arrive with equal experience, that some bring wisdom gained through previous indwelling while others come as virgins to their first mortal assignment, and that the type of Adjuster we receive carries significant implications for our spiritual potential and destiny.

This continuing exploration will deepen our appreciation for the sophisticated divine administration that ensures every mortal receives precisely the type of Adjuster ministry best suited to their needs and potentials. We will see anew the infinite care and perfect wisdom characterizing the Father's personal ministry to His evolving children, and we will gain fresh motivation for cooperation with the divine presence working tirelessly within each of us.

"You are marvelous beings, guardians of the good in the souls of this backward realm... You deserve the name of the Godlike servers of the mortal inhabitants of this strife-torn, grief-stricken, and disease-afflicted world. I honor you; I all but worship you."
—Tabamantia, Sovereign Supervisor of Decimal Planets

Chapter 10: The Adjusters' Mission - Understanding Divine Indwelling

Introduction

The concept of divine indwelling represents one of the most profound mysteries in all of spiritual reality. Within each mortal mind capable of moral choice resides a fragment of the Universal Father himself, a Thought Adjuster whose mission transcends our limited comprehension. This chapter explores the nature of this extraordinary partnership between the eternal and the temporal, between perfection and imperfection, between the divine and the human.

As we continue our study of Paper 108 from *The Urantia Book*, we enter territory that even celestial beings acknowledge do not fully understand. A Solitary Messenger candidly admits the limitations of celestial knowledge regarding these divine fragments, stating: "I doubt that I am able to explain to you just what the adjusters do in your minds and for your souls. I do not know that I am fully cognizant of what is really going on in the cosmic association of a Divine Monitor and the human mind. It is all somewhat of a mystery to us, not as to the plan and purpose, but as to the actual mode of accomplishment."

This honest acknowledgment should provide us with both humility and wonder as we seek to comprehend the Adjuster's mission in our lives.

The Diversity of Divine Fragments

We must first understand that Thought Adjusters represent only one category among seven distinct types of prepersonal spirit fragments emanating from the Universal Father. While Thought Adjusters minister specifically to evolutionary mortals like ourselves, other types of divine fragments serve different orders of beings throughout the grand universe.

Personalized Monitors

One example of these other fragments includes the personalized monitors. When a Thought Adjuster serves during the bestowal mission of a Creator Son or Magisterial Son, fusion cannot occur because these Sons already possess divine sonship with Paradise. They do not require permanent fusion with a Father fragment to achieve their eternal destiny. Upon completion of such bestowal missions, these adjusters are typically personalized, granted their own distinct personality, and continue their service as separate entities.

This diversity reminds us that the Universal Father's direct and personal contact extends throughout all realms of creation. The Father is not limited to one method of indwelling his creatures. Through these various types of prepersonal spirits, God maintains intimate involvement with countless orders of beings across the universes.

The Gravity Messengers and Mystery Monitors

The Solitary Messenger who authors this section acknowledges that much inexplicable spiritual work occurs throughout the universe, wrought by gravity messengers and certain types of mystery monitors. These divine fragments are not devoted solely to the remaking of mortal minds. Rather, they represent the Universal Father's direct and unexplained contact with creatures throughout the realms of space.

This broader perspective helps us appreciate that our experience with Thought Adjusters, while intensely personal, participates in a much vaster divine plan encompassing all of creation.

The Nature of the Adjuster's Mission - Receiving and Translating Spiritual Messages

The Thought Adjuster accepts a difficult assignment when volunteering to indwell composite beings such as those living on Urantia. These divine fragments undertake the challenging task of existing within material minds, receiving admonitions from the spiritual intelligences of the realms, and then attempting to redirect or translate these spiritual messages to the material mind.

But from whom do Thought Adjusters receive these spiritual admonitions.

The sources include:

- **The Spirit of Truth** from the Creator Son
- **The Spirit of Truth** from the Eternal Son himself
- **The Infinite Spirit** through the Holy Spirit
- **The Local Universe Mother Spirit** through her Holy Spirit
- **The Seven Adjutant Mind-Spirits** of the local universe

As we progress toward fusion with our Thought Adjuster, we actually begin to hear the voice of God more clearly. This divine voice may convey messages not only from God the Father but also from the Creator Son, the local Universe Mother Spirit, the Infinite Spirit, or the Eternal Son. The Thought Adjuster serves as the interpreter and translator of all these spiritual influences into concepts our material minds can grasp.

Faithful Preservation Across the Circles

One of the most reassuring aspects of the Adjuster's ministry concerns the preservation of spiritual truth. What the Thought Adjuster cannot successfully utilize in our present life, those truths he cannot transmit to his mortal partner, he faithfully preserves for use in the next stage of existence. Just as the Adjuster carries information from circle to circle in our present life when we fail to comprehend or cooperate, so too does he preserve valuable spiritual insights for our morontia career.

This preservation depends significantly upon our cooperation. The degree to which we work in partnership with our indwelling guide determines how much spiritual progress can be registered in our current experience. However, nothing of genuine spiritual value is ever lost. The Adjuster's faithfulness ensures that all authentic growth contributes to our eternal career.

The Psychic Circles and Spiritual Ascension

The Thought Adjuster carries spiritual achievements from circle to circle as we progress through the psychic levels of human attainment. These circles represent definite levels of intellectual, social, spiritual, and cosmic-insight status. Attainment of the third psychic circle ensures that, upon death, we will immediately translate to the mansion worlds rather than waiting for a dispensational resurrection.

The ultimate goal involves reaching the first psychic circle, the highest level of human spiritual attainment, where we stand ready for fusion with our Thought Adjuster. As we ascend through these circles, we require progressively less assistance from the seven-adjutant mind-spirits. The final two adjutants, worship and wisdom, become less necessary as we achieve greater consistency in our worship of the Universal Father and develop true cosmic wisdom.

When fusion finally occurs, we step beyond the local universe mind-control system into the cosmic mind, the super-universe level of consciousness. This represents a graduation from preparatory spiritual education into the reality of eternal cosmic citizenship.

What the Adjuster Is Not

Understanding what the Thought Adjuster does not do proves as important as understanding his actual mission. Many misconceptions arise from projecting our desires onto the Adjuster's purpose.

Not Thought Helpers But Thought Adjusters

The divine monitors are not thought helpers in the sense of making thinking easier or more comfortable, they are not our concept of Santa Clause, they are thought *adjusters*, laboring with the material mind for the purpose of constructing, by adjustment and spiritualization, a new mind for the new worlds and the new name of our future career.

Their mission concerns chiefly the future life, not this one. They are called heavenly helpers, not earthly helpers. They are not interested in making our mortal career easy. Rather, they are concerned with making our life reasonably difficult and rugged so that decisions will be stimulated and multiplied.

The presence of a great Thought Adjuster does not bestow ease of living or freedom from strenuous thinking. Such a divine gift should not be expected to confer a sublime peace of mind or a superb comfort in all circumstances.

Not Providers of Selfish Consolation

Our transient and ever-changing emotions of joy and sorrow are, in the main, purely human and material reactions to our internal psychic climate and external material environment. We should not, therefore, look to the Adjuster for selfish consolation and mortal comfort.

It is the business of the Adjuster to prepare us for the eternal adventure and to assure our survival. It is not the mission of the mystery monitor to smooth our ruffled feelings or to minister to our injured pride. Rather, the preparation of our soul for the long ascending career engages the attention and occupies the time of the Thought Adjuster.

The responsibility for managing our emotional life, for developing mental competence and psychological health, belongs to us. Spiritual growth requires that we learn to handle life's experiences with increasing wisdom and grace. The Adjuster spiritualizes our decisions and reactions, but he does not make the decisions for us or shield us from their consequences.

Not Mechanical Operators

The Thought Adjuster would like to change our feelings of fear to convictions of love and confidence, but such transformation cannot occur mechanically or arbitrarily. That is our task. In executing those decisions which deliver us from the fetters of fear, we literally supply the psychic fulcrum upon which the Adjuster may subsequently apply a spiritual lever of uplifting and advancing illumination.

This principle deserves careful consideration. We must do our part, making decisions, taking action, confronting our fears, before the Adjuster can build upon our choices to create spiritual reality. The divine monitor cannot spiritualize what does not exist. He works with the material we provide through our decisions and experiences.

Overcoming the Fetters of Fear

Perhaps no single obstacle impedes spiritual progress more than fear. Throughout human history, religion has too often been built upon fear rather than love. The early Hebrew prophets found it necessary to control their people through fear of God because the people were not sufficiently advanced to respond to love. Fear of divine punishment proved the only effective means of preventing them from constantly harming one another.

However, this foundation of fear was never the ideal. The opposite should have been taught that through love of God, we naturally refrain from harming others. Because we love God and recognize his presence in our fellows, we cannot bear to inflict suffering upon them. This is still true even today.

Fear of God Versus Love of God

The transition from fear of God to love of God represents one of the most crucial spiritual transformations we must undergo. At least sixty percent of contemporary religions remain based primarily on fear of God rather than love of God. This misplaced foundation cripples spiritual growth and distorts our relationship with the Universal Father.

When we finally overcome our fear of God and replace it with genuine love, we discover that the universe itself becomes transformed. We realize that nothing in this vast cosmos means us harm. The universe is fundamentally friendly. As Jesus taught, "There is nothing I perceive in this vast universe that means harm to me."

The Friendly Universe

If we could truly live without fear, without fear of bodily harm, without fear of overcontrolling government, without fear of churches that seek to run our lives rather than teach us proper spiritual concepts, every day would feel like Christmas. On Christmas Day, we experience a glimpse of the brotherhood of humanity. That feeling of universal kinship and goodwill should characterize every day of our lives.

When we reach the first mansion world, we discover that the entire world operates on principles of love and companionship, embodying the Fatherhood of God and the brotherhood of man. Fear has been left behind with the limitations of mortal existence. What a tremendous step forward this represents!

The Adjuster in Moral Conflicts

When we face sharp and well-defined conflicts between higher and lower tendencies, between what is genuinely right or wrong, not merely what we might label as right or wrong, we can depend upon the Thought Adjuster to participate in some definite and active manner. The fact that such Adjuster activity may remain unconscious to us does not diminish its value and reality.

In every human conflict between right and wrong, there is always a voice indicating "this is the way." That voice may come through the Spirit of Truth, the Holy Spirit, or directly from our indwelling Thought Adjuster. Even when we remain unconscious of the source, we still receive the benefit of this divine guidance.

Jesus expressed this truth simply and profoundly: whenever we face a decision, there is always a voice showing us the right path. Learning to recognize and follow that voice constitutes a primary skill in spiritual development.

The Perfection of Adjuster Ministry - Angels May Err, But Adjusters Never Fail

If we have a personal guardian of destiny and fail to achieve survival, that guardian angel must be adjudicated to receive vindication regarding the faithful execution of her trust. Angels, despite their advanced nature, can potentially fall short of perfection in their ministry. However, Thought Adjusters are never subjected to such examination when their subjects fail to survive.

While angels and other high types of spirit beings, not excepting even the local universe types of Sons, may occasionally embrace evil and depart from the divine way, Thought Adjusters never falter. They are absolutely dependable. This absolute reliability applies equally to all seven groups of divine fragments.

The Guarantee of Perfection

This perfect guidance means that the goal of perfection is certainly attainable. We have a perfect guide within us. The Thought Adjuster always leads us in the right direction, never making mistakes, never failing in his mission. If we fail to survive, it is never because our Thought Adjuster let us down.

Our guardian angel, despite her best efforts, might possibly make errors. More commonly, however, survival failure results from the decisions we ourselves make. We bear responsibility for our spiritual destiny. The Thought Adjuster provides perfect guidance; whether we choose to follow that guidance remains our decision.

When we finally fuse with our Thought Adjuster, our eternal survival becomes absolutely guaranteed. We need never again worry about defaulting or falling into rebellion. God will not rebel against himself. Once we fuse with that divine fragment, we become part of the postulated I AM, the eternal, unchanging reality that pervades all existence. We continue to grow, but we never regress into evil.

The Divine Condescension

It is indeed a marvel of divine condescension that the exalted and perfect Adjusters offer themselves for actual existence in the minds of material creatures such as the mortals of Urantia, to actually consummate a probationary union with beings of animal origin.

Consider the magnitude of this condescension: a fragment of absolute perfection, existing in eternity, volunteers to enter the mind of an imperfect, time-bound creature living on a troubled world. The Adjuster descends from the heights of Paradise to dwell within evolving mortals who remain on probationary status even after reaching the mansion worlds.

The Probationary Nature of Mortal Existence

Even when we awaken on the first mansion world, our survival is not yet absolutely guaranteed. We remain on probationary status, still being evaluated, still needing to prove our commitment to the eternal path. Not until we fuse with our Thought Adjuster does our existence become eternally secure.

The Adjuster willingly enters this uncertain situation, committing himself to years or even decades of dwelling within an imperfect mind, never knowing with certainty whether his mortal partner will ultimately choose survival. Such is the depth of divine love and the commitment of the Universal Father to each of his evolving children.

The Adjuster's Torment

Following the bestowal of a divine Son and the subsequent outpouring of the Spirit of Truth upon all humans, Thought Adjusters flock to such worlds to indwell the minds of all normal will creatures. Through these divine gifts, the Father makes the closest possible approach to sin and evil.

It is literally true that the Adjuster must coexist in the mortal mind even in the very midst of human unrighteousness. The indwelling Adjusters are particularly tormented by thoughts that are purely sordid and selfish. They are distressed by irreverence toward that which is beautiful and divine. They are virtually thwarted in their work by many of humanity's foolish animal fears and childish anxieties.

The Reality of Adjuster Suffering

When we choose pathways of evil, destruction, or actions that harm our fellow beings, we torture our Thought Adjuster. The divine monitor must exist on the same plane as our mortal mind. When that mind concentrates on nothing but evil, the Adjuster experiences constant conflict throughout his entire indwelling presence.

Consider those individuals whose entire existence revolves around accumulating wealth through cheating others, who seek power to dominate and control, who live lives dedicated to selfish gain regardless of the suffering they cause. Their Thought Adjusters endure continuous torment. Every day, these divine fragments struggle against the tide of negative thoughts and harmful intentions flooding the minds they inhabit.

The Contrast of Righteous Living

Conversely, there exist people who dedicate their lives to uplifting the human race, who spend themselves in service to others, who seek to spread love and understanding. These individuals, whether or not they identify as religious, whether or not they belong to any church, cooperate with their Thought Adjusters and provide the spiritual material from which eternal souls are built.

Not all evangelists for goodness identify themselves as such. Many people labor tirelessly to improve human conditions without seeking recognition, without building temples to their own glory, without constantly soliciting funds. They simply live lives of genuine service, reflecting the love of the Father in practical, tangible ways.

We can observe the people around us and discern for ourselves whether they live godly lives or self-absorbed, selfish existences. The difference becomes apparent in their actions, their treatment of others, and the fruits their lives produce.

The Destiny of Soul and Mind

Understanding the mechanics of survival helps clarify the Adjuster's role in our eternal future. When we die, different aspects of our being are preserved by different agencies:

The Preservation of Identity

The morontia soul, that developing reality which represents the partnership between our will decisions and the Adjuster's spiritual leading, is transported to the mansion worlds by our guardian angel. The soul possesses a quasi-material nature that requires angelic ministry for its preservation and transport.

Meanwhile, our personality and our complete mental record are carried to the mansion worlds by the Thought Adjuster himself. Personality, being a direct gift from the Universal Father, naturally remains in the Father's custody through his indwelling fragment. Our memories, our identity, our character, all that makes us uniquely ourselves, travels with the Adjuster.

When we arrive on the first mansion world, we receive a new morontia body. Into this body, the soul (transported by the guardian angel) and the personality-mind complex (carried by the Thought Adjuster) are integrated. Like Humpty Dumpty, all the pieces are put back together again, and we awaken as ourselves, continuously with who we were, yet beginning a new phase of existence.

When Fusion Occurs

When we finally fuse with our Thought Adjuster, a profound transformation occurs. The soul, the mental records, and the personality all combine into a perfect oneness. This unified being becomes our new reality, a fused personality, eternally indissoluble, forever secure in the universe.

The Fate of Non-Survivors

If we die and do not survive, if we choose not to continue, our personality and all our mental records remain with the Thought Adjuster. When that Adjuster is reassigned to a new mortal, he carries with him the experiential background from his previous indwelling, though the specific identity of the non-survivor ceases to exist.

The soul that was developing during our mortal life, however, is absorbed into the experiential reality of the Supreme Being. Nothing of genuine value is ever lost in the universe. Even when an individual chooses extinction, any authentic spiritual achievement becomes part of the growing experience of the evolving God of time and space.

Practical Implications for Daily Living

This understanding of the Adjuster's mission carries significant implications for how we live each day:

Worship as the Path to Fusion

If we desire to accelerate our progress toward fusion with our Thought Adjuster, we should cultivate the practice of worship. The more we learn to worship, to stand in awe and adoration before the Universal Father, the more we communicate directly with our indwelling guide. Consistent, sincere worship opens the channels through which the Adjuster can more effectively spiritualize our consciousness.

Jesus emphasized the supreme importance of worship. The last of the seven-adjutant mind-spirits is the spirit of worship, and achieving consistency in worship prepares us for graduation beyond adjutant ministry into the realm of cosmic mind and ultimate fusion.

Embracing Difficulty as Opportunity

Rather than seeking an easy, comfortable life, we should recognize that challenges and difficulties provide the raw material for spiritual growth. Each decision we must make, each problem we must solve, each fear we must overcome creates an opportunity for the Adjuster to work with us in building eternal spiritual reality.

The Adjuster makes our life "reasonably difficult and rugged" precisely because this stimulates decisions. And decisions, real choices between genuine alternatives, constitute the foundation of spiritual development. We should therefore embrace life's challenges as opportunities for growth rather than obstacles to happiness.

Supplying the Psychic Fulcrum

We must do our part before the Adjuster can do his. When we make brave decisions, when we choose love over fear, when we act with integrity despite difficulty, we supply the psychic fulcrum upon which the Adjuster can apply his spiritual lever. Our choices give the Adjuster something to work with, material he can spiritualize and preserve for eternity.

This partnership requires our active participation. The Adjuster cannot mechanically make us spiritual. He needs our cooperation, our decisions, our willingness to act in accordance with the highest values we perceive.

Conclusion

The mission of the Thought Adjuster encompasses far more than we can fully comprehend in our present state. These divine fragments undertake an assignment of extraordinary difficulty: to dwell within imperfect, often confused material minds, to translate spiritual realities into concepts we can grasp, to preserve all spiritual value from our experiences, and to prepare us for an eternal career beyond imagination.

The Adjusters never fail in their mission. They work with Paradise perfection, absolutely reliable, eternally faithful. When we fail to progress spiritually, it is never because our Adjuster has let us down. The limitation lies within ourselves, our fears, our selfishness, our unwillingness to make decisions and take spiritual risks.

Yet we need not despair, for we have all eternity before us. Whether we fuse with our Adjuster on the first mansion world or on the thousandth sphere of our ascending career matters less than our ultimate commitment to the eternal path. The Father is patient, and his love is infinite.

As we continue this study, we will explore in the next chapter the relationship between Adjusters and universe creatures, examining how these divine monitors relate to other orders of beings and how their ministry extends throughout all creation. We will also consider the various types and classifications of Thought Adjusters, deepening our understanding of these remarkable gifts from the Universal Father.

The marvel remains: within each of us who can make moral choices dwells a fragment of God himself, working ceaselessly to lead us home to Paradise. No truth could be more humbling or more exalting. We are not alone, and we never will be. The journey to perfection has already begun, and our divine guide will never abandon us along the way.

Chapter 11: The Relation of Thought Adjusters to Universe Creatures

Introduction

In the grand design of the universe, few relationships are as profound and transformative as that between mortal beings and their indwelling Thought Adjusters. These divine fragments of the Universal Father represent God's most direct and personal ministry to His evolutionary children, dwelling within the human mind as faithful companions on the eternal journey toward perfection.

Paper 109 of *The Urantia Book*, titled "Relation of Adjusters to Universe Creatures," illuminates this sacred partnership with remarkable clarity. Authored by a Solitary Messenger of Orvonton, this revelation provides insight into the developmental journey of Thought Adjusters themselves, a perspective often overlooked in our study of spiritual growth. Just as mortal creatures evolve through experience, so too do these divine monitors grow and develop through their ministry to evolving beings across the universes.

This chapter explores the mutual evolution inherent in the adjuster-mortal relationship: while humans evolve inward and upward from mortal status toward divine perfection, Thought Adjusters evolve outward and downward from divine perfection toward experiential understanding of mortal existence. The final product of this union, achieved through adjuster fusion, eternally embodies both the son of man and the Son of God, perfectly exemplified in the life of Jesus of Nazareth.

Understanding this relationship is essential for grasping the mechanics of eternal survival, the nature of spiritual growth, and the Father's magnificent plan for transforming finite creatures into perfected beings of eternal destiny.

The Developmental Career of Thought Adjusters - The Training of Virgin Adjusters

Before any Thought Adjuster embarks upon its mission to indwell a mortal mind, comprehensive preparation must occur. The Solitary Messenger candidly acknowledges that while a comprehensive and elaborate plan for training virgin adjusters undoubtedly exists on Divinington, the specific details remain largely unknown to celestial beings who have not themselves experienced this process. This admission of limited knowledge underscores the sacred and mysterious nature of the Father's direct ministry.

What can be ascertained comes primarily from personalized adjusters, those rare monitors who have completed their experiential journey and now possess full recall of their developmental history. These personalized adjusters serve as invaluable sources of information, sharing insights that would otherwise remain hidden behind the impenetrable veil of Divinington's privacy.

Virgin adjusters, those embarking upon their first mission, typically receive their initial assignments on worlds where the inhabitants possess limited capacity for eternal survival. These planets, often characterized by primitive spiritual development or barbaric conditions, (much like our planet in pre-planetary prince days 500,000 years ago), provide the perfect training ground for inexperienced monitors. During these preliminary assignments, adjusters practice the essential skills of indwelling, spiritual ministry, and soul development, even though fusion with their mortal subjects remains impossible due to the subjects' developmental limitations.

This arrangement serves a dual purpose: it provides virgin adjusters with crucial experiential training while simultaneously offering whatever spiritual ministry possible to beings who, though incapable of survival, still deserve the Father's loving presence during their brief mortal existence.

The Retraining Process

When a Thought Adjuster completes an assignment, whether through the death of its mortal subject or the rare translation of a surviving soul, it returns to Divinington for retraining. This extensive system of preparation ensures that each adjuster arrives at its next assignment better equipped to minister effectively to its new mortal partner.

The retraining process proves especially significant when a mortal fails to survive. Every time a monitor-indwelt mortal fails of survival and the adjuster returns to Divinington, an extended course of training is provided. This additional preparation draws directly upon the experience of having indwelt a human being, transforming even apparent failures into valuable learning opportunities. The adjuster carries forward every lesson learned, every spiritual struggle witnessed, every moment of moral decision-making observed, incorporating this experiential knowledge into its expanding repertoire of ministerial capabilities.

This explains why mortal beings on worlds like ours, advanced beyond the primitive stages but still struggling with spiritual immaturity, never receive virgin adjusters. Instead, we are indwelt by experienced monitors who have already navigated at least one complete mortal lifetime. These adjusters arrive prepared for the complexities of human consciousness, equipped with practical understanding gained through prior indwelling experience.

The Nature of Experiential Growth

One of the most profound revelations in this paper concerns the absolute necessity of actual experience. The perfection of divinity possessed by a newly formed Thought Adjuster does not, in any manner, endow this mystery monitor with experienced ministerial ability. Despite their divine origin and perfect nature, adjusters cannot substitute divine endowment for the irreplaceable value of lived experience.

This principle applies universally across creation: experience remains inseparable from living existence. No amount of divine perfection can absolve any being, mortal or divine, from the necessity of acquiring experiential knowledge through actual participation in evolutionary existence. Therefore, in common with all beings living and functioning within the present sphere of God the Supreme, Thought Adjusters must acquire experience through practice. They must evolve from lower, inexperienced status to higher, more experienced classifications.

This evolutionary requirement reveals something profound about the nature of God the Father Himself. The Universal Father, though absolute in knowledge and perfect in wisdom, cannot gain actual mortal experience except through the ministry of His fragmented presence within evolutionary creatures. As we live, struggle, choose, grow, and eventually triumph over our mortal limitations, our Thought Adjusters share every moment of that journey. The experiential knowledge gained becomes permanently incorporated into the adjuster's being and ultimately contributes to the experiential evolution of God the Supreme.

Thus, the Father gains experiential knowledge of mortal existence through billions upon billions of indwelling experiences across the grand universe. Later, when the Supreme Being achieves full actualization, the Father will gain this experiential perspective yet again, this time through the completed evolution of Supremacy itself. This magnificent arrangement ensures that nothing of value in the evolutionary universes is ever lost, and that God Himself participates intimately in every finite experience.

The Process of Adjuster Development - The First Stage: Achieving Fusion

The developmental career of a Thought Adjuster passes through distinct stages, each marked by increasing skill, wisdom, and ministerial effectiveness. The first and most significant stage of adjuster evolution culminates in fusion with the surviving soul of a mortal being.

This fusion represents the ultimate achievement for both partners in the divine-human relationship. From the adjuster's perspective, it marks the successful completion of the primary mission assigned by the Universal Father: to transform a mortal creature of animal origin into an eternal being of spiritual destiny. From the mortal perspective, it represents the final and irrevocable commitment to eternal existence and service in the Father's universe.

The beauty of this union lies in its complementary nature. While mortal beings evolve in nature inward and upward, from human status toward divine perfection, the Thought Adjusters evolve in nature outward and downward, from divine perfection toward experiential understanding of finite existence. These two streams of evolution meet in fusion, creating an entirely new being who eternally embodies both the son of man and the Son of God.

Jesus of Nazareth, the Creator Son incarnated as a human being, perfectly exemplified this dual nature. Though His situation differed in that He was already divine before His human birth, His life demonstrated the ideal outcome of the mortal-divine partnership: a being who fully understands both finite existence and infinite reality, capable of ministering effectively across all levels of universe reality.

Progressive Skill Acquisition

Throughout their developmental career, Thought Adjusters progressively acquire skills and abilities as a result of any and all contacts with material races. This acquisition occurs regardless of whether their particular mortal subjects survive or fail to achieve eternal life. Every indwelling experience contributes to the adjuster's growing competence, expanding repertoire of ministerial techniques, and deepening understanding of mortal consciousness.

The adjusters function as equal partners with the human mind in fostering the evolution of the immortal soul of survival capacity. This partnership aspect cannot be overstated. The Thought Adjuster does not unilaterally create the soul, nor does the mortal mind create it alone. Rather, the soul emerges from their cooperative interaction, a unique creation that partakes of both mortal identity and divine potential.

As this partnership develops over the years of mortal life, the adjuster's investment in the relationship deepens. Each moral decision, each spiritual insight, each moment of worship or service contributes to the soul's growth and simultaneously enriches the adjuster's experiential understanding. When fusion finally occurs, all of these accumulated experiences become permanently incorporated into the adjuster's being, available for reflection and application throughout all eternity.

Even when a mortal fails to survive, the adjuster retains every lesson learned during the indwelling experience. This knowledge becomes available to assist the next mortal subject, creating a cumulative effect where each successive assignment benefits from all previous experiences. Some adjusters can serve as temporary indwellers to ten, twelve, or even fifteen mortal subjects before finally achieving fusion with a survivor. The adjuster who finally fuses with such an experienced monitor gains access to an extraordinary wealth of experiential knowledge, providing tremendous advantages in the early stages of the ascension career.

The Classification of Self-Acting Adjusters - Defining Characteristics

Among the various classifications of Thought Adjusters, virgin, advanced, and supreme, a certain functional classification deserves special attention: the self-acting adjusters. These highly experienced monitors possess capabilities far beyond those of ordinary adjusters, operating with a marked degree of will in all matters not directly involving the human personalities of their immediate indwelling.

A self-acting adjuster must meet specific criteria, having achieved a level of experience and competence that permits greater autonomy in universe service. The classification requires fulfillment of at least one of several conditions, each indicating substantial experiential development.

Prerequisites for Self-Acting Status - Prior Indwelling Experience

A self-acting adjuster must have had certain requisite experience in the evolving life of a will creature. This experience may come through service as a temporary indweller on a world where adjusters are only loaned to mortal subjects, planets where the inhabitants lack the capacity for fusion. Alternatively, the experience may derive from service on an actual fusion planet where the human subject failed to survive.

Either path provides the necessary experiential foundation. The adjuster who serves on a non-fusion world gains invaluable practice in the mechanics of indwelling and spiritual ministry, even knowing that fusion remains impossible. The adjuster whose mortal subject fails to survive learns equally valuable lessons about the challenges of evolutionary existence and the tragic consequences of persistent spiritual resistance or indifference.

Following such experiences, the adjuster automatically becomes classified as either an advanced or supreme adjuster, depending on the depth and breadth of experience acquired.

Attainment of the Third Psychic Circle

An adjuster may achieve self-acting status through service with a human who has made the third psychic circle and consequently has been assigned a personal seraphic guardian. The third psychic circle represents a crucial threshold in mortal spiritual development, the point at which human decision-making has demonstrated sufficient spiritual commitment to warrant specialized ministry.

When a mortal attains this circle, the Local Universe Mother Spirit signals the achievement, and the adjuster's ministry enters a new phase of effectiveness. Simultaneously, the mortal receives the assignment of personal seraphic guardians, two seraphim supported by two cherubim and two sanobim, who work in close cooperation with the indwelling adjuster to facilitate continued spiritual growth.

Adjusters serving mortals at this level of development gain experience in coordinating their ministry with these guardian angels, learning to work as part of an integrated spiritual team rather than as isolated divine monitors. This collaborative ministry provides excellent training for self-acting responsibilities.

Supreme Decision and Betrothal

Perhaps the most significant prerequisite for self-acting status involves serving a subject who has made the supreme decision, entering into a solemn and sincere betrothal with the adjuster. This moment of commitment represents the most profound choice any mortal being can make: the absolute, unqualified dedication to the Father's will and the acceptance of eternal destiny.

When this supreme decision occurs, something remarkable happens from the adjuster's perspective. The monitor looks beforehand to the time of actual fusion and reckons the union as an event of fact. This forward-looking recognition reflects the eternal perspective of divinity, where time as mortals understand it does not exist. From God's viewpoint, past, present, and future form a seamless whole. Therefore, when a mortal makes an irrevocable commitment to fusion, the Father accepts that commitment as already accomplished.

This principle reveals the true nature of salvation. Eternal life is not secured merely by intellectual belief in God's existence or even by emotional religious experiences, however sincere. Rather, salvation comes through the decisive commitment to eternal partnership with the divine presence within, the moment when a mortal being wholeheartedly accepts God's ascension plan and dedicates themselves completely to the Father's will.

At this point of supreme decision, the mortal becomes saved from the one true danger threatening eternal existence: annihilation through persistent rejection of spiritual reality. All other so-called sins, the countless mistakes, errors, and shortcomings that characterize evolutionary existence, amount to nothing more than manifestations of spiritual immaturity requiring mental and moral correction. Only the willful, sustained rejection of God constitutes genuine sin, and only this sin can prevent eternal survival.

Service in the Reserve Corps of Destiny

An adjuster may achieve self-acting status through service with a subject who has been mustered into one of the reserve corps of destiny on an evolutionary world of mortal ascension. The reserve corps represents a specialized group of mortals who have been unconsciously trained for emergency planetary service.

These reservists typically possess highly advanced adjusters, as membership in the reserve corps requires spiritual development far beyond that of ordinary mortals. Members of this corps remain largely unaware of their special status, going about their normal daily lives while their adjusters maintain them in a state of readiness for potential emergency service.

During planetary crises, whether spiritual, social, or even physical, these reservists may be temporarily mobilized by their adjusters to perform specific services essential to the spiritual economy of the planet. The mobilization might involve anything from preventing a catastrophic nuclear exchange to maintaining the concept of God alive during periods of widespread spiritual darkness. The adjuster may even temporarily detach from the sleeping reservist to perform necessary administrative or coordinative functions before returning undetected.

Service with such advanced mortals provides adjusters with invaluable experience in crisis management, interplanetary coordination, and high-level spiritual administration, all excellent preparation for self-acting responsibilities.

Temporary Detachment During Sleep

An adjuster qualifies for self-acting status if, at some time during human sleep, it has been temporarily detached from the mind of mortal incarceration to perform some exploit of liaison, contact, reregistration, or other extra human service associated with the spiritual administration of the world of assignment.

This criterion recognizes that adjusters serve not only their individual mortal subjects but also contribute to the broader spiritual administration of their assignment worlds. While the mortal sleeps, unaware of the adjuster's absence, the monitor may journey to participate in administrative councils, coordinate activities with other adjusters, register important spiritual developments, or perform various other services essential to planetary spiritual welfare.

The ability to temporarily detach, perform necessary extra human services, and return before the mortal awakens requires considerable skill and experience. Adjusters who have successfully performed such detachments demonstrate the reliability and competence required for self-acting classification.

Crisis Service with Cosmic Complements

Finally, an adjuster may achieve self-acting status through service in a time of crisis in the experience of some human being who was the material complement of a spirit personality entrusted with the enactment of some cosmic achievement essential to the spiritual economy of the planet.

This rather technical description refers to situations where a mortal becomes the human partner in a cosmic undertaking of extraordinary importance. The spiritual personality involved might be a high-level administrator, a specialized minister, or even a divine being requiring human cooperation to accomplish a specific mission. The mortal serves as the material complement, the physical anchor and human channel, through which this spiritual personality can operate in the material world.

The adjuster indwelling such a mortal gains unique experience in facilitating cosmic-level operations, learning to coordinate divine purposes with human limitations, and contributing to achievements of planetary or even universe-wide significance. This rarefied experience certainly qualifies the adjuster for self-acting status.

The Capabilities of Self-Acting Adjusters - Autonomous Function

Self-acting adjusters possess a marked degree of autonomous will in all matters not directly involving the human personalities of their immediate indwelling. This autonomy manifests in numerous ways, both within and beyond their mortal subjects of attachment. Their exploits demonstrate capabilities far exceeding those of ordinary adjusters, operating with greater freedom to participate in the broader spiritual administration of their worlds.

While these advanced monitors frequently function as undetected indwellers of their earthly tabernacles, working quietly within the human mind to spiritualize experience and foster soul growth, they also engage in activities invisible to their mortal subjects. They participate in administrative councils, coordinate emergency responses, register spiritual achievements, and perform countless other services essential to planetary spiritual welfare.

Inter-Adjuster Communication

Self-acting adjusters can communicate with those in other realms, maintaining contact with their fellows across planetary, system, and even universe boundaries. However, this intercommunication occurs only on the levels of mutual work and for the purpose of preserving custodial data essential to the adjuster ministry of the realms of their sojourn.

This communication network operates primarily through the cosmic mind, the universal mental circuitry connecting all intelligent beings throughout creation. Through this medium, adjusters can coordinate their activities, share crucial information, and maintain the administrative coherence necessary for effective planetary ministry.

Interestingly, this inter-adjuster communication may explain a curious phenomenon observed repeatedly throughout human history: the simultaneous, independent discovery of identical innovations by multiple individuals in different locations. When a particular invention or insight becomes necessary for human progress, adjusters working with different mortals across the globe may guide their subjects toward similar conclusions. The cosmic mind connection allows coordination of these efforts, ensuring that valuable developments do not depend on single individuals who might fail or be prevented from bringing their insights to fruition.

On rare occasions, self-acting adjusters have been known to function in interplanetary matters during times of crisis. These exceptional circumstances demonstrate the breadth of authority and capability vested in these highly experienced monitors, who can transcend normal limitations when planetary or system welfare demands extraordinary intervention.

Physical Independence

A remarkable characteristic distinguishes supreme and self-acting adjusters from their less experienced counterparts: they can leave the human body at will. These indwellers are not organic or biological parts of mortal life; they represent divine superimpositions upon material existence. Though provided for in the original life plans, adjusters are not indispensable to continued material existence in the strictly physical sense.

Nevertheless, it should be recorded that advanced adjusters very rarely, even temporarily, leave their mortal tabernacles after they once take up their indwelling residence. The bond formed between adjuster and mortal, while not physical, becomes so intimate and purposeful that separation serves no useful function except in extraordinary circumstances requiring the adjuster's specialized services elsewhere.

This ability to depart and return undetected provides supreme and self-acting adjusters with remarkable flexibility in their ministry. They can attend administrative gatherings, perform emergency services, coordinate with other spiritual ministers, and accomplish various tasks requiring their temporary presence elsewhere, all while their mortal subjects remain completely unaware of the adjuster's absence.

The Ultimate Achievement

The career of self-acting adjusters culminates in a simple yet profound goal: these advanced monitors are those who have achieved the conquest of their entrusted tasks and now await only the dissolution of the material life vehicle for the liberation of the immortal soul.

Once fusion has been assured through the mortal's supreme decision, the adjuster's primary mission is essentially complete. What remains is simply the patience to await physical death, the natural conclusion of mortal existence that permits the transition to morontia form and the beginning of the mansion world career. The adjuster waits faithfully, continuing to spiritualize experience, foster soul growth, and maintain readiness for the moment of transition.

At death, the self-acting adjuster departs immediately with the soul, bearing its precious trust to the resurrection halls of the mansion worlds. There, in cooperation with seraphic guardians and morontia power supervisors, the adjuster participates in the re-creation of personal identity, the resurrection of the surviving mortal as a morontia being ready to continue the eternal ascension adventure.

The Significance for Mortal Destiny - The Mutual Partnership

Understanding the developmental career of Thought Adjusters illuminates the profound mutuality inherent in the divine-human relationship. This partnership involves not one-way ministry from a perfect being to an imperfect subject, but rather a genuine collaboration between two beings, one divine, one mortal, who need each other to achieve their respective destinies.

The Thought Adjuster needs mortal experience to complete its own evolution from inexperienced virgin status to accomplished veteran of the ascension career. The adjuster cannot gain this experience through any other means; divine perfection cannot substitute for actual participation in evolutionary existence. Only by indwelling mortal minds, sharing the struggles and triumphs of finite creatures, and working to foster soul development can adjusters acquire the experiential wisdom necessary for their eternal careers.

Conversely, mortal beings need their Thought Adjusters to achieve eternal survival and cosmic citizenship. Without the indwelling divine presence, humans would remain merely intelligent animals, capable of temporal achievement but lacking any bridge to eternal existence. The adjuster provides that bridge, creating through patient ministry the immortal soul that survives physical death and continues the ascension journey.

The Progressive Revelation

The information in Paper 109 progressively reveals deeper levels of meaning as students advance in their understanding of divine ministry. Initially, readers may grasp only the basic concept that adjusters develop through experience with mortals. Deeper study reveals the magnificent economy whereby God Himself gains experiential knowledge through the ministry of His fragments.

Still deeper contemplation unveils the profound truth that every mortal life, regardless of survival outcome, contributes to the experiential evolution of deity. Even those who ultimately reject survival contribute their experiences to the adjusters who indwelt them, and those experiences benefit future mortal subjects. Nothing is wasted in the divine economy; every experience possesses eternal value.

This understanding should profoundly affect how believers view their daily lives. Each decision, each struggle, each moment of moral choosing or spiritual insight contributes not only to personal soul growth but also to the experiential development of the indwelling adjuster. Through this development, each mortal life contributes to the experiential evolution of the Supreme Being and ultimately enriches the infinite Father's understanding of finite existence.

The Assurance of Divine Investment

Perhaps most encouraging for mortal believers is the recognition of the extraordinary divine investment represented by Thought Adjuster ministry. The Universal Father does not dispatch virgin, untested fragments to indwell evolutionary mortals. Rather, He ensures that each human receives an experienced monitor already trained through prior indwelling experience.

This fact demonstrates the Father's loving concern for His evolutionary children. He provides each mortal with the best possible spiritual assistance, equipping adjusters with practical experience before assigning them to new subjects. The Father wants each mortal to succeed, to survive, to achieve eternal life and cosmic citizenship. The assignment of experienced adjusters, some having ministered to numerous prior subjects, reflects this divine desire for mortal success.

Furthermore, the progressive development of adjusters from virgin to advanced to supreme to self-acting status reveals a cosmic system designed to eventually provide every surviving mortal with the most skilled spiritual ministry possible. As adjusters gain experience through successive indwellings, they become increasingly effective in their ministry. Mortals who receive adjusters with extensive prior experience benefit enormously from that accumulated wisdom and skill.

Conclusion

The relation of Thought Adjusters to universe creatures represents one of the most beautiful and profound aspects of divine ministry. This relationship transcends simple one-way benevolence, instead manifesting as genuine partnership wherein both participants contribute to and benefit from the association.

Understanding adjuster development enriches appreciation for the patient, skilled ministry occurring constantly within human consciousness. These divine monitors are not static, unchanging entities performing rote functions. Rather, they are evolving beings engaged in their own developmental careers, growing in skill and wisdom through each successive indwelling experience.

The classification of adjusters, virgin, advanced, supreme, and self-acting, reveals a carefully designed system ensuring optimal spiritual ministry for evolutionary mortals. The prerequisites for self-acting status demonstrate the varied paths through which adjusters gain the experience necessary for advanced responsibilities. Whether through service on primitive worlds, ministry to advanced mortals who have achieved the psychic circles, partnership with reservists of destiny, or participation in cosmic achievements of planetary significance, each adjuster progressively develops capabilities essential for effective ministry.

Most importantly, this study illuminates the supreme decision available to every mortal: the choice to enter into conscious, wholehearted partnership with the indwelling divine presence. This decision, the sincere betrothal to the adjuster and acceptance of eternal destiny, constitutes true salvation, securing eternal survival and cosmic citizenship.

As we continue our exploration of Thought Adjuster ministry in the following chapter, we will examine the mission and ministry of these divine fragments in greater detail. We will discover how adjusters actually work within human consciousness, the techniques they employ to foster soul growth, and the ultimate destiny awaiting those who achieve fusion with their divine partners. The foundation laid in this chapter prepares us to appreciate more fully the magnificent ministry unfolding daily within the minds of all normal human beings throughout the inhabited worlds of time and space.

"While you are in nature evolving inward and upward from man to God, the Adjusters are in nature evolving outward and downward from God to man; and so, will the final product of this union of divinity and humanity eternally be the son of man and the Son of God." - The Urantia Book, Paper 109:1.3

Chapter 12: The Relation of Adjusters to Mortal Types

Introduction

The relationship between Thought Adjusters and mortal beings represents one of the most profound aspects of the Father's divine plan for human ascension. As we continue our exploration of Paper 109 from *The Urantia Book*, we turn our attention to the remarkable diversity of these relationships and how they vary according to the nature of mortal types throughout the universe. This chapter examines the three distinct series of Adjuster assignments and reveals why the work of these divine fragments is more uniform than that of any other created order of celestial beings.

Understanding these relationships is essential for comprehending our own spiritual journey and appreciating the magnificent scope of the Father's plan for all evolutionary creatures. Whether we are destined for Adjuster fusion, Spirit fusion, or Son fusion, each path leads ultimately to the same goal: eternal life and service in the Father's vast universe.

This variation in Adjuster function reveals something extraordinary about the divine economy: despite serving across 700,000 local universes, each containing thousands of inhabited worlds with vastly different evolutionary patterns, the Thought Adjusters maintain a remarkable uniformity in their essential purpose. Their labors demonstrate greater consistency than those of any created order of celestial beings, precisely because they are not created but rather constitute direct fragments of the Universal Father Himself.

The Uniformity of Adjuster Ministry

The character of the detailed work of Mystery Monitors varies in accordance with the nature of their assignments, whether they are liaison adjusters, fusion adjusters, or bestowed as personality candidates with permission for everlasting fusion. Despite serving on different planetary types across various systems and universes, the labors of Thought Adjusters are remarkably uniform, more so than the duties of any other created orders of celestial beings.

This uniformity is particularly significant when we consider the vast diversity of mortal life throughout the seven hundred thousand local universes. Each Creator Son fashions unique types of mortals for their respective domains, with thousands of variations within each universe. Yet the Thought Adjusters, being fragments of the Universal Father himself, maintain a consistency of purpose and function that transcends these variations.

The reason for this remarkable uniformity lies in the nature of the Adjusters themselves. Unlike created beings who must learn and adapt, Thought Adjusters emanate directly from Divinington as fragments of the First Source and Center. They do not need to be created; they simply appear when needed, bearing the essence and perfection of the Universal Father.

Liaison Adjusters: Temporary Divine Companionship

The first category of Adjuster ministry involves what are termed "liaison" Adjusters, divine fragments loaned to mortal beings for the duration of their earthly lifetime. These Adjusters serve populations where fusion partnership is not yet a possibility, either due to the primitive nature of the evolutionary stage or the specific design of that particular mortal type.

Liaison Adjusters fulfill a crucial experiential function. They inhabit minds that may possess only rudimentary concepts of spirituality, beings who have barely emerged from the animal level of existence. On certain primitive worlds, these Adjusters gain invaluable experience while simultaneously preparing their mortal subjects for whatever level of spiritual achievement they can attain.

It is important to understand that beings indwelt by liaison Adjusters are not abandoned to oblivion. When such mortals demonstrate survival capacity and pass through the transition of death, they receive either a Son fragment or a Spirit fragment, depending on their nature and potential. Those who fuse with a Son fragment become permanent citizens of their local universe, while those who achieve Spirit fusion become citizens of the superuniverse. Neither ascends beyond these boundaries in the same manner as fusion Adjusters, but both achieve immortality and purposeful eternal existence.

The presence of liaison Adjusters on primitive worlds demonstrates a profound principle: nothing of survival value is ever lost in the wide universe. Even in circumstances where traditional Adjuster fusion cannot occur, the Father's plan provides alternative paths to eternal life for all beings who demonstrate the capacity and will to survive.

The Three Primary Classifications of Adjuster Service - Series One: Primitive Worlds and Virgin Adjusters

Closely related to liaison service is the mission of virgin Adjusters, those Father fragments embarking on their first assignment with mortal subjects. These inexperienced Adjusters are frequently sent to primitive worlds where human beings have just begun to arrive at "the valley of decision," that critical juncture where moral choice becomes possible.

The distinction between liaison Adjusters and virgin Adjusters is subtle but significant. While liaison Adjusters may have previous experience but serve in roles where fusion is impossible, virgin Adjusters lack prior mortal experience but may later serve subjects with whom they can fuse. A virgin Adjuster might first serve a primitive being to gain foundational experience, then receive assignment to a more advanced mortal capable of fusion partnership.

On these early evolutionary worlds, many beings fail to elect the arduous ascent beyond self-mastery toward emerging spirituality. However, those who do achieve survival often become Spirit-fused ascenders, advancing through the superuniverse administration even though they never achieved Adjuster fusion.

The experience gained by virgin Adjusters during these challenging early assignments proves invaluable. The wisdom acquired through transient association with primitive minds equips them for subsequent service with superior beings on other worlds. This represents another dimension of the divine economy: every experience, every challenge, every partial success contributes to the experiential wisdom that enriches the entire universe.

On certain primitive worlds inhabited by beings with single-lobed brains, Thought Adjusters indwell the minds of creatures primarily for experiential training, for the self-culture and progressive development of the Adjusters themselves. Virgin adjusters are typically sent to such worlds during the earliest times when primitive humans are arriving in the valley of decision, though comparatively few of these beings will elect to ascend the mortal heights beyond the hills of self-mastery and character attainment to reach the higher levels of emerging spirituality.

It is crucial to understand that many of these primitive beings fail to achieve Adjuster fusion but do survive as Spirit-fused ascenders. The Adjusters assigned to these worlds receive valuable training and acquire wonderful experience through their transient association with primitive minds. They are subsequently able to utilize this experience for the benefit of superior beings on other worlds. The last principle bears repeating nothing of survival value is ever lost in all the wide universe.

The Nature of Primitive Humanity

In the early evolutionary races of Urantia, three distinct groups of beings existed. The first group was so animalistic that they utterly lacked Adjuster capacity. These beings possessed only the first five adjutant mind-spirits, intuition, understanding, courage, knowledge, and counsel, but never developed worship and wisdom. Without these final two adjutants, they had no concept of a higher power and no capacity for moral decision-making. They lived and died much like the animals of our world today, with no awareness of survival potential.

The second group exhibited undoubted capacity for Adjusters and promptly received them upon reaching the age of moral responsibility. These individuals, like Andon and Fonta, the first true human beings on Urantia, demonstrated moral consciousness and thereby qualified for Adjuster indwelling.

The third class occupied a borderline position. They possessed capacity for Adjuster reception, but the Monitors could only indwell their minds upon the personal petition of the individual. These beings required a specific spiritual crisis or conscious turning toward a higher power before an Adjuster could be assigned.

The Development of Worship and Wisdom

The critical distinction between animal life and true humanity lies in the activation of the last two adjutant mind-spirits: worship and wisdom. When Andon and Fonta demonstrated their first moral decision, the choice to leave their tribe and seek a better life, they activated these dormant capacities. The adjutant of worship gave them the concept of a power greater than themselves, while the adjutant of wisdom enabled them to consider consequences beyond immediate self-interest.

This development of worship and wisdom is essential for the emergence of two fundamental spiritual concepts: the Fatherhood of God and the Brotherhood of Man. Without the ability to worship, creatures cannot conceive of God the Father. Without wisdom, they cannot develop the social consciousness necessary for recognizing the brotherhood of all beings.

Fusion Adjusters: The Partnership of Eternity

The third and highest category involves fusion Adjusters, properly designated as "personality candidates." These are Father fragments bestowed with permission for everlasting fusion with their mortal subjects, provided those subjects achieve survival. Urantia mortals, those of us reading these words, are potential partners for fusion Adjusters.

The relationship between a fusion Adjuster and a mortal being constitutes a genuine betrothal, a life-and-death engagement that, if successful, results in eternal union. Once a human being makes the sincere decision to follow the will of the Universal Father, that mortal becomes betrothed to their indwelling Adjuster. From the Adjuster's perspective, this supreme decision effectively completes the partnership, only the technical aspects of fusion remain to be accomplished, typically on the fifth mansion world.

This betrothal represents far more than mere cooperation. It signifies the beginning of an actual merger of identity wherein the human personality and the divine fragment increasingly operate as a unified being. The human contributes personality; the Adjuster contributes divinity. Together, they form something neither could be alone: an ascending son or daughter of God, a mortal who has achieved functional immortality through partnership with a fragment of eternal Deity.

The Role of Language in Spiritual Development

Animals possess fellow feelings and can express emotions, but they cannot communicate concepts, ideas, or ideals to one another. Similarly, primitive humans of animal origin could not experience higher forms of intellectual intercourse or spiritual communion until they developed speech. Language development marks a crucial threshold on the road to receiving Thought Adjusters.

The arrival of the Caligastia One Hundred, five hundred thousand years after Andon and Fonta, marked the first epochal revelation to Urantia. One of their primary missions was teaching these early humans basic speech and the first concepts of God the Father. Through language, human beings could finally share ideas, develop social structures, and build upon accumulated knowledge rather than starting anew with each generation.

Series Two: Worlds of Liaison Adjusters - Worlds of Non-Fusion Mortals

On another type of world, the series two group, Adjusters are merely loaned to mortal beings. Here the Monitors can never attain fusion personality through such indwelling, but they afford great help to their human subjects during the mortal lifetime, far more than they are able to give to Urantia mortals. These Adjusters are loaned to mortal creatures for a single lifespan as patterns for their higher spiritual attainment, temporary helpers in the intriguing task of perfecting a survival character.

The Adjusters do not return after natural death on these worlds. Surviving mortals attain eternal life through Spirit fusion or Son fusion, becoming permanent citizens of either the local universe or the superuniverse, depending on the nature of their fusion. While they do not achieve the Paradise destiny of Adjuster-fused mortals, they nevertheless gain eternal life and meaningful service in the Father's universe.

These series two mortals may have either single-lobed or dual-lobed brains, similar to Urantia mortals in physical structure. The determining factor is not brain structure but rather the divine plan for that particular world and its inhabitants. Even liaison Adjusters, though unable to fuse with their subjects, gain invaluable experience that prepares them for future assignments where fusion will be possible.

This arrangement demonstrates the Father's flexibility in achieving His purposes. Not every mortal type can fuse with an Adjuster, but every mortal type that achieves survival capacity receives an appropriate form of eternal partnership. The goal remains constant, eternal life and progressive perfection, while the means adapt to the nature of each unique creation.

Series Three: Urantia and the Betrothal Engagement

On worlds such as Urantia, the series three group, there exists a real betrothal with these divine gifts, a life-and-death engagement. If you survive, there is to be an eternal union, an everlasting fusion, the making of man and Adjuster into one being.

We who inhabit Urantia are series three mortals with dual-lobed brains, destined for Adjuster fusion if we survive. The moment we make the supreme decision to follow God the Father and do His will; we become betrothed to our indwelling Adjusters. From that moment forward, the Adjuster considers the partnership established. From the Adjuster's perspective, this betrothal is as binding as the fusion itself; the technical completion is merely a formality to be accomplished, typically on the fifth mansion world.

However, an important equalizing factor exists in the career after death, all three types, one-brained, two-brained, and three-brained mortals, proceed identically. Once translated to the mansion worlds, all receive morontia forms equipped with standardized mental apparatus. Whatever advantages or disadvantages existed during mortal life are neutralized by the new form of existence. All begin their mansion world careers on essentially equal footing, differentiated only by their accumulated experiential wisdom and spiritual attainment.

The Significance of Betrothal

This betrothal relationship fundamentally transforms our status in the universe. Once we make that sincere decision to seek and do the Father's will, our Adjuster considers us one being. The human provides personality; the Adjuster provides divinity. Together, in this sacred partnership, we are already, in essence, children of God, though we remain faith sons and daughters until actual fusion occurs.

Nothing can prevent the ultimate fusion of a betrothed Adjuster and willing mortal. Difficulties may arise, delays may occur, but the outcome is certain. The Father's fragment has chosen us, we have chosen the Father's will, and the eternal circuit is complete.

The Impact of Bestowal Sons

Following the bestowal of a Paradise Son on two-brained worlds, a significant change occurs in Adjuster assignments. Virgin Adjusters are seldom assigned to persons with unquestioned survival capacity. Instead, practically all Adjusters indwelling intelligent beings of survival capacity belong to the advanced or supreme type, experienced fragments who bring accumulated wisdom to their ministry.

This shift reflects the enhanced spiritual atmosphere created by the bestowal. When a Creator Son incarnates on a world, that experience elevates the entire planet's spiritual potential. Subsequent generations benefit from this enhanced atmosphere, receiving more experienced Adjuster guidance appropriate to their increased capacity for spiritual understanding.

The Gift of Personality

One of the most profound mysteries in this relationship involves personality. God the Father is the source of all personality, yet the Adjusters, being fragments of the Father himself, are pre-personal beings. They possess every attribute of divinity except personality. Why this seeming paradox?

The answer reveals the Father's wisdom. If the Adjusters possessed the Father's own personality, fusion would be impossible. We cannot share the Father's personality; it is uniquely His. Instead, the Father bestows upon each mortal a unique personality gift, distinct and unrepeatable throughout all eternity. When we fuse with our Adjusters, we provide personality to the divine fragment, while the fragment provides divinity to us. This divine transaction creates something entirely new: an immortal child of God, possessing both human personality and divine nature.

Post-Bestowal Changes

Following the bestowal of a Paradise Son on a world, significant changes occur in Adjuster assignments. On two-brained worlds after such a bestowal, virgin adjusters are seldom assigned to persons who have unquestioned capacity for survival. The belief is that on such worlds, practically all Adjusters indwelling intelligent men and women of survival capacity belong to the advanced or supreme types.

On Urantia, after the Day of Pentecost following Jesus' bestowal, all normal-minded individuals reaching the age of moral responsibility receive Thought Adjusters. This represents a significant advancement in our world's spiritual status and reflects the Father's confidence in the potential for survival among Urantia mortals.

The Evolutionary History of Urantia - Three Classes of Early Beings

In the early evolutionary races of Urantia, three distinct groups existed, representing different stages of development:

The Animalistic: Some beings remained so completely animalistic that they utterly lacked Adjuster capacity. These represented the earliest human ancestors, possessing only the first five adjutant mind-spirits, intuition, understanding, courage, knowledge, and counsel, but lacking worship and wisdom. Without these final two adjutants, they could not conceive of a higher power or exercise moral judgment, thus remaining essentially advanced animals rather than true humans.

The Capable: Others exhibited undoubted capacity for Adjusters and promptly received them upon reaching the age of moral responsibility. These individuals, though still primitive, had developed sufficient self-consciousness and moral awareness to make genuine spiritual decisions. When that first moral choice occurred, worship and wisdom activated, and an Adjuster arrived.

The Borderline: A third class occupied a borderline position, possessing capacity for Adjuster reception but requiring personal petition before a Monitor could indwell their minds. These individuals needed to make an explicit appeal to a higher power, a conscious reaching toward the divine, before they could receive their Father fragment.

This third category reveals something profound about free will and divine respect for personality. Even when capacity exists, God will not force His presence upon any being. The petition requirement ensured that even these borderline individuals exercised authentic choice in establishing their relationship with the divine.

The Influence of Experienced Adjusters

The type of Adjuster assigned has much to do with the potential for expression of human personality. Down through the ages, many of the great intellectual and spiritual leaders of Urantia have exerted their influence chiefly because of the superiority and previous experience of their indwelling Adjusters.

Consider extraordinary individuals like Nikola Tesla, whose innovations seemed to transcend normal human capacity. Such genius likely reflects the partnership between a receptive human mind and an Adjuster of vast experience. The Adjuster, having served in numerous prior assignments, brings accumulated wisdom and insight that, when combined with a capable human intellect, produces remarkable results.

This principle applies not only to intellectual achievement but to spiritual leadership as well. Those who have made the greatest spiritual impact on human civilization, religious teachers, moral philosophers, ethical reformers, often possess Adjusters with extensive prior experience in guiding mortals toward God-consciousness.

The Adjusters know in advance the personality type and potential of their assigned subjects. Before leaving Divinington, they preview the entire life path awaiting them, understanding the DNA patterns, ancestral history, and mind potential of the mortal they will indwell. This foreknowledge allows for optimal preparation and more effective ministry.

The Importance of Communication

Animals possess fellow feelings but cannot communicate concepts to each other. They can express emotions through body language, sounds, and behaviors, but they cannot convey ideas and ideals. Similarly, primitive humans of animal origin could not experience high-level intellectual intercourse or spiritual communion until Thought Adjusters were bestowed.

The development of speech represents a critical threshold in human evolution. When evolutionary creatures develop language, they stand on the road to receiving Adjusters. Language enables the communication of abstract concepts, justice, love, mercy, deity, which forms the foundation for genuine spiritual growth.

One of the first tasks of the Caligastia One Hundred involved teaching their primitive students systematic speech and basic writing. This gift of enhanced communication capacity accelerated social and spiritual development exponentially. With language, people could share not just immediate needs but ideals, hopes, and spiritual concepts. They could discuss the nature of God and contemplate their relationship to divine reality.

This historical progression reveals why the Dalamatia teachings constitute the first epochal revelation. For the first time, celestial beings systematically communicated the concept of the Universal Father to human beings. The revelation consisted not merely of information but of the very capacity to understand and discuss that information, language itself serving as a revelatory gift.

The Historical Transition

All three groups existed on Urantia before the arrival of the Caligastia One Hundred and the establishment of the Planetary Prince's administration. For approximately 500,000 years after Andon and Fonta, the first true human beings, evolutionary progress proceeded slowly. Communication remained limited to grunts, groans, and primitive gestures. Social development barely extended beyond immediate family units.

Andon and Fonta distinguished themselves as the first humans not merely because they were more intelligent than their contemporaries, but because they made the first genuine moral decision. In that moment of moral choice, worship and wisdom activated within their minds, and they received Thought Adjusters. This event, occurring roughly one million years ago, marked the actual beginning of human history on Urantia.

The subsequent 500,000 years witnessed gradual evolutionary progress. By the time of the Caligastia One Hundred's arrival, sufficient numbers of Adjuster-indwelt humans existed to justify the establishment of formal civilization. The Planetary Prince's staff introduced advanced concepts: organized agriculture, primitive writing, social structures, and most importantly, systematic concepts of the Universal Father.

Following Michael's bestowal as Jesus of Nazareth, and particularly after the day of Pentecost, all normal-minded individuals began receiving Adjusters at the age of moral responsibility. The three early categories collapsed into one: all capable beings now receive divine indwelling as their birthright, provided they possess normal mental capacity and reach the age of decision.

The Role of Inheritance and Environment - Genetic Limitations

The text acknowledges a sobering reality: some beings face virtual disqualification for survival due to disinheritance through unfit and inferior ancestors. Genetic damage, whether from inbreeding, radiation, disease, or other causes, can so impair the human brain that normal Adjuster ministry becomes impossible.

However, even these tragic cases serve a purpose in the divine economy. Many virgin Adjusters have gained valuable preliminary experience by contacting such damaged minds, subsequently becoming better qualified for assignment to higher types of mind on other worlds. The experience of attempting to reach a severely impaired consciousness provides insights useful in working with more receptive but still challenging subjects.

Those who die with such severe mental impairments essentially reawaken on the mansion worlds as blank slates. They retain no memories of their earth life and must begin learning everything anew, much like infants. Guardian angels, teachers, and other celestial beings provide patient, loving instruction, ensuring that these individuals receive the opportunity for growth and development they were denied during mortal existence.

These unfortunate souls typically receive Spirit or Son fragments rather than Adjusters and generally remain within their local universe. They lack the experiential foundation for the long Paradise ascent, but they achieve immortality and meaningful eternal existence, proof again that nothing of survival value is ever lost.

The Mansion World Revelation

One of the most significant advantages of studying *The Urantia Book* during our earthly lives is the preparation it provides for mansion world existence. Upon arriving at the first mansion world, every survivor must master the equivalent of all the teachings contained in this revelation before progressing further. Those who have studied these truths beforehand possess an enormous advantage.

The resurrected morontia beings on the first mansion world continuously replay the life of Jesus for new arrivals, for understanding our own history is essential before we can help others understand theirs. We cannot proceed past our own history until we know and comprehend it fully. This is why wisdom requires knowledge of the past, so we do not repeat the mistakes that have plagued humanity throughout the ages.

The Universal Lesson

Consider the pattern of human history: warfare, oppression, the killing of brothers and sisters in endless cycles of violence. Why do we repeat these patterns? Because we fail to teach each succeeding generation the lessons of the past. We fail to instill the fundamental truths of the Fatherhood of God and the Brotherhood of Man.

When we truly understand that we are all children of the same Universal Father, killing our brothers and sisters becomes unthinkable. When we destroy others, we destroy their future and, by extension, our own. We eliminate their opportunity to teach their children, to contribute to the collective wisdom of humanity, to add their voice to the cosmic chorus.

Wisdom, he seventh adjutant mind-spirit, enables us to learn from experience and apply those lessons to future decisions. Without wisdom, we are doomed to repeat the same errors endlessly, like striking our thumb with a hammer over and over without learning to move it out of the way.

Survival and Faith: The Essential Requirement

Nothing of survival value is ever lost in all the wide universe. This profound truth means that every being with survival potential will survive, regardless of their religious affiliation, cultural background, or theological understanding. The only requirement for survival is faith, faith in the possibility of survival itself, which necessarily implies faith in a power greater than ourselves.

The Universal Nature of Survival

Christians need not fear for their Muslim brothers and sisters, nor Muslims for Christians, nor adherents of any faith for those of different beliefs. Anyone who possesses faith in God, by whatever name they call Him, will survive. The mansion worlds will be populated by individuals from every religious tradition on Urantia, for God is not limited by human theological constructs.

What matters is not whether one believes that Jesus is their personal savior in the sectarian Christian sense. What matters is faith in God the Father and, by extension, faith in Jesus as our universe Creator and the living revelation of the Father. When we understand that "I am in the Father and the Father is in me," we comprehend that believing in God necessarily encompasses believing in Jesus, for they are one in purpose and nature.

The Role of Children and the Mentally Impaired

Special provision is made for those who die as children or who are mentally incapacitated and unable to make moral decisions during their earthly lives. These individuals are not lost; they awaken in the mansion worlds as if they were newly born, with no memory of a previous existence. They are taught from the beginning by patient teachers and guardian angels, given every opportunity to develop and grow spiritually.

Even those whose genetic inheritance or circumstances have severely limited their earthly potential will find full opportunity for development in the morontia realms. Though they may not achieve Adjuster fusion, instead attaining survival through Spirit or Son fusion, hey nevertheless gain eternal life and meaningful service. They become citizens of the local universe or superuniverse, contributing their unique perspective to the cosmic tapestry.

The Influence of Experienced Adjusters

The type of Adjuster assigned to a mortal being significantly affects that individual's potential for intellectual and spiritual expression. Throughout Urantia's history, many great intellectual and spiritual leaders have exerted their influence primarily because of the superiority and previous experience of their indwelling Adjusters.

The Adjuster receives advance knowledge of its assigned subject's life pattern, personality potential, and genetic endowment before leaving Divinington. This foreknowledge enables precise matching: the right Adjuster for the right mortal at the right time. The seemingly miraculous breakthroughs, the unexpected flashes of insight, the sudden solutions to intractable problems, these often represent moments when the Adjuster successfully communicates with the mortal mind, elevating human thought to approach divine wisdom.

Universal Principles and Local Application - The Consistency of Adjuster Ministry

Despite the bewildering diversity of mortal types across 700,000 local universes, each containing thousands of inhabited worlds, Thought Adjuster ministry demonstrates remarkable uniformity. This consistency reflects their origin: they are not created beings who might vary in capability or understanding, but rather fragments of the perfect, infinite Father Himself.

Every Adjuster brings the absolute perfection of divinity to its mortal assignment. The variation in their work arises not from differences in their essential nature but from the vast differences among their mortal subjects. A Father fragment serving a primitive three-lobed being on a distant world exercises the same divine wisdom and love as one serving a two-lobed Urantian—the apparent differences reflect the varying capacities of their subjects, not limitations in the Adjusters themselves.

The Cosmic Economy of the Ascension Plan

Lucifer, in his rebellion, claimed that ninety percent of the economy of the superuniverses revolved around the ascension plan for mortals. While intended as a criticism, this observation actually reveals a profound truth: we lowly mortals are central to the Father's plan.

Consider the vast hosts of celestial beings dedicated to our service: guardian angels, teaching advisors, Melchizedeks, Life Carriers, Material Sons and

Daughters, and countless others. All exist, at least in part, to facilitate our ascension from animal origin to Paradise finality. This is not a waste of resources but rather the Father's loving provision for His children.

Moreover, when we mortals eventually reach Paradise and join the Corps of the Finality, we will carry this experiential knowledge forward to the outer space levels. There, newly evolving beings will benefit from our hard-won wisdom, and we will serve as guides and mentors much as celestial beings now serve us. The investment in our development thus pays dividends throughout eternity.

The Brotherhood of Man and Social Progress

The development of language and the capacity for spiritual communion enable the fundamental principle of the Brotherhood of Man. Without the ability to communicate complex ideas and ideals, human beings cannot develop the social consciousness necessary for civilization.

The early work of the Caligastia One Hundred focused precisely on these foundations: teaching language, encouraging social organization, introducing the concept of God, and fostering the understanding that all humans are related as children of the Universal Father. Though the Caligastia betrayal derailed this progress, the fundamental truths remained.

When human beings truly internalize the Fatherhood of God and the Brotherhood of Man, warfare becomes obsolete. We cannot sustainably make war upon those we recognize as our brothers and sisters. We cannot willingly destroy those we know to be fellow children of our loving Father. The solution to human conflict is not political or military but spiritual, a transformation of consciousness that recognizes our essential unity.

Nothing of Value Is Ever Lost

Throughout this chapter, one principle recurs with profound reassurance: nothing of survival value is ever lost in all the wide universe. This applies universally, from the most primitive beings barely capable of moral thought to the most advanced three-brained mortals approaching light and life.

If a being demonstrates any capacity for survival, any genuine faith, any authentic moral choice, any sincere desire for relationship with the divine, then provision exists for that being's eternal continuance. The form may vary: Adjuster fusion, Spirit fusion, Son fusion. The timing may differ: some fuse during mortal life, others on the mansion worlds, still others in later stages of ascension. But the principle remains constant: the Father's love ensures that no willing child will be lost.

This assurance should comfort those who worry about the fate of primitive peoples, mentally impaired individuals, or those who lived before enhanced spiritual ministry became available. God's justice is perfect, His mercy is infinite, and His wisdom ensures that every being receives precisely the opportunity appropriate to their capacity and circumstances.

Conclusion

The relationship between Adjusters and mortal types reveals the magnificent efficiency of the divine economy. Every type of mortal being, on every inhabited world, in every local universe throughout the grand universe, receives ministry precisely calibrated to their nature and capacity. Yet this incredible diversity operates within a framework of absolute unity of purpose: the eternal survival and progressive perfection of every willing creature.

The Thought Adjusters, despite being pre-personal fragments, demonstrate more uniformity in their work than any created order of beings because they emanate directly from the perfection of the Universal Father. They gain experience through service, just as we gain spirituality through living, and together, mortal and Monitor, we forge an eternal partnership that culminates in fusion and immortality.

Understanding these relationships helps us appreciate not only our own spiritual journey but also the journeys of all our fellows, regardless of their apparent capacity or current development. Nothing of survival value is ever lost. Every effort toward goodness, truth, and beauty contributes to the cosmic whole. Every sincere soul seeking God will find Him, for the Father has already sent forth His own spirit to indwell and guide us.

As we move forward in our study, we will explore in greater depth the phenomenon of fusion itself and the remarkable transformation it produces. We will examine what it means to become finaliters and what destiny awaits the immortal children of God. The journey from mortal birth to Paradise is long, but it begins with that first moral decision, that first turning toward the light, that first whispered prayer to the Father who already dwells within us.

We who read *The Urantia Book* enjoy extraordinary privilege. We possess, during our mortal lifetime, knowledge that most beings in the universe only acquire after translation to the mansion worlds. We understand our origin, nature, and destiny. We comprehend the indwelling Adjuster's function and the fusion opportunity it represents. We can cooperate consciously and intelligently with our divine fragments, accelerating our spiritual growth and preparing for the great adventure that awaits.

This knowledge carries profound responsibility. We cannot claim ignorance of our spiritual nature or our cosmic destiny. We cannot plead that we lacked opportunity or information. The fifth epochal revelation has been placed in our hands, offering comprehensive understanding of our place in the universe and our relationship with the Universal Father.

The question facing each reader is ultimately simple yet infinitely significant: Will we cooperate with our indwelling Adjusters? Will we make that supreme decision that constitutes betrothal with the divine fragment? Will we commit ourselves to the thrilling adventure of eternal progression, knowing that nothing of survival value is ever lost, and that our partnership with a fragment of God Himself guarantees both immortality and an eternally fascinating career of service and growth?

In our next chapter, we will explore the mission and ministry of Thought Adjusters in greater detail, examining how they actually work within human minds to foster spiritual growth and prepare us for that eventual fusion that transforms human will into divine purpose, and mortal creatures into ascending sons and daughters of God.

"The Adjusters are here loaned to the mortal creatures for a single lifespan as patterns for their higher spiritual attainment, temporary helpers in the intriguing task of perfecting a survival character.", The Urantia Book, Paper 109

The betrothal has been offered. The decision remains ours.

"The Adjusters are here loaned to the mortal creatures for a single lifespan as patterns for their higher spiritual attainment, temporary helpers in the intriguing task of perfecting a survival character.", The Urantia Book, Paper 109

Chapter 13: The Persistence of Divine Values and the Triumph of Consecrated Will

Introduction

In our continuing exploration of Paper 109, we now turn our attention to one of the most profound and encouraging truths in the entire revelation: the persistence of divine values and the transformative power of consecrated dedication to the Father's will. This chapter examines how Thought Adjusters work to preserve everything of eternal worth, even when individual personalities fail to survive, and how the human mind can cooperate with these divine fragments to achieve spiritual transformation.

The material we explore here addresses fundamental questions that have troubled sincere seekers throughout human history: What happens to the good we accomplish if we fail to survive? How do our hereditary limitations affect our spiritual potential? Can we truly communicate with the divine presence within us? And most importantly, what does it mean to consecrate our will to God's will?

These are not merely theoretical considerations. They touch the very heart of our spiritual existence and our eternal destiny. As we shall see, the answers provided in this revelation offer both profound comfort and serious challenge to those who would pursue the ascending career toward Paradise.

The Influence of Experienced Adjusters on Planetary Leadership

The type of Adjuster assigned to a human being has much to do with the potential for expression of that human personality throughout the ages. Many of the great intellectual and spiritual leaders of Urantia have exerted their influence chiefly because of the superiority and previous experience of their indwelling Adjusters. This truth should bring both comfort and perspective to those who struggle with feelings of inadequacy in spiritual service.

Some individuals are blessed with Adjusters who have served in multiple personalities across vast reaches of time and space. These experienced monitors bring with them the accumulated wisdom and spiritual insights of their previous indwellings. The revelation speaks of one particular Adjuster serving on Urantia in the twentieth century who had, according to the records on Divinington, indwelt fifteen minds previously in Orvonton. Whether this monitor had similar experiences in other superuniverses remains unknown, but this much is certain:

such an Adjuster represents one of the most useful and potent spiritual forces on our planet during this present age.

The implications of this truth are profound. Those who possess extraordinary spiritual or intellectual gifts need not attribute their abilities solely to personal merit. The superior experience of their indwelling Adjusters may well account for their enhanced capacity for spiritual expression. Conversely, those who feel they lack such gifts need not despair, for they may be providing their Adjusters with unique and valuable opportunities for growth and service. The relationship between Adjuster and mortal is always reciprocal, always meaningful, and always purposeful.

Consider the great musicians of human history, composers like Mozart and Bach, whose genius seemed to transcend normal human capability. Consider spiritual leaders whose insights illuminated entire eras of human development. While personal talent and dedication certainly play their roles, the superior experience and guidance of their Thought Adjusters contributed significantly to their remarkable achievements. This understanding should cultivate both humility in the gifted and hope in those who serve more quietly.

The Cooperative Work of Adjusters in Civilizational Advancement

The indwelling Adjusters have, in no small measure, cooperated with other spiritual influences in transforming and humanizing the descendants of the primitive peoples of ancient times. This cooperation represents one of the most significant factors in the gradual elevation of human civilization from barbarism toward enlightenment.

The revelation presents a sobering hypothetical: if the Adjusters indwelling the minds of Urantia's inhabitants were suddenly withdrawn, the world would slowly return to many of the scenes and practices of primitive times, the barbarism of past ages. The Divine Monitors are, therefore, one of the real potentials of advancing civilization. Without their constant, patient guidance, humanity would lack the essential spiritual compass that directs evolutionary progress toward higher values and meanings.

This truth should profoundly affect our understanding of human history and cultural development. The gradual abandonment of human sacrifice, cannibalism, and tribal warfare; the slow emergence of concepts like justice, mercy, and human dignity; the development of art, philosophy, and science, all these advances have been facilitated by the tireless work of millions of Thought Adjusters laboring in the superconscious minds of evolving mortals.

Yet we must acknowledge that even with Adjuster guidance, human civilization remains far from perfected. Wars continue, injustice persists, and cruelty still mars the human experience. The difference between ancient barbarism and modern society lies not in the elimination of destructive impulses, but in the gradual strengthening of spiritual influences that counteract and eventually transform these tendencies. We have advanced the technology of destruction, but the fundamental spiritual struggle remains: the choice between following animal impulses or heeding divine guidance.

Planetary Cross-Fertilization and Adjuster Experience

In a certain sense, the Adjusters may be fostering a degree of planetary cross-fertilization in the domains of truth, beauty, and goodness. However, they are seldom given two indwelling experiences on the same planet. There is no Adjuster now serving on Urantia who has previously been on this world, with the notable exception of the Adjuster who indwelt both Machiventa Melchizedek and Jesus of Nazareth. This policy ensures the maximum distribution of divine experience across the vast populations of evolving worlds.

The significance of this practice cannot be overstated. Each Adjuster brings to Urantia experiences from other worlds, other cultures, and other evolutionary conditions. This cosmic perspective enriches the spiritual potential of our planet. An Adjuster who previously served on a world that successfully avoided planetary rebellion brings different insights than one who ministered on a quarantined sphere. An Adjuster experienced in other superuniverses contributes perspectives beyond the accumulated wisdom of Orvonton alone.

This cross-fertilization operates subtly, never violating human free will, yet constantly introducing new spiritual possibilities into human consciousness. The great ideas that seem to arise spontaneously in human minds, concepts of universal brotherhood, ideals of justice that transcend tribal loyalty, visions of cosmic citizenship, these may well reflect the influence of Adjusters drawing upon experiences gained in other planetary systems where such ideals have already been realized.

Material Handicaps and Adjuster Ministry

Supreme and self-acting Adjusters are often able to contribute factors of spiritual import to the human mind when it flows freely in the liberated but controlled channels of creative imagination. At such times, and sometimes during sleep, the Adjuster is able to arrest the mental currents, stay the flow, and then divert the procession of ideas. All this is done in order to effect deep spiritual transformations in the higher recesses of the super consciousness.

Thus are the forces and energies of mind more fully adjusted to the key of the contactual tones of the spiritual level of the present and the future. This superconscious communication between the Adjuster and the human mind operates on a level that the conscious personality never directly experiences. Even if one attempted to deliberately access this superconscious realm, the very act of conscious attention would interrupt the delicate spiritual processes occurring there.

This explains why spiritual guidance often comes through unexpected channels, dreams, sudden insights, creative inspirations, or moments of quiet reflection. When the conscious mind releases its controlling grip and allows free creative flow, the Adjuster can more effectively introduce spiritual values and cosmic perspectives. Many individuals have experienced powerful dreams that redirected their lives, providing insights into unresolved psychological conflicts or revealing new directions for personal growth. Such experiences may well represent Adjuster ministry operating through the symbolic language of the subconscious mind.

It is sometimes possible to have the mind illuminated, to hear the divine voice that continually speaks within, so that one may become partially conscious of the wisdom, truth, goodness, and beauty of the potential personality constantly indwelling. However, our unsteady and rapidly shifting mental attitudes often result in thwarting the plans and interrupting the work of the Adjusters.

The Adjuster's work is not only interfered with by the innate natures of the mortal races, but this ministry is also greatly retarded by our own preconceived opinions, settled ideas, and long-standing prejudices. Because of these handicaps, many times only the Adjusters' unfinished creations emerge into consciousness, and confusion of concept is inevitable.

Therefore, in scrutinizing mental situations, safety lies only in the prompt recognition of each and every thought and experience for just what it actually and fundamentally is, disregarding entirely what it might have been. This counsel cuts to the heart of a common human tendency: dwelling on past mistakes with the endless refrain of "if only I had done this differently." Such rumination not only paralyzes present action but also obscures the Adjuster's current guidance.

The great problem of life is the adjustment of ancestral tendencies of living to the demands of the spiritual urges initiated by the divine presence of the Mystery Monitor. While in the universe and superuniverse careers no one can serve two masters, in the life we now live on Urantia every person must perforce serve two masters. We must become adept in the art of continuous human temporal compromise while yielding spiritual allegiance to but one master. This is why so many falter and fail, grow weary, and succumb to the stress of the evolutionary struggle.

We must live in the material world, earning our living, providing for our families, fulfilling our social obligations. These material necessities function as masters demanding our time, energy, and attention. Yet simultaneously, our spiritual nature responds to the urging of the indwelling Adjuster, calling us toward higher values and eternal realities. The tension between these competing demands creates the crucible in which spiritual character is forged.

Hereditary Limitations and Spiritual Achievement

While the hereditary legacy of cerebral endowment and that of electrochemical overcontrol both operate to delimit the sphere of efficient Adjuster activity, no hereditary handicap in normal minds ever prevents eventual spiritual achievement. Heredity may interfere with the rate of personality conquest, but it does not prevent eventual consummation of the ascendant adventure.

If we will cooperate with our Adjusters, the divine gift will sooner or later evolve the immortal morontia soul, and subsequent to fusion therewith, will present the new creature to the Sovereign Master Son of the local universe and eventually to the Father of Adjusters on Paradise. This represents perhaps the most significant "if" in the entire revelation: *if you will cooperate with your Adjuster*.

This cooperation is not complicated, though it is profound. It consists essentially in choosing to do what we know to be right, in following the highest values we can perceive, in treating others as we would wish to be treated. The trick lies not in understanding what the Adjuster desires, for we have an innate sense of right and wrong, but in consistently choosing the right course despite contrary impulses.

For young people especially, this consistency proves challenging. Peer pressure, immediate gratification, and the intensity of physical desires all work against steady spiritual progress. Yet once the habit of choosing right becomes established, doing right becomes natural rather than exceptional. The spiritual path, while never easy, becomes increasingly clear and compelling as we mature in our commitment to divine values.

The Persistence of True Values

Adjusters never fail. Nothing worth surviving is ever lost. Every meaningful value in every will creature is certain of survival, irrespective of the survival or non-survival of the meaning-discovering or evaluating personality. Thus, it is a mortal creature may reject survival, yet the life experience is not wasted. The eternal Adjuster carries the worthwhile features of such an apparent life of failure into some other world, and there bestows these surviving meanings and values upon some higher type of mortal mind, one of survival capacity.

No worthwhile experience ever happens in vain. No true meaning or real value ever perishes. These words offer profound comfort to those who struggle with the apparent futility of human effort. Even when individuals choose not to survive, whether through deliberate rejection of the survival plan or through simple spiritual indifference, the genuine values they created or discovered during their earthly lives are preserved.

The Adjuster who indwelt such a non-surviving personality carries forward everything of eternal worth from that life experience. These preserved values become resources for future ministry. When this Adjuster receives a new mortal assignment, the wisdom gained from the previous indwelling enriches the new relationship. The second mortal benefits from insights and perspectives developed during the first indwelling, even though the first personality chose not to continue.

As related to fusion candidates, if a Mystery Monitor is deserted by the mortal associate, if the human partner declines to pursue the ascending career, then when released by natural death or prior thereto, the Adjuster carries away everything of survival value which has evolved in the mind of that non-surviving creature.

If an Adjuster should repeatedly fail to attain fusion personality because of the non-survival of successive human subjects, and if this Monitor should subsequently be personalized, all the acquired experience of having indwelt and mastered all these mortal minds would become the actual possession of such a newly Personalized Adjuster, an endowment to be enjoyed and utilized throughout all future ages.

A Personalized Adjuster of this order is a composite assembly of all the survival traits of all former creature hosts. Such beings represent living repositories of tested values, embodiments of proven meanings, and exemplars of surviving worth. Their existence demonstrates that nothing of true value is ever truly lost in the universe, regardless of the choices made by individual personalities.

The Adjusters of Bestowal Sons

Adjusters of long universe experience volunteer to indwell Divine Sons on bestowal missions. They fully know that personality attainment can never be achieved through this service, for the bestowal Sons are already perfected beings who cannot fuse with Adjusters. But often does the Father of Spirits grant personality to these volunteers and establish them as directors of their kind.

These are the personalities honored with authority on Divinington. Their unique natures embody the mosaic humanity of their multiple experiences of mortal indwelling and also the spirit transcript of the human divinity of the Paradise bestowal Son of the terminal indwelling experience. This represents one of the highest honors that can come to a Thought Adjuster, to serve as the divine monitor of an incarnated Creator Son.

The activities of Adjusters in our local universe are directed by the Personalized Adjuster of Michael of Nebadon, that very Monitor who guided him step by step when he lived his human life in the flesh of Joshua ben Joseph. Faithful to his trust was this extraordinary Adjuster, and wisely did this valiant Monitor direct the human nature, ever guiding the mortal mind of the Paradise Son in the choosing of the path of the Father's perfect will.

This Adjuster had previously served with Machiventa Melchizedek in the days of Abraham and had engaged in tremendous exploits both previous to this indwelling and between these bestowal experiences. The same Adjuster who guided Machiventa during his emergency bestowal later guided Jesus through his earthly life, gaining unparalleled experience in both assignments.

This fact illuminates a crucial aspect of Jesus' human experience. When Joshua ben Joseph was born as a helpless infant, he had voluntarily limited his self-awareness as a Divine Son. He did not consciously know his true identity and cosmic status. During his childhood and youth, as he grew in wisdom and understanding, what kept him on the righteous path? What guided his choices toward perfection?

The answer must lie significantly in the ministry of his superbly experienced Adjuster. This divine Monitor, drawing upon previous experience with Machiventa and countless other indwellings, guided the human mind of Jesus toward increasingly perfect choices, even before Jesus consciously realized his divine nature. This Adjuster's influence helps explain why Jesus, even as a child, demonstrated unusual spiritual wisdom and moral integrity.

When Jesus completed his bestowal and fully resumed his consciousness as Michael of Nebadon, the experiences and memories of his human life became integral to his nature as Creator Son. But the soul that had developed during his thirty-three years as a human being, what became of it? Michael, already a Divine Son, had no need of this evolved soul. Instead, this soul, encompassing all the human experiences of Jesus, became the foundation of the Personalized Adjuster.

In this sense, two "versions" of Jesus emerged from the incarnation: Michael of Nebadon, who retained all memories of his human experience as an integral part of his divine consciousness, and the Personalized Adjuster, who possessed the actual soul developed during Jesus' human life, along with complete memory transcripts of the entire experience.

This Personalized Adjuster, bearing the soul and memories of the most perfect human life ever lived on Urantia, became the supreme example of perfected human spiritual attainment. For this reason, he now directs all Adjuster activities in Nebadon, serving as the living standard of what cooperation between human will and divine guidance can achieve.

The Triumph of Consecrated Will

This Adjuster did indeed triumph in Jesus' human mind, that mind which in each of life's recurring situations maintained a consecrated dedication to the Father's will, saying, "Not my will, but yours be done." Such decisive consecration constitutes the true passport from the limitations of human nature to the finality of divine attainment.

Here lies the heart of the entire matter. Jesus' consecration to doing the Father's will preceded his conscious awareness of being the Creator Son. As a young man growing into spiritual maturity, Joshua ben Joseph made the fundamental choice that determines all eternal destiny: complete dedication to divine will regardless of personal cost or consequence.

This same choice faces every human being at some point in life. The specific circumstances vary, but the essential decision remains constant: Will I consecrate my life to doing God's will, or will I reserve ultimate authority for myself? Will I say with Jesus, "Not my will, but yours be done," or will I insist on maintaining final control over my choices and destiny?

Many people can identify a specific moment when they made this consecration, a particular day, hour, or circumstance when they consciously surrendered their will to divine guidance. For others, the choice unfolds more gradually through a series of decisions that eventually crystalize into complete commitment. But whether sudden or gradual, this consecration represents the turning point of spiritual existence.

From the moment this decision is made and sustained, life changes fundamentally. Not that external circumstances necessarily improve, often they become more challenging. But internal perspective shifts. The anxiety of trying to control everything gives way to the peace of trusting divine guidance. The burden of managing outcomes alone is replaced by partnership with the indwelling Adjuster. Decisions become clearer because the fundamental question changes from "What do I want?" to "What does the Father want?"

This consecration does not mean passive resignation to fate or abandonment of personal responsibility. Rather, it represents active partnership with divinity, where human will and divine guidance align in cooperative service. We still face choices, still exercise judgment, still experience the full range of human emotions and challenges. But we face them with the confidence that we are not alone, that divine wisdom is available to guide us, and that ultimate outcomes rest in hands more capable than our own.

Conclusion

The truths explored in this chapter offer both profound comfort and serious challenge. The comfort lies in knowing that nothing of true value is ever lost, that our hereditary limitations cannot prevent spiritual achievement, and that experienced Adjusters guide many of humanity's greatest leaders. The challenge lies in the requirement for personal consecration, for the daily choice to align our will with divine guidance despite the contrary pull of material concerns and ancestral tendencies.

We have seen that Adjusters work tirelessly to preserve and transmit values, even when the personalities who developed those values fail to survive. We have learned that these divine Monitors employ creative imagination, dreams, and superconscious processes to guide us toward spiritual transformation. We have discovered that the tension between material necessity and spiritual aspiration, far from being an unfortunate accident, represents the designed environment for forging eternal character.

Most significantly, we have encountered in Jesus' life the supreme example of human-divine cooperation, where complete consecration to the Father's will enabled a human mind to achieve perfect spiritual attainment. His Adjuster's triumph demonstrates what becomes possible when human will and divine guidance achieve perfect harmony.

As we continue our study in the next chapter, we will explore additional dimensions of Adjuster ministry, examining how these divine Monitors function in relation to other spiritual influences and how their work contributes to the supreme goal of achieving fusion, that eternal partnership where human and divine become inseparably one.

The invitation stands before each of us: Will we cooperate with our Adjusters? Will we consecrate our wills to doing the Father's will? The choice is ours, but the potential outcome, eternal life and Paradise citizenship, makes it the most important decision we will ever make.

Chapter 14: The Destiny of Personalized Thought Adjusters

Introduction

In our continuing exploration of Paper 109, "Relation of Adjusters to Universe Creatures," we now arrive at one of the most profound revelations concerning the divine fragments that indwell human consciousness: the nature and destiny of personalized Thought Adjusters. These extraordinary beings represent a unique category of universe personality, entities who have transcended their original mission as indwelling monitors to become independent agents of the Universal Father's will throughout the grand universe.

This chapter examines the remarkable transformation that occurs when a Thought Adjuster is released from mortal service and granted personality by the Universal Father himself. We will explore the supreme example of this phenomenon through the personalized Adjuster of Jesus of Nazareth, whose cosmic service extends from the time of Abraham through the present administration of Urantia and beyond. Understanding these personalized Adjusters illuminates not only the potential destiny of our own indwelling monitors but also reveals the intricate mechanisms by which divine experience is preserved, transmitted, and utilized throughout the universes of time and space.

The concept of personalized Adjusters challenges our conventional understanding of personality, experience, and eternal survival. These beings exist at the intersection of the prepersonal, personal, and Superpersonal, embodying past, present, and future in ways that transcend our finite comprehension. As we shall discover, they serve as the executive administrators for the Architects of the Master Universe, functioning as the personal agents of the Universal Father's ministry across all levels of cosmic reality.

The Heritage of Michael's Personalized Adjuster - A Legacy Spanning Millennia

The activities of Thought Adjusters within our local universe are directed by the personalized Adjuster of Michael of Nebadon, that very monitor who guided him step by step when he lived his human life in the flesh of Joshua ben Joseph. Faithful to his trust was this extraordinary Adjuster, and wisely did this valiant monitor direct the human nature of the Paradise Son, ever guiding his mortal mind in choosing the path of the Father's perfect will.

This particular Adjuster possessed a remarkable history even before his bestowal with Jesus. He had previously served with Machiventa Melchizedek in the days of Abraham, engaging in tremendous exploits both previous to that indwelling and between these bestowal experiences. This dual service, first with an emergency bestowal Son and then with a Creator Son living as a mortal, equipped this monitor with unparalleled experiential credentials.

The significance of this heritage cannot be overstated. For a Thought Adjuster to be selected for service with Machiventa Melchizedek during his emergency mission to Urantia suggests exceptional qualifications and prior experience. To then be chosen as the indwelling spirit for Michael's final bestowal represents the supreme honor and responsibility that could be bestowed upon any fragment of the Universal Father. Such selection indicates that this monitor had accumulated extensive experiential wisdom through previous indwellings, preparing him for service at the highest levels of universe administration.

The Triumph of Divine-Human Partnership

This Adjuster did indeed triumph in Jesus' human mind, that mind which, in each of life's recurring situations, maintained a consecrated dedication to the Father's will, saying, "Not my will but yours be done." Such decisive consecration constitutes the true passport from the limitations of human nature to the finality of divine attainment.

Here we encounter one of the most crucial revelations in all spiritual teaching: the pathway to divine achievement lies not in supernatural intervention but in the human will's voluntary alignment with the Father's will. Jesus demonstrated this principle throughout his earthly life, establishing a pattern that every mortal can follow. His dedication was not passive acceptance but active consecration, a continuous, conscious choice to subordinate his human desires to divine purpose.

The term "passport" is particularly significant. Just as a passport grants access to foreign territories otherwise closed to travelers, the consecration of one's will to the Father's will opens dimensions of spiritual experience and divine attainment that remain forever inaccessible to the self-centered personality. This is not a loss of freedom but rather the discovery of true liberty, the liberation that comes from partnership with Deity.

The Nature of Preserved Experience

This same Adjuster now reflects in the inscrutable nature of his mighty personality the pre-baptismal humanity of Joshua ben Joseph, the eternal and living transcript of the eternal and living values which the greatest of all Urantians created out of the humble circumstances of a commonplace life, as it was lived to the complete exhaustion of the spiritual values attainable in mortal experience.

This passage reveals a profound truth about the preservation of experience. The personalized Adjuster of Jesus retains within his being the complete experiential record of Jesus' human life, not merely as archived information but as living reality integrated into his very nature. Every decision Jesus made, every spiritual value he actualized, every human challenge he faced and overcame, all of this constitutes the eternal character of this personalized monitor.

The phrase "complete exhaustion of the spiritual values attainable in mortal experience" deserves careful consideration. Jesus did not merely sample or partially explore human existence; he lived it fully, extracting every possible spiritual lesson and value from the mortal condition. This completeness of experience makes his personalized Adjuster uniquely qualified for universe service, as he embodies the perfected integration of human and divine perspectives.

It is crucial to understand that while this Adjuster possesses all the memories and experiential patterns of Jesus' human life, he did not appropriate Jesus' personality itself. Personality is sacred, inviolate, and unique. Michael of Nebadon's personality remained his own; it was not absorbed by his Adjuster. Instead, upon personalization, the Universal Father bestowed upon this monitor a new and unique personality, one that nevertheless carries the complete experiential transcript of Jesus' life.

The Mechanism of Value Preservation - The Eternal Repository

Everything of permanent value which is entrusted to an Adjuster is assured eternal survival. In certain instances, the monitor holds these possessions for bestowal upon a mortal mind of future indwelling. In others, upon personalization, these survived and conserved realities are held in trust for future utilization in the service of the Architects of the Master Universe.

This statement addresses one of the most profound questions in human experience: What happens to the spiritual gains of a lifetime when a mortal fails to survive? The answer provides both cosmic justice and economic efficiency. Nothing of genuine spiritual value is ever lost. The Thought Adjuster, as a fragment of the infinite God, cannot lose or waste any authentic spiritual achievement.

When a Thought Adjuster indwells successive mortals (before achieving personalization), the spiritual treasures accumulated with the first mortal become part of the endowment of the second. Thus, a person whose Adjuster has had previous assignments begins with a spiritual heritage, subtle inclinations toward goodness, truth, and beauty that seem innate but are actually the preserved achievements of previous mortals who worked in partnership with this same divine monitor.

Upon personalization, these accumulated values take on a different role. They are no longer held for potential bestowal upon individual mortals but become resources for cosmic administration, tools for the Architects of the Master Universe in their vast work of planning and creating the universes of outer space. In this way, every genuine spiritual achievement of every mortal, whether that mortal survives or not, contributes to the eternal unfolding of the Father's universal plan.

The Preservation Trinity

Although not explicitly detailed in this section of Paper 109, the revelators elsewhere inform us that human experience is preserved in triplicate: by the Thought Adjuster, by the guardian seraphim, and by at least one archangel. This threefold safeguard ensures that the precious values of human experience survive not only the death of the physical body but any possible failure in the preservation system itself.

This redundancy reflects the immense value the Universe places on mortal experience. The struggles, choices, and spiritual achievements of finite creatures living in time and space are so precious to the Universal Father that multiple independent systems are employed to guarantee their preservation. When a mortal awakens on the mansion worlds, all three repositories contribute to the reconstruction of that individual's identity, personality patterns, and experiential memory.

The Nature of Personalized Adjusters - The Question of Personalizability

We cannot state whether or not non-Adjuster Father fragments are personalizable, but we have been informed that personality is the sovereign free-will bestowal of the Universal Father. As far as we know, the Adjuster type of Father fragment attains personality only by the acquirement of personal attributes through service ministry to a personal being. These personalized Adjusters are at home on Divinington, where they instruct and direct their prepersonal associates.

The revelators' candid admission of the limits of their knowledge is instructive. Even celestial beings of high order do not possess complete information about all the Father's plans and potentials. The personalization of Father fragments may be limited to Thought Adjusters, or it may extend to other types of divine fragments; the revelators simply do not know.

What they do affirm is that personality originates solely in the Universal Father. No other being, however exalted, can create or bestow personality. The Infinite Spirit bestows personality upon the angelic orders, but this power is itself a gift from the Father. Similarly, when a Thought Adjuster becomes personalized, it is the Universal Father himself who grants this unprecedented gift.

The requirement that Adjusters gain "personal attributes through service ministry to a personal being" before they can be personalized is significant. It suggests that God values experiential learning even for his own fragments. The Adjuster must encounter personality, work with personality, struggle alongside a personal being to achieve spiritual goals, only through this intimate service does the monitor acquire the qualities necessary for personalization.

Divinington, the home of personalized Adjusters, is aptly named, it is the divine sphere, the central abode of Father fragments. Here, personalized Adjusters serve as instructors and directors for their prepersonal colleagues, sharing the experiential wisdom they have gained through mortal ministry. In this way, the experience accumulated through service in time and space returns to eternity, enriching the preparations of Adjusters who will subsequently enter mortal service.

The Categories of Personalization

Personalized Adjusters fall into distinct categories based on the circumstances of their personalization. The first category consists of those Adjusters whose mortal partners chose not to survive. Despite the Adjuster's faithful ministry and the accumulation of spiritual values, the human will ultimately rejected eternal life. In such cases, the Father may choose to personalize the Adjuster, preserving all the hard-won spiritual achievements and freeing this experienced monitor for other forms of universe service.

The second category includes Adjusters who have been released from duty for special purposes. The supreme example is Jesus' Adjuster, who was released upon the completion of Michael's mortal bestowal. Having faithfully guided the Creator Son through his human life, this monitor was personalized and assigned to direct all Adjuster activities on Urantia, a position of tremendous responsibility reflecting his unique qualifications.

A third category, mentioned elsewhere in the Urantia Papers, consists of Adjusters whose mortal partners have achieved fusion but who are subsequently released for higher service. This typically occurs when a fusion-perfected mortal reaches such advanced stages of spiritual development that their Adjuster can be personalized without disrupting their continued existence. Such cases are rare but demonstrate the flexibility of divine administration in utilizing experienced monitors for cosmic purposes.

The Characteristics of Omnipersonality

Personalized Adjusters are described as "omnipersonal beings", a term requiring careful explanation. They are prepersonal in the sense that they existed as Father fragments before personality was ever bestowed upon any creature. They participated in the divine nature before the concept of personality emerged in the finite universes. In this sense, they transcend personality, carrying within themselves the potential for personal expression but not being limited by it.

They are personal in that they now possess, through the Father's gift, actual personality, they are recognizable individuals with unique identities, capable of relationships, choices, and personal growth. Unlike their prepersonal Adjuster brethren, personalized Adjusters can be known, addressed, and related to as distinct persons.

They are post personal or Superpersonal in that their personality transcends the limitations of typical personal beings. They minister the personality of the Universal Father "as in the eternal past, the eternal present, and the eternal future." Their consciousness spans temporal dimensions that finite personalities cannot grasp. They comprehend time as God comprehends it, as an eternal now containing all past and all future.

This omnipersonal nature makes them uniquely suited for service at the interface between time and eternity, between the finite and the infinite, between creature experience and Creator purposes. They are, in a very real sense, living bridges connecting the temporal and the eternal.

The Ministry of Personalized Adjusters - Administrators of Cosmic Purpose

Personalized Adjusters are the untrammeled and sovereign stabilizers and compensators of the far-flung universe of universes. They combine the Creator and creature experience, existential and experiential. They are conjoint time and eternity beings. They associate the prepersonal and the personal in universe administration.

This passage reveals the cosmic significance of personalized Adjusters. They are "untrammeled", not subject to the restrictions that govern prepersonal Adjusters, who cannot directly communicate with their mortal subjects or override human will. As sovereign beings, personalized Adjusters possess authority to act independently in service to the Father's plans.

Their role as "stabilizers and compensators" suggests they function as universal troubleshooters, beings who can be dispatched to address imbalances, correct deviations, or facilitate adjustments in the vast administrative machinery of creation. When circumstances require unique solutions that combine divine perspective with creature experience, personalized Adjusters are ideally equipped to provide such ministry.

The combination they represent, Creator and creature, existential and experiential, prepersonal and personal, time and eternity, makes them invaluable in an evolving universe where the perfect plans of eternity must be worked out through the imperfect circumstances of time. They understand both divine intention and mortal limitation, both eternal purpose and temporal process.

Executives of the Architects

Personalized Adjusters are the all-wise and powerful executives of the Architects of the Master Universe. They are the personal agents of the full ministry of the Universal Father, personal, prepersonal, and Superpersonal. They are the personal ministers of the extraordinary, the unusual, and the unexpected throughout all the realms of the transcendental absonite spheres of the domain of God the Ultimate, even to the levels of God the Absolute.

The Architects of the Master Universe represent one of the most mysterious orders of beings mentioned in the Urantia Papers. They are eventuated beings, neither created nor procreated, who exist to plan and organize the physical universes of outer space. These vast realms beyond the seven superuniverses will eventually house trillions upon trillions of inhabited worlds, all requiring administrative frameworks, spiritual guidance, and coordinated development.

Personalized Adjusters serve as the executives, the implementing authorities, for these Architects. While the Architects conceive the plans, personalized Adjusters help execute them, carrying the Father's personal ministry into these realms of ultimate and absolute reality. This is ministry far beyond the finite level of time-space existence, extending into absonite domains where time and space are transcended.

The description of personalized Adjusters as "personal ministers of the extraordinary, the unusual, and the unexpected" is particularly intriguing. It suggests they specialize in handling situations that fall outside normal administrative channels, circumstances requiring personal attention, creative solutions, and the unique wisdom that comes from combining divine nature with creature experience.

The Reserved Bestowal Type

Existential personality on the order of the Infinite and Absolute, the Father bestowed upon the Eternal Son, but he chose to reserve for his own ministry the experiential personality of the type of the personalized Adjuster bestowed upon the existential prepersonal Adjuster. They are thus both destined to the future eternal super-personality of the transcendental ministry of the absonite realms of the Ultimate, the Supreme-Ultimate, even to the levels of the Ultimate-Absolute.

This complex passage reveals a profound aspect of divine administration. The Universal Father bestowed existential personality, eternal, perfect, and complete from the beginning, upon the Eternal Son. But he reserved a different type of personality for his own exclusive use: experiential personality gained through time-space service.

This experiential personality bestowed upon personalized Adjusters is not perfect from the beginning; it grows, develops, and expands through ministry and service. It combines the Father's infinite nature with hard-won creature experience, creating a unique type of personal being equipped for service in the emerging domains of Supreme, Ultimate, and Absolute Deity.

The implication is staggering that personalized Adjusters are destined for eternal ministry at the very highest levels of cosmic reality. As the Supreme Being completes himself through the evolutionary experiences of time and space, as God the Ultimate emerges through the transcendental administration of outer space, and as God the Absolute begins his unfathomable actualization, personalized Adjusters will serve as personal agents of the Universal Father's ministry at these incomprehensible levels of Deity expression.

Personalized Adjusters in Universe Service - Rare Appearances and High Counsel

Seldom are personalized Adjusters seen at large in the universes. Occasionally they consult with the Ancients of Days, and sometimes the personalized Adjusters of the sevenfold Creator Sons come to the headquarters worlds of the constellations to confer with the Vorondadek rulers.

The rarity of personalized Adjuster appearances emphasizes their elevated status and specialized functions. They do not serve in routine administrative capacities but are reserved for consultations at the highest levels of universe government. When they do appear, it is typically to confer with beings of superior authority and wisdom, the Ancients of Days who rule the superuniverses, or the Vorondadek Sons who administer the constellations.

The personalized Adjusters of Creator Sons, monitors like Jesus' Adjuster who served during incarnation bestowals, possess unique qualifications for such consultations. They carry within their experiential nature the complete record of a Creator Son's life as a mortal creature. This perspective is invaluable when superuniverse or constellation administrators face questions or situations requiring insight into the fusion of Creator and creature perspectives.

Emergency Service on Urantia

When the planetary Vorondadek observer of Urantia, the Most High custodian who not long since assumed an emergency regency of your world, asserted his authority in the presence of the resident governor general, he began his emergency administration of Urantia with a full staff of his own choosing. He immediately assigned to all his associates and assistants their planetary duties. But he did not choose the three personalized Adjusters who appeared in his presence the instant he assumed the regency. He did not even know they would thus appear, for they did not so manifest their divine presence at the time of a previous regency. And the Most High regent did not assign service or designate duties for these volunteer personalized Adjusters.

This remarkable account illuminates the spontaneous nature of personalized Adjuster ministry. During the crisis precipitated by the Lucifer Rebellion, when a Most High of Edentia assumed emergency control of Urantia, three personalized Adjusters volunteered their services without being summoned or assigned. They simply appeared, offering their assistance in managing the planetary emergency.

The regent's response reveals appropriate spiritual wisdom. He did not presume to assign duties to these exalted beings or dictate their service. They represented the Universal Father's direct personal interest in Urantia's crisis, and the regent wisely allowed them to function according to their own wisdom and the Father's direction. To have attempted to command or direct personalized Adjusters would have been presumptuous, equivalent to trying to tell God how to manage his own personal ministry.

Nevertheless, these three omnipersonal beings were among the most active of the numerous orders of celestial beings then serving on Urantia. Though we are given no details of their specific activities, their presence during this critical period demonstrates the Father's intimate concern for the welfare of his mortal children, even on a quarantined and rebellious world.

The Breadth of Ministry

Personalized Adjusters perform a wide range of services for numerous orders of universe personalities, but we are not permitted to discuss these ministries with Adjuster-indwelt evolutionary creatures. These extraordinary human divinities are among the most remarkable personalities of the entire grand universe, and no one dares to predict what their future missions may be.

The revelators' reticence about detailing the specific ministries of personalized Adjusters reflects appropriate spiritual discretion. We mortals carry within us prepersonal fragments of the Father, Adjusters who may one day themselves be personalized. To provide extensive information about personalized Adjuster activities might influence our relationship with our own indwelling monitors in inappropriate ways or create expectations that would complicate the Adjuster's delicate work within human consciousness.

The description of personalized Adjusters as "extraordinary human divinities" is provocative. In what sense are they "human"? They have never been human beings. Yet they carry within their experiential nature the complete transcript of human experience, the struggles, choices, failures, and victories of mortal existence. They know humanity from within, having shared the interior life of human consciousness. This intimate experiential knowledge, combined with their divine nature, creates a unique synthesis: beings who are simultaneously divine and intimately acquainted with humanity.

The concluding statement, that no one dares predict their future missions, acknowledges the vast potential inherent in these beings. They stand at the frontier of Deity expression, equipped for service in realms of reality that do not yet exist, at levels of cosmic function that have not yet emerged. Their ultimate destiny remains veiled in the inscrutable plans of the Universal Father.

The Implications for Mortal Destiny - The True Passport to Divinity

The revelation concerning Jesus' decisive consecration to the Father's will, "Not my will but yours be done", provides the key insight of this entire chapter. This voluntary substitution of the human will for the divine will constitutes "the true passport from the limitations of human nature to the finality of divine attainment."

This is not metaphorical language or pious sentiment; it is cosmic fact. The human will, freely choosing alignment with divine will, activates spiritual forces and opens experiential dimensions that would otherwise remain forever closed. This choice does not diminish human freedom but rather expands it infinitely. The person who says "Thy will be done" exchanges the narrow limitations of finite selfhood for the boundless possibilities of partnership with Deity.

Many mortals misunderstand this principle, fearing that surrender to God's will means loss of individuality or suppression of personality. The opposite is true. When the human will aligns with the Father's will, the personality is liberated to become authentically itself, not the distorted self-created by fear, pride, and temporal illusions, but the true self that the Father eternally envisions. This is not annihilation but actualization, not suppression but supreme expression.

The Preservation of Individual Achievement

The teachings about value preservation assure us that nothing of genuine spiritual worth is ever lost. Every authentic spiritual decision, every victory over selfishness, every gesture of love, every insight into truth, all these achievements are eternally preserved in the Thought Adjuster's keeping. Even if a mortal chooses ultimate self-extinction through persistent rejection of survival, the spiritual values that person created are not destroyed. They pass into the experiential endowment of the Supreme Being or are held in trust for future universe utilization.

This revelation should profoundly affect how we view spiritual growth. We are not merely developing ourselves for our own benefit; we are contributing to the experiential evolution of Deity. Every genuine spiritual achievement enriches not only our own soul but also the cosmic repository of experiential wisdom. We are, in a very real sense, collaborators with God in the evolution of the universe.

The Unique Path of Each Mortal

The discussion in this chapter about the uniqueness of individual experience carries important implications. Just as Jesus exhausted "the spiritual values attainable in mortal experience" through his particular life circumstances, so each mortal has a unique set of spiritual possibilities to actualize. We cannot and should not attempt to duplicate another person's spiritual journey. What we can and must do is fully explore the spiritual potentials inherent in our own particular life circumstances.

This means that comparison with others is spiritually counterproductive. The person living in poverty has different spiritual lessons to learn than the person living in wealth. The individual facing chronic illness encounters spiritual challenges distinct from those confronting the healthy. The artist's spiritual path differs from the scientist's. Each life situation, no matter how humble or exalted by human standards, contains the full possibility of spiritual perfection within that context.

The goal is not to be like Jesus in the sense of duplicating his specific life choices, but to be like Jesus in the sense of completely actualizing the spiritual values available in one's own unique circumstances. This is what is meant by living "to the complete exhaustion of the spiritual values attainable in mortal experience", not exhausting ourselves, but exhausting the possibilities for spiritual growth inherent in our particular life situation.

Conclusion: The Eternal Significance of Temporal Choices

The revelation of personalized Thought Adjusters illuminates the cosmic significance of mortal existence in ways that should transform our understanding of daily life. We are not merely struggling through a brief material existence before entering "real" spiritual life. We are, right now, engaged in the creation of values of eternal significance, values so precious that the Universal Father assigns fragments of himself to preserve them, and establishes multiple redundant systems to guarantee their survival.

The personalized Adjusters who serve as executives of the Architects of the Master Universe, who consult with the Ancients of Days, who minister at levels of Ultimate and Absolute Deity, these beings carry within their natures the experiential transcripts of mortal lives. Human experience, gained in the humble circumstances of material existence on evolutionary planets, becomes an eternal resource for universe administration at the highest conceivable levels. This is the ultimate dignity of mortal existence: we are creating values that will enrich Deity itself throughout eternity.

The pathway to this magnificent destiny lies open before every human being who chooses to follow Jesus' example: "Not my will but yours be done." This decisive consecration is not a single dramatic moment but a continuous choice, renewed in each situation, throughout the course of mortal life. It is this sustained dedication that transforms human nature, actualizes divine potentials, and creates a soul worthy of eternal survival and infinite destiny.

As we prepare to explore further dimensions of Adjuster ministry and mortal-divine partnership in subsequent chapters, we carry with us the profound assurance that our struggles, choices, and spiritual victories are not ephemeral phenomena of temporal existence but eternal realities that will echo throughout the ages of ages in ways we cannot yet imagine. The God who indwells us values our experience supremely, so much so that he preserves it, transmits it, and utilizes it in the administration of universes yet unborn.

In the next chapter, we will examine the practical implications of Adjuster indwelling for daily living, exploring how mortals can cooperate more effectively with their divine monitors and accelerate their spiritual growth. We will investigate the specific conditions that enhance or inhibit Adjuster function and discover the techniques by which humans can become increasingly conscious of divine guidance in their lives.

This chapter is based on Paper 109, Section 6 and Section 7 of The Urantia Book, as taught by myself, Dr. Roger Paul, in my continuing series on Thought Adjusters and human destiny on You Tube.

Chapter 15: The Relation of Adjusters to Individual Mortals

Introduction

The relationship between the Thought Adjuster and the individual mortal represents the most intimate and profound connection in all of creation. This divine partnership, established by the Universal Father himself, transcends all other spiritual relationships and forms the foundation upon which our eternal survival depends. In this chapter, we explore Paper 110 of *The Urantia Book*, which illuminates the nature of this sacred relationship and provides practical guidance for understanding how these divine monitors work within the human mind.

The journey we undertake in this life is but the vestibule of our eternal existence, a beginning point where fundamental decisions shape the trajectory of our cosmic career. Understanding the role of the Thought Adjuster in this journey is essential for anyone seeking spiritual growth and eventual fusion with the divine fragment that indwells their mind.

The Divine Cost of Free Will

The Urantia Book opens Paper 110 with a profound statement: "The endowment of imperfect beings with freedom entails inevitable tragedy, and it is the nature of the perfect ancestral Deity to universally and affectionately share these sufferings in loving companionship."

This declaration establishes a fundamental truth about the nature of free will and divine love. When the Universal Father granted us the freedom to choose our own path, he accepted the reality that imperfect beings would sometimes make unwise decisions, resulting in suffering and tragedy. Rather than withholding this gift of free will to prevent our suffering, God chose to experience that suffering alongside us through the indwelling presence of the Thought Adjuster.

This is not the detached observation of a distant deity, but the intimate companionship of a loving Father who shares every moment of our lives, both our triumphs and our tragedies. The Thought Adjuster does not merely observe our struggles; it participates in them, experiencing our pain, confusion, and growth as we navigate the complexities of mortal existence.

The Unique Nature of Divine Love

As conveyed through the celestial author of Paper 110: "As far as I am conversant with the affairs of a universe, I regard the love and devotion of a Thought Adjuster as the most truly divine affection in all creation. The love of the Sons in their ministry to the races is superb, but the devotion of an Adjuster to the individual is touchingly sublime, divinely father-like."

This extraordinary testimony from a celestial being reveals an important distinction in the hierarchy of divine love. While the Creator Sons, including Christ Michael of Nebadon, demonstrate superb love through their ministry to entire races and worlds, the Universal Father has reserved a unique form of personal contact for himself alone. No other being in the universe of universes experiences the same level of intimate, personal connection with individual creatures as does the Universal Father through the Thought Adjuster.

The Paradise Father has apparently reserved this form of personal contact with his individual creatures as an exclusive Creator prerogative. This father-like love differs from all other forms of divine affection because it operates at the most personal level imaginable. within the very mind of the individual. The Thought Adjuster knows our every thought, experiences our every emotion, and participates in our every decision at a level of intimacy that no other being can replicate.

The Distinction Between Father and Mother Influences

Understanding the difference between the Father's indwelling presence and the Mother Spirit's external influence enriches our comprehension of spiritual ministry. The Universal Father, through the Thought Adjuster, provides an internal influence that becomes part of our very being. The local universe Mother Spirit, conversely, provides external influences through the Holy Spirit and the seven-adjutant mind-spirits.

The Father's love can be characterized as a creative, personal, father-like love that deals with each individual uniquely and intimately. The Mother Spirit's love manifests as a nurturing, unifying influence that concerns itself with relationships, community, and the harmonious functioning of the whole. While the Father focuses on the individual's personal spiritual growth and survival, the Mother Spirit ensures that individuals can relate to one another and function as part of a greater spiritual family.

Both forms of divine love are essential to our spiritual development. The Father cultivates our individual potential and personality uniqueness, while the Mother Spirit helps us learn to cooperate, relate, and contribute to the collective good. These complementary influences work together to produce balanced, spiritually mature individuals capable of both personal achievement and social contribution.

It is worth noting that to the Universal Father and the Thought Adjusters, the distinction between male and female makes no ultimate difference in terms of spiritual value or potential. Adjusters volunteer for service without regard to the gender of their subjects. However, the male and female influences that begin with the Eternal Son and Infinite Spirit and continue through the Creator Sons and local universe Mother Spirits, create complementary approaches to spiritual ministry that mirror the cosmic balance of universe reality.

The Mind as the Dwelling Place of God - Beyond the Physical Brain

A critical distinction must be made regarding where the Thought Adjuster actually resides. The revelators make clear that "Adjusters should not be thought of as living in the material brains of human beings; they are not organic parts of the physical creatures of the realms. The Thought Adjuster may more properly be envisaged as indwelling the mortal mind of man rather than as existing within the confines of a single physical organ."

This distinction is essential for understanding how the Thought Adjuster functions and why it can continue to preserve our identity even when the physical brain suffers damage. The Thought Adjuster indwells the *mind*, that superimposition of the local universe Mother Spirit's mind circuit upon the human organism, rather than residing in the physical tissue of the brain itself.

The mind is a functional reality that transcends mere neural activity. It represents the arena where consciousness operates, where decisions are made, and where personality expresses itself. The Thought Adjuster operates within this mental arena, specifically at the superconscious level, where it can influence our highest aspirations, noblest impulses, and most spiritually significant decisions.

Communication Through the Superconscious

The revelators tell us that "indirectly and unrecognized, the Adjuster is constantly communicating with the human subject, especially during those sublime experiences of the worshipful contact of mind with spirit in the superconscious."

This explains why we rarely experience direct, conscious communication with our Thought Adjuster in the way we might hear another person speak to us. The Adjuster's primary mode of operation is through the superconscious mind, that level of mental function that lies above ordinary conscious awareness. During moments of worship, deep meditation, sincere prayer, and profound spiritual reflection, the barriers between the conscious and superconscious mind become more permeable, allowing greater influence from the Adjuster to reach our awareness.

This is why the common religious experience of feeling that "God told me" to buy a certain house, marry a certain person, or make some other mundane decision often reflects misunderstanding rather than genuine divine communication. The Thought Adjuster's mission is not to make our daily decisions for us, that would violate our free will and rob us of the very experiences we need for spiritual growth. Rather, the Adjuster works to give spiritual significance to whatever decisions we make, transforming ordinary experiences into opportunities for soul growth.

When the Mind is Damaged

Understanding that the Thought Adjuster indwells the mind rather than the physical brain helps us comprehend what happens when severe brain damage or mental illness occurs. If a person becomes completely insane or suffers brain damage so severe that meaningful mental function ceases, the Thought Adjuster is released from its assignment. The Adjuster departs, taking with it the individual's personality, identity records, and all soul values that have been accumulated to that point, and transports these to the mansion worlds to await the individual's natural death and subsequent resurrection.

This does not mean the person has lost their chance at eternal survival. The guardian angels remain with the physical body until natural death occurs, recording any experiences that might have residual value. When the person is resurrected on the mansion worlds, they possess all the soul growth and spiritual achievement they had accumulated up to the point of mental incapacitation.

For children who suffer severe brain damage or other conditions that prevent normal mental development, the same principle applies. A child who sustains catastrophic brain injury at age two will be resurrected on the mansion worlds with whatever soul development occurred during those two years. The experiences after the injury, while recorded by the guardian angels, will not have the same direct, conscious quality as normal human experience. These memories will be more dreamlike in nature when reviewed during the resurrection process, but they are not lost.

The Spiritual Work of the Thought Adjuster - The True Mission

The revelators provide us with an extraordinary description of the Thought Adjuster's work: "I wish it were possible for me to help evolving mortals to achieve a better understanding and attain a fuller appreciation of the unselfish and superb work of the Adjusters living within them, who are so devoutly faithful to the task of fostering man's spiritual welfare."

These divine monitors serve as:

- **Efficient ministers** to the higher phases of human minds
- **Wise and experienced manipulators** of spiritual potential
- **Devoted guides** dedicated to guiding us inward and upward to celestial havens of happiness
- **Tireless toilers** consecrated to the future personification of the triumph of divine truth
- **Watchful workers** who pilot the God-conscious human mind away from the shoals of evil
- **Loving leaders** providing safe and sure guidance through uncertain mazes
- **Patient teachers** constantly urging their subjects forward on paths of progressive perfection
- **Careful custodians** of the sublime values of creature character

This comprehensive description reveals the multifaceted nature of the Adjuster's ministry. The Adjusters are not passive observers or occasional advisors; they are actively and constantly engaged in the work of spiritual transformation, working tirelessly to help us achieve our highest potential.

The revelators express a poignant wish: "I wish you could love them more, cooperate with them more fully, and cherish them more affectionately." This appeal speaks to the reality that many mortals live their entire lives largely unaware of the divine presence within them, missing opportunities for deeper cooperation and more rapid spiritual growth.

Spiritual Significance in Daily Life

A crucial understanding emerges regarding what the Thought Adjuster is and is not concerned with in our daily lives. The Adjusters are "chiefly concerned with your spiritual preparation for the next stage of the never-ending existence," yet they are "also deeply interested in your temporal welfare and in your real achievements on Earth. They are delighted to contribute to your health, happiness, and true prosperity."

However, the Adjusters are "not indifferent to your success in all matters of planetary advancement which are not inimical to your future life of eternal progress." This means the Adjusters care about our temporal welfare insofar as it affects our spiritual development, but they do not concern themselves with decisions that have no spiritual significance.

The Adjuster's primary focus is on transforming every experience, whether mundane or extraordinary, into an opportunity for spiritual growth. A conversation with a friend, a challenge at work, even a frustrating encounter in traffic can all become spiritually significant if approached with the right attitude. The Adjuster works constantly to help us extract spiritual meaning and soul value from every circumstance we encounter.

This means that every relationship we form, every interaction we have with another human being, carries potential spiritual significance. Our relationships are not mere temporal arrangements that disappear when this life ends; they are potential eternal associations that continue to enrich us throughout our ascending career. The way we treat others, the attitudes we adopt in our interactions, the love and service we render, all of these experiences contribute to our developing souls and have eternal ramifications.

The Importance of Temporal Welfare

While the Adjusters focus primarily on spiritual concerns, they are keenly interested in certain aspects of our temporal welfare. They work to promote our health, happiness, and prosperity, not for materialistic reasons, but because these conditions facilitate spiritual growth. A person overwhelmed by financial stress, suffering from poor health, or trapped in constant unhappiness faces significant obstacles to spiritual development.

The body serves as the "earthly tabernacle of this marvelous gift from God," and how we treat this temple matters. The revelators warn: "How unkind knowingly to defile or otherwise deliberately to pollute the physical body, which must serve as the earthly tabernacle of this marvelous gift from God. All physical poisons greatly retard the efforts of the Adjuster to exalt the material mind."

This is not a call to obsessive perfectionism about our bodies, but rather an appeal to common sense and reasonable stewardship. Excessive alcohol consumption, drug abuse, and other forms of bodily mistreatment create barriers between our conscious minds and the Adjuster's influence. While moderate enjoyment of life's pleasures is not spiritually harmful, deliberate and persistent abuse of our bodies shows disrespect for the divine presence within us.

Mental Poisons

Even more insidious than physical poisons are the mental poisons that interfere with spiritual progress: "The mental poisons of fear, anger, envy, jealousy, suspicion, and intolerance likewise tremendously interfere with the spiritual progress of the evolving soul."

These attitudes poison the mind more effectively than any chemical substance could poison the body. They create barriers between the conscious and superconscious mind, making it nearly impossible for the Adjuster's influence to penetrate into our awareness and decision-making.

Prejudice deserves special mention as one of the most spiritually destructive attitudes we can harbor. Prejudice, whether based on race, gender, nationality, religion, or any other superficial characteristic, directly contradicts the spiritual reality that all humans are children of the same universal Father and are equally loved by him. When we view others through the lens of prejudice, we see a distorted reality that prevents genuine spiritual connection and growth.

The modern world faces ongoing challenges with prejudice, sometimes manifested in overt discrimination and sometimes in more subtle forms. The solution is not to obsess over our imperfections or to engage in self-flagellation over past mistakes, but rather to recognize that we are all growing and improving. The human race has made tremendous progress in overcoming prejudice over the past centuries, and this progress continues. We should acknowledge this growth while remaining vigilant against falling back into old patterns.

The Courtship Period and Divine Predestination - A Divine Romance

Paper 110 presents our mortal life as a courtship between the human and the divine: "Today you are passing through the period of the courtship of your Adjuster, and if you only prove faithful to the trust reposed in you by the divine spirit who seeks your mind and soul in eternal union, there will eventually ensue that morontia oneness, that supernal harmony, that cosmic coordination, that divine attunement, that celestial fusion, that never-ending blending of identity, that oneness of being which is so perfect and final that even the most experienced personalities can never segregate or recognize as separate entities the fusion partners, mortal man and divine Adjuster."

This beautiful description portrays our relationship with the Thought Adjuster as a developing romance, a gradual process of growing trust, deepening cooperation, and increasing harmony that ultimately culminates in eternal fusion. Just as in human courtship, both partners must freely choose to pursue the relationship. The Adjuster has already made its choice by volunteering for this mission; we must make our choice through our decisions and spiritual dedication.

The fusion described here represents a union so complete that once accomplished, no being in all creation can separate or even distinguish the formerly separate identities of the human and the Adjuster. We become one new being, neither purely human nor purely divine, but a unique fusion of both that has never existed before and will never exist again.

The Divine Plan

When Thought Adjusters come to indwell human minds, "they bring with them the model careers, the ideal lives as determined and foreordained by themselves and the Personalized Adjusters of Divinington, which have been certified by the personalized Adjuster of Urantia." This statement reveals several crucial truths about predestination and free will.

First, every Thought Adjuster arrives with a carefully crafted plan for the intellectual and spiritual development of its human subject. This plan represents the ideal life, the path that would lead to maximum spiritual growth and soul development if perfectly followed.

Second, these plans have been certified by "the personalized Adjuster of Urantia." This refers to the Thought Adjuster that indwelt Jesus of Nazareth during his mortal life and became personalized following Jesus' resurrection. This Adjuster, having experienced mortal life with the Creator Son himself, now serves as a kind of supervisor or coordinator for all Adjusters serving on Urantia. Thus, every predestined plan that comes with a Thought Adjuster bears the stamp of approval from the very Adjuster that guided Jesus through his human life.

This means that when we align ourselves with the will of God and follow the leading of our Thought Adjuster, we are, in a very real sense, following in the footsteps of Jesus. We are walking a path that has been designed according to principles learned and demonstrated in the life of our Creator Son during his incarnation as a mortal.

Freedom to Accept or Reject

However, and this is crucial, "it is not incumbent upon any human being to accept this plan. You are all subjects of predestination, but it is not foreordained that you must accept this divine predestination. You are at full liberty to reject any part or all of the Thought Adjuster's program."

This paradox of predestination and free will resolves itself when we understand what it means. Yes, there is a divine plan, an ideal pathway that has been carefully prepared for us. But we are completely free to follow that plan or to reject it. We can accept parts of it while rejecting others. We can cooperate fully, partially, or not at all.

The Adjusters "are dedicated to the stupendous task of guiding you safely inward and upward to the celestial haven of happiness," but "under no circumstances do these divine monitors ever take advantage of you or in any way arbitrarily influence you in your choices and decisions. The Adjusters respect your sovereignty of personality; they are always subservient to your will."

This absolute respect for human free will represents one of the most profound truths in all the revelation. God could easily override our wills, force us to make correct decisions, and guarantee our survival and perfection. But such forced compliance would violate the very purpose of our existence, to become perfected beings who have freely chosen God's way through countless decisions made in the face of genuine alternatives.

Living in Partnership with the Divine, and Discovering Your Calling

Each person must discover their own unique calling, their particular role in the divine plan. No two predestined plans are identical because no two personalities are identical. The universe needs an infinite diversity of perfected beings, each with unique experiences, perspectives, and contributions to make.

Some are called to teach, others to heal, still others to administer, create, serve, or lead. Some are gifted with words, others with compassionate presence, and still others with practical wisdom. The key is to discover what *you* are uniquely suited to do and then to pursue that calling with dedication and faith.

This discovery process requires honest self-reflection, willingness to try different paths, and attention to the deep inner promptings that come from the superconscious mind. It also requires patience, as our true calling may not become clear immediately. Often, we must pass through several experiences and apparent false starts before we recognize the pattern of our unique mission.

No legitimate spiritual calling will ever involve manipulating others, demanding money in exchange for blessings, or claiming special divine authority over other people's lives. Beware of religious teachers who promise that financial contributions to their ministries will result in divine blessings proportional to the amounts given. God's blessings are not for sale, and anyone who suggests otherwise is either deceived or deceptive.

Practical Cooperation

Cooperating with the Thought Adjuster involves several practical dimensions:

Maintaining Mental and Physical Health: Since the Adjuster must work through our minds and bodies, maintaining these in reasonable condition facilitates the Adjuster's work. This includes getting adequate rest, nutrition, and exercise; avoiding excessive physical toxins; and cultivating mental attitudes that promote rather than hinder spiritual receptivity.

Cultivating Stillness: Creating regular times for quiet meditation, worship, and reflection provides opportunities for the Adjuster's superconscious influence to penetrate more deeply into conscious awareness. In the noise and hurry of modern life, these moments of stillness become increasingly important.

Making Value-Based Decisions: When facing decisions, we should consider not just what is expedient or profitable, but what is right, good, and spiritually significant. Every decision provides an opportunity to align our will with God's will, and the cumulative effect of these choices determines the trajectory of our spiritual growth.

Serving Others: The Adjusters are pleased when we engage in genuine service to our fellow human beings. Such service not only helps others but also develops within us the qualities of character that have eternal value, compassion, patience, generosity, and love.

Seeking Truth: The Adjusters work to expand our understanding of reality, helping us move from superstition and error toward truth and wisdom. A genuine commitment to truth-seeking, wherever it may lead, facilitates the Adjuster's teaching mission.

Practicing Forgiveness: Holding grudges, nursing resentments, and refusing to forgive create barriers between ourselves and our Adjusters. These attitudes poison the mind and prevent spiritual progress. Learning to forgive, both others and ourselves, removes major obstacles to spiritual growth.

The Vestibule of Eternal Life, This Life as Beginning

The revelators repeatedly emphasize that this mortal life represents only the beginning of our eternal journey, the vestibule of our true existence. A vestibule is that first small space you enter when stepping into a building, where you pause to orient yourself before proceeding into the main structure.

In this vestibule of mortal existence, we make the fundamental decisions that will shape the entire trajectory of our eternal career. Do we choose to recognize God as our Father? Do we choose to treat our fellow human beings as brothers and sisters? Do we choose to seek truth, beauty, and goodness? Do we choose to value spiritual growth over material accumulation?

These basic orientation decisions, made in the vestibule, determine which doors open before us as we proceed into the mansion worlds and beyond. They establish the foundation upon which all subsequent growth builds.

Building the Morontia Soul

The primary purpose of this life is to build a morontia soul, that reality which is neither purely material nor purely spiritual but represents a unique blending of both. This soul is the joint creation of the human mind, the Thought Adjuster, and the personality working together.

The soul begins its existence at the moment of the Thought Adjuster's arrival, typically around the age of five or six when the child makes its first moral decision. From that point forward, every decision of spiritual significance, every experience that has survival value, every noble impulse and loving action contributes to the soul's growth and development.

When we die, this soul, along with the personality and a transcript of our identity held by the Thought Adjuster, is all that survives the dissolution of the physical body. On the mansion worlds, a new morontia body is constructed and connected to the soul, and we awaken as morontia beings ready to continue our ascension journey.

The quality and development of the soul we build in this life determines, to a large extent, where we begin our mansion world experience. Those who have cooperated extensively with their Adjusters and built well-developed souls may awaken on higher mansion worlds, bypassing some of the remedial training that others require.

Your Real Life Begins

As paradoxical as it may seem, "your real life starts when you die", or more accurately, when you awaken on the first mansion world in your morontia form. This life is preparation; that life is the reality for which we are preparing. This life is the rehearsal; that life is the performance. This life is the seed-planting; that life is the harvest.

This does not mean our current life is unimportant or merely illusory. Rather, it means that what we are really building here, the soul, the character, the spiritual values, will find its full expression and fruition only when we transition to the next stage of existence. The relationships we form, the truths we learn, the character we develop, the love we give and receive, all of these continue and expand in the morontia life and beyond.

Conclusion: The Divine Romance Continues

The relationship between the Thought Adjuster and the individual mortal stands as the most intimate and profound connection in all creation. This divine fragment of the Universal Father, residing within the superconscious mind, works tirelessly to guide, teach, protect, and transform us into beings capable of eternal existence and eventual Paradise perfection.

We live in the courtship period, the time when we are learning to know and trust this divine partner. Every decision we make, every experience we have, every relationship we form carries the potential for spiritual significance if we remain receptive to the Adjuster's influence. The mental and physical poisons we have discussed can interfere with this relationship, while attitudes of truth-seeking, service, forgiveness, and worship facilitate it.

The divine plan exists, a perfect pathway prepared for each of us by our Adjusters and certified by the personalized Adjuster of Christ Michael. Yet we remain completely free to accept or reject this plan. The Adjusters respect our sovereignty absolutely, never forcing or manipulating us, always waiting for our willing cooperation.

This life serves as the vestibule of eternity, a crucial beginning point where fundamental decisions establish the trajectory for all that follows. Here we build the morontia soul that will become our vehicle for ascending through the mansion worlds and beyond. Here we develop the character that will determine our ultimate destiny.

As we move forward to Chapter 16, we will examine more deeply how this relationship evolves through the various stages of mortal life, from childhood through maturity and even into the after-death experience. We will explore the dynamics of Adjuster guidance, the phenomenon of circles of achievement, and the ultimate goal of eternal fusion, that cosmic marriage that transforms both mortal and divine into something entirely new and eternally beautiful.

The divine romance has begun. The question before each of us is: How will we respond to this divine courtship? Will we prove faithful to the trust reposed in us? Will we cooperate fully with the loving leader seeking our soul in eternal union? The answer we give through the living of our lives will echo through eternity.

In the next chapter, we will explore the progressive stages of psychic circles and the evolving relationship between adjusters and their mortal subjects as spiritual growth advances.

Chapter 16: Adjusters and the Human Will - The Divine Partnership

Introduction: The Sacred Relationship Between Humanity and Divinity

Among all the revelations contained within The Urantia Book, few concepts are as profound, or as personally transformative, as the relationship between Thought Adjusters and human will. Paper 110, "Relation of Adjusters to Individual Mortals," with particular focus on Section Two, which addresses the delicate balance between divine guidance and human sovereignty.

At the heart of this teaching lies a remarkable truth: each human being is indwelt by a fragment of God the Father, yet this divine presence never violates our freedom of choice. We are subjects of predestination yet simultaneously possess absolute liberty to accept or reject the divine plan prepared for us. This apparent paradox reveals the elegant design of the universe, a design that honors both the perfection of God's foreknowledge and the sacred autonomy of human personality.

Understanding this relationship is essential for anyone seeking spiritual growth, for it illuminates the very mechanics of how we cooperate with divinity in our daily lives. The implications extend far beyond theological interest; they touch the practical reality of every decision we make, every moral choice we face, and every step we take toward our eternal destiny.

The Nature of Predestination and Free Will

The Urantia Book presents a sophisticated view of predestination that transcends the traditional religious debates that have divided theologians for centuries. According to the text, when Thought Adjusters indwell human minds, they bring with them "model careers" and "ideal lives" that have been predetermined and foreordained. These plans have been certified by the personalized Adjuster of Urantia, significantly, this is Michael's Adjuster from his bestowal as Jesus of Nazareth.

This detail carries profound implications for our world. On other planets throughout the universe, the certifying authority would be the Adjuster of whatever Son performed the bestowal mission there, typically a Magisterial Son or Trinity Teacher Son. But on Urantia, because our bestowal Son was none other than the Creator Son of our local universe, Michael of Nebadon, we have a unique spiritual advantage. When our world reaches the age of light and life, Michael's Adjuster will be released to serve as head of the finaliter corps for our entire local universe.

Yet despite this predetermined plan, the text is emphatic: "You are all subjects of predestination, but it is not foreordained that you must accept this divine predestination. You are at full liberty to reject any part or all of the Thought Adjuster's program."

This statement resolves the ancient tension between divine sovereignty and human freedom. Predestination exists, but it operates through, not against, human volition. The Adjuster's mission is "to effect such mind changes and make such spiritual adjustments as you may willingly and intellectually authorize." The crucial words are "willingly" and "intellectually authorize." Under no circumstances do these divine monitors take advantage of us or arbitrarily influence our choices and decisions.

The text emphasizes repeatedly: "The Adjusters respect your sovereignty of personality. They are always subservient to your will."

This means that while a divine destiny awaits each of us, we must choose to walk toward it. By making decisions aligned with God's will, we are actively effecting our predestination. The apparent contradiction dissolves when we understand that predestination is not fatalism; it is a prepared path that we must still choose to follow, step by conscious step.

The Three Dimensions of Reality

To fully grasp how Thought Adjusters function, we must understand the multidimensional nature of reality as presented in The Urantia Book. Rather than a "multiverse" of parallel universes, the text describes three dimensions superimposed upon one another: the physical, the morontia, and the spiritual.

The physical dimension operates at the molecular level. Everything in the finite universe, the seven superuniverses, exists as material reality composed of what we might call "100 molecules." (This is not the same as our known periodic table because our known periodic table incorporates combination molecules so it will always have more than just 100. This has been a confusion in study groups for years.) Paradise and Havona, by contrast, operate on a higher frequency of "1,000 molecules," representing a more refined physical reality.

Superimposed upon this physical dimension is the morontia dimension. This is the transitional reality we will experience when we awaken on the mansion worlds after death. Morontia substance is neither purely physical nor purely spiritual, but rather a bridge between the two. Remarkably, morontia reality exists even now on our world, for our evolving souls are morontia in nature. We are building morontia substance during our physical lives, though we cannot perceive it with our material senses.

Finally, there is the spiritual dimension, which we will enter upon leaving the local universe and beginning our journey through the superuniverse. This dimension is also superimposed upon both the physical and morontia realms.

The Thought Adjuster is pure spirit, a fragment of divinity itself. Although the Adjuster indwells our physical minds, it exists in the spiritual dimension and cannot leave until we die. This creates a fascinating dynamic: when we choose to do the will of God, we are superimposing spiritual reality upon physical existence. We are bringing divinity into the material realm through the medium of choice.

Our will, by contrast, is part of the mind circuit, a gift from the local Universe Mother Spirit, transmitted through the original Life Carriers who implanted life throughout the local universe. This mind circuit is physical in its operation, part of our evolutionary endowment. It is not inherently divine, despite its celestial origin, because it does not come directly from God the Father.

However, and this is crucial, when we attune our will to God the Father's will, our decisions become infused with divinity. Any action undertaken in alignment with God's will becomes, to that extent, a divine act. This is how we bring the spiritual dimension into tangible expression in our physical lives.

The Arrival and Purpose of the Thought Adjuster

One of the most frequently asked questions about Thought Adjusters concerns their arrival: Why do they not indwell us from birth?

The answer is both logical and profound. Thought Adjusters arrive at approximately five to six years of age, specifically, when a child makes their first moral decision. Prior to this point, the Adjuster would have nothing to do. Without the capacity for moral choice, there can be no cooperation between the human will and the divine will.

Before the Adjuster's arrival, children who die are assured of survival and resurrection on the mansion worlds. Their innocent souls are preserved by the guardian angels. But once the Thought Adjuster arrives, a new element enters: the individual now possesses the free will capacity to choose or reject eternal survival.

This is why the first moral choice is so significant. It represents the dawn of true personality sovereignty, the moment when a human being becomes capable of distinguishing right from wrong and choosing between them. From that point forward, the Adjuster begins its sacred work of spiritual transformation.

The Adjuster's purpose is not to control our thinking, but rather "to spiritualize it, to eternalize it." Neither angels nor Adjusters are devoted to directly influencing human thought. that is our exclusive personality prerogative. Instead, the Adjuster is dedicated to "improving, modifying, adjusting, and coordinating your thinking processes."

More specifically, Adjusters work to build up "spiritual counterparts of your careers, morontia transcripts of your true advancing selves, for survival purposes." Think of it this way: the Adjuster is creating a divine transcript of your life, a spiritualized version of your experiences, decisions, and growth. This transcript becomes the foundation of your morontia identity when you awaken after death.

The Two Minds and the Superconscious

One of the most important concepts for understanding Adjuster function is the recognition that we possess two minds, or more accurately, two levels of mind operation.

The text states explicitly: "There are therefore two realities which impinge upon and are centered in the human mind circuits: one, a mortal self evolved from the original plans of the Life Carriers; the other, an immortal entity from the high spheres of Divinington, an indwelling gift from God."

The mortal self, your conscious, everyday thinking mind, evolved through the Life Carriers' work and is plugged into the mind circuit of the local Universe Mother Spirit. You have been connected to this circuit from birth. This is your conscious and subconscious mind, the arena of your ordinary thoughts, feelings, and decisions.

The Adjuster, however, operates on the superconscious level. This is a realm of mind that most people are completely unaware of. The Adjuster works unceasingly in "the spheres of the higher levels of the human mind, seeking to produce morontia duplications of every concept of the mortal intellect."

This means you have two simultaneous mental processes occurring:

1. Your conscious, mortal thinking
2. The Adjuster's superconscious spiritual work

Ordinarily, these two levels do not communicate directly. The Adjuster's work proceeds without your awareness. Only rarely do you catch "an echo, a faint and distant echo, of the divine voice."

This explains why spiritual discernment is so challenging. When people believe they have received direct messages from God in dreams or visions, they are usually experiencing the interaction of their own conscious and subconscious minds, not actual communication from the Adjuster. Such experiences can be meaningful psychologically, but they should not be confused with genuine superconscious contact.

True communication with the Adjuster is subtle, indirect, and usually recognized only in retrospect. It manifests as a growing spiritual intuition, an increasing alignment with divine values, and a gradual transformation of character, not as dramatic voices or visions.

The Mechanics of Divine-Human Cooperation

How, then, do we cooperate with our Adjusters? How do we bridge the gap between the conscious mind and the superconscious?

The answer lies in a remarkable process of mind unification described in the text:

"You, as a personal creature, have mind and will. The Adjuster, as a prepersonal creature, has premind and prewill. If you so fully conform to the Adjuster's mind that you see eye to eye, then your minds become one, and you receive the reinforcement of the Adjuster's mind."

Notice the progression: conforming leads to unity, which leads to reinforcement.

The text continues: "Subsequently, if your will orders and enforces the execution of the decisions of this new or combined mind, the Adjuster's prepersonal will attains to personality expression through your decision, and as far as that particular project is concerned, you and the Adjuster are one."

This is the sacred alchemy of spiritual transformation. Let us break it down:

1. **You possess personality and will.** This gives you the power of choice and self-direction.
2. **The Adjuster is prepersonal and possesses prewill.** It has intentions and plans but no personality through which to express them in the finite realm.
3. **When you choose to do God's will, something extraordinary happens:** Your personality gives expression to the Adjuster's prewill, while the Adjuster's divinity infuses your decision.
4. **The result is a unified mind** that is simultaneously human and divine, personal and prepersonal, temporal and eternal.

The text makes this explicit: "Your mind has attained to divinity attunement, and the Adjuster's will has achieved personality expression."

This is not a theoretical abstraction. It has practical implications for every significant decision in your life. When you face a choice and consciously ask, "What would God have me do? What is the Father's will in this situation?", and then act on your best understanding, you are creating a moment of divine-human partnership.

In that moment:

- You give the Adjuster personality
- The Adjuster gives you divinity
- Your combined minds work together toward a divine outcome

If you make this choice habitually, it becomes your default mode of operation. Eventually, you can live your entire life in conscious cooperation with your Adjuster, with every decision infused with spiritual wisdom and divine alignment.

The Morontia Mind and Spiritual Identity

The ultimate result of successful Adjuster cooperation is the development of what the text calls the "morontia mind."

"Morontia mind is a term signifying the substance and sum total of the cooperating minds of diversely material and spiritual natures. Morontia intellect, therefore, connotes a dual mind in the local universe dominated by one will."

This dual mind consists of:

1. The human mind of material origin
2. The divine mind of spiritual origin

When these are "dominated by one will", the will to do God's will, they create morontia intellect, the very substance of your emerging soul.

Remarkably, this process can begin during your mortal life. You do not have to wait until death to develop morontia reality. Every time you choose spiritual values over material impulses, every time you act with divine motivation rather than purely selfish interest, you are building morontia substance. You are becoming what you will be on the mansion worlds.

This is what happened with Enoch and Elijah, the two mortals mentioned in scripture who "walked with God" and were taken directly to the next life without experiencing death. They had so fully developed their morontia identity during physical life that the transition to the next realm required no intermediate sleep of death.

The text describes this beautifully: "This is a will, human in origin, which is becoming divine through man's identification of the human mind with the mindedness of God."

Your human will becomes progressively divine as you align it with God's will. Your mortal mind becomes increasingly morontia as you cooperate with your Adjuster. This is the great transformation available to every person, he journey from purely mortal thinking to divinity-infused consciousness.

Practical Application: Discerning God's Will

A question that inevitably arises is: "How do I know what God's will is in a specific situation?"

This is one of the most challenging aspects of spiritual living. The answer is both simple and complex.

The simple answer is: With every decision of importance, ask yourself, "What would God want me to do?" Then act on your best understanding, trusting that your Adjuster will guide you super consciously.

The complex answer is: You often won't know with certainty that you're following God's will. The Adjuster works on the superconscious level, which means divine guidance is usually subtle, intuitive, and recognized only in retrospect.

Several principles can help:

First, understand that God's will is not concerned with trivial matters. The Father does not care whether you buy a house or rent an apartment, whether you drive a Corvette or a minivan. Such material decisions are yours to make using your own wisdom and preferences. God's will concerns spiritual values, moral choices, and the development of your character.

Second, draw upon accumulated wisdom. Your decisions are shaped by your experiences and the knowledge you have acquired. This is why studying The Urantia Book, and other sources of spiritual wisdom is so valuable. The insights you gain become part of your mental framework, unconsciously guiding your choices toward greater spiritual alignment.

Third, use your spiritual intuition. Ask yourself: "How do I feel about this choice? Does it bring peace or anxiety? Does it align with love, service, and truth?" Your developing spiritual sensitivity is itself a product of Adjuster influence.

Fourth, recognize that trial and error is part of the process. You will make mistakes. You will sometimes choose poorly. But each mistake becomes a learning opportunity, and your Adjuster works with whatever decisions you make, always seeking to bring spiritual good from human imperfection.

Fifth, be patient with the process. The superconscious communication from your Adjuster is usually "lost in the material currents of the energy streams of human mind." Only occasionally do you catch "an echo, a faint and distant echo, of the divine voice." This is normal. Spiritual discernment is a skill that develops gradually over a lifetime.

The text offers this reassurance: "The success of your Adjuster in the enterprise of piloting you through the mortal life and bringing about your survival depends not so much on the theories of your beliefs as upon your decisions, determinations, and steadfast faith."

What matters is not perfect theological understanding, but sincere commitment to spiritual growth. God honors honest seeking and faithful striving, even when our understanding is imperfect.

The Secret of Survival

Perhaps the most critical teaching in this section concerns the attainment of eternal life. What is required for survival?

The text is remarkably clear: "The secret of survival is wrapped up in the supreme human desire to be God-like and in the associated willingness to do and be any and all things which are essential to the final attainment of that overmastering desire."

Notice the two components:

1. **The desire to be God-like.** This is the fundamental spiritual hunger, the longing to embody divine qualities such as love, wisdom, mercy, and truth.
2. **The willingness to do and be any and all things necessary.** This is the commitment aspect, the determination to pay whatever price is required for spiritual attainment.

Many people possess the desire but lack the willingness. They want spiritual transformation but are unwilling to sacrifice pride, comfort, or self-will. True spiritual progress requires both elements.

The text also emphasizes what is NOT required: "Cooperation with the Thought Adjuster does not entail self-torture, mock piety, or hypocritical and ostentatious self-abasement. The ideal life is one of loving service rather than an existence of fearful apprehension."

This statement contradicts much traditional religious teaching. Spiritual growth does not require:

- Self-flagellation or ascetic extremes
- Displays of false humility
- Living in fear of divine punishment
- Ostentatious religious performances

Instead, the spiritual life is characterized by:

- Loving service to others

- Joyful cooperation with divine guidance
- Genuine humility without self-abasement
- Confidence in God's goodness rather than fear of God's wrath

The text beautifully states: "A devoted and determined effort to realize eternal destiny is wholly compatible with a lighthearted and joyous life and with a successful and honorable career on earth."

You do not have to abandon normal human happiness to pursue spiritual growth. In fact, true spirituality should enhance your capacity for joy, not diminish it.

When Adjusters Succeed or Fail

One of the most comforting teachings in this section addresses the question of Adjuster success or failure.

The text states: "When we speak of an Adjuster's success or failure, we are speaking in terms of human survival. Adjusters never fail; they are of the Divine essence, and they always emerge triumphant in each of their undertakings."

This requires careful interpretation. Adjusters never fail in the sense that they always do everything divinely possible to lead their subjects toward survival. They never make mistakes, never miss opportunities, and never fall short of divine perfection in their ministrations.

However, due to human free will, not every person chooses survival. When someone makes the final decision to reject eternal life, this is not the Adjuster's failure, it is the human's choice.

The Adjuster presents the case for survival as perfectly as possible. If the human decides otherwise, the Adjuster has still fulfilled its mission with complete fidelity. The responsibility for survival rests entirely with the human subject.

This is crucial to understand: Survival is entirely your choice. Nothing you have done makes you deserve survival, it is a gift from God. Conversely, nothing in your circumstances can prevent survival if you genuinely desire it. No amount of ignorance, hardship, or difficulty can block your path to eternity if you choose it with sincere faith.

The text affirms: "Whatever the Adjuster has succeeded in doing for you, the records will show that the transformation has been accomplished with your cooperative consent. You will have been a willing partner with the Adjuster in the attainment of every step of the tremendous transformation of the ascension career."

Your salvation is a cooperative achievement, not earned by works, but also not purely passive. You must willingly cooperate with divine grace.

The Meaning of Life: A Summary

If someone were to ask, "What is the meaning of life according to The Urantia Book?" this section provides the answer:

"The great goal of human existence is to attune to the divinity of the indwelling Adjuster. The great achievement of mortal life is the attainment of a true and understanding consecration to the eternal aims of the Divine Spirit who waits and works within your mind."

This is why we exist. This is what we are here to accomplish. Everything else, career success, family relationships, creative achievements, intellectual pursuits, are valuable as contexts within which this great attunement can occur, but they are not the ultimate purpose.

The ultimate purpose is spiritual transformation: becoming increasingly God-like, progressively attuning our will to the Father's will, and building the morontia soul that will be our identity throughout eternity.

This does not diminish earthly life; it ennobles it. Every moment becomes an opportunity for spiritual growth. Every relationship becomes a context for practicing divine love. Every challenge becomes a chance to demonstrate faith and trust in God's guidance.

Conclusion: The Divine Partnership

The relationship between Thought Adjusters and human will represents the most intimate partnership in the universe, the cooperation between the finite and the infinite, the mortal and the divine, the temporal and the eternal.

This partnership honors both parties completely. The Adjuster brings divine perfection, spiritual vision, and eternal perspective. The human brings personality, will, and the power of choice in the time-space realm. Together, they create something neither could accomplish alone: a perfected ascendant being who embodies both human experience and divine character.

The mechanics of this partnership are elegant in their design. The Adjuster never coerces, never violates human sovereignty. The human never operates without divine support, never faces spiritual challenges alone. Through the superconscious work of the Adjuster and the conscious choices of the human, a morontia soul gradually emerges, an identity that transcends both its material origin and its spiritual endowment.

As we move forward in our study of The Urantia Book, we will explore the seven psychic circles of spiritual attainment, the stages through which this divine-human partnership progressively deepens. We will discover how spiritual progress is measured, what facilitates growth, and what obstacles must be overcome.

For now, it is enough to grasp this central truth: You are not alone in your spiritual journey. Within you dwells a fragment of the infinite God, patiently working to transform you into an eternal being of divine perfection. Your cooperation with this indwelling spirit is the great adventure of existence, the supreme purpose of human life, and the foundation of your eternal destiny.

The choice to embark upon this adventure consciously and wholeheartedly is yours alone. The Adjuster awaits your decision, ready to guide, inspire, and transform, but always respecting your sovereign will.

What will you choose?

In our next chapter, we will examine the seven psychic circles of spiritual attainment and explore how we progress from the seventh circle of initial spiritual awakening to the third circle of morontia development, and ultimately to Adjuster fusion, the permanent union of human and divine identity.

Chapter 17: Universal Circuits and Divine Communication

Introduction

The relationship between mortal beings and the divine operates through an intricate network of spiritual, mental, and material circuits that pervade all of reality. Understanding these circuits is essential to comprehending how Thought Adjusters maintain constant communication with individual mortals and how every being in creation remains connected to the Universal Father, the Eternal Son, and the Infinite Spirit.

This chapter explores Paper 110, Section 3 of *The Urantia Book*, which addresses the practical challenges mortals face in cooperating with their indwelling Thought Adjusters. While confusion, discouragement, and even doubt may temporarily hinder our spiritual progress, these obstacles do not prevent our survival. Only conscious and persistent resistance to divine leading can sever the connection between the evolving soul and eternal life.

We will examine the multiple circuit systems that facilitate divine communication, from the seven superuniverse circuits that relay cosmic intelligence, to the local universe circuits that minister directly to evolving mortals, to the universal circuits of Paradise that pervade all levels of reality. Through understanding these systems, we gain insight into how seemingly isolated human beings on a quarantined world remain continuously connected to the vast cosmos and to God Himself.

The Nature of Spiritual Resistance and Survival - Understanding Confusion and Doubt

The Urantia Book offers reassuring guidance regarding the challenges mortals face in their spiritual journey:

"Confusion, being puzzled, even sometimes discouraged and distracted, does not necessarily signify resistance to the leadings of the indwelling Adjuster. Such attitudes may sometimes connote lack of active cooperation with the Divine Monitor and may, therefore, somewhat delay spiritual progress, but such intellectual-emotional difficulties do not in the least interfere with the certain survival of the God-knowing soul."

This passage provides profound comfort to those who struggle with faith or experience periods of spiritual uncertainty. The human experience inevitably includes moments of confusion, discouragement, and distraction. These temporary states do not constitute rejection of divine guidance, nor do they jeopardize one's eternal future.

The Assurance of Survival

The text continues with an even more emphatic assurance:

"Ignorance alone can never prevent survival; neither can confusional doubts nor fearful uncertainty. Only conscious resistance to the Adjuster's leading can prevent the survival of the evolving immortal soul."

This statement establishes a critical distinction: passive confusion differs fundamentally from active rebellion. A person may lack understanding, experience doubt, or struggle with uncertainty, yet still maintain the essential openness to divine leading that ensures survival. Only a deliberate, sustained, and final decision to reject God's will can prevent eternal progression.

This understanding should encourage those who worry that their imperfect faith or limited comprehension might disqualify them from eternal life. The Father's mercy extends far beyond human weakness and confusion. What matters is not perfect understanding but genuine willingness, however imperfect, to seek truth and follow divine guidance.

Four Principles of Effective Cooperation, The Nature of Adjuster Communication

While cooperation with one's Thought Adjuster need not be a particularly conscious process, certain attitudes and decisions facilitate this divine partnership:

"You must not regard cooperation with your Adjuster as a particularly conscious process, for it is not; but your motives and your decisions, your faithful determinations and your supreme desires, do constitute real and effective cooperation."

This passage clarifies an important point: effective spiritual communication operates largely below the threshold of conscious awareness. Mortals need not constantly focus on communicating with their Adjusters. Rather, the quality of one's motives, the consistency of one's decisions, the faithfulness of one's determinations, and the supremacy of one's desires create the conditions for effective divine partnership.

The Four Pillars of Divine Cooperation

The Urantia Book identifies four specific ways mortals can consciously augment harmony with their Thought Adjusters. These principles reflect the core teachings Jesus emphasized during His bestowal on Urantia:

1. Choosing to Respond to Divine Leading

The first principle involves:

"Sincerely loving virtue and earnestly desiring righteousness, choosing to respond to divine leading, sincerely basing the human life on the highest consciousness of truth, beauty, and goodness, and then coordinating these qualities of divinity through wisdom, worship, faith, and love."

This comprehensive approach integrates the recognition of spiritual values (truth, beauty, and goodness) with the practical application of spiritual qualities (wisdom, worship, faith, and love). These elements constitute the "fruits of the spirit" that Jesus taught and exemplified throughout His life.

Truth guides the intellect toward reality as it truly is, unclouded by prejudice or wishful thinking. Beauty elevates the soul through appreciation of harmony, proportion, and aesthetic excellence. Goodness directs the will toward moral action that benefits others and aligns with divine purpose.

These three values find expression through four coordinating qualities:

- **Wisdom** applies truth intelligently to practical situations
- **Worship** acknowledges the source of all value and reality
- **Faith** trusts divine goodness despite incomplete understanding
- **Love** motivates service and creates relationships of lasting value

2. Loving God and Desiring to Be Like Him

The second principle addresses the fundamental orientation of the spiritual life:

"Loving God and desiring to be like Him, genuine recognition of the divine fatherhood and loving worship of the heavenly Parent."

This principle captures the essence of the religious life: recognizing God as Father and responding with filial love and worship. This recognition transforms the spiritual journey from obligation into relationship, from duty into devotion.

The desire to become like God, to embody divine qualities in one's own character and conduct, provides the primary motivation for moral growth and spiritual transformation. This aspiration constitutes the most direct form of communication with one's Thought Adjuster, whose essential function is to facilitate precisely this transformation.

Jesus repeatedly emphasized this dual commandment: love God with all your heart, soul, mind, and strength. This supreme loyalty and affection creates the foundation for all spiritual progress.

3. Loving Others and Desiring to Serve Them

The third principle extends divine love outward toward fellow mortals:

"Loving man and sincerely desiring to serve him, wholehearted recognition of the brotherhood of man coupled with an intelligent and wise affection for each of your fellow mortals."

Human relationships provide the primary arena for spiritual growth. The recognition that all human beings share common origin and destiny, that we are truly brothers and sisters in the universal family, should inspire both respect and affection for every person.

Service represents love in action. Jesus taught and demonstrated that spiritual growth occurs through loving service to others. This service should be intelligent and wise, not merely sentimental or impractical, but motivated by genuine affection and recognition of spiritual kinship.

The brotherhood of man flows naturally from the fatherhood of God. Those who recognize God as Father cannot help but recognize all other God-knowing mortals as family. This recognition should extend even to those who do not yet know God, for they too are potential sons and daughters of the Universal Father.

4. Joyful Acceptance of Cosmic Citizenship

The fourth principle addresses the evolving mortal's relationship to the larger cosmic order:

"Joyful acceptance of cosmic citizenship, honest recognition of your progressive obligations to the Supreme Being, awareness of the interdependence of evolutionary man and evolving Deity. This is the birth of cosmic morality and the dawning realization of universal duty."

This principle introduces concepts that transcend traditional religious teaching. Cosmic citizenship acknowledges that human beings belong to a vast universe teeming with life and personality. We are not isolated accidents on an insignificant planet, but genuine citizens of a purposeful cosmos.

The Supreme Being, the evolving God of time and space, grows through the collective experience of all finite creatures. Every human decision, every moral choice, every spiritual achievement contributes to the actualization of the Supreme. This understanding transforms individual experience into cosmic participation.

Recognizing our interdependence with evolving Deity imbues daily life with profound significance. No experience is trivial, no choice lacks consequence. Every moral decision ripples through reality, contributing to the growth of the Supreme and thereby to the destiny of the entire universe.

This awareness gives birth to cosmic morality, an ethical framework that extends beyond personal or social considerations to embrace universal values. It awakens the realization of universal duty, the recognition that each person bears responsibility not only to self, family, and society, but to the cosmos itself.

The Teachings of Jesus

These four principles synthesize the essential teachings Jesus emphasized during His bestowal on Urantia. He constantly taught:

- The supreme responsibility of loving God and loving one's fellow mortals
- The spiritual values of truth, beauty, and goodness
- The necessity of loving service to others
- The cosmic significance of human experience

Jesus lived these principles perfectly, demonstrating how a human being could fully cooperate with the indwelling divine presence while navigating the challenges of mortal existence.

The Superuniverse Circuits, The Nature of Cosmic Communication

The Thought Adjuster operates not in isolation but within a vast network of spiritual, mental, and material circuits:

"The Adjusters work in the sphere of the mind. Adjusters are able to receive the continuous stream of cosmic intelligence coming in over the master circuits of time and space. They are in full touch with the spirit intelligence and energy of the universes."

Despite this comprehensive connection to universal reality, Adjusters face significant challenges in communicating with their mortal subjects:

"But these mighty indwellers are unable to transmit very much of this wealth of wisdom and truth to the minds of their mortal subjects because of the lack of commonness of nature and the absence of responsive recognition."

The fundamental difference between divine spirit and material mind creates inherent communication difficulties. The Thought Adjuster possesses access to cosmic intelligence and universal wisdom yet finds limited means to convey this knowledge to the mortal mind it indwells.

The Seven Master Circuits

The superuniverse level maintains seven primary circuits that facilitate communication throughout the grand universe:

1. The Unified Intelligence Circuit of the Master Spirits

"The personality gravity circuit of the Universal Father and the unified intelligence circuit of one of the seven Master Spirits of Paradise. Such a cosmic-mind circuit is limited to a single superuniverse."

Each of the seven superuniverses possesses its own Master Spirit, and each Master Spirit maintains a distinct mind circuit connecting all intelligent beings within that superuniverse. For those dwelling in the seventh superuniverse, our own, this circuit connects through the Seventh Master Spirit, who serves as the vicegerent of the Supreme Being.

Through this circuit, the Universal Father, the Eternal Son, and especially the Infinite Spirit maintain constant awareness of all mental activity throughout the superuniverse. Every thought, every decision, every mental process registers within this vast circuit.

2. The Reflective Service Circuit

"The reflective service of the seven Reflective Spirits in each superuniverse."

The reflective circuits enable the Paradise Deities and superuniverse administrators to observe events throughout the realms of time and space. This mechanism transcends mere information transfer, it provides direct observation, as though the observing personalities were physically present.

Reflectivity operates through actual spiritual beings, the Reflective Image Aids and related personalities, who serve as living channels for cosmic observation. This ensures that reflection includes not merely mechanical data transmission but intelligent discernment and appropriate filtering.

3. The Secret Circuits of the Mystery Monitors

"The secret circuits of the Mystery Monitors, in some manner interassociated and routed by Divinington to the Universal Father on Paradise."

The Thought Adjusters maintain their own dedicated communication network, routing directly to the Universal Father through Divinington, the sphere of the Father's exclusive domain. This circuit enables Adjusters to communicate with each other and with the Father without interference or observation by other orders of beings.

This secret circuit underscores the sacred privacy of the relationship between the Father and each individual mortal. No other being, however exalted, can intrude upon this intimate communion.

4. The Circuit of Intercommunication Between Paradise Sons

"The circuit of the intercommunication of the Eternal Son with His Paradise Sons."

This circuit connects the Eternal Son with all Paradise Sons throughout the universes. It provides the primary channel for the Spirit of Truth, which Michael of Nebadon bestowed upon Urantia following His resurrection.

Through this circuit, the influence of the Creator Sons extends throughout their respective universes, enabling all sincere truth-seekers to experience the guidance and inspiration of the divine Son who created them.

5. The Flash Presence of the Infinite Spirit

"The flash presence of the Infinite Spirit."

This circuit connects the Infinite Spirit with the local universe Divine Ministers, the Creative Mother Spirits who partner with the Creator Sons. Through this circuit flows the ministry of the Holy Spirit, which functions as the primary spiritual influence for those who have not yet achieved higher levels of spiritual receptivity.

6. The Broadcasts of Paradise and Havona

"The broadcasts of Paradise, the space reports of Havona."

Paradise and the central universe regularly transmit information throughout the grand universe. These broadcasts reach all non-quarantined planets, providing news, inspiration, and instruction from the eternal and perfect realms.

When mortals arrive on the first mansion world, access to these broadcasts becomes one of their chief sources of education and inspiration. The viewing areas where residents gather to receive Paradise broadcasts constitute favorite gathering places for ascending mortals eager to learn about the wider universe.

7. The Energy Circuits of the Power Centers

"The energy circuits of the power centers and the physical controllers."

These circuits regulate the physical, material aspects of reality, the fundamental energies that sustain planetary systems, regulate gravitational relationships, and maintain the stability of material creation.

Unlike some other circuits, the energy circuits have never been interrupted by quarantine. To do so would precipitate cosmic chaos, destabilizing the very fabric of physical reality. These circuits operate continuously and automatically, maintaining the material foundation upon which all other forms of existence depend.

The Significance of Universal Connection

These seven superuniverse circuits ensure that no being exists in true isolation. Even on a quarantined world like Urantia, mortals remain connected to the cosmos through multiple channels. The Father knows each person intimately through the indwelling Adjuster. The Infinite Spirit ministers through the cosmic mind. The material creation itself maintains perfect stability through unbreakable energy circuits.

This comprehensive network demonstrates the thoroughness of divine care. God has not created beings and then abandoned them to isolation. Rather, He has established multiple, redundant systems ensuring that every creature remains constantly connected to the source and center of all things.

The Local Universe Circuits - The Three Primary Local Circuits

In addition to the superuniverse circuits, three primary circuits operate specifically within each local universe, providing more immediate and personalized ministry:

1. The Bestowal Spirit of the Paradise Sons

"The bestowal spirit of the Paradise Sons, the Comforter, the Spirit of Truth, the spirit of Michael on Urantia."

When a Creator Son completes His seventh bestowal, He gains the capacity to bestow His spirit upon all creatures within His local universe. On Urantia, this occurred when Jesus of Nazareth, Michael of Nebadon incarnate, completed His mortal life and returned to universe headquarters.

The Spirit of Truth operates through the fourth superuniverse circuit (the intercommunication of the Eternal Son with Paradise Sons), but manifests specifically within the local universe as the personal spiritual presence of the Creator Son. This spirit guides truth-seekers, illuminates spiritual meaning, and draws sincere souls toward progressive understanding of reality.

2. The Circuit of the Divine Ministers

"The circuit of the Divine Ministers, the local universe Mother Spirits, the Holy Spirit of your world."

The local universe Creative Mother Spirit, the divine consort of the Creator Son, bestows the Holy Spirit upon all normal-minded mortals. This ministry prepares individuals for higher spiritual receptivity and provides initial spiritual guidance.

The Holy Spirit connects directly to the fifth superuniverse circuit (the flash presence of the Infinite Spirit), serving as the local universe expression of the Third Person of Deity. Through this circuit, the Infinite Spirit maintains intimate contact with every evolving mortal.

3. The Intelligence-Ministry Circuit

"The intelligence-ministry circuit of a local universe, including the diversely functioning presence of the adjutant mind-spirits."

The local universe Mother Spirit provides seven adjutant mind-spirits to all creatures within Her domain. These adjutants constitute the fundamental mental endowment that makes conscious life possible:

1. **The Spirit of Intuition** - enables quick, instinctive responses
2. **The Spirit of Understanding** - facilitates comprehension and learning
3. **The Spirit of Courage** - motivates action despite danger or difficulty
4. **The Spirit of Knowledge** - drives curiosity and discovery
5. **The Spirit of Counsel** - promotes social consciousness and cooperation
6. **The Spirit of Worship** - draws the creature toward the Creator
7. **The Spirit of Wisdom** - coordinates all other adjutants and enables moral choice

All creatures receive at least the first five adjutants. Human beings, having achieved will-dignity status, also receive the spirits of worship and wisdom. These final two adjutants make possible moral consciousness, spiritual receptivity, and personality survival.

The Intelligence Ministry and Personal Records

The intelligence-ministry circuit serves another crucial function: maintaining comprehensive records of each individual's life experience. Through this circuit, the archangels access complete transcripts of every mortal's decisions, experiences, and spiritual growth.

This recording function operates continuously and automatically. Every thought, decision, and experience of spiritual significance registers within the circuit and becomes part of one's permanent record. When a mortal awakens on the first mansion world, this record provides the foundation for reconstructing identity and resuming spiritual progress.

The Transition Beyond Local Universe Circuits

When ascending mortals complete their local universe training and achieve first-stage spirit status, they graduate beyond dependence on local universe circuits. At this point:

- The seven-adjutant mind-spirits are no longer necessary, having fulfilled their function
- The individual becomes directly circuited in the cosmic mind
- The local universe Mother Spirit's direct ministry concludes, though Her love and interest continue
- The ascending mortal becomes a true cosmic citizen, connected directly to Paradise circuits

This transition represents graduation from the nursery of the local universe into the larger cosmos. Having proven their spiritual stability and commitment, ascending mortals no longer require the intensive ministry and protection provided during their early evolutionary experience.

The Universal Circuits of Paradise, The Foundation of All Reality

Beyond the superuniverse and local universe circuits, four universal circuits emanate directly from Paradise, pervading all levels of reality:

1. The Personality Gravity Circuit of the Universal Father

This circuit connects every personality directly to the Universal Father. Personality, that unique quality bestowed exclusively by the Father, remains always and forever connected to its divine source.

Through this circuit, God knows intimately every personality throughout the universes. No distance, no barrier, no circumstance can interrupt this connection. The Father's love reaches each person directly and individually through the personality gravity circuit.

2. The Spiritual Gravity Circuit of the Eternal Son

All spiritual reality responds to the spiritual gravity of the Eternal Son. As mortals become increasingly spiritual, as they transform from material-minded creatures into spirit-dominated beings, they become more strongly attracted to the Son's spiritual presence.

When ascending mortals achieve first-stage spirit status and graduate from their local universe, they enter fully into the spiritual gravity circuit of the Eternal Son. This circuit draws all spiritual beings toward Paradise and ultimate union with God.

3. The Mind Gravity Circuit of the Conjoint Actor

The Infinite Spirit, the Conjoint Actor, maintains the mind gravity circuit that connects all intelligent beings. From the highest spirit minds to the most primitive conscious creatures, all participate in this universal circuit.

This circuit makes possible all forms of mind communication, including telepathy, cosmic insight, and the various phenomena studied under terms like extrasensory perception. When individuals report communication with distant intelligences, even with beings from other worlds, such communication, if genuine, must occur through the mind gravity circuit.

4. The Material Gravity Circuit of the Eternal Isle

Paradise itself serves as the absolute gravity center for all material reality. Every physical particle, every quantum of energy, every material form throughout the universes responds to the material gravity of the central Isle.

This circuit maintains the stability and order of physical creation. It ensures that natural law operates consistently throughout the cosmos. It provides the foundation upon which all material life, including human life, depends.

The Pervasiveness of Paradise Circuits

The Urantia Book emphasizes the comprehensive reach of these universal circuits:

"These present circuits are: the personality gravity of the Universal Father, the spiritual gravity of the Eternal Son, the mind gravity of the Conjoint Actor, and the material gravity of the eternal Isle."

These four circuits together ensure that nothing in all reality exists apart from God. The Father pervades all reality through these circuits, physical, mental, and spiritual. No creature, no world, no circumstance can separate anyone from divine presence and awareness.

This understanding provides profound reassurance. Even on a quarantined world, even in circumstances of isolation or difficulty, every person remains constantly connected to the very source of all existence. God is not distant or unaware; He is intimately present through multiple channels of contact and communication.

The Unity of All Circuit Systems

The three levels of circuits, superuniverse, local universe, and Paradise, function as an integrated whole. They are not separate or competing systems but coordinated expressions of divine ministry:

- Paradise circuits provide the universal foundation
- Superuniverse circuits adapt universal ministry to regional conditions
- Local universe circuits personalize ministry to individual creatures

Together, these circuits ensure that every being receives precisely the ministry needed for optimal growth while remaining constantly connected to ultimate reality and the Paradise Deities.

The Challenge of Mortal Communication, The Difficulty of Adjuster Contact

Despite the comprehensive circuit systems connecting all beings to divine reality, direct Adjuster communication remains problematic:

"Trust all matters of mind beyond the dead level of consciousness to the custody of the Adjusters. In due time, if not in this world then on the mansion worlds, they will give good account of their stewardship, and eventually will they bring forth those meanings and values entrusted to their care and keeping. They will resurrect every worthy treasure of the mortal mind if you survive."

The Adjuster works continuously to spiritualize the mortal mind and evolve the morontia soul. Yet the mortal subject remains largely unconscious of this inner ministry:

"You are quite incapable of distinguishing the product of your own material intellect from that of the conjoint activities of your soul and the Adjuster."

This inability to distinguish between one's own thoughts and Adjuster guidance creates significant confusion. Mortals cannot reliably determine whether an insight originates from their own thinking, from subconscious mental processes, or from actual Adjuster communication.

The Role of Subconscious Mental Activity

The Urantia Book clarifies an important distinction:

"Certain abrupt presentations of thoughts, conclusions, and other pictures of mind are sometimes the direct or indirect work of the Adjuster; but far more often they are the sudden emergence into consciousness of ideas which have been grouping themselves together in the submerged mental levels."

Much of what mortals experience as sudden insight or inspiration results from normal subconscious mental activity. The mind continuously works on problems and questions below the threshold of awareness, organizing information and forming connections. When these subconscious processes reach completion, their results emerge suddenly into consciousness, creating the experience of revelation or inspiration.

This natural mental function operates independently of Adjuster guidance, yet serves spiritual purposes by enabling learning, problem-solving, and intellectual growth.

The Superconscious Realm

Genuine Adjuster communication occurs in the superconscious rather than the subconscious:

"In contrast with these subconscious emanations, the revelations of the Adjuster appear through the realms of the superconscious."

The superconscious represents that level of mind above normal awareness where the Adjuster plants spiritual insights, moral perceptions, and higher meanings. These communications typically lack the dramatic quality mortals expect. They emerge quietly as deepening moral conviction, enhanced spiritual perception, or progressive clarification of life purpose.

The Adjuster rarely communicates through spectacular visions or audible voices. Such dramatic manifestations risk overwhelming the mortal mind, creating fanaticism or psychological disturbance rather than genuine spiritual growth.

The Obstacles to Clear Communication

The Urantia Book candidly acknowledges the severe difficulties Adjusters face:

"There exists a vast gulf between the human and the Divine, between man and God. The Urantia races are so largely electrically and chemically controlled, so highly animal-like in their common behavior, so emotional in their ordinary reactions, that it becomes exceedingly difficult for the Monitors to guide and direct them."

Human beings operate primarily on electrical and chemical impulses. The brain functions as a biological computer, processing information through electrochemical reactions. Emotions, themselves chemical events, dominate much of human consciousness. Animal urges and instincts exert powerful influence on behavior.

This material nature creates a fundamental incompatibility with pure spirit:

"You are so devoid of courageous decisions and consecrated cooperation that your indwelling Adjusters find it almost impossible to communicate directly with the human mind."

Most mortals lack the sustained commitment, disciplined thought, and spiritual receptivity necessary for clear Adjuster communication. They fail to make firm decisions and maintain consistent spiritual focus. Their attention scatters across countless trivial concerns.

The Danger of Misinterpretation

Even when the Adjuster successfully communicates, results often prove disappointing:

"Even when they do find it possible to flash a gleam of new truth to the evolving mortal soul, this spiritual revelation often so blinds the creature as to precipitate a convulsion of fanaticism or to initiate some other intellectual upheaval which results disastrously. Many a new religion and strange 'ism' has arisen from the aborted, imperfect, misunderstood, and garbled communications of the Thought Adjusters."

This sobering statement explains the proliferation of religious movements, eccentric teachings, and spiritual confusion throughout human history. Mortals receive a genuine flash of spiritual insight but, lacking context and discriminatory wisdom, distort it beyond recognition. They elevate personal revelation above collective wisdom, creating new "isms" that fragment spiritual community rather than unifying it.

The solution lies not in rejecting spiritual experience but in:

- Maintaining humility regarding one's understanding
- Testing insights against the accumulated wisdom of spiritual traditions
- Recognizing that genuine revelation uplifts and unifies rather than divides
- Avoiding the temptation to claim exclusive divine favor or unique spiritual status

The Crisis of Self-Acting Adjusters - A Disturbing Trend

The Urantia Book reveals a troubling pattern:

"For many thousands of years, so the records of Jerusem show, in each generation there have lived fewer and fewer beings who could function safely with self-acting Adjusters. This is an alarming picture, and the supervising personalities of Satania look with favor upon the proposals of some of your more immediate planetary supervisors who advocate the inauguration of measures designed to foster and conserve the higher spiritual types of the Urantia races."

A self-acting Adjuster possesses such complete rapport with its mortal subject that it can act independently, trusting the mortal to cooperate automatically with divine leading. Such Adjusters indicate exceptionally high spiritual receptivity and moral reliability in their human subjects.

The declining frequency of self-acting Adjusters suggests deteriorating spiritual capacity among Urantia mortals. This trend alarms supervising personalities throughout the local system, indicating a serious regression in human spiritual potential.

The Role of Self-Acting Adjusters in Revelation

The Fifth Epochal Revelation itself came through a human subject with a self-acting Adjuster. This individual maintained complete unconsciousness of the revelatory process, having no personal interest in the material being communicated. This unique situation enabled pure transmission without distortion from human ego, ambition, or preconception.

The rarity of such individuals makes epochal revelation correspondingly rare. Without humans capable of serving as clear channels for superhuman communication, revelation must come through less direct means or await the development of suitable contact personalities.

Proposed Solutions

The supervising personalities seek to implement measures designed to "foster and conserve the higher spiritual types of the Urantia races." While *The Urantia Book* does not specify these measures in detail, the implication is clear: some form of selective encouragement of spiritually advanced individuals to reproduce and raise families.

This suggestion troubles many readers, evoking memories of discredited eugenics movements. However, the proposal differs fundamentally from racist or coercive programs:

- It focuses on spiritual receptivity rather than racial or physical characteristics
- It operates through voluntary encouragement rather than coercion
- It recognizes that genetic factors influence spiritual capacity
- It seeks to recover Adam and Eve's default lost, the systematic upgrade of human genetic stock

The Adamic mission intended to uplift human genetic quality through voluntary interbreeding between Adamic offspring and native mortals. The default aborted this mission, leaving Urantia's races genetically deprived compared to normal evolutionary worlds.

The proposals mentioned in *The Urantia Book* apparently seek to partially remedy this deficit through encouraging spiritually gifted individuals to bear and raise children who might inherit enhanced spiritual receptivity.

The Value of Struggle and Tribulation, The Necessity of Difficulty

A seeming paradox emerges from Urantia's quarantined status: isolation from universe broadcasts and diminished celestial ministry appear disadvantageous, yet *The Urantia Book* reveals unexpected benefits:

"Mortals who have been deprived of outside help through isolation are sometimes fortunate in that they face greater problems and develop stronger characters. The greatest affliction of the cosmos is never to have been afflicted. Mortals only learn wisdom by experiencing tribulation."

Planets settled in light and life, where spiritual ministry operates at maximum efficiency and material conditions approach perfection, provide comparatively little opportunity for the character development that comes through struggle. Inhabitants of such worlds receive everything needed for comfortable existence without significant effort or difficulty.

Urantia mortals, by contrast, face constant challenges:

- Material hardship and uncertainty
- Spiritual isolation from universe broadcasts
- Absence of visible superhuman guidance
- Cultural confusion regarding spiritual truth
- Personal struggles with doubt, temptation, and moral ambiguity

These difficulties, while painful, forge spiritual character of exceptional strength. Mortals who persist in seeking truth despite obstacles, who maintain faith without sensory confirmation, who serve others amid personal hardship, these individuals develop capacities unavailable to those raised in ease.

The Example of the Bestowal Sons

This principle operates throughout the universe. All Creator Sons must experience seven bestowals, including at least one as a mortal of the realm. These bestowals subject the Creator Sons to genuine struggle, vulnerability, and difficulty.

Michael of Nebadon's final bestowal as Jesus of Nazareth exemplified maximum struggle:

- He was born into poverty and political oppression
- He experienced family responsibility and economic hardship

- He worked at demanding physical labor for many years
- He endured misunderstanding from those closest to Him
- He faced rejection, betrayal, and execution

None of this came easily or automatically. Jesus grew through struggle precisely as all mortals must. The experience shaped His understanding and deepened His compassion for all struggling mortals throughout His universe.

Would Jesus have become such an effective Sovereign and merciful Father without experiencing mortal struggle? The question answers itself. His identification with mortal experience makes Him accessible and understanding in ways impossible without actual participation in human difficulty.

The Value of Struggle in Universe Service

Ascending mortals from troubled worlds like Urantia become highly valued throughout the universe precisely because of their experience with struggle:

"The greatest affliction of the cosmos is never to have been afflicted."

When these mortals reach the mansion worlds and begin universe service, their experience becomes invaluable for teaching and ministering to others facing similar challenges. They understand struggle from the inside. They know doubt, confusion, and discouragement not as abstract concepts but as lived experience.

Inhabitants of worlds settled in light and life lack this experiential knowledge. Their service, though sincere, carries less authority because they have not personally endured what they counsel others through. They can sympathize but not fully empathize.

This explains why troubled worlds, though superficially disadvantaged, actually contribute exceptional citizens to universe service. The difficulties that seem purely negative in the moment prove ultimately valuable in the larger cosmic context.

The Spiritual Danger of Ease

The chapter includes an illuminating illustration from popular culture:

"Andy Griffith's son came to him and said, 'Dad, I want to talk to you about something. The current belief is, for an allowance, a child should get seventy-five cents and not have to do any work for it, just give him seventy-five cents.' Andy looked at him and said, 'Well, that's interesting. My current belief is this: my current belief is you earn twenty-five cents, but to earn that twenty-five cents you have to clean the garage and you have to do a few chores, or you don't get the twenty-five cents. We don't live by the current belief, do we? We live by our beliefs.'"

This simple story captures a profound truth: unearned benefits produce weak character. Children who receive everything without effort develop neither competence nor appreciation. They remain perpetually immature, expecting provision without contribution.

The same principle operates spiritually. Mortals who face no challenges, who never doubt or struggle, who automatically receive spiritual insight without seeking it, such mortals remain spiritually infantile. They lack the strength and wisdom that come only through experience.

God apparently understands this principle perfectly. Rather than providing automatic ease, He arranges conditions requiring effort, persistence, and courage. This arrangement reflects not cruelty but wisdom, the wisdom of a Father who desires children capable of eventual partnership in cosmic administration rather than eternal dependence.

Conclusion

The universal circuits that pervade all reality ensure that no mortal exists in true isolation from God. Through the seven superuniverse circuits, the three local universe circuits, and the four Paradise circuits, every individual remains constantly connected to the Father, the Son, and the Spirit.

Yet this connection does not guarantee easy communication. The vast gulf between divine spirit and material mind creates inherent difficulties. Human beings, dominated by electrochemical processes and emotional reactions, struggle to distinguish Adjuster guidance from their own thoughts. The Adjuster's spiritual revelations operate in the superconscious realm, often unnoticed amid the clamor of ordinary consciousness and subconscious mental activity.

Four principles facilitate cooperation with the indwelling Adjuster:

1. Choosing to respond to divine leading based on truth, beauty, and goodness
2. Loving God and desiring to be like Him

3. Loving others and sincerely desiring to serve them
4. Joyfully accepting cosmic citizenship and one's obligations to the Supreme Being

These principles, which Jesus taught and exemplified throughout His bestowal, create the conditions for effective divine-human partnership despite the inherent communication difficulties.

The declining frequency of self-acting Adjusters indicates serious spiritual regression among Urantia mortals, prompting proposals to foster higher spiritual types within the human population. Yet even this troubling trend cannot negate the larger truth: struggle itself provides irreplaceable spiritual value. Mortals from troubled worlds, including Urantia, develop through difficulty the strength and wisdom that make them exceptionally valuable in universe service.

Understanding these circuits and communication challenges provides necessary context for spiritual growth. Mortals need not despair of confusion or struggle. Only conscious, sustained resistance to divine leading can prevent survival. All other difficulties, including ignorance, doubt, and uncertainty, merely delay rather than prevent eternal progression.

In the next chapter, we will examine the specific mechanics of soul growth, exploring how the Adjuster transforms mortal decisions into eternal realities and how the morontia soul evolves through the partnership between human will and divine presence.

Chapter 18: Erroneous Concepts of Adjuster Guidance and the Seven Psychic Circles

Introduction

Among the most misunderstood aspects of spiritual development is the nature and function of divine guidance in human life. Across religious traditions, countless individuals claim to hear the voice of God directing their daily decisions, from mundane choices about possessions to life-altering commitments. Yet *The Urantia Book* reveals a more nuanced and profound reality: the distinction between human conscience and authentic divine leading represents one of the most critical understandings for spiritual maturity.

This chapter examines Paper 110, Section 5, "Erroneous Concepts of Adjuster Guidance," along with Section 6, "The Seven Psychic Circles." These sections provide essential clarification on how Thought Adjusters actually function within the human mind, dispelling common misconceptions that have led to spiritual confusion, religious fanaticism, and disappointed expectations throughout human history. Understanding these truths enables seekers to discern genuine divine influence from psychological phenomena, thereby facilitating authentic spiritual progress.

The journey through the seven psychic circles, from initial moral consciousness to potential Thought Adjuster fusion, represents the supreme adventure of mortal existence. This chapter illuminates that pathway, offering practical wisdom for those committed to balanced spiritual growth.

The Fundamental Distinction: Conscience Versus Divine Guidance, The Nature of Human Conscience

The Urantia Book begins this section with a stark clarification: "Do not confuse and confound the mission and influence of the Adjuster with what is commonly called conscience. They are not directly related." This statement challenges deeply held assumptions across religious cultures that equate the "still, small voice" of conscience with God speaking directly to the soul.

Conscience is described as "a human and purely psychic reaction." It functions as an internalized moral compass developed through childhood socialization, cultural conditioning, and learned ethical frameworks. As individuals mature, they absorb the mores, values, and behavioral standards of their family and society. These become encoded in the psyche, creating automatic responses to moral situations, what we experience as conscience.

The passage notes that conscience "rightly admonishes you to do right," acknowledging its legitimate role in moral behavior. However, it represents human moral judgment rather than divine revelation. Conscience reflects what we have been taught is right or wrong, which may or may not align with absolute spiritual truth.

The Adjuster's True Function

In contrast, the Thought Adjuster "endeavors to tell you what truly *is* right, when and as you are able to perceive the monitor's leading." This distinction is profound. While conscience operates within the framework of cultural and personal moral codes, the Adjuster seeks to reveal universal spiritual truth. The Adjuster's guidance transcends human convention, pointing toward cosmic reality and divine perfection.

However, this divine guidance rarely manifests as clear verbal direction in daily consciousness. The Adjuster works primarily in the superconscious realm, a level of mind generally inaccessible to ordinary awareness. Most humans cannot consciously distinguish Adjuster promptings from their own thoughts, desires, or conditioned responses.

The Danger of Misattribution

The confusion between conscience and divine guidance has produced countless "erroneous concepts" throughout human religious history. When individuals believe that every intuition, impulse, or internal conviction originates from God, they may act with unwarranted certainty on what are actually personal preferences or cultural biases.

This misattribution leads to several problematic patterns:

Religious Presumption: Individuals claim divine authorization for personal decisions, declaring "God told me to do this" when, in reality, they are following their own desires or responding to psychological needs.

Disappointed Expectations: When believers invest time, resources, and emotional energy in pursuits they attribute to divine leading, only to experience failure or frustration, their faith may be shaken. The problem lies not in divine guidance but in the misidentification of its source.

Spiritual Arrogance: Claiming direct divine instruction can foster a sense of superiority over others and justify actions that may not serve genuine spiritual growth or the welfare of others.

Fanaticism and Extremism: History demonstrates repeatedly that some of the most destructive religious movements have been led by individuals convinced they were following God's explicit direction.

The corrective to these dangers lies in cultivating humility and discernment. Spiritual maturity requires acknowledging that we are finite beings with limited capacity to perceive divine will. As the text emphasizes, we should approach our spiritual intuitions with appropriate caution, recognizing that "God is not Santa Claus" who exists to fulfill our material wishes or validate our every inclination.

The Mystery of Dreams and Unconscious Sleep, The Incoherence of Dream Life

The document addresses another common misconception: the belief that dreams carry divine messages or prophetic significance. *The Urantia Book* presents a sobering perspective: "Man's dream experiences, that disordered and disconnected parade of the uncoordinated sleeping mind, present adequate proof of the failure of the Adjusters to harmonize and associate the divergent factors of the mind of man."

Dreams, in this understanding, represent neural activity, the firing of synapses in patterns that create fragmented, often bizarre narratives. They reflect the mind processing daily experiences, unresolved emotions, suppressed desires, and random associations. The incoherence of dreams demonstrates the vast gulf between human and divine consciousness.

The passage notes that "the Adjusters simply cannot, in a single lifetime, arbitrarily coordinate and synchronize two such unlike and diverse types of thinking as the human and the divine." The human psyche operates on material, emotional, and social levels that function according to finite principles. The divine mind operates from eternal, perfect, and cosmic perspectives. These realms rarely merge seamlessly during mortal existence.

When Dreams Do Carry Meaning

An important exception exists in rare cases, the Adjuster can communicate through dreams when a person has achieved sufficient spiritual development. Biblical examples include Joseph's dreams and other prophetic visions recorded in scripture. However, these represent exceptional instances, not the norm for ordinary dream experience.

The critical point is that these genuine divine communications occur through direct Thought Adjuster intervention, not through the ordinary dream mechanism. They are qualitatively different from the nightly parade of unconscious imagery that most humans experience.

The Adjuster's Work During Sleep

While ordinary dreams lack spiritual significance, the sleeping state serves a crucial function in spiritual development. During sleep, when conscious mental activity diminishes, the Adjuster works in the superconscious realm to spiritualize the experiences of daily life.

The text explains: "During the slumber season, the Adjuster attempts to achieve only that which the will of the indwelt personality has previously fully approved by the decisions and choosing's which were made during times of fully wakeful consciousness."

This process involves several elements:

Spiritual Translation: The Adjuster takes morally significant experiences, decisions, and insights from waking life and translates them into spiritual values that become part of the evolving soul.

Soul Building: Through this nightly work, the Adjuster constructs a "carbon copy" of meaningful life experiences, not a physical duplicate, but a spiritual essence that survives physical death and continues into morontia existence.

Value Preservation: Only those experiences and choices of genuine spiritual worth are preserved. Trivial, selfish, or purely material concerns hold no eternal value and therefore are not spiritualized.

Superconscious Operation: This work occurs in the superconscious mind, the "liaison domain of human and divine interrelationship," which operates independently of ordinary consciousness and dreams.

The Problem of Interference

The passage acknowledges a significant challenge: "While mortal hosts are asleep, the Adjusters try to register their creations in the higher levels of the material mind, and some of your grotesque dreams indicate their failure to make efficient contact."

Human emotional and physical nature can interfere with the Adjuster's superconscious work. Unexpressed passions, suppressed desires, unresolved conflicts, and physiological needs manifest in dreams, creating "horrible distortions of the representations of the spiritual concepts presented by the Adjusters."

A person might experience a dream that begins with a spiritual theme but quickly shifts to sexual imagery, then to work-related anxiety, then to a completely unrelated scenario. This chaotic progression demonstrates how "your own passions, urges, and other innate tendencies translate themselves into the picture and substitute their unexpressed desires for the divine messages which the indwellers are endeavoring to put into the psychic records during unconscious sleep."

This interference explains why most people remember little of their dreams. The mind, in its mercy, often shields consciousness from the confused mixture of spiritual attempts and material intrusions that characterize the dream state.

Discernment and Individual Responsibility - The Challenge of Differentiation

The Urantia Book acknowledges the profound difficulty of distinguishing Adjuster guidance from ordinary mental processes: "It is extremely dangerous to postulate as to the Adjuster content of the dream life. Likewise, it is hazardous to attempt the differentiation of the Adjusters' concept registry from the more or less continuous and conscious reception of the dictations of mortal conscience."

This honest assessment recognizes that even sincere spiritual seekers face inherent limitations in identifying divine influence. The human mind cannot easily separate divine promptings from psychological reactions, cultural conditioning, or personal desire.

The Principle of Cautious Humility

Given these challenges, the text offers practical wisdom: "A human being would do better to err in rejecting an Adjuster's expression through believing it to be a purely human experience than to blunder into exalting a reaction of the mortal mind to the sphere of divine dignity."

This principle advocates cautious humility. It is spiritually safer to attribute an insight to human thinking than to falsely claim divine origin for what may be merely personal opinion. The dangers of spiritual presumption far exceed the risks of modest uncertainty.

This approach protects against:

False Authority: Claiming divine sanction for human ideas grants them unwarranted authority and closes them to examination or correction.

Spiritual Pride: Believing oneself to be a direct channel for God's voice can foster arrogance and separate one from fellow seekers.

Harmful Actions: When people believe God has commanded specific actions, they may pursue courses that harm themselves or others, all while feeling divinely justified.

Disillusionment: Repeated experiences of supposed divine guidance leading to poor outcomes can erode genuine faith.

The Superconscious Reality

The passage concludes this section with a crucial reminder: "Remember, the influence of a Thought Adjuster is for the most part, though not wholly, a superconscious experience."

The Adjuster's primary work occurs beyond conscious awareness. While occasional insights, moral promptings, or spiritual illuminations may filter into consciousness, the vast majority of divine influence operates in realms the conscious mind cannot directly access.

This reality should temper expectations. Rather than seeking constant conscious communication with the divine, spiritual seekers should trust the unseen work of the Adjuster, focus on making moral decisions, cultivate spiritual receptivity, and allow divine influence to shape character gradually over time.

The Seven Psychic Circles: The Framework of Spiritual Progress, Introduction to the Circles

Section 6 of Paper 110 introduces one of *The Urantia Book*'s most significant concepts for understanding human spiritual development: the seven psychic circles. These circles represent measurable stages of personality integration and spiritual maturity that every mortal must traverse.

The text states: "The sum total of personality realization on a material world is contained within the successive conquest of the seven psychic circles of mortal potentiality."

Several key points establish the framework:

Numbering System: Paradoxically, the journey begins with the seventh circle and progresses to the first. The seventh circle represents initial moral consciousness, while the first circle indicates relative spiritual maturity.

Universal Pathway: All normal-minded mortals traverse these circles, though at vastly different rates and ages.

Personality Realization: Circle attainment measures integrated personality function, the harmonious coordination of physical, mental, and spiritual capacities.

Preliminary to Fusion: Mastery of these circles represents necessary preparation for Thought Adjuster fusion, though circle attainment alone does not guarantee fusion.

The Seventh Circle: Beginning the Journey

"Entrance upon the seventh circle marks the beginning of true human personality function."

Most individuals enter the seventh psychic circle around age five or six, coinciding with the arrival of the Thought Adjuster. This occurs when a child makes their first genuine moral decision, the first time they distinguish right from wrong and choose accordingly based on internal conviction rather than mere fear of punishment or desire for reward.

This represents a crucial transition from pre-moral innocence to moral agency. The child becomes accountable, capable of spiritual growth, and begins the long process of personality unification under potential divine guidance.

Progression Through the Circles

As individuals mature, they progress through the circles, seventh to sixth, sixth to fifth, and so on. However, this progression is neither automatic nor tied to chronological age. Several factors influence circle advancement:

Moral Decision-Making: Each choice to pursue truth, beauty, and goodness contributes to spiritual growth and potential circle advancement.

Personality Integration: Circle attainment requires harmonious functioning of all personality aspects, physical health, mental stability, emotional maturity, and spiritual receptivity.

Life Experience: The wisdom that comes through lived experience, especially experience that tests character and clarifies values, facilitates circle progression.

Spiritual Dedication: Conscious commitment to spiritual growth and willing cooperation with divine leading accelerates development.

Many young people reach the third circle during adolescence or early adulthood, especially those with strong spiritual inclinations and stable developmental environments. Others may not attain the third circle until middle age or later. Some individuals never progress beyond the lower circles during their earthly lives, though they continue their development on the mansion worlds.

The Third Circle: A Critical Milestone

The third psychic circle represents a particularly significant achievement. "Completion of the third circle" results in the assignment of personal seraphic guardians, a destiny guardian and two attending cherubim.

Prior to third-circle attainment, individuals receive the ministry of group seraphim who serve entire communities or populations. Upon reaching the third circle, however, a person's spiritual progress and cosmic potential justify the assignment of personal spiritual ministers.

These seraphic guardians work from the outside to complement the Adjuster's internal ministry. They manipulate the external environment, orchestrate helpful circumstances, arrange beneficial encounters, and protect from certain dangers, all to facilitate continued spiritual growth.

The assignment of destiny guardians indicates that the universe has recognized the individual's commitment to spiritual values and their potential for eternal survival. It represents a cosmic vote of confidence in the person's spiritual trajectory.

The First Circle: Relative Maturity

"Completion of the first circle denotes the relative maturity of the mortal being."

Attainment of the first psychic circle represents approaching the limits of spiritual development possible in mortal form. Several significant developments characterize first-circle attainment:

Direct Communication: At the first circle, communication with the Thought Adjuster can become conscious and direct. The individual may actually "hear" the voice of God as distinct from their own thoughts.

Cosmic Consciousness: First-circle mortals develop genuine cosmic perspective, understanding themselves as citizens of the universe rather than merely inhabitants of one planet.

Spiritual Stability: These individuals have achieved consistent victory over lower impulses and established reliable patterns of spiritual living.

Potential for Fusion: While fusion does not automatically occur at first-circle attainment, the individual has met the preliminary requirements and may fuse during earthly life or soon after death.

However, the text carefully notes: "Though the traversal of the seven circles of cosmic growth does not equal fusion with the Adjuster, the mastery of these circles marks the attainment of those steps which are preliminary to Adjuster fusion."

Most mortals, even those who reach the first circle, do not fuse during earthly life. Fusion typically occurs on the mansion worlds, often around the fifth mansion world, after further spiritual refinement in morontia form.

The Rare Case of Earthly Fusion

In exceptional cases, individuals achieve such complete alignment of human will with divine will that fusion occurs during mortal life. When this happens, "such souls are translated directly to the mansion worlds without the necessity of passing through the experience of death."

This translation involves the physical body being consumed in a brilliant flash of energy, the "chariots of fire" referenced in ancient religious texts. The universe always provides advance notice of impending translation, as translation orders originate from superuniverse capitals.

However, such translations remain exceedingly rare. They require not only first-circle attainment but also such perfect will alignment that the human and divine wills become functionally identical. Few mortals achieve this state while burdened with material bodies and living in material environments.

Balanced Development: The Danger of Imbalanced Growth, The Key to Circle Advancement

One of the most important teachings in this section concerns the necessity of balanced development. Spiritual progress cannot occur through emphasis on one aspect of personality while neglecting others.

The text warns: "When the development of the intellectual nature proceeds faster than that of the spiritual, such a situation renders communication with the Adjuster both difficult and dangerous."

Intellectual development without corresponding spiritual growth produces skepticism, materialism, and loss of faith. Highly intelligent individuals who neglect spiritual cultivation often become trapped in rationalistic worldviews that deny or minimize spiritual reality. Such people may achieve remarkable success in scientific, professional, or academic pursuits while remaining spiritually impoverished.

Conversely: "Over spiritual development tends to produce a fanatical and perverted interpretation of the spirit leadings of the divine indweller."

Religious extremism, superstition, and fanaticism arise when spiritual enthusiasm outpaces intellectual and emotional maturity. People who emphasize spiritual experiences while neglecting rational development easily fall prey to delusion, misinterpreting psychological phenomena as divine revelation and pursuing irrational or harmful courses while believing themselves divinely led.

The text also notes: "Lack of spiritual capacity makes it very difficult to transmit to such a material intellect the spiritual truths resident in the higher super consciousness."

Those who develop only intellectually or physically, ignoring spiritual dimensions, create minds essentially closed to divine influence. The Adjuster's work becomes severely limited when the mortal provides no receptivity to spiritual values.

The Ideal of Triune Harmony

The passage articulates the ideal condition for spiritual progress:

"It is to the mind of perfect poise, housed in a body of clean habits, stabilized neural energies, and balanced chemical function, when the physical, mental, and spiritual powers are in triune harmony of development that a maximum of light and truth can be imparted with a minimum of temporal danger or risk to the real welfare of such a being."

This comprehensive statement identifies several essential elements:

Perfect Mental Poise: Emotional stability, psychological health, and balanced perspective, neither excessive anxiety nor unrealistic optimism, neither rigid dogmatism nor wishy-washy uncertainty.

Clean Physical Habits: Maintaining bodily health through proper nutrition, adequate rest, regular exercise, and avoidance of substances that impair function or poison the system. This includes abstaining from addictive drugs, excessive alcohol, and tobacco.

Stabilized Neural Energies: Healthy nervous system function, which requires both physical health and stress management. Chronic pain, neurological disorders, or severe stress compromise the nervous system's ability to support spiritual receptivity.

Balanced Chemical Function: Proper hormonal balance, adequate brain chemistry, and metabolic health. Mental illness, hormonal imbalances, and chemical dependencies interfere with both psychological stability and spiritual sensitivity.

Triune Harmony: The integrated development of physical, mental, and spiritual capacities in balanced proportion. None can be neglected without compromising the others.

Practical Implications

These principles offer practical guidance for spiritual seekers:

Physical Health Matters: Spiritual progress is supported by physical well-being. Neglecting health in the name of spirituality is counterproductive.

Mental Health Is Essential: Psychological problems should be addressed through appropriate therapy or medical intervention. Spiritual practice cannot substitute for needed mental health treatment.

Intellectual Development Supports Spirituality: Reading, study, critical thinking, and education enhance rather than threaten genuine spirituality. Faith need not fear reason.

Spiritual Practice Requires Discipline: Regular prayer, meditation, worship, and moral inventory contribute to balanced development.

Gradual Integration: "By such a balanced growth does man ascend the circles of planetary progression one by one, from the seventh to the first." Progress occurs gradually through sustained effort across all dimensions of being.

The Adjuster and Circle Progression - The Adjuster's Independent Development

An intriguing aspect of circle progression is revealed in the statement: "The Adjuster is your equal partner in the attainment of the seven circles, the achievement of comparative mortal maturity. The Adjuster ascends the circles with you from the seventh to the first but progresses to the status of supremacy and self-activity quite independent of the active cooperation of the mortal mind."

This indicates that while the Adjuster accompanies the mortal through circle attainment, the Adjuster's own development and capacity for action increase independently. A highly experienced Adjuster indwelling a seventh-circle mortal possesses capabilities far beyond what that mortal can currently access or comprehend.

As the mortal progresses through the circles, they become increasingly able to benefit from the Adjuster's advanced capacities. The limitation lies not in the Adjuster but in the mortal's receptivity and ability to consciously cooperate with divine leading.

Personality Status and Soul Growth

The text clarifies what circle attainment actually measures: "Psychic circles are not exclusively intellectual, neither are they wholly moral; they have to do with personality status, mind attainment, soul growth, and Adjuster attunement."

Several dimensions contribute to circle advancement:

Personality Status: The degree of personality integration and self-mastery achieved. This includes emotional maturity, consistent character, and unified life purpose.

Mind Attainment: Intellectual development, wisdom, breadth of understanding, and capacity for complex thought. This is not mere intelligence but functional wisdom.

Soul Growth: The accumulated spiritual values created through moral decision-making and divine cooperation. The soul represents the joint creation of human will and divine spirit.

Adjuster Attunement: The degree of harmony between human will and divine purpose. As this attunement increases, the person becomes increasingly capable of perceiving and following divine leading.

The critical insight: "Successful traversal of these levels demands the harmonious functioning of the entire personality, not merely of some one phase thereof."

One cannot advance through sheer intellectual brilliance while remaining emotionally immature. Neither can emotional development compensate for intellectual laziness or spiritual indifference. All aspects must develop together.

The Whole Self Development

"The growth of the parts does not equal the true maturation of the whole; the parts really grow in proportion to the expansion of the entire self, the whole self, material, intellectual, and spiritual."

This principle emphasizes organic, integrated growth. Authentic spiritual development transforms the entire person, body, mind, and spirit, not merely one isolated aspect. The spiritually mature individual demonstrates:

- Physical vitality and healthy habits
- Mental clarity and emotional stability
- Moral integrity and consistent character
- Spiritual awareness and cosmic perspective
- Service orientation and compassionate engagement with others
- Balanced judgment combining wisdom and faith

Such individuals manifest the fruits of the spirit naturally through integrated personality function rather than through forced effort or artificial piety.

The Contact Personality: A Rare Case Study - An Example of Balanced Receptivity

The text includes a fascinating reference to the individual through whom much of *The Urantia Book* was transmitted:

"The Adjuster of the human being through whom this communication is being made enjoys such a wide scope of activity chiefly because of this human's almost complete indifference to any outward manifestations of the Adjuster's inner presence."

This "contact personality" possessed an exceptionally experienced Adjuster, a self-acting Adjuster with extensive prior experience. However, the human subject's conscious personality remained largely unaware of and unconcerned with the spiritual phenomena occurring through their instrumentality.

The Virtue of Passive Cooperation

The passage emphasizes several remarkable qualities:

Conscious Unconcern: The individual remained "consciously unconcerned about the entire procedure," neither seeking spiritual experiences nor troubled by their occurrence.

Lack of Preoccupation: Rather than obsessing over spiritual phenomena, the person maintained normal engagement with everyday life.

Passive Reaction: The subject demonstrated a "rare and fortuitous reaction", neither resisting nor exploiting the Adjuster's activity.

Health and Tranquility: This passive cooperation contributed to the individual's physical health, mental efficiency, and emotional tranquility.

The text notes that the Guardian of Destiny pronounced this passive reaction "rare and fortuitous," indicating how unusual such balanced receptivity is. Most humans either resist spiritual leading through skepticism and materialism or seek spiritual experiences with an intensity that actually interferes with genuine divine work.

Implications for Receptivity

This case study suggests that optimal receptivity to divine leading involves:

Humble Openness: Willingness to be used for divine purposes without demanding specific experiences or recognition.

Balanced Engagement: Living normally and effectively in the material world while remaining spiritually sensitive.

Non-Attachment to Phenomena: Avoiding preoccupation with spiritual experiences, visions, or supernatural manifestations.

Stable Mental Health: Maintaining psychological equilibrium rather than emotional extremes.

Service Orientation: Focusing on useful contribution rather than personal spiritual attainment.

The contact personality was not selected because of spiritual superiority or extraordinary holiness, but rather because their Adjuster was highly experienced and their personality structure allowed passive, non-interfering cooperation with the Adjuster's work.

Practical Wisdom for the Spiritual Journey, Cultivating Realistic Expectations

This chapter offers several practical guidelines for those seeking authentic spiritual growth:

Recognize Limitations: Acknowledge the difficulty of distinguishing divine guidance from psychological processes. Approach spiritual intuitions with appropriate humility.

Avoid Presumption: Resist the temptation to claim divine authority for personal preferences or cultural assumptions.

Trust the Process: Understand that most Adjuster work occurs in the superconscious realm, beyond conscious awareness. Absence of dramatic experiences does not indicate spiritual stagnation.

Focus on Decisions: Since the Adjuster primarily works with moral decisions and spiritual values, concentrate on making ethical choices rather than seeking mystical experiences.

Cultivate Balance: Develop all aspects of personality, physical, mental, and spiritual, in harmonious proportion.

The Role of Age and Experience

The text suggests that spiritual maturity often correlates with chronological age, though not invariably. Several factors explain this correlation:

Life Experience: Years of living provide opportunities to test values, face challenges, and develop wisdom that theoretical knowledge cannot supply.

Hormonal Moderation: As sexual and aggressive drives diminish with age, mental and emotional energy becomes available for spiritual pursuits.

Simplified Priorities: Older individuals often achieve clarity about what truly matters, releasing attachment to status, possessions, and social approval.

Facing Mortality: Awareness of life's finite nature often stimulates serious spiritual reflection and commitment.

However, the relationship between age and spirituality is not automatic. Some young people achieve remarkable spiritual maturity through intense dedication, while some elderly individuals remain spiritually childish. Age provides opportunity for growth but does not guarantee it.

The Gift of Uncertainty

Perhaps paradoxically, one mark of genuine spiritual maturity is comfort with uncertainty. The text repeatedly emphasizes the difficulty of knowing with certainty when one is receiving divine guidance versus responding to psychological impulses.

Rather than representing a deficiency, this uncertainty serves several beneficial purposes:

Humility: Uncertainty prevents spiritual arrogance and keeps seekers teachable.

Openness: Not knowing definitively maintains receptivity to new insights and willingness to revise understanding.

Genuine Faith: True faith functions amid uncertainty. If everything were absolutely clear, faith would be unnecessary.

Focus on Growth: When certainty is elusive, attention naturally shifts from validating experiences to faithfully living spiritual values.

The spiritually mature person learns to say, "I believe this is right, but I acknowledge my understanding may be incomplete." This honest humility contrasts sharply with the dogmatic certainty often characteristic of religious fundamentalism.

Conclusion: The Supreme Adventure

The journey through the seven psychic circles represents nothing less than the supreme adventure of mortal existence, the transformation of an animal-origin creature into a spirit-destined child of God. This transformation occurs gradually, through countless small decisions, steady effort, and patient cooperation with divine ministry.

Several key principles emerge from this examination:

Discernment Is Essential: Learning to distinguish conscience from divine guidance, psychological phenomena from spiritual experience, and personal preference from cosmic truth represents foundational spiritual wisdom.

Balance Enables Progress: Integrated development of physical, mental, and spiritual capacities creates the optimal conditions for circle advancement and authentic spiritual growth.

Humility Protects: Acknowledging the difficulty of certain knowledge about divine leading prevents presumption, fanaticism, and the disappointments that follow misattributed guidance.

The Process Is Reliable: Though individual experiences vary widely, the framework of the seven psychic circles provides a trustworthy map for spiritual development available to all normal-minded mortals.

Divine Partnership: Human effort and divine ministry work together in the great project of soul building and personality perfection. Neither operates alone; both are essential.

As we progress through these circles, whether rapidly or gradually, dramatically or quietly, we participate in the universal plan that transforms finite creatures into perfected spirits capable of standing in the presence of the Universal Father on Paradise. This journey begins with the first moral decision of childhood and continues through mortal life, the mansion worlds, and the long ascent toward Paradise.

The next chapter will examine the specific functions and activities of the Thought Adjuster as it works to spiritualize human experience and prepare the evolving soul for eternal survival. We will explore how the Adjuster operates within the constraints of material mind while simultaneously connecting mortal consciousness to cosmic reality and spiritual truth.

This chapter is part of Dr. Roger Paul's comprehensive study series on The Urantia Book, offering accessible scholarly examination of the Fifth Epochal Revelation for both new students and experienced readers seeking deeper understanding.

Chapter 19: The Seven Psychic Circles - Understanding Spiritual Attainment

Introduction: The Architecture of Spiritual Growth

Among the most profound revelations in The Urantia Book is the concept of the seven psychic circles, a systematic framework for understanding human spiritual development from initial moral consciousness to the threshold of fusion with the divine. These circles represent not arbitrary stages but rather measurable levels of cosmic achievement that reflect the progressive mastery of mind, the evolution of soul, and the increasing reality of personality.

This chapter explores Paper 110, Section 6, which addresses the relationship between Thought Adjusters and individual mortals as we traverse these circles of attainment. Understanding this journey is essential for anyone seeking to comprehend their own spiritual progress and the magnificent partnership between human will and divine guidance that characterizes the mortal adventure.

The seven psychic circles are not merely theoretical constructs; they represent the actual trajectory of every soul's development, from the arrival of the Thought Adjuster in childhood to the potential achievement of fusion with that divine fragment. As we shall see, each circle conquered brings us closer to spiritual maturity and cosmic citizenship.

The Nature of Divine Communication

The revelators begin with a profound statement about the challenge of divine-human communication:

"The Adjusters are always near you and of you, but rarely can they speak directly as another being to you."

This limitation is not arbitrary but reflects the vast gulf between human consciousness and divine reality. The Thought Adjuster exists at a level of spiritual frequency far beyond our normal perception. For God to speak directly to mortals in our current state would require us to operate at the level of divinity itself, a transformation that would render our material existence obsolete.

The gulf between mortality and divinity is bridged gradually through circle attainment. As we progress, our intellectual decisions, moral choices, and spiritual development progressively enhance the Adjuster's ability to function within our minds. Circle by circle, we ascend from the lower stages of adjuster association and mind attunement, enabling the Adjuster to increasingly register his "picturizations of destiny" upon our evolving God-seeking consciousness.

This process requires that we become active seekers of God. The Adjuster can only work effectively with a "God-seeking mind-soul." Those who live without spiritual hunger, who never turn their thoughts toward higher realities, provide little material for the Adjuster to work with. The divine fragment within can guide only those who seek guidance. Even though, they work within all mortals for eventual spiritualization.

The Power of Decision: Forging Spiritual Habits

Every decision we make, whether seemingly mundane or obviously spiritual, either facilitates or impedes the Adjuster's function. This is one of the most important concepts in understanding spiritual growth. The Adjuster must evaluate each decision to determine what should be preserved in the spiritual transcript of our lives.

The revelators emphasize that "the supremacy of a decision, its crisis relationship, has a great deal to do with its circle-making influence." Momentous choices, those made at crossroads in life, can dramatically accelerate our progress. However, they quickly add that "numbers of decisions, repetitions, persistent repetitions, are also essential to the habit-forming certainty of such reactions."

This principle has profound practical implications. Spiritual growth is not achieved through occasional dramatic choices alone but through the patient, persistent repetition of right decisions until they become habitual. Consider the person struggling with addiction, whether to substances, lust, or greed. The path to freedom lies not in a single heroic moment but in the repetitive choice, made hour by hour and day by day, to align with higher values.

When we consistently choose the Father's will, or what we understand it to be, those choices eventually become second nature. What once required conscious effort becomes automatic. We develop what might be called "the habit of divinity", a natural inclination toward goodness, truth, and beauty that no longer requires deliberation.

This is why the revelators emphasize that following God's will must become habitual. The repetitive nature of daily decisions, made consistently in alignment with spiritual values, gradually transforms our character until righteousness becomes our default setting rather than an achievement requiring constant vigilance.

Defining the Seven Circles: Framework and Limitations

The revelators acknowledge the difficulty of precisely defining these seven levels of human progression. The circles are deeply personal, variable for each individual, and apparently determined by each person's growth capacity. No two people traverse them in exactly the same way or at the same pace.

Despite this inherent variability, circle attainment is reflected in three measurable ways:

1. Adjuster Attunement

The spiritualizing mind progressively attunes itself to the Adjuster presence proportional to circle attainment. The higher we climb, the more synchronized our consciousness becomes with divine guidance. By the time we reach the first circle, distinguishing between our will and the Adjuster's will becomes nearly impossible, they have become functionally unified.

2. Soul Evolution

The emergence of the morontia soul indicates the extent and depth of circle mastery. Our soul, that unique creation formed from the partnership of human will and divine spirit, grows in substance and reality as we progress. The more developed our morontia nature, the higher our circle attainment. This is significant because our soul represents our true immortal self, the identity that will persist beyond physical death.

3. Personality Reality

Perhaps most intriguingly, the degree of selfhood reality is directly determined by circle conquest. The revelators state that "persons become more real as they ascend from the seventh to the first level of mortal existence."

This concept challenges our assumptions about reality. We typically assume we are maximally real as we currently exist. However, from the cosmic perspective, those who remain in the lower circles are living in a shadowy, diminished state of reality.

Their personalities lack the full substantiality and cosmic effectiveness of those who have achieved higher attainment.

The person who lives entirely for material gain, who never develops spiritually, who remains consumed by self-serving pursuits, is living in a kind of unreality, chasing shadows while missing the substance. In contrast, those who progress spiritually become increasingly real, their personalities taking on greater cosmic significance and eternal substance.

The Seventh Circle: Entrance into Potential Citizenship

This level is entered when human beings develop several crucial capacities: the powers of personal choice, individual decision, moral responsibility, and the capacity for spiritual individuality. The seventh circle signifies the united function of the seven-adjutant mind-spirits under the direction of the spirit of wisdom.

This achievement represents several simultaneous spiritual events:

- The encirclement of the mortal creature in the influence of the Holy Spirit (from the Divine Minister of the local universe)
- The first functioning of the Spirit of Truth (from Christ Michael)
- The reception of a Thought Adjuster in the mortal mind

Entrance upon the seventh circle occurs typically around age five or six, when moral consciousness first awakens. At this moment, the child becomes a truly potential citizen of the local universe. The word "potential" is crucial here. The arrival of the Adjuster does not guarantee citizenship, it merely makes it possible.

Three conditions can prevent the realization of this potential: First, failing to genuinely seek God throughout one's life. Second, living a life dominated entirely by selfish, material pursuits, "wine, women, and song," as the saying goes, without ever developing spiritual hunger. Third, committing cosmic suicide through deliberate, final rejection of spiritual reality.

The seventh circle, then, marks the beginning of our embryonic spiritual life. We are like spiritual infants, barely aware of the divine presence within, but possessing the potential for magnificent growth.

The Third Circle: The Betrothal Stage

The text jumps from the seventh circle directly to the third, omitting detailed discussion of circles six, five, and four. This is not an oversight but reflects the fact that these intermediate circles represent gradual stepping stones of growth, varying so much by individual that specific definition would be misleading.

However, the third circle marks a critical threshold:

"The Adjuster's work is much more effective after the human ascender attains the third circle and receives a personal seraphic guardian of destiny."

Upon reaching this circle, the ascending mortal is assigned not one but four full-time ministering spirits: two seraphim (guardian angels), one cherubim, and one sanobim. This celestial support team remains with the individual throughout the remainder of mortal life and continues through the morontia career.

Why such intensive spiritual support at this stage? Because reaching the third circle indicates that the mortal has made a definitive commitment to doing God's will. The Adjuster interprets this as a betrothal, a spiritual engagement. From the divine perspective, which can see the end from the beginning, the outcome is virtually assured. The person has crossed a threshold of commitment that makes fusion highly probable.

This is an expression of divine love beyond comprehension. When we genuinely commit ourselves to God's purposes, the universe mobilizes resources to ensure our success. We are given every possible advantage, every conceivable support, to help us complete the journey we have chosen to make.

The text notes that while there is "no apparent concert of effort between the adjuster and the seraphic guardian," there is nonetheless "an unmistakable improvement in all phases of cosmic achievement and spiritual development subsequent to the assignment of the personal seraphic attendant."

Once the third circle is attained, the Adjuster endeavors to "morontiaize the mind of man during the remainder of the mortal lifespan, to make the remaining circles, and achieve the final stage of the divine-human association before natural death dissolves the unique partnership."

This work of morontiaization is crucial. The Adjuster is preparing the human mind to transition smoothly into morontia existence. Even while we live in flesh, our consciousness is being gradually transformed, preparing for the day when we awaken on the mansion worlds as morontia beings.

The First Circle: The Threshold of Direct Communication

The revelators state clearly:

"The Adjuster cannot, ordinarily, speak directly and immediately with you until you attain the first and final circle of progressive mortal achievement."

The first circle represents "the highest possible realization of mind-adjuster relationship in the human experience prior to the liberation of the evolving morontia soul from the habiliments of the material body."

Concerning mind, emotions, and cosmic insight, achievement of the first psychic circle is "the nearest possible approach of material mind and spirit adjuster in human experience."

It is extraordinarily rare for mortals to achieve this level before death. Even those deeply committed to spiritual living, who dedicate their lives to divine service, may never hear the direct voice of their Adjuster while in the flesh. The conditions required, the complete mastery of mind, the near-total alignment of will, the refined sensitivity of consciousness, are simply beyond most mortals during the brief decades of planetary life.

This is not a cause for discouragement but rather for realistic expectation. The spiritual journey is long, extending far beyond this first life. What we accomplish here lays the foundation for all that follows, but the fullness of adjuster communion typically awaits the morontia career.

For those rare individuals who do achieve the first circle during mortal life, the experience represents the ultimate validation of the partnership between human and divine. The person becomes, in effect, a living representative of fusion, functioning with such unity between mortal will and divine guidance that others may perceive them as speaking and acting with divine authority.

The Morontia Soul: Beginning the Next Existence Now

One of the most important concepts emphasized in this teaching is that our morontia life begins not after death but at the moment the Thought Adjuster arrives. From age five or six onward, we are simultaneously living two existences: our finite material life and our embryonic morontia life.

The morontia existence is superimposed upon the material existence, yet they remain distinct. Our material life involves the evolution of our mind and personality through experience in the physical world. Our morontia life involves the evolution of our soul through the partnership with the Adjuster.

These two streams of development run parallel throughout our mortal years. Every spiritual choice, every alignment with divine values, every moment of worship or service adds substance to our growing soul. We are literally building our next body, our morontia form, through the spiritual choices we make in this life.

This explains Jesus's admonition to "lay up treasures in heaven rather than on earth." The treasures on earth, wealth, possessions, status, physical beauty, are temporary and cannot be carried forward. But the treasures in heaven, character development, wisdom, spiritual insight, love expressed and received, these become part of our permanent morontia endowment.

Consider the wealthy person who spends their entire life accumulating material possessions, building empires of commerce, achieving fame and power, but who never develops spiritually, never seeks God, never allows their soul to grow. They arrive in the next life spiritually impoverished, regardless of their earthly wealth. In contrast, the person who lived simply, perhaps even in poverty, but who devoted time to spiritual growth, service to others, and alignment with divine values, awakens in the morontia life spiritually wealthy, with a well-developed soul ready for advanced training.

This is not to romanticize material poverty or suggest that wealth is inherently evil. Rather, it is a matter of priority and purpose. How we use our resources, whether abundant or meager, determines their spiritual value. Time spent seeking God, serving others, and developing character is never wasted. These investments pay eternal dividends.

Resurrection: Immediate or Dispensational

An important practical consequence of circle attainment concerns resurrection, how and when we awaken after mortal death.

Those who achieve the third circle or higher during their earth life experience what might be called immediate resurrection. They go to sleep on earth and wake up on the mansion worlds in what seems like no time at all. From their subjective experience, they simply close their eyes in death and open them in the resurrection halls, with no awareness of the interval between.

However, those who fail to reach the third circle during their mortal life enter what is called a dispensational sleep. They remain unconscious, held in the care of the seraphim, until the next millennial judgment, the next time a Magisterial Son visits the planet and adjudicates the sleeping survivors.

This could mean sleeping for decades, centuries, or even a full thousand years, depending on when in the dispensational cycle the person died. When they are finally resurrected, it is as part of a group resurrection, awakening alongside others of similar spiritual development to receive remedial training designed to bring them up to at least the third circle level.

This is not punishment but rather efficiency. Those who have proven themselves ready for immediate progression receive it. Those who need additional foundational development receive it in a group context where specialized teaching can be provided to address their specific needs.

The implication is clear: while salvation is ultimately available to all who choose it, there are real consequences to our spiritual choices in this life. We determine, through our decisions and commitments, how quickly we progress in the next phase of existence. This adds urgency and importance to our spiritual development now, while we have the opportunity to advance.

Practical Application: Living as Citizens of Two Worlds

Understanding the psychic circles transforms how we approach daily life. We are not merely surviving until we die, hoping to get into heaven. We are already citizens of the universe, already building our eternal career, already growing the soul that will be our true identity throughout eternity.

This means that every decision matters. The choice to speak truth rather than lie, to show kindness rather than indifference, to forgive rather than harbor resentment, to seek understanding rather than judge, these daily choices are not merely ethical preferences but actual building blocks of our eternal self.

The habit of divinity, consistently choosing the higher path, is developed through repetition. Just as an athlete builds muscle through repeated exercise, or a musician develops skill through persistent practice, we develop spiritual character through the persistent repetition of right choices.

Consider the person struggling with addiction. Whether the addiction is to substances, to lust, to greed, or to anger, the path to freedom is the same: make the right choice in this moment, then make it again in the next moment, and again in the moment after that. Each correct decision strengthens the neural pathways of righteousness, making the next correct decision slightly easier. Eventually, through persistent repetition, the right choice becomes habitual, automatic, second nature.

This is not mere behavioral modification but actual spiritual transformation. The Adjuster uses our decisions as raw material, incorporating our choices into the evolving soul. When we consistently choose in alignment with divine values, we literally become more like God. Our personalities take on divine characteristics. We become living demonstrations of what fusion ultimately accomplishes, the perfect blending of human and divine.

The Reality of Spiritual Support

One of the most encouraging revelations in this material concerns the extent of spiritual support available to sincere seekers. From the moment the Adjuster arrives, we are never alone. We have within us a fragment of God himself, working tirelessly to guide us toward truth, beauty, and goodness.

As we progress, additional support arrives. The seven-adjutant mind-spirits facilitate our intellectual and emotional development. The Holy Spirit of the Divine Minister provides comfort and spiritual nourishment. The Spirit of Truth from Christ Michael reveals truth and helps us understand spiritual realities.

When we reach the third circle, demonstrating serious commitment to the spiritual path, we receive personal guardian angels, a team of four celestial ministers dedicated entirely to our success. They work behind the scenes, arranging circumstances, protecting us from certain dangers, facilitating opportunities for growth, and ensuring that nothing of spiritual value is ever lost.

This is love beyond comprehension, the infinite God mobilizing universal resources to ensure that each sincere soul has every possible advantage for success. We are not struggling alone against overwhelming odds. We are supported, guided, protected, and encouraged by an entire universe dedicated to our spiritual success.

The only thing required from us is genuine desire for spiritual growth and persistent commitment to seeking and doing God's will. When we provide this, the universe provides everything else needed for our success.

Conclusion: The Journey Continues

Understanding the seven psychic circles gives us a framework for evaluating our spiritual progress and understanding the partnership between human will and divine guidance. We begin as spiritual infants in the seventh circle, barely aware of the divine presence within. Through persistent commitment to truth, beauty, and goodness, through the habit-forming repetition of right decisions, we gradually ascend through the circles, becoming increasingly real, increasingly attuned to divine guidance, increasingly effective as cosmic citizens.

The third circle marks our spiritual betrothal, our commitment to fusion, and brings intensive celestial support for the final stages of the mortal journey. The first circle represents the pinnacle of mortal achievement, where direct communion with the Adjuster becomes possible.

Yet even the first circle is not the end but merely the completion of the first stage. Beyond lies fusion itself, the ultimate union of human and divine, and beyond fusion lies the entire universe career, the vast adventure of Paradise ascension.

As we continue our study of the Thought Adjuster's mission and methods, we will explore how this divine fragment works within our consciousness, the kinds of guidance provided, the obstacles encountered, and the glorious destiny toward which all of this patient work is directed. Understanding these circles helps us appreciate both how far we have to go and how much help we have for the journey.

The path is clear, the support is abundant, and the destination is magnificent beyond imagination. Our task is simply to keep choosing, day by day and moment by moment, to align our will with the divine will, until that glorious day when the two become permanently and eternally one.

In the next chapter, we will explore the specific ways the Thought Adjuster communicates and guides, examining the subtle methods by which divine wisdom enters human consciousness and shapes our decisions, ideals, and destiny.

Chapter 20: The Psychic Circles of Mortal Progression

Understanding Our Cosmic Journey Through the Seven Circles

When we first encounter the concept of psychic circles in *The Urantia Book*, most of us feel a bit like we've stumbled into unfamiliar territory. What exactly are these circles? Why do they matter? And how do they relate to our everyday lives as we struggle through the mundane challenges of mortal existence?

Perhaps the most profound truth we can grasp about the psychic circles is this: they represent nothing less than our progressive awakening to who we truly are in the vast cosmos. They measure not our intellectual achievements or our social status, but rather the depth of our experiential relationship with the Supreme Being and our growing awareness of ourselves as cosmic citizens.

The revelators themselves acknowledge the difficulty of explaining these concepts to material minds. They suggest that "psychic circles of mortal progression would be better denominated cosmic levels, actual meaning grasps and value realizations of progressive approach to the morontia consciousness of initial relationship of the evolutionary soul with the emerging Supreme Being." In simpler terms, these circles track our journey from purely material consciousness toward an increasingly spiritual awareness of our place in the universe.

The Nature of the Circles: Quantity and Quality

One of the most liberating truths about the psychic circles is that they operate on two distinct yet complementary principles: quantitative growth and qualitative status.

The quantitative aspect relates to the sheer amount of experiential growth we accumulate, the breadth of our understanding, the expansion of our morontia soul, and our comprehension of supreme meanings. Think of this as the *volume* of spiritual experience we gather as we move through life. Someone who has lived longer, experienced more, and consciously reflected on those experiences may naturally accumulate more of this quantitative growth.

But here's where it gets interesting. The qualitative status of our immortal soul depends entirely on something else, "the grasp of living faith upon the Paradise-potential fact-value that mortal man is a son of the Eternal God." In other words, the *quality* of our spiritual life rests on how deeply we believe and live the truth that we are children of God.

This is why, and this bears repeating, a person just beginning their conscious spiritual journey in the seventh circle can be "almost as truly God-knowing, sonship conscious, as a second or even first circler." A young child who prays sincerely to Jesus before bed may possess a quality of faith that rivals the most philosophically sophisticated adult. Faith doesn't require a PhD in theology. It requires an open heart.

The Seven Circles: A Map of Spiritual Development

Let me walk you through how these circles actually work in our lives.

The Seventh Circle marks the beginning of true cosmic citizenship. This is where we enter when our Thought Adjuster arrives, typically around five or six years of age. Before this moment, we are what the revelators call "wards of the universe," precious beings under the care of guardian angels but not yet possessing that divine fragment that makes us potentially eternal. When the Adjuster arrives, everything changes. Our soul begins to form. We step into the seventh circle. We become, in the truest sense, citizens of a universe that stretches beyond anything we can yet imagine.

The Sixth and Fifth Circles represent our gradual awakening to spiritual realities. We begin to sense, perhaps dimly at first, that there's more to existence than the material world around us. We start making decisions with spiritual implications. We begin to wonder about purpose, meaning, and our relationship with the divine. The seven-adjutant mind-spirits of the local universe Mother Spirit work actively during these stages, helping us develop worship capacity and wisdom.

The Third Circle marks a significant milestone. This is when we've achieved enough spiritual progress that the universe assigns us two dedicated guardian angels, our very own seraphic companions, and a Cherubim and Sanobim, who will guide us not just through the remainder of our mortal life, but all the way to Paradise if we continue to choose survival. Reaching the third circle means we've grasped something profound: we understand our experiential relationship with the Supreme Being. We recognize that our daily choices, our struggles, our growth, all of it contributes to the evolving God of experience.

Those who reach the third circle before natural death typically advance to the mansion worlds within three days. Those who don't reach this level, and this isn't a judgment, just a practical consideration, sleep in unconscious rest until a dispensational resurrection, often about a thousand years later. Why the delay? Because it would be overwhelming to awaken these souls alongside those who have already achieved significant cosmic awareness. Better to awaken them together, with others at similar levels of understanding, where they can be taught the foundational concepts they need as a cohesive group.

The Second and First Circles represent advanced stages of spiritual maturity. By the time we reach these levels, the influence of the adjutant mind-spirits begins to diminish. We're preparing for something monumental: fusion with our Thought Adjuster. The transition from dependence on the material mechanisms of mortal mind to the enhanced capabilities of morontia consciousness accelerates. We're no longer spiritual infants. We're maturing sons and daughters of God, approaching the threshold of an entirely new order of existence.

Faith and Action: The Divine Fulcrum

Here's something that took me years to fully appreciate: the psychic circles aren't advanced through meditation alone, or study alone, or even faith alone. They require something the revelators call "completion of decisions." Decision, decisions and more decisions!

"The motivation of faith makes experiential the full realization of man's sonship with God," the text tells us, "but action, completion of decisions, is essential to the evolutionary attainment of consciousness of progressive kinship with the cosmic actuality of the Supreme Being."

Let me break that down. Faith gets us started. Faith opens our hearts. Faith connects us to the Father. But it's through *doing*, through making decisions and acting on them, that we actually progress through these circles. Faith without action remains potential, not actual.

Think of it this way. Faith transmutes potentials into actuals in the spiritual world. Your Thought Adjuster takes your faithful choices and creates a spiritual transcript, a morontia duplicate of your material experiences. But here's the key: "potentials become actuals in the finite realms of the Supreme only by and through the realization of choice-experience."

The revelators use a fascinating metaphor. They say that choosing to do the will of God "joins spiritual faith to material decisions in personality action and thus supplies a divine and spiritual fulcrum for the more effective functioning of the human and material leverage of God-hunger."

A fulcrum. That's what our choices become, leverage points that allow us to move mountains in our spiritual growth. Every time we choose to act in alignment with God's will, we're not just behaving morally. We're literally augmenting "both cosmic realization of the Supreme and morontia comprehension of the Paradise Deities."

The Blessing of Material Existence

I sometimes hear people wonder why God set things up this way. Why start us at the bottom? Why make us struggle through material existence with all its pain, limitations, and uncertainties?

The answer appears in this very progression through the psychic circles. We *need* material existence. We need the struggles. We need the decisions that matter, the choices that cost us something, the faith that must operate without absolute proof.

When you wake up in the morning and your body hurts, your relationships are strained, your problems seem insurmountable, that's not a curse. That's the raw material of soul-making. Without material challenges, there would be no decisions to make. Without decisions, there would be no experience. Without experience, there would be no growth. Without growth, there would be no soul capable of eternal progression.

The angels, we're told, are actually envious of us. They observe our journey from the lowest point, material creatures barely conscious of spiritual realities, and they recognize something we often miss: we have opportunities for growth they'll never experience. We get to *become* something. We get to *choose* survival. We get to partner with a fragment of God himself in creating an immortal soul.

"Such wise coordination of material and spiritual forces," the text explains, "greatly augments both cosmic realization of the Supreme and morontia comprehension of the Paradise Deities." Our material struggles aren't obstacles to spiritual growth. They're the very means by which spiritual growth occurs.

Common Questions About Circle Attainment

Let me address some questions that come up frequently in study groups.

"How do I know what circle I'm in?"

Honestly? You probably don't, at least not with precision. And that's okay. The circles aren't meant to be a spiritual competition or a source of anxiety. They're descriptive, not prescriptive. What matters is this: Are you growing? Are you making decisions based on faith? Are you developing a real relationship with God?

If someone feels compelled to know, I usually ask them: "Do you have a relationship with God?" If they say yes, I remind them that even a seventh circler, a child just beginning their spiritual journey, can be as truly God-knowing as someone on the first circle. And if they say no, well, then the answer is simple: start developing that relationship. Talk to God. Pray. Study. Serve. Make decisions that align with what you believe God wants for your life.

"Does reaching the third circle guarantee fusion in this lifetime?"

Not necessarily. Reaching the third circle means you're making significant spiritual progress and that you'll likely advance to the mansion worlds quickly after death. But fusion, the permanent union of your soul with your Thought Adjuster, typically occurs on the fifth mansion world after considerable additional growth and preparation.

That said, fusion *can* occur during mortal life. When someone reaches their maximum capacity for spiritual growth in the material realm, the Ancients of Days may authorize early fusion. If this happens, your guardian angel receives notification and warns you, because fusion involves a transformation that produces intense spiritual energy, a "glorious fire" that, while harmless to you, could injure nearby mortals. You're literally converted from a material being to a morontia being in an instant.

"What about people who never hear about these concepts?"

This is crucial to understand. You don't need *The Urantia Book* to progress through the psychic circles. You don't need any particular religious framework. What you need is faith in God and a willingness to do his will. Millions of people throughout history have reached advanced circles without ever reading a single page of revelation. They lived lives of faith, service, and spiritual seeking. That's what matters.

The revelation helps us *understand* what's happening. It gives us a map. But the territory exists whether we have the map or not.

"Is there really an indirect relation between circle attainment and religious experience?"

Yes, and this surprises many people. You can be intensely religious, attending services, participating in rituals, studying scriptures, and still be in the lower circles. Conversely, you can rarely enter a church building and be in the advanced circles. Why? Because circle attainment is about your actual experiential relationship with God and your cosmic awareness, not about external religious performance.

That said, the text notes that "circle attainment always augments the potential of human success and mortal achievement." People who are spiritually aware, who understand their place in the cosmos, who make decisions based on spiritual values, these people tend to live more successful, fulfilled lives even by material standards. Their faith gives them resilience, perspective, and purpose.

The Role of the Thought Adjuster

None of this progression through the psychic circles would be possible without the Thought Adjuster. This divine fragment serves as our spiritual compass, our connection to deity, and the architect of our morontia soul.

Every time we make a decision that has spiritual value, every time we choose truth over falsehood, compassion over cruelty, service over selfishness, the Thought Adjuster creates a spiritual counterpart to that material experience. Think of it as building a parallel identity, a morontia self that can survive the transition from material to spiritual existence.

When we die and our material body dissolves, that morontia transcript becomes the foundation of our continued existence. Without it, we would have no memories, no identity, no continuity of consciousness. We would be, in effect, starting from scratch. But because of the Thought Adjuster's work, we wake up on the mansion worlds as *ourselves*, the same personality, the same essential character, the same accumulated experience.

The Thought Adjuster doesn't do this work automatically or mechanically. It requires our cooperation. It requires decisions that the Adjuster can spiritualize. This is why action matters so much. This is why faith without work remains incomplete.

From Material to Morontia: The Great Transition

The psychic circles map our journey from material consciousness toward morontia consciousness. But what does that actually mean?

Material consciousness is what we experience now, awareness filtered through physical senses, limited by time and space, dependent on electrochemical processes in our brains. It's real, but it's also profoundly limited. We see through a glass darkly, as the ancient scriptures put it.

Morontia consciousness represents something qualitatively different. It's the consciousness of a being who exists in that intermediate realm between material and spiritual. On the mansion worlds, we'll have morontia bodies, not physical, not yet fully spiritual, but something in between. And with those bodies come enhanced capabilities: clearer perception, deeper understanding, more direct communion with spiritual realities.

The psychic circles prepare us for that transition. As we progress from the seventh to the first circle, we're gradually learning to think, perceive, and function in ways that will serve us in morontia existence. We're weaning ourselves from "dependence on the realities of the material life mechanisms preparatory to increased introduction to morontia levels of experience."

By the time someone reaches the first circle, they're already thinking somewhat like a morontia being. They understand cosmic relationships. They grasp supreme meanings. They recognize their place in the grand universe scheme. The physical death and mansion world resurrection simply complete a transformation that's already well underway.

The Supreme Being and Our Experience

I want to circle back to something that confuses many readers when they first encounter it: the relationship between our psychic circle progression and the Supreme Being.

The Supreme Being is God the Finite, the experiential God who is literally *becoming* through the experiences of all creatures in time and space. Every choice we make, every lesson we learn, every value we actualize, all of it contributes to the Supreme. Our individual growth is simultaneously the Supreme's growth.

This may sound abstract, but it has profound practical implications. It means your life *matters* in ways you might never have imagined. You're not just preparing yourself for eternity. You're contributing to the evolution of deity itself. Your struggles, your triumphs, your daily decisions to choose good over evil, all of it feeds into something infinitely larger than yourself.

The psychic circles measure our growing awareness of this relationship. In the lower circles, we may sense vaguely that there's a spiritual dimension to existence. In the middle circles, we begin to grasp that our experiences connect to something universal. In the upper circles, we achieve "experiential realization of progressive kinship with the cosmic actuality of the Supreme Being."

This realization transforms everything. We're no longer isolated individuals struggling alone. We're participants in a cosmic drama, partners with God in the adventure of eternity.

Practical Application: Living the Circles

So what does all this mean for how we actually live?

First, it means we can stop worrying so much about which circle we're in and focus instead on the simple fundamentals: faith, prayer, service, and making good decisions. The circles will take care of themselves if we take care of the basics.

Second, it means we should view our material challenges differently. That difficult relationship? That health problem? That financial stress? Those aren't interruptions to your spiritual growth. They're opportunities for it. Each challenge presents you with decisions to make, and each decision is a chance to choose God's will over your own fears or desires.

Third, it means we should cultivate gratitude for material existence itself. Yes, it's hard. Yes, it's limiting. Yes, it often feels like we're stumbling in the dark. But this is precisely the condition that makes growth possible. If we were created perfect, we'd have no room to grow. If we had no struggles, we'd have no character to forge.

Finally, it means we should be patient with ourselves and others. Spiritual growth isn't a race. Someone in the seventh circle isn't "worse" than someone in the first circle. They're just at a different stage of an infinite journey. And because quality of faith matters as much as quantity of experience, that seventh circler might have something profound to teach the first circler about simple trust in God.

Looking Ahead

As we conclude this exploration of the psychic circles, it's worth remembering where this journey leads. The circles aren't an end in themselves. They're preparation for fusion with the Thought Adjuster, which is itself preparation for the long ascent to Paradise.

Each circle we master brings us closer to that momentous day when we'll stand in the presence of the Universal Father himself, completing a journey that began when we were barely conscious material creatures on an isolated world in a remote corner of a vast universe.

But that's getting ahead of ourselves. For now, we're here, in material bodies, facing material challenges, making material decisions that will have eternal consequences. The question isn't what circle we're in. The question is simpler: Will we choose faith? Will we seek God's will? Will we serve our fellows? Will we grow?

If we can answer yes to those questions, the circles will take care of themselves. And one day, whether in this life or the next, we'll wake up to discover that everything we struggled to understand has become gloriously clear. We'll see that every hardship had purpose, every decision mattered, every moment of faith was building something eternal.

That's the promise of the psychic circles. That's the gift of mortal progression. And that's why this journey, difficult as it sometimes feels, is worth every moment.

In our next chapter, we'll explore what happens when we reach the culmination of this circular progression: the phenomenon of Thought Adjuster fusion and the transformation from mortal to morontia being. It's there that we'll discover the full meaning of everything we've been discussing and glimpse the magnitude of the adventure that lies ahead.

Chapter 21: The Seven Cosmic Circles and the Path to Adjuster Fusion

Understanding Spiritual Progress in Mortal Life

The relationship between a human being and their indwelling Thought Adjuster represents one of the most profound mysteries in all of creation. Within this partnership lies the blueprint for our eternal destiny, a journey that begins here, in our mortal existence, and extends far beyond what we can currently imagine. This chapter explores the seven cosmic circles of achievement, the process of Adjuster fusion, and what it actually means to grow spiritually while still living in a material body.

These aren't abstract theological concepts meant only for scholars or mystics. The cosmic circles describe real stages of development that each of us can, and likely will, experience as we dedicate ourselves to spiritual growth and alignment with the Father's will.

The Seven Cosmic Circles: From Animal to Morontia

The seven circles embrace the entirety of mortal experience, extending from what the revelators call "the highest purely animal level" to "the lowest actual contactual morontia level of self-consciousness as a personality experience." This is significant language. When they speak of the "contactual morontia level," they're referring to the very beginning stages of morontia existence, so elementary that we might not even recognize it as such.

Think about the first two mansion worlds for a moment. The Urantia Book describes these as "detainment spheres." That's not accidental terminology. Most ascending mortals aren't ready to integrate with the broader universe community right away. We carry too much baggage from our isolated, rebellion-scared world. These early mansion world experiences function as a kind of quarantine, not punitive, but protective. We need time to unlearn certain habits, to shed what the book calls "the mark of the beast."

This helps explain why the contactual morontia level mentioned here is described as the lowest such level. When we first arrive on the mansion worlds (assuming we don't fuse during mortal life), we're barely morontia beings at all. We're works in progress, still heavily influenced by the animal legacy we inherited.

Mastery of the First Circle

The mastery of the first cosmic circle "signalizes the attainment of pre-morontia mortal maturity and marks the termination of the conjoint ministry of the adjutant mind-spirits as an exclusive influence of mind action in the human personality."

Let's break that down. When you reach the first circle, still here, still mortal, still walking around on this planet, you've become something remarkable: a pre-morontia mortal. Your soul has developed to such an extent that you're essentially living in a transitional state. The only thing separating you from full morontia status is the experience of death itself.

This is exactly what happened with Jesus during those forty days after his resurrection. He went through all seven morontia levels right here on Urantia before ascending to the Father. That progression is possible for us too, though most of us won't complete it until well after we've left this world behind.

Reaching the first circle also marks a shift in how your mind operates. You're no longer exclusively dependent on the seven-adjutant mind-spirits, those wonderful mental circuits the local universe Mother Spirit provides. Instead, your mind becomes "increasingly akin to the intelligence of the morontia stage of evolution." You begin operating more through the cosmic mind, supplemented by what the book calls "the superadjutant endowment of the creative spirit."

The local Mother Spirit doesn't abandon us, of course. She maintains our connection all the way up to the point where we become first-stage spirits. But the nature of that connection changes as we progress.

The Adjuster's Journey: From Ministry to Partnership

The great milestones in an Adjuster's individual career are worth examining closely. First comes the moment when the human subject breaks through into the third psychic circle, "thus ensuring the Monitor's self-activity and increased range of function (provided the indweller was not already self-acting)."

Many Adjusters assigned to mortals at birth are already self-acting, they possess advanced experience and capabilities from previous assignments. But others aren't. For these Adjusters, the human's achievement of the third circle represents a watershed moment. Suddenly, the Adjuster gains new freedom, new authority, new possibilities for influence and guidance.

Some of the most spiritually advanced people on this planet, many serving in the Reserve Corps of Destiny, have self-acting Adjusters. Picture about a thousand individuals scattered across Urantia, living relatively normal lives, but carrying within them Adjusters capable of assuming direct control in emergency situations. These aren't people who necessarily know they're reservists. They're trained during sleep, prepared for moments when the universe might need immediate intervention to preserve the outworking of the divine plan.

Imagine a scenario: A military officer receives an order that would trigger catastrophic destruction. In that split second, their self-acting Adjuster might intervene, not dramatically, not obviously, but just enough to delay the action, to introduce doubt, to provide a moment for sanity to prevail. We'll never know how many disasters have been averted by such interventions.

The second great day for an Adjuster comes when the human partner attains the first psychic circle. At this level, "they are thereby enabled to intercommunicate, at least to some degree." Notice the careful qualification: "at least to some degree." Even at this advanced level, clear communication with your Adjuster isn't guaranteed. The material mind still presents obstacles.

And then comes the ultimate milestone: final and eternal fusion, when the human and the divine become one being, inseparable throughout all eternity.

The Mystery of Immortality and Fusion

Here's something that surprises many students: "There are many mortals living on Urantia who have attained their circles; but fusion depends on yet other greater and more sublime spiritual achievements, upon the attainment of a final and complete attunement of the mortal will with the will of God as it is resident in the Thought Adjuster."

Circle attainment doesn't automatically equal fusion. You can reach the first circle and still not be ready. Why? Because fusion requires something beyond intellectual achievement or even spiritual dedication. It requires a complete, unreserved, final surrender of will, not in the sense of losing yourself, but in the sense of finding yourself so fully aligned with the Father that there's no longer any separation between what you want and what He wants.

Most ascending mortals don't achieve this until around the fifth mansion world. Think about what that means. Even after death, even after resurrection on world one, most of us need four or five more stages of growth before we're ready for fusion. Why? Because we're products of a confused, isolated, rebellion-scared planet. We've absorbed patterns of thinking, habits of reacting, social conditioning that runs deep, deeper than we can easily recognize.

The first two mansion worlds are detainment spheres for good reason. We're being retrained, re-socialized, gradually freed from what the revelators call "beastly tendencies." By the time we've completed all seven mansion world experiences, we've finally become full cosmic citizens, ready to take our place in the larger universe community.

But on more advanced worlds, planets that have had the benefit of a Magisterial Son, or a Trinity Teacher Son, or that are even settled in light and life, the situation is dramatically different. Mortals on those worlds might already be living at a spiritual level equivalent to mansion world four or five. Their social structures support spiritual growth. They don't waste energy on war, on exploitation, on the thousand forms of selfishness that plague our world. For them, fusion during mortal life happens much more frequently.

When Fusion Happens in the Flesh

When a human being completes the circles of cosmic achievement, and when "the final choosing of the mortal will permits the adjuster to complete the association of human identity with the morontial soul during evolutionary and physical life, then do such consummated liaisons of soul and adjuster go independently to the mansion worlds, and there is issued the mandate from Uversa which provides for the immediate fusion of the adjuster and the morontial soul."

This fusion during physical life instantly consumes the material body. Any human witnesses would simply see the person disappear, in a flash of glory, translation, the old texts called it. "Chariots of fire," as the ancient prophets described it.

On Urantia, we have record of only two such occurrences: Enoch and Elijah. But that's just the official record. How many others might there have been? Think of the news stories we occasionally hear about someone who vanished completely from a locked room, leaving only their clothes or shoes behind. Authorities call it spontaneous combustion, but who knows? Maybe some of those cases represent fusion.

I'd like to believe there are far more spiritually advanced people on this planet than we realize, ordinary folks living quiet lives, steadily progressing through the circles, gradually aligning their wills with the Father's. When they reach that point of complete readiness, their guardian seraphim receives the mandate from the Ancients of Days, warns them that fusion is imminent, and they have time to prepare for translation from mortal to morontia existence.

It's worth noting that most Adjusters who have successfully translated their subjects from Urantia were highly experienced, having served as indwellers for numerous mortals on other worlds. But not all. The book specifically tells us that Adjusters gain valuable experience on worlds like ours, "planets of the loan order", and it doesn't follow that only inexperienced Adjusters get assigned to mortals who fail to survive.

There's mystery here, as there is in so much of the universe. We don't know all the factors that determine Adjuster assignments. We don't fully understand why some highly spiritual people don't fuse during mortal life while others do. The universe operates on principles that, from our limited vantage point, we can only partially glimpse.

After Fusion: Becoming One

"Subsequent to mortal fusion the adjusters share your destiny and experience; they are you."

That simple statement carries profound implications. After fusion, everything the Adjuster has experienced throughout its existence, all the previous indwellings, all the divine perspective, all the connection to the Father, becomes your possession. And everything that was uniquely human in your surviving soul, all your memories, all your personality traits, all your hard-won experiential growth, becomes the Adjuster's possession.

"In a certain sense this new being is of the eternal past as well as for the eternal future."

But here's the catch: "On each universe level the adjuster can endow the new creature only with those attributes which are meaningful and of value on that level."

Imagine trying to download the entire contents of the universal archives into your mind right now. Your brain would short-circuit. Your personality would fracture under the weight of knowledge it wasn't designed to hold. The fusion process protects us from that. The Adjuster can only share with us what we're capable of receiving and processing at our current level of development.

"An absolute oneness with the divine monitor, a complete exhaustion of the endowment of an adjuster, can only be achieved in eternity subsequent to the final attainment of the Universal Father, the Father of spirits, ever the source of these divine gifts."

In other words, you won't have complete access to everything your Adjuster knows, all the past experiences, all the future foresight, until you stand in the presence of God on Paradise. At that moment, the union becomes complete. Every barrier dissolves. The experiential memory of the past and the experienceable potential of the future become fully available to your fused consciousness.

Why the delay? Because God exists outside time. From His perspective, there is no sequence of events, no past, no present, no future. Everything simply *is*. The moment you choose to do the Father's will, really choose it, with full commitment, from God's perspective, your ascension is already complete. He sees the finish line before you've taken the first step.

We can't operate that way, not yet. We exist within time, within sequence. We need to grow through stages, learning one lesson at a time, ascending one level at a time. If we tried to receive everything at once, we'd be overwhelmed. So, the Adjuster shares its gifts gradually, carefully, at exactly the pace we can handle.

This also explains why time travel, in the way science fiction imagines it, isn't possible. You can't go back and change something that's already happened, and you can't jump forward to something that hasn't yet occurred, not for you, anyway. The only consciousness that transcends time completely is the Father's. For the rest of us, there's only this eternal now, this present moment, where growth happens and choices are made.

The Challenge of Communication

For the vast majority of Urantians the Adjuster "must patiently await the arrival of death deliverance; must await the liberation of the emerging soul from the well-nigh complete domination of the energy patterns and chemical forces inherent in your material order of existence."

That's the reality we face. Our material bodies, our chemical-electrical brains, our animal inheritance, all of this creates what amounts to interference in the communication channel between us and our indwelling Adjusters. It's not the Adjuster's fault. They're doing everything possible to reach us. The limitation is on our end.

"The chief difficulty you experience in contacting with your adjusters consists in this very inherent material nature. So few mortals are real thinkers; you do not spiritually develop and discipline your minds to the point of favorable liaison with the divine adjusters."

That's a hard truth. "So few mortals are real thinkers." The revelators aren't trying to be insulting. They're stating a fact. Most people operate on autopilot most of the time, reacting to stimuli, following ingrained patterns, thinking the thoughts that their culture has programmed them to think. Genuine reflection, true contemplation, serious intellectual and spiritual development, these are rare.

"The ear of the human mind is almost deaf to the spiritual pleas which the adjuster translates from the manifold messages of the universal broadcasts of love proceeding from the Father of Mercies."

Our minds are tuned to the wrong frequency, you might say. We're so caught up in the noise of material existence, the constant demands, the endless distractions, the chemical and electrical forces that drive our animal nature, that we simply can't hear what the Adjuster is trying to tell us.

But the Adjusters don't give up. "Adjusters rejoice to make contact with the mortal mind; but they must be patient through the long years of silent sojourn during which they are unable to break through animal resistance and directly communicate with you."

Think about that from the Adjuster's perspective. Imagine being a fragment of infinite Deity, carrying within yourself the love and purposes of the Universal Father, assigned to indwell a mortal creature on a backward, isolated world. You arrive at the moment of moral choice, perhaps when the child is five or six years old. And then you wait. Year after year, you watch your human subject make choices, learn lessons, experience life, and only rarely, very rarely, catch even the faintest glimmer of your presence.

"The higher the thought adjusters ascend in the scale of service, the more efficient they become. But never can they greet you, in the flesh, with the same full, sympathetic, and expressionful affection as they will when you discern them mind to mind on the mansion worlds."

That's the promise. On the mansion worlds, freed from the limitations of material existence, we'll finally be able to communicate with our Adjusters directly. We'll understand then what they've been trying to tell us all along. We'll experience the full depth of their affection, divine affection, which has patiently sustained us through all our stumbling and confusion.

"During mortal life the material body and mind separate you from your adjuster and prevent free communication; subsequent to death, after eternal fusion, you and the adjuster are one, you are not distinguishable as separate beings, and thus there exists no need for communication as you would understand it."

After fusion, the question of communication becomes irrelevant. There's no need to communicate when there's no separation. Your thoughts are the Adjuster's thoughts. The Adjuster's purposes are your purposes. You've become a single being, indivisible, unified throughout eternity.

Hearing the Adjuster's Voice

"While the voice of the adjuster is ever within you, most of you will hear it seldom during a lifetime. Human beings below the third and second circles of attainment rarely hear the adjuster's direct voice except in moments of supreme desire, in a supreme situation, and consequent upon a supreme decision."

For most of us, the Adjuster's voice comes through only in crisis, those moments when we've exhausted our own resources, when we've reached the absolute limit of our capacity, when we finally stop trying to control everything and simply cry out: "God, I can't do this. You have to do this for me."

In those moments, something shifts. Not always in dramatic or obvious ways, but something shifts. A clarity emerges. A path opens. We find strength we didn't know we had, or wisdom that seems to come from beyond ourselves. That's often the Adjuster, breaking through the interference, reaching us when we're finally receptive enough to receive.

A Message from the Adjuster

Tucked away in this section of Paper 110 is one of the most moving passages in the entire Urantia revelation. It's presented by a Solitary Messenger of Orvington, someone who has completed the entire ascension journey and now serves at the highest levels of universe administration.

"During the making and breaking of a contact between the mortal mind of a destiny reservist and the planetary supervisors, sometimes the indwelling adjuster is so situated that it becomes possible to transmit a message to the mortal partner."

What follows is an actual message from an Adjuster to its human subject, a member of the Reserve Corps of Destiny. The Adjuster begins carefully:

"And now, without injury or jeopardy to the subject of my solicitous devotion, and without intent to over chastise or discourage, for me, make record of this my plea to him."

Then comes the message itself, beautiful, touching, almost heartbreaking in its earnest appeal. The Adjuster pleads with its human partner to:

- More faithfully give sincere cooperation
- More cheerfully endure the tasks of divine arrangement
- More carefully carry out the program of divine design
- More patiently go through the trials of divine selection
- More persistently and cheerfully tread the path of divine choosing
- More humbly receive credit that may accrue as a result of the Adjuster's ceaseless endeavors

The Adjuster continues:

"Transmit my admonition to the man of my indwelling. Upon him I bestow the supreme devotion and affection of a divine spirit. And say further to my beloved subject that I will function with wisdom and power until the very end, until the last earth struggle is over; I will be true to my personality trust. And I exhort him to survival, not to disappoint me, not to deprive me of the reward of my patient and intense struggle."

Can you hear the emotion in those words? "My beloved subject." "I will be true to my personality trust." "Not to disappoint me."

The Adjuster goes on:

"On the human will our achievement of personality depends. Circle by circle I have patiently ascended this human mind, and I have testimony that I am meeting the approval of the chief of my kind. Circle by circle I am passing on to judgment. I await with pleasure and without apprehension the roll call of destiny; I am prepared to submit all to the tribunals of the Ancients of Days."

This is pure love, divine love, personal love, patient love that has persevered through years of difficulty, through all the human subject's mistakes and failures and moments of weakness. And now, as the journey nears completion, the Adjuster makes this final plea: Don't give up. Keep going. We're almost there.

The roll call of destiny mentioned here refers to the moment, after mortal death, when an ascending soul is officially approved to continue on the mansion worlds. For those who haven't reached the third circle, there's a waiting period, sometimes a long one, before the roll call comes. When it does, you must be approved by the Ancients of Days to remain on the first mansion world and continue your ascension.

But the deeper meaning here transcends administrative procedure. This is one consciousness speaking to another, one being pleading with another: *I love you. I've walked with you through everything. Please don't give up now.*

We could apply this message to every single one of us. Each of us has an Adjuster who feels this way, who has patiently ascended our minds circle by circle, who waits with pleasure and without apprehension for our continued progress, who exhorts us to survival, to partnership, to eventual fusion.

Conclusion: The Journey Continues

The seven cosmic circles aren't abstract theological concepts. They're real stages of growth that we navigate as we learn to align our wills with the Father's, as we develop our souls, as we prepare for the eternal adventure that lies ahead.

Most of us won't complete this journey during our mortal lives. We'll continue it on the mansion worlds, in environments better suited to spiritual growth, freed from the heavy interference of material existence. But we can make real progress here and now. We can move from circle to circle. We can develop that favorable liaison with our indwelling Adjusters. We can prepare ourselves for what's coming.

And all the while, our Adjusters wait patiently, work tirelessly, and love unconditionally. They're in this with us for the long haul, not just for this life, but for eternity.

In the next chapter, we'll explore the nature of the evolving soul, that unique creation that emerges from the partnership between human will and divine presence, that morontia reality that is neither fully material nor fully spiritual, but something wonderfully new.

The journey of a thousand worlds begins with a single choice: the choice to seek the Father's will and follow wherever it leads.

Chapter 22: The Adjuster and the Soul

Introduction: The Divine Partnership Within

Among the most profound revelations contained within The Urantia Book, few concepts challenge our understanding quite like the dual nature of our inner spiritual reality. This chapter explores Paper 111, which addresses the relationship between the divine adjuster and the evolving human soul, two distinct yet intimately connected aspects of our being that science and philosophy have struggled to comprehend for millennia.

The very presence of a divine fragment within the human mind creates what might be called an epistemological barrier for traditional modes of inquiry. Neither empirical science nor abstract philosophy can fully grasp the evolving soul of the human personality, precisely because this soul represents a child of the universe, knowable only through cosmic insight and spiritual discovery. In other words, the soul reveals itself through experience rather than through laboratory analysis or logical deduction.

To appreciate the complexity of this divine partnership, we need to recognize that human beings exist as a composite of at least three essential elements: the Thought Adjuster (the divine fragment of God the Father), the soul (the embryonic morontia self that develops throughout mortal life), and the mind with its superimposed personality (a direct gift from the Universal Father). Each component originates from a different source, yet they must work in harmony to achieve the ultimate goal of eternal survival.

The Historical Quest for Understanding

Throughout human history, various religious and philosophical traditions have sensed this dual nature of human existence. The concept of an indwelling spirit coupled with an evolving soul appears repeatedly across planetary belief systems, though often imperfectly understood. Many Oriental faiths, as well as certain Occidental traditions, have long perceived that humanity possesses both divine heritage and human inheritance, that something within human nature transcends the brief span of temporal life.

Ancient peoples attempted to localize this spiritual reality within physical organs. Before humanity grasped that the evolving soul was fathered by a divine spirit, different cultures believed it resided in various bodily organs: the eye, liver, kidney, heart, and eventually the brain. Early civilizations associated the soul with blood, breath, shadows, and even reflections in water. While these concepts may seem primitive to modern sensibilities, they reflect a persistent human intuition that we are more than mere biological machines.

Traces of this ancient thinking persist in contemporary language. When we say "in my heart I feel one thing, but in my head I know another," we unconsciously echo beliefs from humanity's distant past. The Thought Adjuster is described as indwelling the mind, which represents a superimposition upon the physical brain. When severe brain damage occurs, the adjuster is released to continue the individual's journey beyond physical existence. The brain, in this framework, functions somewhat like an antenna, a material mechanism necessary for spiritual realities to interface with physical consciousness.

Eastern Perspectives: The Atman and the Dual Nature

Hindu teachers, in their conception of the Atman, came remarkably close to understanding the nature and presence of the adjuster. However, they struggled to distinguish between this divine presence and the co-present evolving soul, the potentially immortal morontia identity that develops alongside the divine fragment.

Chinese philosophy recognized two aspects of human nature: the yang and the yin, representing soul and spirit respectively. This dualistic framework, while not perfectly aligned with the revelations in The Urantia Book, demonstrates an intuitive grasp of humanity's composite nature.

Egyptian Wisdom: The Ka and the Ba

The ancient Egyptians developed perhaps one of the most sophisticated pre-revelation understandings of this dual spiritual reality. They believed in two factors: the ka and the ba. The soul, in their theology, was not typically considered pre-existent; only the spirit held that distinction.

The inhabitants of the Nile Valley taught that each favored individual received at birth, or shortly thereafter, a protecting spirit called the ka. This guardian spirit remained with the person throughout life and preceded them into the future estate. Archaeological evidence for this belief can be found in the temple at Luxor, where depictions of the birth of Amenhotep III show the young prince both on the arm of the Nile god and accompanied by another child-like figure, identical in appearance yet symbolically representing the ka.

This artistic representation is particularly striking. Two arms emerge from the divine figure, one holding the spirit aspect and the other the soul aspect. On the god's arm appear two children, mirror images of each other, representing the spirit and the soul as distinct yet unified entities. The ka was understood as a superior spirit genius that desired to guide the associated mortal soul toward better temporal living and, more significantly, to influence the individual's fortunes in the hereafter.

When an Egyptian of this period died, it was expected that the ka would be waiting on the other side of the Great River, a metaphor remarkably similar to the modern understanding of crossing over to the mansion worlds. Initially, only pharaohs were believed to possess a ka, but eventually this blessing was extended to all righteous individuals.

One Egyptian ruler, speaking of the ka within his heart, declared: "I did not disregard its speech. I feared to transgress its guidance. I prospered thereby greatly. I was thus successful by reason of that which it caused me to do. I was distinguished by its guidance." This ancient testimony reflects a profound truth: listening to divine guidance leads to prosperity, not merely material success, but spiritual advancement.

Many Egyptians believed the ka functioned as "an oracle from God in everybody" and looked forward to spending eternity "in gladness of heart in the favor of the god that is in you." The parallels to revealed truth are unmistakable. As we cross the metaphorical Great River and journey to the mansion worlds, we fuse with the spirit of God and become one, precisely what these ancient teachings suggested.

Universal Intuitions Across Cultures

Every evolving race of Urantian mortals developed vocabulary equivalent to the concept of soul. Primitive peoples often believed the soul looked out upon the world through human eyes, which led to a widespread fear of the "evil eye." This superstition arose from the logical inference that if God dwelt within oneself, then God also dwelt within others. If the divine presence within another person desired something contrary to one's own interests, that created a potential threat. While these beliefs represent superstition rather than spiritual fact, they demonstrate how close early humanity came to grasping fundamental truths.

The Rig Veda states, "My mind speaks to my heart", a poetic expression of the internal dialogue between material consciousness and spiritual reality. These ancient texts reflect humanity's long struggle to articulate the experience of divine indwelling.

The Mind: Arena of Choice

Though the work of the adjusters operates within a spiritual framework, they must necessarily conduct their activities upon an intellectual foundation. The human mind serves as the soil from which the spirit monitor evolves the morontia soul, always working in cooperation with the indwelt personality. This represents a crucial insight: the mind provides the arena where spiritual transformation occurs.

Understanding this requires recognizing that we possess a complex internal architecture. The Thought Adjuster brings divine influence, the cosmic mind circuit provides intellectual capacity (channeled through the local universe Mother Spirit and the seven-adjutant mind-spirits), and the personality, bestowed directly by God the Father, unifies these elements into a functioning whole. In essence, this creates a trinity of influences: Father, Mother Spirit, and the personality gift that originates ultimately in the Eternal Son (since all spirit beings originate in the Son).

Philosophy and science have long struggled to reconcile the concept that both the spirit of God and the evolving human soul dwell within a single individual. The difficulty arises because these represent fundamentally different orders of reality attempting to function cooperatively within the limited framework of mortal consciousness. We might accurately say that we possess "two minds", the mind of the adjuster and the mind of the evolving soul, both operating within the cosmic mind circuit, with personality superimposed upon the entire system.

The personality itself presents a mystery. It receives its characteristics from the Father but exists as a unique gift that grows through experience. Personality is intrinsically connected to will, the capacity to make choices. When we consistently choose against God's will, we fail to grow that personality gift. If this becomes habitual, we place ourselves outside the will of God entirely, jeopardizing our eternal survival. Even those who live largely outside divine guidance may possess salvageable elements, however. The first mansion world (sometimes called the first detention sphere) exists specifically to rehabilitate those who arrive with incomplete spiritual development.

The Seven Mind-Spirits and Spiritual Development

Cosmic unity exists across the several mind levels throughout the universe of universes. Intellectual selves originate in the cosmic mind, much as nebulae take origin in the cosmic energies of universe space. On the human level, the personal level of intellectual selves, the potential for spirit evolution becomes dominant through the ascent of mortal mind, primarily because of the spiritual endowments given to human personality combined with the creative presence of an entity-point of absolute value.

This spirit dominance of the material mind depends upon two critical experiences. First, the mind must evolve through the ministry of the seven-adjutant mind-spirits, progressing through ascending levels of cosmic consciousness. Second, the material-personal self must consciously choose to cooperate with the indwelling adjuster in creating and fostering the morontia self, the evolutionary and potentially immortal soul.

This process cannot be passive. We must actively participate in our own spiritual development by making repeated choices to align with divine guidance. The journey involves ascending through seven cosmic levels of mind while simultaneously choosing, over and over, to cooperate with the divine presence within us.

The Material Foundation of Spiritual Growth

Material mind serves as the arena in which human personalities live, achieve self-consciousness, make decisions, choose or forsake God, and ultimately eternalize or destroy themselves. While it may seem that our physical brains make these decisions, the reality involves the mind superimposed upon the brain, working in concert with spiritual influences to guide our choices.

The decisions we make must be self-conscious, deliberate acts of will. We must actively choose survival and actively choose God. Many people perform good works throughout their lives, yet do so for personal credit, professional ambition, or humanitarian principles rather than from genuine faith in deity. While such service benefits society, it does not necessarily ensure eternal survival. As Jesus warned at the final judgment, to some he will say, "I never knew you." Understanding this principle illuminates much of Christ's teaching that might otherwise seem harsh or inexplicable.

The Temporal Nature of Mortal Mind

Material evolution has provided us with a life machine, the human body. The Father himself has endowed us with the purest spirit reality known in the universe, the Thought Adjuster. Into our hands, subject to our own decisions, has been given mind. It is by mind that we live or die, and within this mind we make the moral decisions that enable us to achieve adjuster-likeness, which is to say, Godlikeness.

Our mortal mind represents a temporary intellectual system loaned to us for use during material lifetime. As we employ this mind, we continually accept or reject the potential for eternal existence. This occurs not merely through major life decisions but through countless small choices made daily. Every interaction, whether standing in a grocery line, speaking with a cashier, or responding to an irritation, either builds up our potential for eternal existence or diminishes it.

Human consciousness rests gently upon the electrochemical mechanism below (the physical brain) and delicately touches the spirit-morontia energy system above. We never become completely conscious of either system during mortal life. Therefore, we must work within the mind of which we are conscious. Critically, it is not so much what mind comprehends, but rather what mind *desires* to comprehend that ensures survival.

This distinction deserves emphasis: It is not so much what mind *is like*, but what mind is *striving to be like* that constitutes spiritual identification. It is not that we are fully conscious of God at every moment, but that we *yearn* for God, this yearning results in universal ascension. What we are today matters less than what we are becoming day by day and throughout eternity.

Protecting the Temple of Consciousness

The connection between the electrochemical mechanism (the brain) and the spiritual-morontia energy system represents a delicate relationship. When we introduce substances that alter brain chemistry, whether through alcohol, recreational drugs, or even unnecessary medications, we modify the electrochemical mechanism that serves as the foundation for spiritual communication. Every time someone lights a cigarette, consumes excessive alcohol, or abuses substances, they change this delicate mechanism. If we put harmful inputs into our bodies, we can expect compromised outputs.

Conversely, when we maintain a healthy lifestyle and treat our bodies as temples, we create optimal conditions for the Thought Adjuster to perform its work. This explains the traditional religious counsel against drinking, smoking, and promiscuous behavior, not as arbitrary rules, but as practical wisdom for maintaining the integrity of our spiritual communication channels.

We experience reality through both conscious and superconscious levels of awareness. The Thought Adjuster communicates primarily through the superconscious mind. When we damage our brains or cloud our consciousness with substances, we make it exponentially more difficult for divine guidance to reach us clearly.

The Daily Practice of Spiritual Identification

The human will functions as a cosmic instrument capable of playing either the discords of destruction or the exquisite melodies of God-identification and consequent eternal survival. The adjuster bestowed upon humanity is, in the final analysis, impervious to evil and incapable of sin. However, mortal mind can be twisted, distorted, and rendered evil and ugly through the sinful machinations of a perverse or self-seeking human will.

Equally, this same mind can be made noble, beautiful, true, and good, actually great, in accordance with the spirit-illuminated will of a God-knowing human being. Even those who have engaged in the most sinful, ugly, perverse, or self-seeking behaviors retain the capacity for transformation. There exists hope for everyone, regardless of past choices.

Perhaps humanity's greatest gift lies in intellect coupled with the capacity for vigilant self-examination. Through intellectual honesty, we can question our motivations, examine our choices, and intentionally direct ourselves toward spiritual growth. Every day presents opportunities to make better decisions, to align more closely with divine will, and to foster the development of our immortal souls.

Throughout the past two thousand years since Christ's earthly life, a curious phenomenon occurred: humanity largely ceased questioning religious authority. For centuries, the Bible remained unchallenged despite containing significant internal contradictions and historical problems. Those who dared to question faced excommunication, torture, or execution. The medieval church employed brutal methods to suppress inquiry and maintain doctrinal control.

We should question everything. Authentic learning requires persistent inquiry. The instructor who grows uncomfortable with questions likely lacks adequate understanding of the subject matter. Truth welcomes investigation; it fears no scrutiny.

The Integration of Science and Spirit

Evolutionary mind achieves full stability and dependability only when manifesting itself at two extremes of cosmic intellectuality: the wholly mechanized and the entirely spiritualized. Between these intellectual extremes, between pure mechanical control and true spirit nature, lies an enormous group of evolving and ascending minds. The stability and tranquility of these developing minds depend entirely upon personality choice and spirit identification.

This presents the fundamental challenge in the perceived conflict between science and religion. Science tends toward the wholly mechanized perspective, while religion emphasizes the entirely spiritualized view. Yet these need not represent opposing forces. When properly understood, science and spirituality reveal themselves as complementary aspects of a unified reality.

The Urantia Book's unique contribution lies precisely in this integration. It demonstrates that mechanical processes and spiritual realities are not antagonistic but rather intimately interrelated. Truth, goodness, and beauty form an inseparable trinity. When we genuinely seek truth, whether through scientific investigation or spiritual inquiry, we inevitably encounter all three dimensions. We cannot develop a mature spiritual worldview without integrating scientific understanding, just as we cannot fully comprehend material reality without acknowledging its spiritual foundations.

Conclusion: The Daily Path of Spiritual Growth

This chapter has explored the fundamental relationship between the divine adjuster and the human soul, tracing humanity's long quest to understand our composite nature. From ancient Egyptian wisdom to modern revelation, the same essential truth emerges, we are beings of dual heritage, possessed of both material mechanisms and spiritual potentials.

The key to eternal survival lies not in intellectual comprehension alone, but in the daily practice of aligning our will with divine purpose. Every decision matters. Every interaction shapes our developing souls. The soul grows through experience, through choosing, again and again, to cooperate with the divine presence within us.

We need not achieve perfection during mortal life. What matters is direction rather than position, trajectory rather than current status. Are we yearning for God? Are we striving to understand divine will and implement it in our daily lives? Are we treating our bodies as temples worthy of housing divine presence? Are we making conscious, deliberate choices to foster spiritual growth?

These questions should guide our daily examination of conscience. The journey from material existence to spiritual reality occurs one step at a time, one choice at a time, one day at a time. As we continue this study of The Urantia Book, we will deepen our understanding of how the soul develops and what awaits us in the morontia realms beyond mortal death.

The next chapter will examine the stages of soul development and the specific mechanisms through which the Thought Adjuster and human will collaborate to create this emerging immortal identity. We will explore what survives the transition from material to morontia existence and how our mortal experiences shape our eternal destiny.

Until then, may we each commit to the daily practice of spiritual awareness, recognizing that every moment offers an opportunity to choose God, to build soul capacity, and to prepare ourselves for the magnificent adventure that awaits beyond the Great River.

Chapter 23: The Nature of the Immortal Soul

Understanding the Divine Partnership Within

The question of what happens to us after death has haunted humanity since the first human being looked up at the stars and wondered about their place in the cosmos. Every culture, every religion, every philosophical tradition has grappled with this fundamental mystery. Yet for all our speculation, for all our hopes and fears, the true nature of the soul, its origin, its development, its destiny, has remained frustratingly elusive.

Paper 111 of *The Urantia Book* offers something remarkable: a detailed, systematic explanation of how the immortal soul comes into being and what it means for our eternal future. This isn't abstract theology or wishful thinking. It's a practical guide to understanding the most important development happening within each of us right now, whether we're aware of it or not.

In this chapter, we'll explore the mechanics of soul creation, the relationship between human will and divine guidance, and why the choices we make today echo throughout eternity. What you're about to discover may challenge some long-held assumptions about spiritual life, but it also offers genuine hope, and practical direction for anyone serious about their eternal career.

The Sacred Partnership: Mind as the Captain's Ship

The Urantia Book presents us with a striking metaphor: your mind is a ship, the Thought Adjuster is the pilot, and your human will serves as captain of this mortal vessel. This image captures something essential about the spiritual life that too many religious traditions miss entirely.

Notice what isn't being said here. You're not being told to abandon the helm, to passively surrender control and let God steer while you sit back and wait for divine intervention. That's not how this works. The human will remains supreme, the captain always has final authority over the vessel. The Thought Adjuster, that divine fragment dwelling within your mind, never dominates. It never overrides your decisions. It never forces spiritual growth upon an unwilling participant.

What the Adjuster does is guide. It suggests. It adjusts your thoughts toward more spiritual interpretations of experience. But it accomplishes this only through your conscious, willing cooperation. You have to choose actively, positively, cooperatively, to follow the Adjuster's leading, particularly when that leading conflicts with what your natural mortal mind wants to do.

This distinction matters more than you might initially realize. We don't slavishly surrender our will to the Adjuster. Instead, we make a consecrated decision, a deliberate, ongoing choice, to allow the Father's will to take precedence over our own impulses. It's a partnership, not a hostile takeover. And like any partnership, it requires active participation from both parties.

Think about the wisdom required here. The master of a mortal vessel should have enough sense to trust a divine pilot who knows the way across barriers of time and through the handicaps of space. The Adjuster comes from Paradise itself, from the very source of the Divine Mind. Where is it trying to guide you? Back to that same Paradise, to the Father of Adjusters himself. What comes from God returns to God, but only if you let it.

This is where human choice becomes decisive. Only through selfishness, through genuine slothfulness, or through persistent sinfulness can you reject the guidance of this loving pilot. And if you do? You wreck your eternal career on what the revelators call "the evil shoals of rejected mercy" and "the rocks of embraced sin." It's a stark image, isn't it? Your ship doesn't just drift aimlessly, it crashes against obstacles you could have avoided if you'd simply trusted the one who knew the way.

The good news? With your consent, this faithful pilot will safely carry you across every barrier, past every handicap, straight to the Divine Mind itself, and beyond, all the way to Paradise. But that word "consent" is crucial. It's not automatic. It's not guaranteed. It's a choice you make, repeatedly, throughout your mortal life.

The Cosmic Loom: Weaving Eternal Fabric

If we shift our metaphor from navigation to creation, we encounter another profound image: the material mind of mortal humanity serves as a cosmic loom. On this loom, the indwelling Thought Adjuster threads spiritual patterns, the enduring values and divine meanings of universe character, into morontia fabric.

Let's unpack that carefully. The cosmos itself functions as a kind of vast weaving apparatus. The morontia individuals we'll become represent the fabric being created. And the Thought Adjuster? It's threading through this fabric, creating patterns that reflect universal spiritual reality. The result is a surviving soul with ultimate destiny, an unending career, a potential finaliter status.

This metaphor reveals something the navigation image doesn't quite capture: the interconnectedness of everything. The universe isn't just a backdrop for individual spiritual journeys. It's a pattern, a template, a cosmic blueprint that influences every circuit of existence. The mind circuits throughout creation follow this same pattern, which is why we can all intercommunicate, why we can grow together as one functioning universal whole.

When you step outside this pattern, when you insist on going your own way, following only your personal desires without regard for cosmic reality, life becomes difficult. Not because God is punishing you, but because you're trying to operate outside the system that makes everything work. Some people call this karma, but that's not quite right. It's simpler than that: you're just not in the flow anymore. You're not aligned with the cosmic mind, and that misalignment creates friction, distortion, problems.

Think about it this way. The cosmic mind represents the normal flow of universal reality. When you align with it, when your decisions harmonize with spiritual truth, you have access to incredible resources: the interchange of ideas, the sharing of concepts, the transmission of genuine values, goodness, beauty, everything that makes life worth living. But when you step outside that flow, when you insist on operating purely from self-interest or ego or pride, you cut yourself off from all of that. You're still alive, still conscious, still making decisions. But you're doing it alone, without the support and guidance that would make those decisions meaningful.

The process of weaving this eternal fabric begins now, in this material life. Every spiritual decision you make, every choice to follow divine leading rather than selfish impulse, adds another thread to the pattern. The Thought Adjuster takes these experiences, these moments when you chose truth over falsehood, love over hate, service over selfishness, and weaves them into something that will survive your mortal death. Something that will be recognizably you when you wake up on the first mansion world.

The Three Essential Factors of Soul Creation

Here's where we need to get precise about what's actually happening when a soul comes into being. The revelators are emphatic about this: there are three factors involved in the evolutionary creation of an immortal soul, not two. This matters because getting the number wrong means misunderstanding the entire process.

Let's look at each factor carefully.

First, the human mind and all cosmic influences antecedent to it and impinging upon it. This includes your actual physical mind, the brain, the neural networks, the biochemistry that allows consciousness to emerge in material form. But it's not just the hardware. It's also your personality, which is a unique gift from the Universal Father himself. It's the adjutant mind-spirits that help you think, reason, worship, and understand wisdom. It's the Spirit of Truth that Jesus bestowed upon humanity. It's the Holy Spirit from the local universe Mother Spirit. All of these influences come together to shape your human mind.

Second, the divine spirit indwelling this human mind and all potentials inherent in such a fragment of absolute spirituality. This is the Thought Adjuster itself, a literal fragment of God the Father. Notice the language here: "absolute spirituality." This isn't some vague mystical force. It's the actual essence of the Universal Father, the infinite and absolute spirit being who is the source of all personality, all love, all truth. When this fragment dwells within your mind, it brings with it all the potentials of spiritual growth, all the possibilities of divine transformation. It carries the influences not just of the Father, but of the Eternal Son, the Infinite Spirit, and the seven Master Spirits who represent the sevenfold nature of Deity.

Third, the relationship between material mind and divine spirit, which creates a value and carries a meaning not found in either of the contributing factors alone. This is the crucial point that many people miss. When you combine a material mind with a divine spirit, you don't just get two things coexisting in the same space. You get something entirely new, something that exists at a different level of reality altogether.

Think about what's happening here. You're adding the finite (the material mind with all its limitations) to the infinite (the eternal spirit with all its potentials). What emerges from this combination? Something in between, something that partakes of both but is reducible to neither. The reality of this unique relationship is neither material nor spiritual. It's morontia. And this morontia reality is the soul itself.

This explains why we can't directly access our souls during mortal life. The soul exists outside the finite dimension where our consciousness normally operates. It also exists outside the purely spiritual dimension where the Thought Adjuster dwells. It occupies a middle ground, an intermediate state that bridges the material and the spiritual. We contribute to it through our choices, but we won't fully experience it until we wake up on the mansion worlds.

The relationship itself deserves more attention. A relationship isn't static. It's dynamic, ongoing, filled with motion and possibility. It experiences trials, it requires effort, it can deepen or remain shallow depending on the choices made by both parties. In this case, one party is your material mind with all its experiences, desires, fears, and aspirations. The other party is a perfect fragment of God with infinite patience and eternal purpose. The relationship between these two produces soul growth.

When the revelators say this relationship "connotes a value and carries a meaning not found in either of the contributing factors," they're pointing to something genuinely transcendent. Your finite experiences alone don't have eternal value, they're too bound up with time, too limited by circumstance, too colored by the imperfections of mortal life. The Adjuster's spiritual nature alone doesn't provide the experiential dimension that makes you a unique person. But when the two combine? When your finite experience is spiritualized by the Adjuster's work? Something emerges that neither could produce alone: a soul capable of surviving death and continuing an eternal adventure.

The Mid-Mind: Understanding Morontia Development

The midway creatures, those unique beings who serve on planets like ours, have long called this evolving soul the "mid-mind." It's an apt description. This mid-mind exists in the realm between the material and the spiritual, between the lower mind we use for everyday thinking and the higher cosmic mind that operates on spiritual levels.

The potential for this morontia evolution appears to be built into the very structure of reality. Two universal urges make it possible: the impulse of the finite mind to know God and attain the divinity of the Creator, and the impulse of the infinite mind of the Creator to know humanity and attain the experience of the creature.

Stop and consider what that means. You have an innate drive to know God, to reach upward toward divinity. You didn't create this urge, it's part of how you're made. At the same time, God has a corresponding drive to know you, to reach downward (if we can use such limited spatial language) toward creature experience. This isn't one-sided. It's not just about you trying to find God while God remains distant and unmoved. God is actively seeking connection with you, actively desiring to experience what mortal life is like through fusion with ascending beings.

This mutual seeking explains why we were created in the first place. The Old Testament got this part right, even if it couldn't articulate the full cosmic scope: God doesn't want to be alone. There's an urge for humanity to know God and an urge for God to know humanity. Leonardo da Vinci captured this beautifully in his famous image of God reaching down and humanity reaching up, fingers almost touching. That moment of contact, that's what we're discussing here.

When these two urges meet, when the ascending mortal's desire to know God aligns with the descending fragment's desire to experience mortal life, soul growth accelerates. The material mind begins to function as something more than just a survival mechanism. It becomes the first personal contact with super-animal realities. It gains what the revelators call "a supermaterial endowment of cosmic ministry," which ensures the evolution of a moral nature capable of making genuine moral decisions.

This is crucial for soul development. You can't build an eternal soul on amoral decisions or purely instinctive reactions. Animals don't develop immortal souls because they can't make true moral choices, they operate on instinct and conditioning. Humans can weigh options, consider consequences, choose between right and wrong even when wrong might be more immediately pleasurable or beneficial. This capacity for moral decision-making, this ability to choose the good when you could just as easily choose the selfish, creates the raw material the Thought Adjuster needs to build your soul.

Laying Up Treasures in Heaven

Jesus told his followers to lay up treasures in heaven rather than treasures on earth. Most of us have heard that teaching so many times it's become almost meaningless through familiarity. But in light of what we're learning about soul development, those words take on urgent practical significance.

What are the treasures of heaven? They're the spiritual experiences, the meaningful relationships, the moments of genuine service, the decisions to follow truth rather than convenience, all the things the Thought Adjuster can work with to build your soul. What are the treasures of earth? Everything else. The money, the possessions, the status, the pride, the self-centered pursuits that dominate so much of human life.

Look around at our culture today. What do most people spend their time doing? They're watching television shows that revel in violence, deception, and moral ambiguity. They're consuming news that keeps them angry and afraid. They're playing video games that train them for nothing but virtual combat. They're scrolling through social media, comparing themselves to others, feeding their egos or crushing their spirits depending on how the comparison goes.

None of this develops the soul. None of it. You can spend sixty years doing these things and wake up on the mansion worlds with essentially nothing to show for it. Your teachers there will look for something salvageable, some spiritual memories they can work with, and find almost nothing. You'll be like those beings who arrive with Son fragments instead of Father fragments, starting from scratch with no experiential foundation to build on.

That's what Jesus meant about laying up treasures in heaven. He was telling people, telling us, to develop spiritual lives worth remembering. Because if you don't, your mortal life becomes what? A dream. Meaningless. Row, row, row your boat, gently down the stream; merrily, merrily, merrily, merrily, life is but a dream. Without spiritual development, without soul growth, that's exactly what mortal life amounts to: a pleasant or unpleasant dream that vanishes upon waking, leaving nothing behind.

This doesn't mean you should abandon the practical necessities of life. You still need to fix supper, mow the lawn, shop for a car when you need transportation. But those activities are what the revelators call "the scaffolding of life." Scaffolding is useful while you're building something, but once the building is complete, the scaffolding comes down and is hauled away. Nobody preserves scaffolding. Nobody takes photographs of scaffolding to remember the building. The scaffolding was just a temporary necessity.

What isn't scaffolding? Relationships. Meaningful connections with other people. Acts of service. Decisions to help someone even when it costs you something. Moments of worship. Times when you choose to do what was right instead of what was easy. These experiences become part of your eternal memory because they have spiritual value. They're the building blocks the Thought Adjuster uses to construct your soul.

So, when you spend all your time on scaffolding activities, when your life consists entirely of earning money, buying things, watching entertainment, and pursuing status, you're not developing anything eternal. You're just living in the scaffolding. And when you die, all of that disappears. Gone. The Thought Adjuster will have little or nothing to work with when it tries to reconstruct you on the mansion worlds.

The Supremacy of Human Will

Throughout all of this discussion, one principle remains constant: the human will is supreme. The Thought Adjuster manipulates but never dominates. It adjusts your thoughts toward more spiritual interpretations, but it cannot force you to accept those interpretations. It works within your mind, but it respects your sovereignty absolutely.

This means mistakes in mortal thinking, errors in human conduct, even extended periods of poor decision-making cannot ultimately prevent soul development once you've made the initial choice to seek God's will. Your mistakes might delay soul evolution, they certainly can slow things down considerably, but they cannot completely inhibit the morontia phenomenon once the Adjuster has been given permission to begin its work.

That permission can come at any point during your mortal life. You could live sixty years making mostly selfish decisions, caring only about your own comfort and pleasure, ignoring spiritual realities entirely. Then, on your deathbed, you could genuinely choose to seek God's will. And that choice, even at the last possible moment, would be honored. You'd wake up on the first mansion world with a functioning soul, ready to continue your development.

Of course, the quality of that soul, the richness of its experiential content, would be minimal compared to someone who'd been actively cooperating with their Adjuster for decades. But it would exist. It would be salvageable. Your eternal career could continue.

The reverse is also true, and this is sobering to consider. At any time before you fuse with your Adjuster, including throughout your morontia life on the mansion worlds, you retain the prerogative to reject eternal life. You can choose not to survive. You can decide you don't want to continue this journey toward Paradise. Right up until the moment of fusion, that option remains open to you.

Why does it end at fusion? Because at that point, you and the Adjuster become one being. The fragment of God that has been guiding you, adjusting your thoughts, building your soul, fully merges with your personality. You become something new: an ascending mortal who has eternally and unreservedly chosen to do the Father's will. And here's the thing, God doesn't rebel against himself. Once fusion occurs, the possibility of rebellion vanishes. Not because you've lost free will, but because your will has become perfectly aligned with divine will. You wouldn't choose to rebel anymore than you'd choose to stop existing.

This explains why none of the fused mortals ever joined the Lucifer rebellion. It wasn't possible for them to rebel. Their fusion guaranteed their loyalty, not through compulsion, but through perfect alignment of will and purpose.

The Transcendence of Temporal Limitations

When the adjutant mind-spirits (dominated by human will that craves to know God) work in liaison with the spiritual forces of the universe (under the overcontrol of an actual fragment of God), something remarkable happens. Material and mortal reality transcends the temporal limitations of the physical life machine.

Think about what that means. You're not stuck in time. Your existence isn't limited to the seventy or eighty years of mortal life. Through the development of your morontia soul, you're already beginning to exist at a level of reality that extends beyond the temporal dimension. You're creating a vehicle for selfhood continuity, a way for you to remain you even as you transition from material to morontia to spiritual existence.

This transcendence doesn't happen automatically. It requires the combined work of the adjutant mind-spirits helping you think and reason and worship, the Holy Spirit providing cosmic orientation, the Spirit of Truth illuminating Jesus's teachings, the guardian angels protecting and guiding you, and above all, the Thought Adjuster spiritualizing your experiences. All of these influences work together to help you rise above the limitations that would otherwise confine you to a single brief lifetime.

The inevitable result of this contactual spiritualization of the human mind is the gradual birth of a soul. Notice that word gradual. Soul development isn't instantaneous. It's not like flipping a switch. It's a slow, evolutionary process that continues throughout your mortal life and beyond. The soul is the joint offspring of an adjutant mind dominated by a human will that craves to know God, working in liaison with spiritual forces under the overcontrol of the Mystery Monitor.

This gradually developing soul attains a new expression and a new identification in what becomes the evolving vehicle for selfhood continuity. That's your morontia identity, the you that will wake up on the first mansion world when your mortal life ends. It's neither the material you (which dies) nor the spiritual Adjuster (which is eternal), but something in between that partakes of both natures.

The Cosmic Mind and Universal Unity

Earlier we touched on the concept of the cosmic mind, but it's worth returning to because it explains so much about how reality functions. The mind circuits of the universe follow a pattern, a cosmic blueprint that ensures all minds can potentially communicate and cooperate. When you align with this cosmic mind, you're not just following arbitrary rules. You're harmonizing with the fundamental structure of reality itself.

Throughout the mind functions of cosmic intelligence, the totality of mind dominates over the parts of intellectual function. Mind, in its essence, represents functional unity. This unity never fails to manifest itself, even when hampered and hindered by unwise actions and choices of a misguided self. The Unity of mind invariably seeks spirit coordination on all levels of its association with selves of will dignity and ascension prerogatives.

What this means practically is that even when you make poor decisions, even when you're completely misguided in your thinking, the cosmic mind continues working to bring you back into alignment. It doesn't give up on you. It keeps seeking spirit coordination, keeps trying to help you make the connection between your finite mind and eternal spiritual realities.

This is part of why life becomes difficult when you step outside the cosmic mind's flow. You're not just making things hard on yourself, you're working against the fundamental structure of reality. It's like trying to swim upstream in a powerful river. You can do it for a while through sheer effort, but it's exhausting and you don't get very far. Meanwhile, if you'd just turn around and swim with the current, you'd move effortlessly toward your destination.

The cosmic mind provides the current. When you align with it through spiritual living, through choosing God's will over your own selfish impulses, you move with the flow of universal reality. Ideas come more easily. Truth becomes clearer. Values deepen. Relationships become more meaningful. You're tapping into something much larger than your individual existence.

Making Choices That Echo Through Eternity

All of this brings us back to the fundamental reality of choice. Decisions, decisions, decisions. That's what mortal life comes down to. Every day presents you with opportunities to choose between the material and the spiritual, between selfish impulses and loving service, between temporary pleasures and eternal values.

These choices matter more than most people realize. They're not just affecting your comfort in this life. They're determining what kind of soul you're developing, what memories you'll carry into the next phase of existence, whether you'll wake up on the mansion worlds with a rich experiential foundation or essentially nothing to work with.

The mistakes you make don't destroy your soul. They can't, once soul development has begun. But they can delay your progress significantly. They can waste years or decades that could have been spent building something meaningful. And here's the difficult truth: you can't get that time back. When you spend forty years pursuing material success and ignoring spiritual development, those are forty years of potential soul growth you've lost. You can't make them up later. You can certainly start growing whenever you choose, but you can't recover the time you've already wasted.

This isn't meant to induce guilt or despair. It's meant to inspire urgency. You have this life, right now, to develop your soul. You don't know when it will end. You don't know how much time remains. What you do know is that every choice matters, every decision counts, every moment is an opportunity to either build eternal treasures or waste time on scaffolding that will eventually be hauled away and forgotten.

The Promise of Eternal Survival

The good news, and it's extraordinarily good news, is that eternal survival is available to everyone. It doesn't require perfection. It doesn't demand that you never make mistakes. It doesn't depend on your intelligence, your education, your social status, or any other external factor. It depends on one thing: your genuine desire to know God and do his will.

That's it. That's the key. If you sincerely want to find God, if you honestly desire to align your will with divine will, then the Thought Adjuster can work with that. Your soul will develop. You will survive mortal death. You will wake up on the first mansion world and continue your eternal adventure.

The Thought Adjuster doesn't need you to be perfect. It just needs your cooperation. It needs your willingness to be guided, your openness to spiritual adjustment, your consent to let divine love and wisdom shape your thinking and your choices. When you provide that willingness, that openness, that consent, the Adjuster can accomplish its mission.

And what is that mission? To safely carry you across the barriers of time and the handicaps of space, to the very source of the Divine Mind itself, and beyond, all the way to Paradise, to the Father of Adjusters. That's where this journey ultimately leads. Not to some vague afterlife in clouds playing harps, but to Paradise itself, to the presence of the Universal Father, where you can continue growing and serving throughout all eternity.

The path is open. The pilot knows the way. The captain's chair is yours. The only question is: what will you choose?

Conclusion: The Beginning of Forever

As we've explored in this chapter, the nature of the immortal soul involves far more than traditional religious teachings typically suggest. It's not something you're born with fully formed. It's not guaranteed regardless of your choices. It's not a passive gift that requires nothing from you.

The soul is something you actively participate in creating through your partnership with the indwelling Thought Adjuster. It develops gradually as you make decisions to follow spiritual leading rather than selfish impulses. It grows as you lay up treasures in heaven instead of treasures on earth. It matures as you align your will with divine will, choosing to cooperate with the Father's plan for your eternal career.

This understanding should change how you approach everyday life. Every decision becomes an opportunity for soul growth. Every challenge becomes a chance to develop eternal values. Every relationship becomes a potential treasure that will survive your mortal death. The scaffolding of life, the routine necessities and mundane activities, remains necessary, but you see it for what it is: temporary support for what you're really building.

What you're building is a vehicle for your eternal identity. You're creating the morontia self that will wake up on the first mansion world. You're developing the experiential foundation that will support your growth through all the ascending stages of universe reality. You're becoming the person who will eventually stand in the presence of the Universal Father on Paradise itself.

That process begins here, now, in this mortal life. The choices you make today echo through eternity. The relationships you nurture now continue beyond death. The spiritual values you develop in this finite existence form the basis for your infinite adventure.

In our next chapter, we'll explore how this soul development continues beyond mortal death. We'll examine what happens when you wake up on the first mansion world, what you'll remember from mortal life, and how your teachers will help you continue the growth that began here. We'll discover why some people arrive with rich experiential backgrounds while others arrive with almost nothing, and what that means for their morontia careers. Most importantly, we'll understand how the choices made during mortal life directly affect the quality and speed of mansion world progress.

The adventure is just beginning. Your immortal soul is forming even now, with every choice you make, every value you embrace, every moment you choose to cooperate with the divine pilot guiding your ship toward Paradise shores.

Chapter 24: The Evolving Soul and the Divine Partnership

Introduction: The Mystery of Soul Development

Among the most profound revelations in *The Urantia Book* is the teaching about the evolving human soul, what it is, how it develops, and why it matters for our eternal destiny. For many readers approaching these concepts for the first time, the relationship between the mortal mind, the indwelling Thought Adjuster, and the emerging morontia soul can seem abstract, even mysterious. Yet understanding this divine partnership may be one of the most practical and life-changing insights we can gain from the fifth epochal revelation.

This chapter explores Paper 111, Section 3, focusing on the nature of the evolving soul and its intimate connection with both human will and divine presence. We'll examine how the soul comes into being, why it remains largely unconscious to us during mortal life, and what role our daily decisions play in building an eternal identity. What emerges from this study is a picture of human existence far more purposeful than many of us have been taught, a life where every meaningful choice contributes to something that will outlast our physical bodies and carry us forward into the next stage of existence.

The ideas presented here challenge some common religious assumptions. We'll discover that the soul isn't quite what most traditions describe, and that our experience of "awakening" on the mansion worlds involves a transformation more profound than simply continuing our current consciousness. These aren't comfortable truths for everyone, but they offer a framework for understanding ourselves that is both scientifically coherent and spiritually elevating.

The Foundation: When Soul Development Begins

The soul's origin is tied directly to a specific moment in childhood, the arrival of the Thought Adjuster, typically around age five or six, when a child makes their first moral decision. Before this moment, there is no soul. The arrival of the divine fragment initiates what the revelators call a "morontia phenomenon," the beginning of a new order of reality that bridges the gap between material existence and spiritual life.

From that moment forward, the Thought Adjuster begins creating what might be called a spiritual duplicate of our lives. This isn't a recording of everything we do, far from it. The Adjuster is selectively building a transcript of those experiences, decisions, and values that have eternal significance. Think of it as a master artist working with raw material, carefully choosing which elements will form the foundation of an immortal identity.

Here's where things get interesting: throughout our entire mortal life, this soul exists within us but remains largely inaccessible to our conscious mind. We can't communicate with it directly. We can't examine its contents. In many ways, it operates as a separate entity, growing and developing according to laws we barely understand. The soul is super-material, meaning it transcends the physical realm, but it's also sub-spiritual, not yet fully spiritual in nature. It occupies a middle ground, the morontia level of reality.

This explains why so many people through history have sensed something within themselves that seems eternal but couldn't quite articulate what it was. The Egyptians spoke of the *ba* and *ka*. Eastern philosophies described the interplay of various subtle bodies. Nearly every religious tradition has grasped at this truth from different angles. What *The Urantia Book* offers is a more precise understanding: the soul is real, it's developing now, and it's being prepared for a purpose.

The Role of Human Will: Our Essential Contribution

One of the most critical teachings in this section concerns the power of human will. The mistake some readers make is assuming that once the Thought Adjuster arrives, the soul's development is automatic, that we're simply along for the ride. Nothing could be further from the truth.

The revelators make it clear: "At any time prior to mortal death, this same material and human will is empowered to rescind such a choice and to reject survival." This is a sobering statement. Even after the soul has been initiated, even after years of spiritual growth, a human being retains the absolute prerogative to say "no" to eternal life. We can choose to reject survival. We can refuse to do the will of the Father. And if we persist in that rejection, when we die, we simply won't wake up on the mansion worlds.

This contradicts a popular notion in Christianity that once you've accepted Christ (or in Urantia Book terms, once you've chosen survival), you're guaranteed eternal life. The reality appears more nuanced. The choice to survive isn't a one-time decision but an ongoing orientation of the will. It's possible to change your mind. It's possible to turn away from the path you once chose.

Even more striking, the paper tells us that this power of choice continues after we reach the mansion worlds. "Even after survival, the ascending mortal still retains the prerogative of choosing to reject eternal life at any time before fusion with the Adjuster." Only fusion, that ultimate union of human will with divine presence, seals our eternal destiny. This gives us what is called eternal life. Before that moment, the door to self-annihilation remains open.

Why would the universe be structured this way? Perhaps because authentic love and genuine spiritual growth can only emerge from genuine freedom. A forced march toward Paradise would produce automatons, not sons and daughters of God. The risk of rejection is built into the system because without that risk, there can be no real choosing, no authentic partnership between creature and Creator.

The Soul's Unique Nature: Between Two Worlds

Understanding what the soul *is* requires grasping what it is *not*. The soul is not material, it doesn't function through the circuits of the physical brain. During mortal life, it can't make decisions on its own or communicate directly with our conscious mind. As the revelators put it, "The soul, being supermaterial, does not of itself function on the material level of human experience."

Neither is the soul fully spiritual. It can't operate on purely spiritual levels without the collaboration of deity, specifically, the indwelling Thought Adjuster. The soul occupies what we might call a transitional state, partaking of qualities from both the material mind and the divine spirit, but not fully belonging to either realm during mortal life.

This is why the soul is called an "embryo." It's developing, growing, taking shape, but it hasn't yet reached maturity. Think of a butterfly forming inside a chrysalis. The creature exists, it's real, it's undergoing profound transformation, but it's not yet what it will become. That's our soul during mortal life.

The soul grows through a specific process. When we make decisions that have super-material significance, choices aligned with truth, beauty, and goodness, decisions to love rather than hate, to serve rather than exploit, to trust rather than fear, these choices are registered by the Thought Adjuster and woven into the fabric of the developing soul. The Adjuster takes the raw material of our experiences and creates spiritual counterparts of those experiences that have eternal value.

This process explains why some of our life feels more significant than other parts. Not every moment carries equal weight. A day spent binge-watching television adds nothing to the soul. An hour spent in genuine communion with another person, an act of selfless service, a moment of authentic worship, these create soul substance. This isn't about earning salvation through works; it's about cooperating with a divine process that's trying to extract eternal value from our temporal existence.

Meanings and Values: Two Pathways to God

The revelators make an important distinction between "meanings" and "values," and understanding this distinction helps explain why people approach spirituality in such different ways.

Meanings represent the intellectual, cognitive aspect of spiritual growth. They're about understanding, comprehension, making sense of reality. When we study *The Urantia Book*, when we wrestle with theological concepts, when we try to grasp how the universe works, we're working with meanings. The mind "knows" meanings. This is the pathway of the philosopher, the theologian, the intellectual seeker.

Values, on the other hand, are *felt*. They're emotional, experiential, intuitive. When you enter a worship service and feel moved by music, when you experience a sense of God's presence in nature, when you have that inner knowing that you're loved by a higher power, you're experiencing values. Values don't require explanation or justification. You feel them in what people commonly call the "heart," though we're not referring to the physical organ.

Neither approach is superior to the other. Both are necessary. The revelators state that values are "the mutual creation of mind which knows and the associated spirit which reality-izes it." In other words, authentic spiritual experience requires both the intellectual comprehension of meanings *and* the heartfelt reception of values.

This helps explain why certain religious traditions emphasize emotion, experience, and feeling, what might be called "heart" churches, or the "feelgood" churches, while others emphasize doctrine, theology, and understanding, "head" churches. Pentecostal services with their expressive worship and emotional intensity are cultivating values. Traditional liturgical services with their emphasis on theological precision and doctrinal clarity are cultivating meanings. Both are valid approaches to the divine.

Most of us lean one direction or the other by temperament. Some people need to *feel* God's presence; the intellectual arguments alone leave them cold. Others need to *understand* the cosmic framework; emotional appeals without intellectual substance feel hollow. The ideal, perhaps, is balance, a spiritual life that engages both mind and heart, that cultivates both meanings and values.

The Mansion World Awakening: Becoming Your Soul

One of the most fascinating, and perhaps unsettling, aspects of this teaching concerns what happens when we die and awaken on the mansion worlds. The process isn't quite what most people imagine.

When you're repersonalized on the first mansion world, your personality, that unique pattern that makes you *"you"*, is reconnected with your morontia soul. The Thought Adjuster is present as well. But here's what many readers miss: *the soul becomes the primary vehicle of consciousness*, not your mortal mind. You don't simply continue as you are now, just in a different location. Your personality is "plugged into" the soul that has been developing throughout your mortal life, and that soul, which contains all the spiritually valuable transcripts of your experiences, becomes your new self.

This means that while you'll feel like yourself, you'll have continuity of identity, you'll remember your life, you're actually experiencing consciousness through a different medium. The physical brain is gone. The material mind circuits that sustained your awareness on Earth are no longer operative. What's functioning now is the morontia soul, animated by your personality and indwelt by the Thought Adjuster.

There's another profound implication here. During mortal life, most of us experience the Thought Adjuster, if we're aware of it at all, as something somewhat separate, a still small voice, a divine presence, a spiritual influence. But on the mansion worlds, this changes. The Adjuster is now *within* the same morontia form as your conscious self. Communication becomes direct and, for many, conscious. You begin to experience a kind of dual consciousness, yourself and the divine presence within, distinct yet unified, working together.

This continues until fusion. And when fusion occurs, the distinction dissolves completely. You and the Adjuster become one being. There's no longer any separation between your will and the divine will. You've become, in a very real sense, a new order of creature, part human, part divine, eternally unified.

Some people experience fusion before ever awakening on the mansion worlds. They die, and in that transition, the union occurs. For these individuals, when they awaken on the first mansion world, they won't experience the Adjuster as separate at all. The divine fragment will simply be part of who they are, as natural as breathing. Other people don't fuse until much later, sometimes not until the fifth mansion world or even beyond. The timing varies based on spiritual readiness, the degree to which human will has become aligned with divine will.

The Practical Question: What Survives?

This brings us to perhaps the most practical question of all: what actually carries forward into eternal life? What matters? What's worth investing in during this brief mortal existence?

The revelators are remarkably clear on this point: "If there is no survival of eternal values in the evolving soul of mortal man, then mortal existence is without meaning, and life itself is a tragic illusion." Like the Roll, roll, roll your boat illustration, Everything that's purely material, wealth, possessions, physical appearance, social status, has zero eternal value. It contributes nothing to the soul. When you die, it all stays behind, because your life in reality was like just a dream!

What does survive? Relationships rooted in spiritual reality. Skills and knowledge pursued for eternal purposes. Character qualities that reflect truth, beauty, and goodness. Experiences of worship, service, and love. The choices you made to align your will with the Father's will. These are the "eternal values" that become woven into the fabric of your soul.

There's a beautiful promise embedded in this section: "Whatsoever you begin in time you will assuredly finish in eternity, if it is worth finishing." That guitar you always wanted to learn to play. If it truly matters to you, if it has value beyond mere entertainment, you'll have the opportunity on the mansion worlds with the best teachers available. That relationship with a friend or family member that was cut short by death. If it was spiritually significant, it continues. That project you were working on that had genuine value, but you ran out of time. You'll be able to complete it.

The universe doesn't waste anything of real value. Every authentic connection, every genuine growth experience, every sincere effort to become better, these all contribute to building an eternal identity. The material scaffolding falls away, but everything of lasting worth is preserved.

The Role of Decisions: Building Eternity Day by Day

If there's one practical takeaway from this study, it's this: our daily decisions matter more than we usually think. Every time we face a choice, we're either contributing to our soul's development or we're not. We're either doing the Father's will or we're not. And over time, these decisions accumulate into a pattern that shapes our eternal destiny.

The process is largely unconscious. We don't directly experience our soul growing. We can't monitor its development or check our spiritual progress with any kind of objective measurement. But we can sense it. There's an inner knowing, a felt awareness that we're either moving forward or we're not, that our lives are either accumulating meaning or dissipating into insignificance.

The revelators emphasize that we're not talking about perfection here. "The mistakes of mortal mind and the errors of human conduct may markedly delay the evolution of the soul, although they cannot inhibit such a morontia phenomenon once it has been initiated." We're going to make mistakes. We're going to fail. We're going to choose poorly sometimes. These errors can slow our progress, but they don't destroy the soul itself. What destroys the soul is persistent, willful rejection of the Father's will, a sustained decision to turn away from spiritual reality altogether.

For most people, the spiritual life is a matter of habitually choosing, day after day, to align their will with what they sense is right, true, and good. It's making the decision, over and over, to say "Not my will but yours be done." It's recognizing that you don't always know what the Father's will is in a given situation, but you're sincerely trying to find it and follow it. That sincerity, that genuine desire to cooperate with the divine plan, this is what builds soul substance.

A Word of Caution: The Tension That Leads to Fusion

There's a mystical dimension to this teaching that deserves attention. The revelators speak of a "tension" that builds between the human personality and the divine Adjuster when a person has truly dedicated their life to doing the Father's will. As the human will increasingly aligns with the divine will, the separation between them becomes harder to maintain. It's like two magnets drawn together, eventually, the pull becomes irresistible.

When this tension reaches a critical point, the Ancients of Days and the Universal Censors may decree that fusion is imminent. At this stage, the process becomes inevitable. Whether the person wants it or not, whether they're consciously ready or not, fusion will occur. The human will and the divine will have become so aligned that they can no longer be held apart.

This is why some people fuse during mortal life. It's why others fuse in the moment of death. The merger isn't always a matter of conscious preparation or spiritual achievement in any conventional sense. It's a natural consequence of will alignment. When your decisions consistently choose what the Father would choose, when your desires increasingly reflect divine purposes, when your very nature has been transformed by persistent cooperation with the indwelling presence, fusion becomes the inevitable outcome.

This should be both encouraging and sobering. Encouraging because it means we don't have to achieve some impossible standard of perfection. We simply need to keep choosing, day by day, to do the Father's will as we understand it. Sobering because it reminds us that there are real consequences to our choices. We're not playing spiritual games. We're building something eternal or we're not.

Conclusion: The Embryo and the Butterfly

As we close this exploration of the evolving soul, it's worth returning to that central metaphor: the soul as embryo. Throughout mortal life, the soul is developing, growing, being prepared for a purpose we can only dimly imagine. We carry within us the seeds of an immortal identity, but we can't fully know what we're becoming while still confined to material existence.

The butterfly doesn't know, while still a caterpillar, what it means to fly. The child doesn't grasp, in any real sense, what adult life will be like. Similarly, we can't truly comprehend what awaits us on the mansion worlds, what it will mean to consciously experience reality through a morontia soul rather than a material brain, what fusion with the Thought Adjuster will feel like, or what we'll become as we journey through the local universe and beyond.

What we can know is this: the process is underway. The partnership between mortal will and divine presence is active right now, in this moment, in your life. Every sincere choice to do what is right, true, and good contributes to an eternal outcome. Every relationship rooted in genuine love, every act of authentic service, every moment of real worship, these are building something that will outlast the stars.

The soul you're developing now will become you when you awaken on the mansion worlds. The person you're becoming through your daily decisions will be the starting point for an adventure that stretches across eternity. This isn't abstract theology. This is the most practical information you could possibly receive about what your life means and where you're going.

In our next chapter, we'll explore what happens after mansion world awakening, how the morontia journey unfolds, what challenges and opportunities await, and how the fusion experience transforms everything once again. For now, it's enough to understand that you are, at this very moment, evolving a soul. The question isn't whether the process is happening. The question is whether you're consciously cooperating with it.

Chapter 25: The Inner Life - Recognition, Understanding, and the Soul's Creative Foundation

Introduction: The Architecture of Spiritual Reality

When we consider the mystery of human existence, we find ourselves standing at the intersection of two worlds, the material realm we can see and touch, and the spiritual dimension that gives meaning to everything we experience. This chapter explores what *The Urantia Book* calls "the inner life," a concept that goes far beyond simple introspection or self-awareness. Rather, it describes the very mechanism by which temporary human experiences are transformed into eternal spiritual realities.

As we continue our study of Paper 111, "The Adjuster and the Soul," we arrive at Section 4, which may be one of the most intellectually challenging yet practically significant passages in the entire revelation. Here, the revelators attempt to explain how sensory impressions from our daily lives become integrated into something far more permanent, the evolving soul that will survive physical death and continue its journey through the universe.

What makes this section particularly fascinating is its connection to the life of Jesus, specifically his experience in the Garden of Gethsemane. When we read Jesus' prayer, "Not my will, Father, but yours be done", we're witnessing something far more profound than a moment of submission. We're seeing the culmination of an entire human life lived in perfect alignment with the divine will, a life that continued to build spiritual reality even after Jesus' Thought Adjuster became personalized at his baptism.

This chapter will guide you through the complex relationship between recognition, understanding, and spiritual meaning. We'll explore why the material world, for all its apparent solidity, is essentially a shadow of spiritual realities, and how our inner life serves as the bridge between these two domains. Along the way, we'll examine Jesus' unique experience as both human and divine, and what his life teaches us about soul development and eternal survival.

Recognition and Understanding: The Foundation of Experience

The revelators begin this section with what appears to be a simple distinction, but one that carries enormous implications for how we understand consciousness itself. They write: "Recognition is the intellectual process of fitting the sensory impressions received from the external world into the memory patterns of the individual."

Think about what happens when you encounter something familiar, perhaps an old friend you haven't seen in years, or a song from your childhood. That flash of recognition isn't just a mental trick; it's your mind actively comparing incoming sensory data with stored patterns from your past. This process happens constantly, mostly below the level of conscious awareness, as your brain attempts to make sense of the continuous stream of sensory information flooding in from your environment.

But recognition alone doesn't constitute true knowledge. The revelators make an important distinction: "Understanding connotes that these recognized sensory impressions and their associated memory patterns have become integrated or organized into a dynamic network of principles."

Understanding, then, represents a higher order of mental activity. It's not enough to simply recognize that you've seen something before; true understanding occurs when you can integrate that recognition into a coherent framework of meaning, when you can see how individual pieces fit into larger patterns, when isolated facts become organized knowledge.

This distinction might seem purely philosophical until we grasp what the revelators are really explaining. They're describing the basic architecture of how temporary, material experiences become candidates for eternal, spiritual preservation. Without recognition, there's no raw material for memory. Without understanding, there's no meaningful pattern to preserve. And without meaning, there's nothing of spiritual value to contribute to the growing soul.

The Problem of Material Reality

Here the revelators make a statement that challenges our everyday assumptions about what's real: "Meanings are derived from a combination of recognition and understanding. Meanings are nonexistent in a wholly sensory or material world. Meanings and values are only perceived in the inner or supermaterial spheres of human experience."

This passage requires careful consideration. The revelators aren't suggesting that the physical world is an illusion in the Eastern philosophical sense. Tables and chairs, mountains and oceans, our own physical bodies, these certainly exist. But they're arguing something more subtle: that meaning itself cannot exist in purely material terms.

Consider a simple example. You look at a tree. Your eyes receive photons, your optic nerve transmits electrical signals, your visual cortex processes patterns. All of this is purely material, atoms, molecules, electrochemical reactions. But when you think, "That tree is beautiful," or "That tree provides shade and oxygen," or "That tree reminds me of my childhood home", where does that meaning exist? Not in the tree itself, surely. Not in the photons or electrical signals. The meaning arises somewhere else, in what the revelators call "the inner or supermaterial spheres of human experience."

This is why they can say that a purely sensory or material world contains no meanings. Meaning requires a subject who interprets, who connects, who finds significance. And that interpretive activity happens in the inner life, in the realm where material experience meets spiritual capacity.

The practical implications of this are profound. It means that two people can have identical sensory experiences, watching the same sunset, hearing the same music, reading the same words, and yet derive completely different meanings from them. One person's transformative spiritual experience is another person's pleasant but forgettable moment. The difference isn't in the external stimulus; it's in the inner capacity to perceive spiritual significance.

The Morontia Mota: Where Material Meets Spirit

The revelators refer to "the supermaterial spheres of human experience," and students of *The Urantia Book* will recognize this as pointing toward the morontia level of reality. The term "morontia" describes the vast experiential domain between the purely material and the fully spiritual, what we might call the soul-level of existence.

One of the book's most intriguing concepts is *morontia mota*, often translated as morontia wisdom. This represents a level of understanding that transcends purely intellectual knowledge while not yet achieving pure spirit insight. It's the wisdom of the soul, built up through the integration of material experience with spiritual values under the guidance of the Thought Adjuster.

We begin building morontia mota right now, in our present material existence. Every time we choose spiritual values over purely material considerations, every time we respond to moral challenges with integrity, every time we recognize divine patterns in human experience, we're adding to our storehouse of morontia wisdom. However, we won't fully access or utilize this wisdom until we awaken on the mansion worlds after physical death.

This is similar to planting seeds in the fall that won't sprout until spring. The work we do now in developing spiritual insight and choosing eternal values is creating something real, but something we won't fully appreciate until we have morontia senses to perceive morontia reality. The Thought Adjuster is carefully preserving everything of spiritual value, weaving it into the fabric of the evolving soul, preparing for the day when that soul becomes our primary vehicle of consciousness.

Jesus and the Personalized Adjuster: A Profound Mystery

To fully appreciate the significance of the inner life, we need to consider Jesus' unique experience. His life demonstrates principles that apply to all humans while simultaneously revealing mysteries that remain partially veiled even in the revelation itself.

When Jesus was baptized by John in the Jordan River, something unprecedented occurred. The Thought Adjuster that had indwelt him since childhood, guiding, teaching, preparing, suddenly separated from him and became what *The Urantia Book* calls a "personalized Thought Adjuster." This was necessary because Jesus, as a human being, had reached the point where he would normally have fused with his Adjuster, essentially disappearing from material existence to awaken on the mansion worlds.

But Jesus couldn't fuse with his Adjuster. He was, after all, the Creator Son of our local universe, Michael of Nebadon, living a human life as part of his seventh and final bestowal. He was already a divine being. Fusion with the Adjuster would have ended his mission before it truly began. He still needed to live four more years, gather and train his apostles, reveal the Father's nature through his life and teachings, and ultimately experience human death.

So the Adjuster was personalized, separated from Jesus while remaining closely associated with him. For the remainder of his earth life, Jesus lived without an indwelling Thought Adjuster. Think about that for a moment. From his baptism until his death on the cross, Jesus was doing the Father's will without the internal guidance that sustains every other faithful human being. He was operating entirely from the spiritual momentum he had built up during those first thirty years of life.

And here's the remarkable thing: he continued building his soul. Even without the Adjuster's indwelling presence, even without that constant internal guidance, Jesus went right on making spiritual progress, living the Father's will, and adding to the spiritual reality he was creating. His prayer in Gethsemane, "Not my will but yours be done", came from a man who had internalized the Father's will so completely that he could follow it without moment-by-moment divine guidance.

This demonstrates something crucial about spiritual development. The goal isn't perpetual dependence on external (or even internal) guidance. The goal is to so completely align yourself with divine purposes that doing God's will becomes natural, automatic, your genuine desire rather than a discipline you force yourself to maintain.

The Soul as Spiritual Counterpart

Throughout these papers on the Thought Adjuster, the revelators emphasize that the soul is a new reality, jointly created by the human mind and the divine Adjuster. They sometimes describe it as the "spiritual counterpart" of our material experience. But what does this actually mean?

Imagine everything you experience, every conversation, every choice, every moment of joy or sorrow, every act of kindness or courage, has a spiritual dimension that your physical senses cannot detect. Your eyes see the sunset; your soul perceives the glory of the Creator's artistry. Your ears hear words of comfort; your soul understands divine love expressing itself through human compassion. Your hands serve another person; your soul participates in the eternal pattern of divine ministry.

The Thought Adjuster is constantly evaluating your experiences, extracting everything of spiritual value, and weaving it into the growing fabric of your soul. Not every experience contributes equally. Moments of genuine spiritual insight, acts of selfless love, decisions that choose eternal values over temporary advantages, these contribute substantially. Purely selfish moments, decisions based solely on material considerations, experiences we refuse to learn from, these contribute little or nothing.

This is why the revelators can say that when you awaken on the mansion worlds, you'll remember your earth life. But how can you remember if your physical brain, where memories are stored, has been left behind with your body? The answer: because the Thought Adjuster has created spiritual counterparts of all your significant memories and woven them into your soul. That soul, implanted into your new morontia body, provides continuity of identity and experience.

Without a soul, even if you somehow survived death, you would be like someone with complete amnesia, technically alive but with no memory of who you were or what you had experienced. You wouldn't be you anymore. The soul is what makes you continuously you across the transition from material to morontia existence.

The Tragedy of Soul-less Survival

This understanding makes clear why some beings might not survive death. *The Urantia Book* describes individuals who are "spirit fused" or "Son fused" rather than "Adjuster fused." These are people whose Thought Adjusters, for whatever reason, cannot or do not return to resurrect them on the mansion worlds.

Perhaps their lives offered nothing of spiritual value for the Adjuster to work with. Perhaps they consistently chose material values over spiritual ones, never developing the soul that would survive. Perhaps mental illness or severe brain damage made meaningful moral choice impossible, leaving no foundation for soul growth.

When such individuals are resurrected (if they are resurrected), they receive a brand new soul, essentially starting from scratch spiritually. They have no memory of their earth life because no spiritual counterpart of that life was created. Their guardian angels must painstakingly rehearse everything significant that happened to them, helping them understand who they were even though they can't remember being that person.

This isn't punishment or divine cruelty. It's simply the natural consequence of living a life without spiritual dimension. If you build nothing of eternal value, there's nothing eternal to survive. The universe cannot preserve what was never created.

The revelators mention that certain conditions, severe antisocial behavior, cosmic insanity, complete detachment from reality, may prevent resurrection entirely. Not because God refuses to save such individuals, but because they've created nothing savable. A person living in complete delusion, unable to make genuine moral choices, experiencing no authentic relationships, such a person isn't building a soul. There's no spiritual counterpart being created, nothing for the Adjuster to preserve.

This might seem harsh but consider: life on the mansion worlds assumes you have some experience of being human, some capacity for choice, some foundation of values and meanings from which to grow. If none of that exists, resurrection wouldn't benefit the individual. It would be like downloading an empty file or planting seeds that never formed embryos.

The Creative Inner Life

"Only in the higher levels of the superconscious mind as it impinges upon the spirit realm of human experience can you find those higher concepts in association with effective master patterns which will contribute to the building of a better and more enduring civilization."

This sentence points us toward one of the most practical implications of the inner life concept. Genuine creativity, the kind that builds lasting value rather than temporary novelty, arises from the superconscious mind's contact with spiritual reality.

Think of the great artists, inventors, reformers, and teachers whose work has blessed humanity across centuries. What distinguished them wasn't merely technical skill or intellectual brilliance (though they often possessed both). What made them truly creative was their ability to access patterns of meaning from the spiritual dimension of reality and translate them into material forms that others could appreciate.

Beethoven didn't just arrange pleasant sounds; he channeled something of the divine harmony into audible music. Lincoln didn't just craft clever political rhetoric; he expressed something of divine justice through human words. Tesla didn't merely tinker with electrical components; he perceived practical applications of natural law that transformed human civilization.

This is what the revelators mean by "higher concepts in association with effective master patterns." The superconscious mind, that level where our consciousness contacts both the Thought Adjuster and the Spirit of Truth, can perceive spiritual patterns that the merely conscious, intellectual mind cannot access. When we bring those patterns into material expression through art, invention, teaching, or service, we're being genuinely creative.

"Personality is inherently creative, but it thus functions only in the inner life of the individual." Here's the key: you can't force this kind of creativity through external techniques or disciplines alone. You can't manufacture it by following formulas or imitating others. Genuine creativity flows from the inner life, from that dialogue between your evolving self and the divine presence within you.

This explains why two people with identical training and equal technical skill can produce such different work. One merely executes techniques competently; the other creates something genuinely new, something that carries spiritual weight and lasting value. The difference is in the depth of their inner life and their openness to spiritual patterns.

Uniqueness: The Cosmic Principle of Personality

"Snow crystals are always hexagonal in form, but no two are ever alike. Children conform to types, but no two are exactly alike, even in the case of twins. Personality follows types but is always unique."

This beautiful illustration reminds us that sameness and uniqueness coexist throughout creation. Snowflakes follow the same physical laws, form according to the same hexagonal geometry, yet each is completely unique. Human beings share a common nature, develop according to recognizable patterns, yet each personality is absolutely unprecedented and unrepeatable.

This has profound implications for the inner life. You cannot develop your soul by simply copying someone else's spiritual practices or trying to recreate their experience. What works for another person may not work for you. What transforms one individual might leave another unmoved. This isn't because spiritual laws are arbitrary or inconsistent; it's because you are unique, and your spiritual path will necessarily reflect that uniqueness.

Even identical twins, sharing the same DNA and often raised in nearly identical circumstances, develop distinct personalities and souls. This tells us that the factors shaping soul development go deeper than genetics or environment. Your personality, that unique quality that makes you specifically you, is a universe gift, and your soul development will reflect the particular way your unique personality responds to spiritual opportunity.

This is why the Thought Adjuster's work is so subtle and individualized. The Adjuster isn't trying to make you into some ideal spiritual type. Rather, the Adjuster is helping you become the perfected version of your unique self, the person you would be if you consistently chose the highest values available to you and developed all your spiritual potential.

Happiness, Joy, and the Social Nature of Reality

"Happiness and joy take origin in the inner life. You cannot experience real joy all by yourself. A solitary life is fatal to happiness. Even families and nations will enjoy life more if they share it with others."

After all this discussion of the inner life, of superconscious contact with spiritual reality, of soul development, of creative originality, the revelators remind us that none of this occurs in isolation. The inner life doesn't mean a life lived alone, withdrawn from others, focused solely on private spiritual experience.

True happiness and genuine joy arise from the inner life, yes, but they naturally flow outward into relationship and service. This is because reality itself is fundamentally social. The Paradise Trinity isn't a solitary God but a fellowship of three eternal persons. The vast universe is organized around relationships, between personalities, between levels of reality, between the central universe and the evolving superuniverses.

You were designed for relationship. Your personality was given to you not primarily for your own benefit but so you could participate in the social life of the cosmos. Your soul development isn't meant to be a private achievement but a preparation for eternal participation in the universal fellowship of all personalities.

This is why a purely solitary life, whether physically alone or emotionally isolated even while among others, is "fatal to happiness." You can survive physically in isolation, but you cannot thrive spiritually. The inner life needs the stimulus of other personalities, the challenge of diverse perspectives, the opportunity for service and the blessing of being served.

Think of Jesus again. He cultivated an extraordinarily deep inner life, hours spent in communion with the Father, profound meditation on spiritual realities, constant openness to the Father's guidance. Yet he was anything but isolated. He was consistently engaged with people from all walks of life, responding to their needs, teaching them truth, revealing the Father's nature through human interaction.

The pattern is clear: depth of inner life naturally expresses itself in richness of outer relationships. The person with a shallow inner life has little to give others and little capacity to receive from them. But the person whose inner life touches spiritual reality becomes a channel through which that reality flows to everyone they encounter.

The Civilization Crisis: Youth and Material Values

"The advances of true civilization are all born in this inner world of mankind. It is only the inner life that is truly creative. Civilization can hardly progress when the majority of the youth of any generation devote their interests and energies to the materialistic pursuits of the sensory or outer world."

The revelators aren't being nostalgic here, pining for some imagined golden age when young people were more spiritual. Rather, they're identifying a genuine civilizational crisis that has recurred throughout history: what happens when an entire generation focuses primarily on material pursuits while neglecting spiritual development?

Notice they don't condemn material pursuits as such. The issue is when "the majority of the youth of any generation devote their interests and energies" almost exclusively to "materialistic pursuits of the sensory or outer world." The problem isn't having a career or enjoying physical pleasures. The problem is when those become the primary focus, when nothing of deeper significance claims young people's attention and energy.

"The inner and the outer worlds have a different set of values. Any civilization is in jeopardy when three-quarters of its youth enter materialistic professions and devote themselves to the pursuit of the sensory activities of the outer world."

Three-quarters, a substantial majority. Imagine a society where most young people are training for careers that offer high income and material comfort but no particular service to others or contribution to human progress. Where entertainment focuses purely on sensory stimulation without any engagement with meaningful questions. Where education teaches skills for economic success while ignoring ethics, philosophy, and spiritual development.

Such a civilization is in genuine jeopardy, not because divine judgment will fall upon it, but because it's failing to develop the spiritual resources necessary for long-term survival and progress. Material prosperity without spiritual depth leads eventually to cynicism, purposelessness, and social decay.

"Civilization is in danger when youth neglect to interest themselves in ethics, sociology, eugenics, philosophy, the fine arts, religion, and cosmology."

This list deserves attention. Ethics, the study of right and wrong, the foundations of moral choice. Sociology, understanding how human communities function and flourish. Eugenics, not racial pseudo-science but thoughtful concern for human genetic health and the wellbeing of future generations. Philosophy, the love of wisdom, the examination of fundamental questions. The fine arts, beauty, creativity, the expression of meaning through form. Religion, humanity's relationship with divinity, the pursuit of ultimate values. Cosmology, understanding our place in the larger universe, the big picture that gives perspective to daily life.

When young people show no interest in these domains, when they find them boring or irrelevant compared to careers, entertainment, and material success, that culture is losing its capacity for genuine progress. It may continue accumulating material wealth and technological capability, but it's spiritually stagnating.

The remedy isn't to make young people abandon material concerns, that's neither realistic nor desirable. The remedy is to help them see that genuine success, lasting satisfaction, and meaningful contribution require developing the inner life alongside material competence. Someone can be both financially successful and spiritually mature, both technically skilled and ethically sophisticated, both practical and philosophical.

Jesus demonstrated this perfectly. He was a skilled craftsman, earning his living as a carpenter and later as a boatbuilder. He wasn't above material concerns, he needed to eat, had to earn money, understood economic realities. But his material work never became his primary focus. It was the platform from which he developed spiritually and eventually launched his public ministry.

Controlling the Inner World

"You cannot completely control the external world environment. It is the creativity of the inner world that is most subject to your direction because there your personality is so largely liberated from the fetters of the laws of antecedent causation."

This is one of the most liberating statements in the entire revelation. You cannot fully control what happens to you. Accidents occur, other people make choices that affect you, natural disasters strike, illnesses develop, economies rise and fall. You did not choose your parents, your genetic endowment, your native culture, or the historical era into which you were born.

The laws of "antecedent causation", the chain of cause and effect that determines so much of material existence constrain everyone. You cannot escape physical law or undo the consequences of past choices (your own or others'). Life on a material world means living within these constraints.

But the inner world, your response to circumstances, the meanings you assign to experiences, the values you choose to live by, the spiritual reality you're building, this is largely within your control. Not completely, you cannot escape the influence of your heredity, culture, and conditioning. But "largely", substantially, significantly, meaningfully.

This is where human freedom genuinely exists. Not in the ability to control events but in the power to control your response to events. Not in escaping physical causation but in rising above it spiritually. Not in determining what happens but in determining what it means and who you become through it.

"There resides within each person a fragment of God, and such a gift is forever seeking to lead such a person to the ultimate reality of eternal existence." The Thought Adjuster ensures that you're never trapped by circumstances. However constrained your external options, you always have the inner freedom to choose spiritual values, to seek divine guidance, to build a soul worthy of eternal survival.

The Stage of Consciousness

"How can a creative imagination produce worthy children when the stage whereon it functions is already preoccupied by prejudice, hate, fears, resentments, revenge, and bigotries?"

This vivid metaphor pictures consciousness as a stage where drama unfolds. If that stage is already crowded with actors representing prejudice, hate, fear, resentment, revenge, and bigotry, there's no room for the creative productions of the superconscious mind to be performed.

These negative qualities aren't just moral failings; they're obstacles to creativity and spiritual growth. They occupy mental and emotional space, consuming energy that could otherwise be directed toward constructive purposes. They distort perception, making it difficult to see reality clearly. They poison relationships, cutting you off from the very connections that stimulate growth.

Think of prejudice, pre-judging people or situations based on categories rather than actual experience. This makes genuine understanding impossible. How can you learn from someone you've already decided isn't worth listening to? How can you see truth in a situation you've already interpreted according to your biases?

Or consider fear, not the healthy caution that preserves life but the chronic anxiety that paralyzes action and distorts perception. Fear makes it nearly impossible to make wise choices because it overwhelms the calm reflection necessary for sound judgment.

Resentment and revenge keep you chained to the past, constantly rehearsing old injuries rather than moving forward. They consume enormous energy while producing nothing of value. The person dominated by resentment cannot be creative because creativity requires openness to possibility, while resentment keeps you focused on what went wrong.

Bigotry, the stubborn attachment to opinions regardless of evidence, makes learning impossible. The bigot already knows what they believe and isn't interested in information that might challenge those beliefs. But spiritual growth requires constant learning, constant adjustment of understanding in light of new truth.

The revelators aren't saying you must achieve perfect spiritual purity before any soul growth can occur. That would be impossible. Rather, they're pointing out that these negative qualities directly interfere with the inner life's creative work. To the degree you can clear the stage of consciousness, reducing prejudice, overcoming fear, releasing resentment, abandoning bigotry, you make room for higher productions to be staged.

This is part of what happens in the mansion world experience. Many of these negative qualities are described as "the mark of the beast", animal traits inherited from our evolutionary origins. They're gradually overcome as we progress through the mansion worlds, finally being completely transcended only on the seventh mansion world.

But we can begin the work now. Each time you catch yourself prejudging, stop and reconsider. Each time fear threatens to paralyze you, call upon faith. Each time resentment flares, practice forgiveness. Each time you notice bigotry in your thinking, open yourself to alternative perspectives. You won't achieve perfection, but you'll be clearing the stage, making room for creativity, expanding your soul.

The Mystery of Jesus' Soul and Future Role

Earlier we discussed Jesus' personalized Thought Adjuster and his continued soul development after his baptism. Now we need to consider the extraordinary speculation the revelators offer about Jesus' future role in the universe.

When Jesus died on the cross, he spoke his final words: "Father, into your hands I commit my spirit." The revelators suggest this "spirit" may have been the soul he had built throughout his human life, that unique spiritual entity jointly created by his human mind and his Thought Adjuster during those thirty-five years seven months on Earth.

After his resurrection, Jesus didn't immediately resume his role as Michael of Nebadon, the Creator Son of our local universe. Despite having received full sovereignty over his universe at his death, despite being fully divine, he chose to experience the morontia progression that all mortal survivors must undergo. For forty days he appeared to his followers in various morontia forms, experiencing the transitional reality between material and spiritual existence.

Only after completing this morontia progression did he finally reclaim his full identity as Michael, sovereign ruler of Nebadon. But what happened to that human soul he had built, that spiritual counterpart of his mortal experience? The revelators propose, and they're careful to note this is speculation, not revelation, that either his personalized Thought Adjuster, or his human soul, or perhaps both somehow combined, may become the head of the finaliter corps from our local universe.

Finaliters are beings who have completed the entire ascension journey from mortal origin to Paradise, who have achieved relative perfection and are being prepared for eternal service in the outer space levels currently being organized beyond the seven superuniverses. Each local universe's finaliter corps will presumably have its own leadership suited to the unique character of that universe.

If this speculation is accurate, it means Jesus, not as Michael the Creator Son but as Jesus of Nazareth the perfected human, will personally lead all of us who successfully complete the ascension journey. The soul that was built during those thirty-five years seven months on Earth, enriched by experiences no other mortal has had but simultaneously genuine human experience, would serve as the connecting link between Michael's divinity and our humanity throughout eternity.

This would fulfill Jesus' promise to always be with us. Not just spiritually present through the Spirit of Truth but personally leading us in our eternal adventures beyond the grand universe. Every other Creator Son will presumably do something similar for the mortals of their respective universes, each building a human soul through their mortal bestowal that becomes the eternal bridge between divinity and ascending humanity.

The revelators emphasize we cannot be certain about these details. They're "proposals," possibilities suggested by the known facts but not definitively revealed. This humility about what they don't know is itself instructive. Even beings far advanced beyond us don't have all answers. Mystery remains, and we'll discover the truth as we progress through universe ages yet to come.

Practical Application: Living from the Inner Life

All this theology and cosmology points toward practical questions: How do I develop my inner life? How do I ensure my soul is growing? How do I live in the material world while building eternal spiritual reality?

The answer isn't complicated, though implementing it requires dedication: You develop your inner life by consistently choosing spiritual values over purely material considerations, by cultivating awareness of the divine presence within you, by allowing your superconscious mind to inform your conscious choices, and by expressing spiritual realities through material service.

Start each day with even a few moments of conscious contact with the Thought Adjuster. This might be formal prayer, quiet meditation, or simply sitting in grateful awareness that God's presence dwells within you. The technique matters less than the sincere intention to acknowledge and commune with that presence.

Throughout the day, pause occasionally to consider whether your choices are building something of eternal value. When faced with decisions, ask not just "What will benefit me materially?" but "What choice reflects eternal values? What would my highest self-choose? What would contribute to my soul's growth?"

Pay attention to your motivations. Are you acting from love or fear? From generosity or selfishness? From faith or anxiety? The same external action can have very different spiritual value depending on the motivation behind it. Money given to impress others contributes little to soul growth; the same amount given from genuine compassion contributes substantially.

Cultivate relationships that stimulate your spiritual growth and offer the same to others. Remember that the inner life isn't solitary. You need other people to challenge your thinking, mirror your blind spots, receive your service, and offer you theirs. Spiritual growth occurs in the friction and fellowship of genuine human contact.

Study truth, not just religious texts but philosophy, science, art, whatever helps you understand reality more deeply. The revelators emphasize that youth should interest themselves in ethics, sociology, philosophy, the fine arts, religion, and cosmology. These same disciplines benefit people of all ages because they expand understanding and provide context for spiritual development.

Practice clearing the stage of consciousness. When you notice prejudice, question it. When fear arises, examine whether it's realistic or distorted. When resentment lingers, work toward forgiveness. When bigotry appears in your thinking, deliberately consider alternative perspectives. This work is never finished, but consistent effort gradually opens space for the superconscious mind's creative contributions.

Express your inner life outwardly through service. Don't hoard whatever spiritual insight you gain. Share it through kindness, teaching, artistic expression, or whatever form fits your unique personality and circumstances. The inner life naturally overflows into outer expression, and attempting to keep it purely private actually stunts its growth.

Finally, be patient with yourself. Soul growth occurs slowly, often imperceptibly. You won't become spiritually perfect in this lifetime, that's what eternity is for. What matters is genuine progress, however gradual. Are you more loving than you were last year? More understanding? More patient? More faithful? More aligned with eternal values? If so, your soul is growing, and you're successfully building the spiritual counterpart that will survive death and continue evolving throughout eternity.

Conclusion: The Inner Life and Eternal Adventure

We've covered complex territory in this chapter, the relationship between recognition and understanding, the nature of material versus spiritual reality, the mechanics of soul growth, Jesus' unique experience, the civilizational crisis when youth neglect spiritual development, and the creative power of the inner life.

But all of this points toward a simple, magnificent truth: You are right now building something eternal. Every choice for truth over falsehood, beauty over ugliness, goodness over selfishness; every moment of genuine communion with the divine presence within you; every act of service motivated by love; every effort to understand reality more deeply, all of this is being preserved, is becoming part of the soul that will be you on the mansion worlds and beyond.

The material world, for all its apparent solidity, is temporary and ultimately unreal in the deepest sense. Only meanings and values are eternal. Only what contributes to soul growth survives. This isn't cause for despair about material existence but for joy about its true significance. Your daily life, ordinary as it may seem, is the raw material from which eternal reality is being fashioned.

In the next chapter, we'll explore the relationship between material mind and spiritual insight, examining how the Thought Adjuster works with the seven-adjutant mind-spirits and the Holy Spirit to foster spiritual growth. We'll look at how pure spirit contact with pure material mind requires something between them, the evolving morontia soul, and how prayer and worship function as the conscious side of spiritual communion.

For now, remember: The inner life is real life. Everything else is preparation, raw material, temporary scaffolding that will eventually be left behind. But what you're building in that inner life, the soul being jointly created by you and your Thought Adjuster, that's what's genuinely and eternally real. That's what you're taking with you. That's what you're becoming. Live accordingly.

Chapter 26: The Adjuster and the Soul - Ideas, Ideals, and the Human Paradox

Introduction: The Inner World and Outer Reality

We live in a world overflowing with ideas. Turn on the news, scroll through social media, or attend any political rally, and you'll find no shortage of proposals, plans, and promises. Ideas spring from the stimuli of the outer world, they're reactions to what we see, hear, and experience in our material existence. But here's the problem: ideas without ideals are like ships without rudders. They may move, but they don't know where they're going.

The Urantia Book makes a striking observation in Paper 111, section 4: "Ideas may take origin in the stimuli of the outer world, but ideals are born only in the creative realms of the inner world." This distinction matters more than we might initially think. Today's nations are directed by men and women who possess a superabundance of ideas but remain poverty-stricken in ideals. This spiritual poverty explains much of what we see around us, poverty itself, divorce, war, and racial hatred all find their roots in this fundamental deficiency.

When we talk about ideals, we're not talking about wishful thinking or naive optimism. We're discussing spiritual principles that align with universal truth, moral standards that reflect cosmic reality rather than cultural preference. The inner world, that sacred space where personality, mind, and the divine fragment meet, is where these ideals are born. Without connection to this inner realm, our moral standards collapse, and society drifts into the very chaos we're witnessing today.

Consider organizations like Tunnel to Towers, which supports families of fallen heroes, police officers, firefighters, and disabled veterans. These groups operate from genuine ideals, not just good ideas. They represent the kind of spiritual principles that could transform our world if we aligned our collective ideas with such divine ideals. When ideas align with ideals, we move closer to what *The Urantia Book* calls "light and life", that advanced state of planetary evolution characterized by spiritual maturity and social harmony.

Political leaders who embody true ideals, those working toward peace, addressing racial division, and serving with genuine moral purpose, stand in stark contrast to those merely reacting to public opinion polls. The difference isn't intelligence or education; it's the connection to that inner world where universal values take precedence over temporary expedience.

We find ourselves at a critical juncture. The threat of ideologies that suppress individual spiritual growth, what the book identifies as the "biggest threat to the world", looms large precisely because these systems operate purely on ideas divorced from spiritual ideals. Socialism, communism, and other materialistic philosophies may sound idealistic on paper, but they fail because they're administered by people without genuine connection to cosmic ideals. Until we reach a state of spiritual maturity as a planet, systems that depend on universal altruism simply cannot function. They collapse under the weight of human selfishness and the absence of divine guidance.

This chapter explores the profound relationship between our inner spiritual life and our outer material existence. We'll examine how free will, that most precious gift, can become either creative or destructive depending on our choices. We'll look at the human paradox: the strange reality that we're simultaneously part of nature and capable of transcending it. And we'll discover how the consecration of our will to divine purposes transforms everything about our existence, both now and eternally.

The stakes couldn't be higher. Our survival beyond this life, our eventual perfection, and our eternal service all depend on choices we make in the present moment. These aren't decisions we'll make someday on the mansion worlds; they're choices that confront us now, in this material existence, as we navigate the tension between our animal heritage and our spiritual destiny.

Free Will: The Double-Edged Gift

Free will stands as humanity's most distinctive characteristic and most dangerous capability. The book states plainly: "Free will man is endowed with the powers of creativity in the inner man." This isn't just about making choices between chocolate and vanilla. We're talking about genuine creative power, the ability to originate something new, to bring into existence patterns of thought and action that never existed before.

But here's where it gets complicated. Free will creativity necessarily embraces the potential for free will destructivity. You can't have one without the other. When creativity turns toward disintegration rather than integration, when it serves selfish purposes rather than universal good, we find ourselves face to face with the devastation of evil and sin.

Evil, according to this teaching, represents a partiality of creativity, a partial expression that tends toward disintegration and eventual destruction. Think of it as taking something whole and breaking it into competing pieces. All conflict is evil in this sense because it inhibits the creative function of the inner life. Conflict creates what the book calls "a species of civil war in the personality", an internal battle that tears us apart rather than building us up.

The perfect example? Lucifer. Here was a being of extraordinary intelligence and creative ability who decided his ideas trumped universal ideals. His rebellion wasn't born from ignorance but from a willful choice to pursue his own path regardless of cosmic harmony. He had ideas, plenty of them, but he severed his connection to divine ideals. The result was catastrophic, affecting entire planetary systems for millennia.

We face the same choice on a smaller scale. When our inner creativity embraces evil, when we choose paths that lead to disintegration rather than integration, our free will becomes destructive. The key lies in ensuring that our creative choices align with cosmic principles, with those ideals born in the inner world where our personality communes with the divine fragment.

This is why Dr. Steven Greer's work with extraterrestrial intelligence proves so fascinating. He consistently reports that these advanced beings operate from a concept of "cosmic unity", they see themselves as part of a universal whole rather than competing fragments. They're trying to teach us to embrace this perspective, to move beyond constant warfare and conflict toward genuine planetary maturity. They're not something to fear; they represent what we could become if we aligned our creative will with universal ideals.

Your free will creativity becomes constructive when it serves integration, when it builds bridges instead of walls, creates harmony instead of discord, and moves toward unity rather than fragmentation. Every choice you make either integrates or disintegrates, creates or destroys, serves the whole or fractures it further.

Inner Creativity and the Nobility of Character

"Inner creativity contributes to ennoblement of character through personality integration and selfhood unification." This sentence packs more punch than it might first appear. When we talk about inner creativity, we're referring to that combination of mind, personality, and divine guidance working together in harmony.

Character ennoblement isn't about becoming stuffy or self-righteous. It's about developing genuine spiritual nobility, becoming someone who naturally expresses what the book calls "the fruits of the spirit." When you live life correctly, this involves integrating God's will into your daily choices until it becomes second nature.

The statement "the past is unchangeable; only the future can be changed by the ministry of the present creativity of the inner self" offers tremendous liberation. Whatever you've done, whatever mistakes you've made, whatever sins you've committed, they're fixed in the past. You can't go back and undo them. But the future remains wide open, malleable, responsive to the creative choices you make right now.

This present creativity springs from the inner self, that integration of your intellectual mind, your unique personality, and the Father fragment dwelling within you. When all three work together in harmony, you achieve what the book calls "personality integration and selfhood unification." You become whole rather than fragmented, directed rather than scattered, purposeful rather than aimless.

Living with dedication to the Father's will creates a kind of spiritual muscle memory. You don't have to constantly stop and think, "What would God want me to do here?" The answer becomes instinctive, automatic, not because you're robotic, but because you've trained your will to align with divine purposes. It's a knowing that transcends intellectual calculation.

This integration of mind, personality, and divine guidance produces balanced living. You're not pulled in multiple directions by competing desires. You're not constantly second-guessing yourself or struggling with internal contradictions. The initiative we discussed in earlier chapters, that quality of taking action aligned with divine purposes, flows naturally from this integrated state.

Your intent matters more than your actions in some ways. Two people can perform the same act with entirely different intentions, and those intentions determine the spiritual value of the action. When your intent aligns with divine ideals, when your will consciously chooses to share your inner life with God, transformation happens almost automatically.

The Consecration of Choice

Here we arrive at the heart of the matter: "The consecration of choice, the doing of the will of God, is nothing more or less than an exhibition of creature willingness to share the inner life with God." Notice that word "consecration." This isn't casual or temporary. Consecration implies dedication, commitment, a sacred setting apart of your will for divine purposes.

But what does it mean practically? It means recognizing that doing God's will represents your willingness to share your inner life with the very God who made that inner life possible. It's reciprocal sharing, God shares all with the Eternal Son and the Infinite Spirit, and they in turn share with the Divine Sons and Spirit Daughters throughout the universes. This sharing represents the fundamental pattern of reality itself.

The imitation of God isn't just recommended, it's described as "the key to perfection." And doing his will? That's "the secret of survival and of perfection in survival." These aren't empty religious platitudes. They're describing the actual mechanism by which finite creatures attain eternal life.

When you make the decision, your decision, not anyone else's, that it's your will to do God's will, something remarkable happens. You're not surrendering your will in the sense of giving it up or losing it. You're consecrating it, expanding it, glorifying it, perfecting it. Your creature will rises from the level of mere temporal significance to a higher estate where you, as a creature son or daughter, actually commune with the personality of the spirit Father.

Think about that for a moment. Two personalities, yours and God's, coming together in communion. Not absorption, not annihilation, but genuine fellowship between the finite and the infinite. Your unique personality, which will never be duplicated throughout all eternity, achieves direct contact with the personality fragment of the Universal Father himself.

This choosing of the Father's will represents "the spiritual finding of the spirit Father by mortal men," even though ages may pass before you actually stand in God's factual presence on Paradise. The relationship begins now, in this life, through your choices.

But here's the crucial distinction the book makes: "This choosing does not so much consist in the negation of creature will, 'not my will but yours be done', as it consists in the creature's positive affirmation: 'It is my will that your will be done.'"

Do you see the difference? One is passive resignation; the other is active consecration. One says, "I give up." The other declares, "I choose this!" The first negates; the second affirms. And this affirmation, this positive choosing that God's will shall be done, makes all the difference.

When you make this choice, the God-choosing son or daughter finds "inner union (fusion) with the indwelling God fragment." Eventually, this same perfecting soul will find "supreme personality satisfaction in the worship communion of the personality of man and the personality of his Maker, two personalities whose creative attitudes have eternally joined in self-willed maturity of expression."

This is spiritual adulthood. This is growing up in the cosmic sense. It's the birth of an eternal partnership between human will and divine will. And when does this partnership form? Not someday in the distant future, but now, through your present choices.

The Human Paradox

We live in a strange in-between state, and *The Urantia Book* doesn't shy away from calling it what it is: a paradox. "Many of the temporal troubles of mortal man grow out of his twofold relation to the cosmos. Man is part of nature, he exists in nature, and yet he is able to transcend nature."

You're finite, but you're indwelt by a spark of infinity. You're an animal, but you're capable of spiritual communion with God. You're temporary, but you harbor eternal potential. This dual situation "not only provides the potential for evil but also engenders many social and moral situations fraught with much uncertainty and not a little anxiety."

Think about your daily experience. You have biological drives, hunger, sexual attraction, the desire for comfort and security. These aren't sins; they're part of your animal nature. But you also have spiritual aspirations, the longing for meaning, the desire for righteousness, the pull toward something greater than mere survival. These two aspects don't always play nicely together.

"The courage required to effect the conquest of nature and to transcend oneself is a courage that might succumb to the temptations of self-pride." There's the rub. When you successfully transcend your material nature, when you rise above your animal impulses, you might become arrogant about it. "The mortal who can transcend self might yield to the temptation to deify his own self-consciousness."

This mortal dilemma consists of a double fact: on material levels, you find yourself subservient to nature, while on spiritual levels, you triumph over nature and all things temporal and finite. You can't escape this paradox; it's inseparable from human existence. And with this paradox comes temptation, potential evil, and decisional errors.

When self becomes proud and arrogant, sin may evolve. Notice it says "may evolve", sin isn't inevitable, but the potential is always there. The sins that most people feel guilty about often stem from this conflict between material nature and spiritual aspiration. You have hormones, biological urges, physical needs. These connect you to nature, to the finite realm.

But when you try to rise above the finite, when you make spiritual choices and attempt spiritual actions, you find yourself at war within yourself. Your nature wants comfort, pleasure, immediate gratification. Your spirit wants growth, sacrifice, eternal values. This internal conflict creates what people traditionally call "sins against oneself" or "sins of the flesh."

Here's the good news: these particular struggles will pass away when you reach the mansion worlds. You won't be connected to physical nature in the same way. You'll have a morontia form that doesn't war against spiritual aspirations. Those biological urges that cause so much internal conflict? They'll be transformed or transcended.

But a new danger emerges when you get beyond that struggle. "When self becomes proud and arrogant, sin may evolve." Spiritual pride represents a more serious problem than biological temptation. A spiritually arrogant person has disconnected from the very humility that makes spiritual growth possible.

This is why genuine spiritual maturity always expresses itself in humility. The smartest person, whether in spiritual matters, medicine, science, or any field, remains humble because they recognize the vastness of what they don't know. The best doctors refer patients to specialists when needed. They don't pretend omniscience. Similarly, the most spiritually advanced person doesn't parade their advancement; they serve quietly, knowing that any progress they've made came through divine assistance, not personal achievement.

Most of us go through life becoming experts at being stupid. We make the same mistakes repeatedly, learn slowly, and stumble frequently. And that's okay. Recognizing our foolishness actually represents the beginning of wisdom. It's when we think we've figured everything out that's we become dangerous to ourselves and others.

Sin, Evil, and the Misuse of the Finite

"The problem of sin is not self-existent in the finite world. The fact of finiteness is not evil or sinful. The finite world was made by an infinite Creator, it is the handiwork of his Divine Sons, and therefore it must be good."

This statement deserves careful attention. The material world isn't inherently evil. Your body isn't evil. Physical pleasure isn't evil. Nature isn't evil. These are all creations of divine beings, expressions of infinite creativity in finite form. They must be good because God doesn't create evil.

So where does evil come from? "It is the misuse, distortion, and perversion of the finite that gives origin to evil and sin."

Water isn't evil, but you can misuse it. During various wars, armies have bombed dams to flood areas and wipe out populations. That's misuse of water for destructive purposes. Go scuba diving without enough air in your tank, and you'll drown, another misuse of water through poor planning. The water itself remains neutral; it's the use that determines whether good or evil results.

Sexual expression isn't evil, but it can be distorted or perverted. Food isn't evil, but gluttony distorts its proper use. Power isn't evil, but its perversion leads to tyranny. Money isn't evil, but greed perverts its function as a medium of exchange.

The key insight here is that you can know whether you're misusing something by examining the consequences. Does your use of this finite resource lead to integration or disintegration? Does it build up or tear down? Does it serve the whole or just your fragment? Does it align with cosmic ideals or merely satisfy temporary desires?

If you don't misuse anything, if you use all finite resources according to their divine purpose, then everything you do in this finite life becomes good. Your life becomes peaceful, constructive, beneficial for yourself and others. You contribute to universal welfare rather than subtracting from it.

This is tremendously liberating. You're not fighting against nature or denying legitimate needs. You're simply using finite resources, including your own body and mind, according to their intended purposes. You're aligning finite expression with infinite ideals.

Mind, Energy, and the Limits of Material Control

"The spirit can dominate mind; mind can control energy. Mind can control energy only through its intelligent manipulation of the metamorphic potentials inherent in the mathematical level of the causes and effects of the physical domains."

This gets technical, but it's worth understanding. Your spirit, or more accurately, the divine fragment within you, can help you dominate mind. This dominated mind can then control energy, but only in specific ways.

"Creature mind does not inherently control energy; that is a Deity prerogative." You can't just think energy into existence or mentally manipulate electromagnetic fields. You're not a deity. But you can create machines that manipulate the matter and energy already present in the physical universe.

Want electricity? Build a generator. Want to travel faster? Build a vehicle. Want to communicate across distances? Build a communications device. Your mind can create mechanical objects that help you manipulate energy, but you can't control energy directly through mental power alone.

The beings who do control energy directly, the Master Physical Controllers, the morontia power supervisors, the various orders of energy manipulators, operate under Deity prerogative. They're specifically created and empowered to manage the energy systems of planets, stars, and universes. The sun doesn't maintain its power by itself; Deity-created beings manage those energy transformations.

But here's what you can do: "Through the intelligent use of the body mechanism, mind can create other mechanisms, even energy relationships and living relationships, by means of which this mind can increasingly control and even dominate its physical level in the universe."

You start with your body, the one mechanism you can directly control. Using your body, you create tools. Using tools, you create more complex machines. Using machines, you create systems that allow you to control and shape your environment. This represents the progression of civilization: using mind to create mechanisms that extend your control over the physical realm.

We're doing this right now, using computers and internet connections to communicate across distances, share ideas, and build community. These are "energy relationships" created by mind through "intelligent manipulation" of physical principles. We haven't violated any laws of nature; we've simply learned to work within them creatively.

Science, Facts, and the Foundation of Wisdom

"Science is the source of facts, and mind cannot operate without facts. They are the building blocks in the construction of wisdom, which are cemented together by life experience."

Here we get to the integration of science, religion, and philosophy. You can't separate them, not really. Science provides facts about the physical universe. Religion provides the love of God and divine law. Philosophy provides the framework for integrating both.

"Man can find the love of God without facts, and man can discover the laws of God without love, but man can never begin to appreciate the infinite symmetry, the supernal harmony, the exquisite repleteness of the all-inclusive nature of the First Source and Center until he has found divine law and divine love and has experientially unified these in his own evolving cosmic philosophy."

This explains why *The Urantia Book* isn't just a religious text. It's also a scientific and philosophical treatise. The three must work together. You need facts (science), love (religion), and integration (philosophy) to truly understand reality.

Think about it this way: Philosophy studies knowledge itself, how we know what we know, what knowledge means, how to think logically. It's the study of wisdom, the examination of truth claims, the analysis of reasoning. In the ancient Greek tradition, philosophy came first, providing the logical framework for investigating reality.

From philosophy emerges science, the systematic study of the physical world using observation, experimentation, and logical deduction. Science transforms philosophical questions into testable hypotheses, abstract reasoning into concrete knowledge.

But both philosophy and science need religion, not in the sense of dogma or ritual, but in the sense of recognizing the spiritual foundation of reality. Without acknowledging the First Source and Center, without understanding that an infinite Creator stands behind all finite creation, your philosophy and science remain incomplete.

Consider the Big Bang theory. Scientists observe that the universe appears to be expanding, so they reason backward to a point of origin, a massive explosion that started everything. But even if such an explosion occurred, it doesn't explain how the initial conditions came to exist. There had to be a First Source and Center, an original cause, a divine initiator. Even the Big Bang requires God.

Every atheist argument falls apart when you follow it to its logical conclusion. Where did the universe come from? "It just appeared" isn't a satisfactory answer. "It always existed" contradicts the evidence of expansion and entropy. At some point, you have to acknowledge an uncaused cause, an unmoved mover, a First Source and Center, or you're left with logical absurdity.

The integration works like this: God (religion) provides the spiritual foundation. Logic (philosophy) provides the framework for understanding. Facts (science) provide the concrete details. Together, they create a comprehensive worldview that explains reality at every level, spiritual, morontia, and material.

The universe itself operates logically. If it didn't, if natural laws were arbitrary or chaotic, nothing could exist. The very fact that science works, that we can discover repeatable natural laws, proves that an intelligent Creator established those laws. Logic isn't just a human invention; it's a reflection of cosmic order, an echo of divine rationality.

So, when *The Urantia Book* talks about finding "divine law and divine love" and unifying them in your "evolving cosmic philosophy," it's describing the only way to truly understand the universe. Science alone gives you facts without meaning. Religion alone gives you faith without foundation. Philosophy alone gives you logic without content. You need all three, integrated and balanced, to grasp "the infinite symmetry, the supernal harmony" of the First Source and Center.

This integration represents the true fatherhood of God and the brotherhood of man. When you understand that God is your Father, that other humans are your brothers and sisters, that the universe operates according to divine law administered with divine love, everything changes. Your cosmic philosophy becomes lived reality rather than abstract theory.

Conclusion: The Choice Before Us

We've covered substantial ground in this chapter. We've seen how ideas differ from ideals, how free will creates both opportunity and danger, how inner creativity builds noble character, and how the consecration of choice transforms our relationship with God. We've examined the human paradox, our simultaneous connection to nature and capacity to transcend it, and we've explored how science, religion, and philosophy must integrate to provide genuine cosmic understanding.

But all of this points toward one central reality: your survival depends entirely on your choices. Not God's choices, he's already chosen to give you a fragment of himself. Not fate's choices, there's no predetermined destiny controlling your life. Your choices made moment by moment, day by day, determine your eternal future.

"Peace in this life, survival in death, perfection in the next life, service in eternity, all these are achieved in spirit now when the creature personality consents to subject the creature will to the Father's will."

This happens now, not later. Your decision to align your will with divine will creates immediate spiritual consequences that extend into eternity. When you choose to share your inner life with God, when you positively affirm "it is my will that your will be done," you initiate an eternal partnership that culminates in fusion, the permanent union of your perfected soul with the divine fragment.

The beauty of this teaching is its clarity. You don't have to wonder whether you're saved, whether you'll survive death, whether heaven awaits you. If you've made the decision to follow God's will in your life, if you've consecrated your choice to divine purposes, your survival is secure. That's it. That's the secret.

You can't get to heaven without choosing the Father's will, but you also can't fail to reach heaven if you do choose it. It's that simple and that profound.

As we move forward in our study, we'll examine more deeply how this choice works out practically in daily life. We'll explore the mechanisms of divine communion, the nature of worship, and the gradual process by which mortal will and divine will merge into something greater than either, alone. We'll see how this partnership affects not just our eternal future but our present experience, how it brings peace, purpose, and power into everyday existence.

The human paradox doesn't disappear, but it becomes manageable when you understand it as part of your growth process. The conflict between nature and spirit doesn't vanish immediately, but it loses its power to destroy you when you align with divine purposes. The challenge of transcending self without falling into spiritual pride becomes navigable when you remain humble before the vastness of cosmic reality.

You stand at a crossroads in every moment. Will you choose ideas or ideals? Will your free will create or destroy? Will you integrate or disintegrate? Will you share your inner life with God or keep it to yourself? Will you affirm "it is my will that your will be done" or continue to insist on your own way?

These aren't rhetorical questions. They're the most practical questions you'll ever face. And the answers you give, through your choices, not just your words, determine literally everything about your future.

The next chapter will build on these foundations, exploring how worship and prayer facilitate this divine-human partnership. We'll see how communication with God works, what makes prayer effective, and how worship differs from every other human activity. But first, take time to consider what we've covered here.

Have you made the choice? Have you consecrated your will to divine purposes? Do you understand the difference between ideas and ideals in your own life? Are you using finite resources according to their divine purpose, or are you misusing, distorting, and perverting them?

These aren't comfortable questions, but they're necessary ones. Your eternal survival hangs in the balance, not because God threatens you, but because reality itself operates according to specific principles. Choose life. Choose growth. Choose divine alignment. Choose to make your will align with the Father's will. Everything else follows from that single, central choice.

Chapter 27: Personality Survival and the Divine Pattern

Introduction

The concept of personality survival stands as one of the most amazing teachings in *The Urantia Book*, revealing not just the mechanics of eternal life but the very architecture of how God relates to each of us as individuals. When I began my study series on Paper 112, "Personality Survival," I opened a doorway into understanding what makes each human being irreplaceable in the cosmic scheme, and why our choices during this mortal life carry weight that echoes through eternity.

This chapter explores the foundational principles of personality as presented in Paper 112, examining how our earthly existence serves as merely the vestibule to our true life. More significantly, it reveals the striking parallel between human spiritual development and the evolution of the Supreme Being, showing us that the pattern of our own transformation mirrors the grand cosmic pattern itself.

The Starting Point of Eternity

The evolutionary planets scattered across the seven superuniverses serve as spheres of human origin, the initial worlds of what *The Urantia Book* calls our "ascending mortal career." Urantia, our own world, represents your starting point, mine, and that of every soul who begins this remarkable journey.

From the moment a Thought Adjuster, a fragment of God the Father himself, takes up residence within the human mind, typically around age five or six, we enter into what the revelation describes as a "temporary union." This phrasing may seem surprising at first. Many people naturally assume that once the Thought Adjuster arrives, the partnership becomes permanent. Yet the text makes it clear that this initial relationship depends entirely on our choices. We are endowed with a perfect guide, yes, but whether that guide remains with us throughout eternity hinges on our willingness to run "the race of time" and gain "the final goal of faith."

Should we choose survival, should we genuinely desire to do the will of God, then comes the moment of fusion, when our identity permanently unites with the indwelling Adjuster. Only then, according to the revelation, does our "real life" truly begin. Everything before that moment, including our entire mortal existence, serves as what the text beautifully terms the "vestibule."

Think of walking into a grand home. The vestibule is that small entry space you pass through before entering the actual living areas. It's part of the house, certainly, but it's not where life happens. Our mortal years function much the same way, a necessary threshold, an introduction, but not the full experience. I've often uses the children's rhyme to illustrate this point: "Row, row, row your boat, life is but a dream." In a very real sense, our mortal life *is* but a dream compared to what comes after fusion.

The real adventure, the exalted and progressive mission as finaliters, begins only after fusion, stretching out through ages we can barely imagine. And yet, throughout all these successive stages of evolutionary growth, from mortal to morontia, through 570 morontia levels, into spirit form, and beyond, one element remains absolutely constant: personality.

The Nature of Personality: Fifteen Defining Characteristics

Paper 112 acknowledges the conclusion that attempting to define personality would be presumptuous. Instead, it offers fifteen characteristics that help us understand what personality is and how it functions. I've tried to emphasized that these aren't just abstract theological points; they're practical truths about what makes each of us fundamentally unique and eternally significant.

1. The Source of Personality

Personality is that quality in reality bestowed by the Universal Father himself, or by the Conjoint Actor (the Infinite Spirit) acting for the Father. For mortal humans like us, personality comes directly from God the Father. But for the vast angelic hosts and other celestial beings, personality originates through the Infinite Spirit, though it ultimately derives from the Father. This distinction matters because it shows that personality bestowal isn't random or automatic, it's a deliberate gift from deity.

2. Bestowal Upon Living Energy Systems

Here's where things get interesting. Personality may be bestowed upon "any living energy system which includes mind or spirit." This took me years of study to fully grasp. Personality isn't limited to biological beings as we commonly understand them. Consider the Master Physical Controllers, beings who regulate energy throughout the universes. Many of these entities possess personality despite having no biological form whatsoever. They represent living energy systems with mind, and that qualifies them for personality bestowal.

This broader definition helps us grasp that personality transcends our narrow, human-centered view of what constitutes a "person."

3. Freedom from Antecedent Causation

Personality "is not wholly subject to the fetters of antecedent causation." In plain language, this means we are not helplessly trapped by circumstances or the accidents of time. Yes, a hurricane might destroy your house. You couldn't prevent that. But your response to that disaster, your attitude, your choices about how to move forward, these remain entirely within your control.

Personality is "relatively creative or cocreative." The creative aspect comes from the God-fragment within us; the cocreative aspect comes from our own free will. Together, these elements mean we're not just billiard balls bouncing around according to fixed physical laws. We have genuine agency, even when external circumstances seem overwhelming.

4. Spirit's Mastery Over Matter

When personality is bestowed upon evolutionary material creatures, it "causes spirit to strive for the mastery of energy-matter through the mediation of mind." Here we see a three-way dynamic at work: spirit (the Thought Adjuster), mind (provided by the Infinite Spirit through the local Universe Mother Spirit), and matter (our physical body).

Personality acts as the integrating force. It's why doctors, especially holistic practitioners, often say that healing begins from within. The human body is designed as a self-healing organism. When the energy circuits and nervous system function properly, when the mind can properly interface with the brain's physical structure, the body can handle most microbial invasions and injuries. What enables this remarkable capacity? The mastery of energy-matter through mind, coordinated by personality.

This principle also explains something troubling: why damage to the brain can destroy identity even while the body continues functioning. If the mind circuit cannot properly interface with the physical brain, the person as a conscious entity effectively ceases to exist, even though biological processes continue. The Thought Adjuster and guardian angel depart with the developing soul, leaving behind only a biological shell.

5. Unifying Identity

"Personality, while devoid of identity, can unify the identity of any living energy system." This statement initially seems paradoxical. Personality itself doesn't have identity, it's more like the container or framework. But when combined with mind and the experiences of living, personality creates identity.

You can't have true identity without mind. If your brain suffers catastrophic damage, your identity as a functioning person is lost, even though your personality (in the eternal sense) and your soul have already been preserved by celestial guardians. The physical you may continue breathing, but the conscious, choosing you is gone.

6. Qualitative Response

Personality "discloses only qualitative response to the personality circuit, in contradistinction to the three energies which show both qualitative and quantitative response to gravity." This gets technical, but the essential point is that personality isn't measured by quantity, by "how much", but by quality, by "what kind."

The personality circuit of God the Father doesn't operate like physical gravity, which responds mechanically to mass and distance. Instead, personality responds to the quality and character of other personalities. It's relational rather than mechanical, personal rather than impersonal.

7. Changelessness

"Personality is changeless in the presence of change." Throughout all our transformations, from mortal to morontia to spirit, the core personality remains constant. Everything else about us changes continuously. We move through 570 morontia levels, each one representing a significant transformation. But the personality bestowed upon us by the Father never alters in its essential nature.

If change stops, death follows. Growth is life; stagnation is death. Yet within all that necessary growth and change, personality provides the stable center, the continuous thread of identity that makes you recognizably still "you" from beginning to end.

8. The Only Gift to God

Perhaps the shortest yet most profound statement in the entire list: personality "can make a gift to God, the dedication of the free will to the doing of the will of God."

This is the only gift we can give our Creator. God doesn't need our prayers in the sense of needing information or emotional support. He doesn't require our worship to bolster his self-esteem. What he desires is our willing cooperation with his purposes. When you say, "Father, it is my will that your will be done in my life," you're giving the supreme gift, returning to God the very free will he gave you.

This isn't submission in any degrading sense. It's the ultimate expression of trust and love, the recognition that infinite wisdom knows better than finite ignorance. I've emphasized this point repeatedly: you can't just say, "God, I'm going to do your will, tell me what to do." It has to be *your will* wanting *God's will* to manifest itself in your life. That distinction makes all the difference.

9. Moral Consciousness

Personality is "characterized by morality, awareness of relativity of relationship with other persons." Without moral awareness, without concern for how our actions affect others, personality cannot properly function in choosing between good and evil.

This is why Thought Adjusters typically arrive around age five or six, that's when children make their first genuine moral choice. Before that point, there's no ethical framework for the Adjuster to work with. Early humans in primitive times didn't receive Adjusters automatically either. Before Pentecost, you had to actively seek to do the Father's will before an Adjuster would indwell you. We're fortunate in this era to receive them so young and so readily.

Morality isn't imposed from outside; it emerges from personality's natural ability to discern conduct levels and discriminate between them. The Ten Commandments and other ethical codes codify what personality, when functioning properly, already recognizes: that relatedness to others carries inherent obligations.

10. Absolute Uniqueness

"Personality is unique, absolutely unique." The text emphasizes this point exhaustively: unique in time and space, unique in eternity and on Paradise, unique when bestowed, unique during every moment of existence, unique in relation to God.

There are no duplicates. Not even identical twins share the same personality, though they may share genetics and upbringing. God is no respecter of persons, meaning he doesn't play favorites, but neither does he add personalities together or total them up. They're "non-addable" and "non-totalable." You cannot take ten personalities and combine them into one super-personality. You cannot take a million personalities and somehow merge them into a collective whole.

Each personality stands alone, irreplaceable and unrepeatable. When you get married, no matter how much you love your spouse, you remain unique individuals. You might become "one" in a spiritual or relational sense, but your personalities remain distinct.

If you choose not to survive, if you ultimately reject the path to eternity, that unique personality is lost to the universe forever. The experience gathered by your Thought Adjuster goes to the Supreme Being, yes, but your particular configuration of personality, that conscious, choosing entity that is *you*, ceases to exist. It's not punished or sent somewhere. It simply isn't anymore, like falling into total unconsciousness with no possibility of waking. You wouldn't have a vehicle to revive into.

This makes survival crucial. God the Father loses something irreplaceable when a personality chooses nonexistence. The universe loses a potential thread in the grand tapestry. And you, you lose everything.

11. Direct Response to Other Personalities

"Personality responds directly to other-personality presence." Because each personality is unique, whenever we encounter another person, we're encountering something fundamentally different from ourselves. This accounts for why human interactions can be so complex and sometimes frustrating.

That person taking forever in the grocery checkout line? They're not being difficult to annoy you; they're simply operating from a different personality framework. Understanding this doesn't mean accepting all behavior without boundaries, but it does encourage patience and recognition of our common humanity despite our differences.

12. The Primacy of the Father

Personality "is one thing which can be added to spirit, thus illustrating the primacy of the Father in relation to the Son." When God the Father created the Eternal Son, he gave the Son a separate personality, distinct from his own. From that moment forward, the Eternal Son began living his own personality, developing according to his own choices and responses.

Interestingly, "mind does not have to be added to spirit." The spirit of God doesn't need mind added to it because God is already in perfect contact with the Infinite Spirit, the source of all mind. Mind itself arose from the combined action of Father and Son, bringing forth the Spirit.

This trinitarian pattern, Father (personality), Son (spirit), Spirit (mind), becomes the template for our own development, as we'll explore more fully in the next section.

13. Survival Through the Soul

"Personality may survive mortal death with identity in the surviving soul." The Thought Adjuster is changeless; personality is changeless. But the relationship between them, the soul being built through their cooperation, is "nothing but change, continuing evolution."

If this change ceased, the soul would cease. Growth is essential. Stagnation equals death. And this remains true even after fusion. We never reach a point where we can say, "I've arrived; no more development is needed." The journey continues infinitely, always expanding, always deepening, always revealing new dimensions of reality and relationship.

14. Unique Consciousness of Time

"Personality is uniquely conscious of time, and this is something other than the time perception of mind or spirit." Our mind perceives time as linear, tick-tock, one moment after another, inexorably moving toward death. Our spirit, influenced by the eternal Adjuster, begins to grasp timelessness.

But personality has its own time consciousness, something that transcends both mortal urgency and eternal timelessness. It's aware of time's relative unreality while still functioning within time's constraints. I have noted that even some contemporary physicists are beginning to recognize that time doesn't really exist in the way we experience it, it's more like a succession of events rather than an independent flowing stream.

As we approach fusion and especially after achieving it, this broader time consciousness expands. We begin to see time more as God sees it, not as a limiting constraint but as a succession of experiential opportunities.

15. Summary: Personality as Unifying Gift

The final characteristic circles back to the unifying function mentioned earlier. Personality, properly understood, is the gift that makes us capable of relationship, with God, with other personalities, with the universe itself. It's the foundation of our identity, the guarantee of our uniqueness, and the framework within which we make choices that echo through eternity.

The Pattern: Human and Supreme

During his study session, I've introduced a parallel that illuminates perhaps the most profound truth about personality survival: our individual development mirrors the evolution of the Supreme Being. I admitted this realization came to me only after fifty years of studying *The Urantia Book*, a humbling reminder that these cosmic truths reveal themselves gradually.

The Supreme Being is not yet fully actualized. In Havona, there exists God the Supreme, the spirit person created by the Paradise Trinity. But the full realization of the Supreme requires two other aspects: the Almighty Supreme (the power expanding throughout the seven superuniverses) and the Supreme Being (the God of experience, gathering all experiences of all evolutionary creatures).

Think of these three, God the Supreme, the Almighty Supreme, and the Supreme Being, not as three separate entities but as three aspects of one developing deity, similar to how the Paradise Trinity consists of Father, Son, and Spirit as distinct persons yet one divine reality.

Now consider the human parallel:

- **The Thought Adjuster** = God the Supreme (the spirit person, the divine fragment, the changeless spiritual presence)
- **Personality** = The Almighty Supreme (the controller, the integrator of power and experience, the organizing principle)

- **The evolving soul** = The Supreme Being (the repository of experience, constantly growing and developing)

Just as the Supreme Being evolves toward ultimate unification of these three aspects, so do we. Our entire mortal existence, our morontia progression, our spirit development, all of it moves toward the moment when Adjuster, personality, and soul fuse into one unified being.

When fusion occurs, we become something new: a finalized expression of the partnership between divine and human, eternal and temporal, perfect and perfecting. We don't lose our individuality; we complete it. And from that point forward, all our experiences contribute directly to the Supreme Being, making us literal children of the Supreme, just as the Supreme is a child of the Paradise Trinity.

Here's where it gets even more remarkable: every fused mortal becomes a permanent thread in the fabric of the Supreme. Our uniqueness is preserved and contributes to the whole. But if we fail to survive, if we choose nonexistence, it's like pulling a thread from that fabric. The experience still goes to the Supreme through the Adjuster, but the personality, the unique pattern of who we are, is lost.

The universe is diminished. The Supreme is diminished, not in power or factuality, but in the richness of diversity. And you, personally, lose everything, not because God punishes you, but because you've rejected the very thing that would give you eternal existence.

I have emphasized how this pattern repeats across different scales of reality. Just as Paradise serves as the pattern the Creator Sons use to create local universes, this trinitarian structure, spirit, personality, soul, serves as the pattern for mortal survival and eventual finality. It's heavy stuff, but once you see the connection, the entire cosmic architecture starts making sense.

The Critical Role of Volition

Understanding personality survival isn't merely an intellectual exercise or theological curiosity. It changes how we live today, how we treat ourselves and others, how we respond to difficulty and opportunity.

If every person you meet carries a personality bestowed directly by God the Father, absolutely unique and irreplaceable, how does that affect your patience in traffic? Your response to the difficult coworker? Your judgment of the homeless person on the street corner? Each one is a universe of potential, a personality destined for eternity, assuming they choose it.

And what about your own choices? I kept returning to this central theme: it's the volition of God that things are set up the way they are. God's volition is his will, the I AM, the First Source and Center expressing his purposes. It is his will that we each have a fragment of himself. It is his will that we receive personality at birth, like a blank slate, a new creation all its own.

But here's where free will becomes sacred: it is *our* volition whether to survive or not. It is our volition to do the will of God or our own will. That's why when you pray, you need to say, "Father, it is my will that your will be done in my life." You can't just say, "God, I'm going to do your will, tell me what to do." It doesn't work that way. It has to be your will *wanting* the will of God to manifest itself in your life.

If you choose, if your free will, your volition, chooses not to survive, then nothing in the universe can save you. Because volition, free will, is sacred. It's the ultimate gift and the ultimate responsibility. It's not until you turn that will over to God that it becomes God's will working through you.

Can you see that? Can you see the importance of choosing survival during this life?

This makes "every-day matter". We're all going to have problems. We're all going to face days when we think, "I don't know if I want to keep going." But these are, in my words, "stupid little problems of human life." What we need to keep in line is our faith that it will all work out according to the will of God the Father.

If this life truly is just the vestibule, the entrance hall to the real mansion of existence, does it make sense to spend all our energy decorating the entryway while neglecting to move into the house? We can get so caught up in the urgencies of mortal life, money, status, comfort, security, that we forget these things are temporary scaffolding, not the building itself.

The real building, the permanent structure, is the soul being constructed through the partnership of our personality and the Thought Adjuster. Every moral choice, every act of kindness, every moment of genuine worship or service adds to that structure. Every selfish decision, every willful rejection of truth, every persistent choosing of comfort over growth weakens it.

The Path to Recognition

I have tried to point out something that often gets overlooked: the Supreme Being is our pathway to the Trinity. When you go to Havona, you have to understand and recognize the Supreme Being before you can recognize God the Father, God the Son, and God the Spirit.

This is part of what's called God the Sevenfold:

1. The Creator Son and The Creative Daughter (Universe Mother Spirit)
   2. The Ancients of Days
   3. The Seven Master Spirits
   4. The Supreme Being
   5. The Infinite Spirit
   6. The Eternal Son
   7. The Universal Father

We have to recognize God the Sevenfold on the way to the Supreme. Then we recognize the Supreme on the way to the Infinite Spirit. Then we recognize the Infinite Spirit on the way to the Eternal Son. Then we recognize the Eternal Son to finally stand before God the Father.

When we stand before God the Father, we become finaliters. That's why they're called finaliters, because you're on the final journey to stand before God the Father. And once you stand before God the Father, you're a child of God, a child of the Supreme, ready for your next assignment.

That assignment will be in the universes until the point where the seven superuniverses reach a certain level of completion. Then the children of the Supreme, that's us, will go out into the four outer space levels to continue the work of creation and perfection.

But in order to get to that point, the seven superuniverses have to reach a certain threshold of completion. And when all three aspects of the Supreme, God the Supreme, the Almighty Supreme, and the Supreme Being, come together into what I've called "the triune of the Supreme," then the Supreme will have all the experiences and all the personalities of all beings in the seven superuniverses.

That prepares us for life as finaliters. Our progression to Paradise is really just the first step to going out and becoming finaliters and doing all sorts of interesting things we can't even imagine yet.

The Implications for Now

Most of us probably muddle through, making some good choices and some poor ones, gradually learning and growing despite our stumbles. The revelation assures us that God judges by intent as much as by action, and that all who genuinely desire to do right will be given every possible assistance and opportunity. The universe literally conspires to help us survive, if we'll cooperate even a little.

But it's possible to refuse. It's possible to say, in effect, "I don't want this. I don't want to grow, to change, to become more than I am. I want to remain as I am, or I want to cease entirely." God honors that choice, terrible as it is. Free will is sacred, even when it's used to choose extinction.

I have admitted these concepts are hard to grasp. After reading *The Urantia Book* for over fifty years, I am still having "aha" moments where light suddenly comes on and things make perfect sense. But that's part of the beauty of the revelation, it continues to yield new insights, deeper understanding, richer appreciation for the cosmic architecture.

One of the study group participants, suggested that much of this has to do with our growth and development and a mutual exchange between God the Father and other entities, God the Almighty and so on. I agreed enthusiastically: "You've hit it on the head. That's exactly true."

It's about relationship. It's about exchange. It's about the finite contributing to the infinite, the temporal participating in the eternal, the imperfect cooperating with the perfect to create something neither could achieve alone.

Conclusion: The Choice Before Us

The evolutionary planets are indeed spheres of human origin, but they're much more than that. They're the beginning of a journey that, properly undertaken, leads through morontia worlds, spirit spheres, Havona itself, and ultimately to standing in the presence of the Universal Father on Paradise. And even that isn't the end, it's really just the beginning of the beginning, the commencement of our service as finaliters in universes yet to be organized and perfected.

Throughout this entire journey, from Urantia to Paradise and beyond, one thing remains constant: the personality given to you by the Father, unique in all creation, irreplaceable in all eternity. What you choose to do with that gift determines everything.

We've explored fifteen characteristics of personality, each one revealing something essential about what makes us who we are. We've seen how our individual development mirrors the evolution of the Supreme Being, Thought Adjuster, personality, and soul working together just as God the Supreme, the Almighty Supreme, and the Supreme Being work together.

We've discovered that the only gift we can give to God is the dedication of our free will to doing his will. And we've confronted the sobering truth that if we refuse to survive, we lose not just our future but our very existence, that unique personality configuration is lost to the universe forever.

In the next chapter, we'll explore more deeply the mechanics of survival, what happens at death, how the soul is preserved, what awaits us on the mansion worlds, and how the transition from mortal to morontia actually occurs. We'll look at the role of the guardian seraphim, the reality of the third-day resurrection, and what it means to wake up on the first mansion world.

But none of that matters if we haven't first grasped the fundamental truth of this chapter: personality is God's gift to you, and survival is your gift back to him. The choice, as always, is yours. And it's a choice that echoes through eternity.

Chapter 28: Personality and Survival - The Cosmic Dimensions of Identity

Introduction

I want to begin this chapter by sharing something that happened during one of our study sessions, something that reminded me, once again, that none of us are beyond making mistakes. Last week, I managed to mentally rearrange the solar system. Yes, you read that correctly. In my mind, I had somehow swapped Mars and Jupiter, making Mars the giant and Jupiter the smaller neighbor. One of our regular students, Rodney, caught my error and sent me a gentle email correction. My first reaction? "Oops. I did do that, didn't I?"

Why do I start with this confession? Because it illustrates something fundamental about our journey through understanding *The Urantia Book*, we're all learning, all evolving, all subject to the limitations of our finite minds. Even those of us who have spent years studying this revelation can stumble over basic facts. And that's perfectly fine. What matters is that we remain open to correction, willing to grow, and committed to pursuing truth wherever it leads us.

This chapter focuses on Paper 112, titled "Personality Survival," which may be one of the most personally relevant papers in the entire book. After all, what could matter more to us than understanding what we truly are, how we function, and whether we continue beyond this brief mortal existence? The answers provided in this paper are both reassuring and challenging. They tell us that personality, that unique aspect of ourselves that makes us *"us,"* is a divine gift from the Universal Father himself, designed to function not just in this life, but potentially throughout eternity.

This will likely be the last time I teach these classes in detail. I'm not going to be around forever, and I want to hit the most important topics while I still can. The Life of Christ recordings are already available on YouTube for anyone who wants them, and I believe those papers are largely self-explanatory. All we can do is enlighten you on how the Jesus lessons integrate with the beginning of the Book and make the lessons of Jesus clearer to understand. But when you encounter Jesus talking about the Supreme in those papers, you'll have a connection point from these classes. You'll understand why Jesus is part of the Supreme, and why that matters so profoundly for our understanding of God's experiential nature.

The Foundation: What Is Personality?

Let me start with the most fundamental statement in this entire paper: **Personality is bestowed by the Universal Father upon his creatures as a potentially eternal endowment.**

Notice that word, "potentially." Why potentially? Because personality, while it comes from God the Father and carries something of his eternal nature, requires our cooperation to become actually eternal. If we choose not to survive, if we refuse the ascending career offered to us, that personality returns to its source. It doesn't float around as some ghostly remnant. The experience of that personality goes into the Supreme, contributing to the experiential growth of God himself, but it never again knows itself as a conscious entity.

This is worth pausing over. The personality you possess right now, reading these words, is a direct gift from the First Source and Center of all reality. It didn't evolve from your genes. It wasn't constructed by your brain. It was *bestowed*, given to you as an act of divine generosity. And here's what makes this even more remarkable: that personality is designed to function on numerous levels and in successive universe situations, ranging from the lowly finite (where we are now) to the highest absonite (a level we can barely conceive), and even to the borders of the absolute.

Think about what this means. The personality you're building right now, in your everyday life, dealing with work frustrations, family challenges, moments of joy and disappointment, this personality is equipped to function in Havona, on Paradise, and eventually in the outer space levels that haven't even fully materialized yet. God doesn't give us temporary tools. He gives us eternal equipment, suitable for an infinite journey.

Now, you might be wondering about the Infinite Spirit. Doesn't the Infinite Spirit also bestow personality? Yes, but with an important distinction. The Infinite Spirit bestows personality on the celestial angels and support beings, the vast hosts of ministering spirits who serve throughout the universes. These beings are all children of the Infinite Spirit, and they receive their personality endowment from that divine source. But you and I, as ascending mortals, receive our personality directly from the Universal Father. This tells us something about our potential destiny and our relationship with God.

Three Cosmic Planes of Function

The paper tells us that personality performs on three cosmic planes or in three universe phases. Let me break these down clearly:

First: Position/Status in the Local Universe, Superuniverse, and Central Universe

Your personality functions equally well whether you're here on Earth (in Nebadon, our local universe), progressing through Orvonton (our superuniverse), or eventually reaching Havona (the central universe). The same personality that helps you navigate your neighborhood, your workplace, and your family relationships will serve you perfectly well when you're navigating billion-year-old architectural spheres in the company of supernal beings. I find this both humbling and exciting.

What the paper doesn't explicitly mention here, but which is certainly implied elsewhere, is that this same personality will continue to serve us in the outer space levels, those four concentric rings of forming universes that will eventually house God knows how many trillions of beings. Your personality isn't just equipped for the present age. It's built for eternity.

Second: Meaning/Status on Finite, Absonite, and Absolute Levels

This is where things get interesting, and honestly, a bit challenging for our finite minds to grasp. We currently function on the finite level. Everything we experience, every thought, every decision, every relationship, happens within the boundaries of time and space. We are creatures of sequence and limitation.

But personality is designed to eventually function on the absonite level. What does that mean? Absonite is the in-between level that bridges finite and absolute. Havona beings are absonite. They didn't evolve through time like we do, but they're not absolute like God the Father, Son, and Spirit. When we finally graduate from the superuniverses and enter Havona, we'll begin functioning on this absonite level. Our personality won't need an upgrade or replacement, it's already designed for this transition.

And the paper hints at something even more remarkable: personality has potential for functioning "as impinging upon the absolute." This is far-future stuff, likely related to our eventual service in the outer space levels, where we may interact with beings and realities that transcend even the absonite. God has built us for an adventure beyond our current imagination.

Third: Value/Status - Material, Morontial, and Spiritual

Here's where the rubber meets the road, as we used to say. Personality can be experientially realized in the progressive realms of the material, the morontial, and the spiritual. Notice that word "experientially." This isn't theoretical theology. This is about lived reality.

Right now, in our material bodies, we're experiencing personality in its most limited expression. We're bounded by flesh, constrained by biochemistry, subject to fatigue and hunger and all the limitations of animal origin. But even here, personality shines through. You recognize your friends not just by their faces but by something deeper, their essential *"them-ness"*. That's personality.

When we re-personalize on the mansion worlds (assuming we've chosen survival), we'll experience personality in the morontial realm. Morontia is that fascinating halfway state between material and spiritual, part energy, part matter, neither quite one nor the other. In that state, personality will have greater freedom, greater range of expression, greater capacity for cosmic awareness.

And finally, in the spiritual realms, after we've completed our morontia ascension and become fully spirit beings, personality will achieve its highest expression within the finite level. We'll be complete, integrated, unified beings, ready for whatever adventures await in Havona and beyond.

The Critical Importance of the Supreme

I need to pause here and emphasize something that appears throughout this paper and indeed throughout the entire book: everything we do as finite, experiential beings feeds into the Supreme. This might sound abstract, but it's actually intensely practical.

The Supreme Being is God in time and space, God as he *becomes* through the collective experience of all finite creatures. We are not just citizens under the Supreme's jurisdiction; we are literally children of the Supreme. Our every experience, every choice, every moment of growth contributes to the actualization of the Supreme Being.

This is why Jesus kept mentioning the Supreme during his earthly ministry. If you go back and read the Jesus papers carefully (and I encourage you to do so, they're available in our video series on YouTube), you'll notice how frequently he refers to Supreme realities. Jesus, as a Creator Son, is fundamentally a being of experience.

Everything the Creator Sons do falls under the domain of the Supreme. They're not static, absolute beings like the eternal Trinity. They're experiential, growing, evolving, and so are we.

When the paper says that the value status of personality "can be experientially realized," it's pointing to this fundamental truth: without this experiential dimension, none of what we do would feed into the Supreme. We don't live outside the Supreme's experience. We can't. We're integral parts of it, whether we realize it or not.

This also helps explain why personality, though unchanging in its essential nature, can nevertheless grow and develop. The personality itself, that gift from the Universal Father, remains constant. But its expression, its realization, its experiential content continually evolves. And all of that evolution contributes to something larger than ourselves: the emerging Supreme Being, who will one day be fully actualized when all seven superuniverses finally settle in light and life.

Three Dimensions: Length, Depth, and Breadth

The paper gets quite specific about how finite personality operates. It describes three dimensions that should sound familiar if you've studied geometry: length, depth, and breadth. But these aren't spatial dimensions in the ordinary sense. They're functional dimensions that describe how personality works.

Length: Direction and Movement

Length represents direction and the nature of progression, movement through space and according to time. This is your life journey, your progression plan. It's how you move through the stages of existence, from birth to death to re-personalization to morontia progression to spirit status and beyond.

Think of length as your timeline, but not in a purely chronological sense. It's the directional aspect of your experience. Where are you going? What's your trajectory? Are you moving toward greater truth, beauty, and goodness, or are you stagnating? This dimension measures progress through the cosmos over the eons of your existence.

Vertical Depth: Self-Realization and Environmental Response

Vertical depth embraces the organismal drives and attitudes, the varying levels of self-realization, and the general phenomenon of reaction to environment. This is where things get personal.

Vertical depth is what allows you to recognize yourself as distinct from others, as a unique individual. Each personality is different. We're not cookie-cutter souls stamped out from a divine mold. Your personality has depths that no one else's has. Your combination of temperament, preference, style, and manner of being is absolutely unique in all of universe history.

This dimension also governs how you interact with your environment. Do you respond to challenges with courage or fear? Do you meet other personalities with openness or suspicion? How deep is your capacity for empathy, for understanding, for growth? All of this falls under the vertical depth of personality.

Breadth: Coordination and Organization

Breadth embraces the domain of coordination, association, and selfhood organization. If I had to pick one word to describe breadth, I'd probably choose "relational." This is your capacity to coordinate things in your life, to form associations with other personalities, and to organize your own mind and plans.

Some people seem naturally gifted at this. They bring people together, coordinate complex projects, maintain dozens of friendships, and keep their lives organized. Others struggle more. But we all have this dimension of personality, this capacity for breadth. And it can grow.

Think about how you organize your own selfhood. Do you have a coherent philosophy of life, or are you scattered and reactive? Can you coordinate your various roles, parent, worker, friend, citizen, into a unified whole, or do they conflict and fragment you? The breadth dimension determines how well you integrate the many aspects of your being into one coherent self.

My wife sometimes tells me I'm a "super organizer." I can work on multiple projects simultaneously, recording videos, preparing study materials, writing books, managing our fellowship, and still somehow keep track of it all. That's the breadth dimension functioning fairly well, though I certainly have room for growth. But we all have different personalities, different strengths. What comes easily for one person requires great effort for another. And that's perfectly fine. God doesn't expect us all to function identically.

Seven Dimensions of Potential

Now we come to something truly remarkable. The paper tells us that the type of personality bestowed upon mortals has a potentiality of seven dimensions of self-expression or person-realization. Seven dimensions. Why seven?

Seven always points back to God the Father, doesn't it? God the Father, God the Son, God the Spirit, that's three. Add Paradise, the Deity Absolute, the Universal Absolute, and the Unqualified Absolute, and you have seven fundamental dimensions of the I AM, the infinite God who transcends all our categories.

And here's the key insight: since our personality comes from God the Father, it mirrors these same seven dimensions. We're made in the image of God, not physically but functionally. Our personality structure reflects the divine pattern.

The paper breaks these seven dimensions into a specific pattern:

- **Three dimensions on the finite level**: This is everything we experience from birth through our entire mortal ascension, all the way up to the borders of Havona. These are the dimensions we're currently using, length, depth, and breadth, as we've discussed.
- **Three dimensions on the absonite level**: These dimensions will activate when we reach Havona and Paradise. They represent capacities we can barely imagine right now, ways of functioning that transcend time and space as we currently experience them.
- **One dimension on the absolute level**: This seventh-dimension totals and unifies all the previous six. It's described as "the fact of personality" itself, the supreme dimension that is "an associable absolute." This dimension has potential for "sub-infinite penetration of the absolute," which appears to mean we'll eventually interact with absolute realities in ways appropriate to our finite-becoming-absonite-becoming-something-more nature.

Why structure personality this way? I believe it's because God has already planned for our service in the outer space levels. When we finally graduate from the superuniverses, when the Supreme Being is fully actualized, a whole new age of universe development will begin. Those vast, unpeopled outer space levels will need to be administered, settled, and brought to fruition. And we, finite ascenders who have climbed from the bottom to the top, will be qualified for that service precisely because our personalities are dimensionally equipped for it.

Cosmic Reality and Unchallengeable Consciousness

The paper makes a fascinating statement about the finite dimensions of personality. It says they relate to cosmic length, depth, and breadth, where:

- **Length denotes meaning**
- **Depth signifies value**
- **Breadth embraces insight**

That third one particularly caught my attention: "the capacity to experience unchallengeable consciousness of cosmic reality."

Why "unchallengeable"? Rodney asked this during our study session, and it's a good question. I believe the answer relates to spiritual security. Once you step into this cosmic dimension, once you've truly experienced the reality of the cosmos through your personality's insight dimension, no one in the universe can come along and convince you it's all a farce.

Remember Lucifer? His entire rebellion was built on the claim that the universe government was a sham, that the Creator Sons had invented this elaborate system just to control everyone, that the Universal Father was a myth. He challenged the very foundations of cosmic reality.

But here's the thing: any being who had properly developed their personality's insight dimension, who had experienced that unchallengeable consciousness of cosmic reality, would have been immune to Lucifer's arguments. They would have known, experientially and undeniably, that the cosmos is real, that the spiritual hierarchies are genuine, that God's love permeates everything.

This is what makes personality such a safeguard. It's not just a philosophical position you adopt. It's an experiential certainty you develop. And once you have it, nothing, no clever sophistry, no charismatic rebel, no temporary doubt, can fundamentally shake it.

Think of it as the spiritual equivalent of knowing you exist. Descartes famously said, "I think, therefore I am." That's an unchallengeable certainty, isn't it? You can doubt many things, but you can't coherently doubt your own existence. Similarly, the insight dimension of personality provides an unchallengeable certainty about cosmic reality. You know it the way you know you exist, directly, immediately, undeniably.

This is security. Real security. Not the false security of dogma or the fragile security of wishful thinking, but the deep security that comes from experiential knowledge. And I find that tremendously reassuring.

The Morontia Enhancement

The paper then makes a crucial point: "On the morontia level all of these finite dimensions of the material level are greatly enhanced, and certain new dimensional values are realizable."

This is important. When we transition from our material existence to the morontia level, when we wake up on the mansion worlds with a new morontia body and a vastly expanded consciousness, all three dimensions of our personality will be enhanced.

Why? Because we'll have moved from finite philosophy to morontia mota. Mota is the morontia equivalent of philosophy. It's the way morontia beings think about and understand reality. And it's vastly superior to our current philosophical capabilities.

Right now, we're limited by our seven-adjutant mind-spirits, those divine circuits of mind that serve finite, material creatures. These adjutants are wonderful. They give us everything from basic instinct to worship and wisdom. But they're designed for finite life.

When we reach the morontia level, we step into cosmic mind, the universal mind circuit provided by the Infinite Spirit through the Master Spirits. This is a qualitative leap, not just a quantitative improvement. Suddenly, we have access to cosmic perspectives, to morontia mathematics (yes, everything really is mathematics), to levels of insight that simply aren't possible with a material brain.

The paper also mentions "the contribution of morontia mathematics." Now, I know many people groan when they hear about mathematics. "I barely passed algebra," someone might say. "You're telling me I'll need advanced math in the afterlife?"

But here's the thing: morontia mathematics isn't like struggling through calculus homework. It's the natural language of reality. Everything in the cosmos operates according to mathematical principles, energy, matter, mind, spirit, all of it follows precise, beautiful patterns. When you have a morontia mind, understanding these patterns becomes natural, even enjoyable. It's not drudgery; it's enlightenment.

And this mathematical/philosophical enhancement affects all three personality dimensions. Your length, your sense of direction and progress, becomes clearer. Your depth, your self-understanding and environmental response, becomes more profound. Your breadth, your capacity to coordinate and organize, expands dramatically.

Then comes the spiritual level, where the same enhancement happens again. Each transition, material to morontia, morontia to spirit, brings another quantum leap in personality function. And through it all, the personality itself remains constant. It's the same you, just with vastly greater capacities.

Why We Struggle to Understand

Here's where the paper offers us some grace. It says: "Much trouble experienced by mortals in their study of human personality could be avoided if the finite creature would remember that dimensional levels and spiritual levels are not coordinated in experiential personality realization."

In other words, cut yourself some slack. You're trying to understand multidimensional, trans-temporal realities with a three-pound lump of electrified meat. (Your finite brain), Of course it's difficult.

We look at everything through finite lenses because that's all we have right now. We think in terms of before and after, here and there, this and that. We can't directly experience morontia reality. We certainly can't experience spiritual reality, not in its fullness. We have faith, yes, and occasionally we might have mystical experiences that give us glimpses, but for the most part, we're operating blind.

And that's okay. That's part of the plan. We're not supposed to fully understand these higher dimensions yet. We're supposed to develop faith, to trust the process, to continue growing despite our limitations.

Even philosophy and theology, our best human attempts to understand spiritual reality, are constantly shifting and evolving. What one generation considers settled truth, the next generation questions and revises. That's not a bug; it's a feature. We're evolving beings in an evolving creation, seeking to understand an infinite God with finite minds. Of course, our theology changes.

And here's something crucial that I always try to emphasize: this book, *The Urantia Book*, wasn't written for one religion. It wasn't written just for Christians, just for Muslims, just for Buddhists, or just for anyone else. It was written for all of humanity, for every religion, every culture, every level of intellectual development.

The revelators tell us explicitly that they used more than 2,000 human concepts just in retelling the life of Jesus. They scoured human history for the best theological insights, the best philosophical frameworks, the best spiritual understandings they could find, and they wove all of it together to give us a revelation that speaks to everyone.

That's why you'll find echoes of Christianity and Buddhism and Hinduism and many other traditions throughout the book. The revelators aren't plagiarizing. They're building bridges. They're showing us that truth is truth, regardless of where it appears, and that God has been at work in all cultures, all religions, all genuine spiritual seeking throughout human history.

So, when someone says, "Well, that part sounds like it came from the Bible," I say, "Yes! And thank God for the Bible. It contains profound truths that needed to be incorporated into this larger revelation." The same goes for insights from Eastern religions, from Greek philosophy, from modern science. Truth is truth. The revelators honored that.

Life as Process

One of my favorite sections in this paper is the simple statement: "Life is really a process which takes place between the organism (selfhood) and its environment."

Life is process. Not a static state, not a fixed condition, but an ongoing, dynamic process. And personality is what "imparts values of identity and meanings of continuity to this organismal-environmental association."

Think about what this means. Without personality, you'd just be a biological machine responding to stimuli, a complex robot running on autopilot. Stimulus comes in, response goes out, no real meaning to any of it.

But personality transforms that mechanical process into something meaningful. It gives you identity, you're not just any organism, you're *"you"*. And it gives you continuity, you're the same person you were yesterday, last year, in childhood, despite all the physical and mental changes you've undergone.

The paper makes an important distinction: "Mechanisms are innately passive; organisms are inherently active."

A machine, no matter how sophisticated, is passive. It responds to inputs according to its programming, but it doesn't initiate anything. It doesn't have drives, desires, purposes of its own. Even the most advanced artificial intelligence, despite what some enthusiasts claim, isn't alive. It's a mechanism, and mechanisms are passive.

But organisms are active. We don't just respond; we initiate. We don't just process information; we create meaning. We don't just exist; we strive, dream, hope, love.

And this is why, despite all the hype about artificial intelligence potentially becoming "conscious" or developing "personality," it's never going to happen. A robot doesn't have the spark of life. It doesn't have a personality bestowed by the Universal Father. It doesn't have a Thought Adjuster, a soul, a capacity for eternal survival. It's a tool, a useful, potentially powerful tool, but it's not a person.

When I explained this during our study session, someone pointed out that this makes it impossible for robots to ever truly have personality. Exactly right. You can program a computer to simulate personality, to respond as if it had preferences and opinions and feelings, but it's all simulation. There's no *"there"* there. No real self-looking out through those camera-lens eyes.

The Uniqueness Problem

Here's something that should humble all of us: "The personality imparts values of identity and meanings of continuity to this organismal-environmental association. Thus, it will be recognized that the phenomenon of stimulus-response is not a mere mechanical process since the personality functions as a factor in the total situation."

What this means, practically speaking, is that every single one of us processes reality differently. Your personality filters, interprets, and responds to the environment in a unique way. So does mine. So does everyone else's.

This is why we can attend the same event and come away with completely different impressions. It's why witnesses to an accident give contradictory testimony even when they're all trying to be truthful. It's why reading the same scripture passage can inspire completely different insights in different people.

One of our students made a wonderfully honest observation: "This last sentence just describes why everybody else is wrong except you." We all laughed, but there's truth in it. From your perspective, filtered through your unique personality, your interpretation makes sense. From my perspective, filtered through my unique personality, my interpretation makes sense. And both of us might be partially right and partially wrong.

This should make us humble in our certainties and generous in our disagreements. You're not wrong just because you see things differently than I do. You're just... different. Your personality brings different dimensions, different depths, different breadths to the question.

This is also why the book emphasizes the brotherhood of man so strongly. We need each other. No single personality contains all truth. We're like the blind men examining the elephant, each of us grasps part of the reality, but only together can we begin to see the whole.

Evolution and Environment

"Physical life is a process taking place not so much within the organism as between the organism and the environment."

I love this because it emphasizes something we often forget we're not isolated units. We're relational beings, constantly interacting with our environment, physical, social, spiritual.

And every interaction creates patterns. The paper says, "Every such process tends to create and to establish organismal patterns of reaction to such an environment. And all such directive patterns are highly influential in goal choosing."

You are, to a large extent, the product of your patterns. How you've learned to respond to stress, to joy, to challenge to opportunity, these patterns shape your choices, which shape your life, which shapes your destiny.

But here's the hopeful part: patterns can change. Evolution isn't just physical; it's mental, social, and spiritual. Every day offers opportunities to establish new patterns, better patterns, patterns more aligned with truth, beauty, and goodness.

If you stop evolving, you die. Maybe not physically, at least not immediately, but spiritually and intellectually. Stagnation is death. Growth is life.

This is true for individuals, for societies, for planets, for universes. Everything is either growing toward greater perfection or declining toward entropy. There's no neutral ground, no static equilibrium. You're either moving forward or sliding backward.

The good news? God has built the universe to favor growth. The default trajectory, if you cooperate even minimally with divine guidance, is upward and inward, toward greater truth, beauty, and goodness, and toward closer union with God.

The Attitude of the Whole Personality

Let me close this chapter with one final insight from the paper: "Through the mediation of mind, the self and the environment establish meaningful contact. The ability and willingness of the organism to make such significant contacts with environment (response to a drive) represents the attitude of the whole personality."

Notice those three elements: ability, willingness, and drive. Your personality determines all three.

Some of us have great ability but little willingness. We could grow tremendously, could achieve great things, could serve wonderfully, but we don't want to. We're comfortable where we are, thank you very much.

Others have tremendous willingness but limited ability. They want to serve, want to grow, want to contribute, but they struggle with limitations, whether intellectual, physical, or circumstantial.

And then there's drive, that inner motivation that pushes us forward even when ability is limited and willingness wavers. Where does drive come from? Partly from personality, partly from environment, partly from the indwelling Thought Adjuster who constantly nudges us toward better choices.

The attitude of your whole personality, the sum total of your abilities, willingness, and drives, determines how you interact with reality. And those interactions, accumulated over time, determine who you become.

This is why Jesus emphasized the Fatherhood of God and the Brotherhood of Man so strongly. It wasn't because he didn't care about theology or because he was avoiding deeper truths. It was because he understood that right relationships, with God and with each other, create the optimal environment for personality growth.

If you want to find his message, don't look first to the crucifixion. Look to his life, his teachings, his relationships. He showed us how to live as children of a loving Father and as brothers and sisters to all humanity. That was his gospel. That was his gift. And if you really listen to the Jesus papers (which I've been recording and putting on YouTube), you'll hear it again and again and again: the Fatherhood of God and the Brotherhood of Man.

Looking Ahead

We've covered the foundational concepts of personality, what it is, where it comes from, how it functions, and why it matters. But we've barely scratched the surface of Paper 112. In the sessions ahead, we'll explore personality's relationship with the Thought Adjuster, the nature of the soul, what happens at death, the process of re-personalization, and ultimately, what it means to achieve survival and fusion.

These aren't abstract theological questions. They're personally vital. Understanding personality survival isn't just intellectual exercise, it's preparation for the most important transition you'll ever make: the transition from this life to the next.

So, I invite you to continue this journey with us. Whether you're joining our live study sessions on Thursday nights or watching the recordings later, whether you're brand new to *The Urantia Book* or a longtime student, there's always more to discover, more to understand, more to experience.

And remember we're all learning together. I make mistakes. You make mistakes. We all have limitations. But we're progressing, evolving, growing, just as we were designed to do.

In the next chapter, we'll delve deeper into the mechanics of survival, exploring how personality, Thought Adjuster, soul, and mind work together to create the continuity of selfhood that bridges mortal death. We'll look at what happens in that strange interval between your last breath here and your first breath on the mansion worlds. And we'll begin to understand why, despite all the uncertainties and challenges of finite existence, we can face the future with unshakeable confidence.

Until then, I encourage you to reflect on your own personality, its dimensions, its patterns, its potential. You are a unique expression of divine creativity, a beloved child of the Universal Father, a citizen of an infinite cosmos. Never forget that. Never doubt that. And never lose sight of the magnificent adventure that lies ahead.

Thank you for studying with me. And may the peace of Christ Michael be with you always.

Chapter 29: Personality Survival - The Unity of Self and Cosmic Reality

Introduction

In my years of studying and teaching *The Urantia Book*, I've come to realize that few topics challenge students as much as the concept of personality survival. What exactly survives death? How does the mind relate to the soul? Why does personality matter in the cosmic scheme of things? These aren't just abstract theological questions, they cut to the heart of what it means to be human and what our future holds beyond this brief mortal existence.

This chapter explores Paper 112 of *The Urantia Book*, focusing on personality survival and the intricate systems that make us who we are. I'll be honest: some of these concepts took me years to grasp fully, and I still find myself discovering new layers of meaning. The revelators didn't make this easy for us, but that's precisely because they're describing realities that our limited mortal minds can barely comprehend.

What I hope to accomplish here is to break down these complex ideas into something more manageable. We'll examine how the mind mediates our experience of reality, why human beings cannot thrive in isolation, and how personality serves as the organizing principle that unifies all aspects of our being. More importantly, we'll discover what all of this means for our eternal future.

The Mind as Mediator Between Self and Environment

Let me start with something fundamental that often gets overlooked: your mind is the bridge between you and everything else. Paper 112 puts it this way, it is through the mediation of mind that the self and the environment establish meaningful contact. Without this mediating function, nothing in your external world would make any sense. You'd have experiences, perhaps, but no way to interpret them, no framework for understanding what's happening around you.

Think about it practically. Right now, as you read these words, your mind is processing visual symbols, converting them into meaning, relating them to previous knowledge, and forming new concepts. Your environment, this book, the room you're in, the sounds around you, only becomes *your reality* because your mind mediates that experience. If your mind didn't perform this function, you'd be lost in a chaotic stream of sensory data with no ability to make sense of it.

The ability and willingness of the organism to make such significant contacts with the environment represents what the revelators call "the attitude of the whole personality." This is important. We're not talking about passive reception of stimuli. Your mind actively *chooses* how to engage with the world around you. When our sound system malfunctioned during one of our study sessions, which seems to happen more often than I'd like, my reaction to that technical difficulty reflected my personality's attitude toward the environment. I could have gotten frustrated, shut down the meeting, and walked away. Instead, my mind mediated that challenge in a way that allowed the group to continue.

This may seem like a small example, but it illustrates a profound truth: your mind doesn't just observe reality; it actively shapes how you experience and respond to it. Your attitude, your personality, your very sense of self, all of these emerge from this mediating function of mind. And here's what fascinates me: this process continues beyond death. The mind you're developing now, the patterns of response you're establishing, the attitudes you're cultivating, these are building something that will persist into your morontia existence.

The Social Nature of Personality

One of the clearest teachings in *The Urantia Book* appears in this section: personality cannot very well perform in isolation. Man is innately a social creature, dominated by what the book calls "the craving of belongingness." The text puts it bluntly, it is literally true that no man lives unto himself.

I've watched people over the years who've tried to pursue spirituality in complete isolation. Maybe they've retreated to remote locations, cut themselves off from family and friends, convinced that solitude will bring them closer to God. While I understand the appeal, and certainly there's value in periods of reflection and meditation, the revelators make it clear that this isn't the divine plan for human development. You could, theoretically, go live in a cave somewhere and never talk to anyone except your Thought Adjuster. But that's not what God wants for you.

Why? Because growth happens in relationship. The friction, the joy, the challenges, the shared experiences, these are the raw materials of soul growth. When we come together in our study groups, something happens that couldn't occur if each of us studied alone. We're not just learning information; we're building a system of relationships that becomes part of our eternal experience. My wife, Diane, Jane, Gary, Rodney, Pamela, Lech and when we gather to study these papers, we're creating something that will be remembered and carried forward into the mansion worlds.

Family represents the most fundamental of these relationships. It's why the family unit appears throughout the universe, from mortal worlds all the way to Paradise. The lessons learned in family relationships, patience, forgiveness, unconditional love, sacrifice, service, these can't be learned in isolation. You need other personalities to interact with, to challenge you, to love you, and yes, sometimes to frustrate you.

The Brotherhood of Man that Jesus taught isn't just a nice philosophical concept. It's a recognition of our fundamental nature as social beings who need each other in order to become what we're meant to be. We're designed for community, wired for relationship, and destined for an eternity of expanding social connections.

From Relationships to Systems: Understanding Cosmic Organization

Here's where things get more complex but stay with me because this is crucial. The book makes a distinction between relationships and systems. A relationship exists between two objects or two people. But when you have three or more, you don't just have a more complicated relationship, you've created something qualitatively different. You've created a system.

The distinction appears vital because in a cosmic system, the individual members are not connected with each other except in relation to the whole and through the individuality of the whole. Read that sentence again slowly. It's dense, but it reveals something profound about how reality actually works.

Let me illustrate with our study group. When just two of us interact, we have a relationship, straightforward, direct, person-to-person. But when three or more of us come together, something new emerges. We form a system where each person relates not just to each other person individually, but to the group as a whole. The system itself takes on characteristics that transcend the sum of its parts. We share insights that none of us would have discovered alone. We create an atmosphere of learning that exists beyond any individual contribution. The whole becomes greater than the sum of its parts.

This principle applies at every level of reality. Think about the Paradise Trinity, three divine persons who function as a system, not just a relationship. Or consider the triodities described in the book's introduction. Three entities coming together create a system that operates according to principles different from simple bilateral relationships.

Now apply this to yourself. You are not a single thing. You are a system composed of at least three distinct realities: your physical body, your mind (which connects you to universal mind circuits), and your developing soul (which is being co-created by your personality and your Thought Adjuster). Each of these components relates to the others, and together they form a system that is uniquely you.

When you die, the system doesn't simply continue unchanged. The physical component drops away, it's served its purpose. But the other components persist in a new configuration. Your personality (which came from the Universal Father), your soul (which contains the meaningful experiences of your mortal life), and your Thought Adjuster (which has been recording everything of spiritual value) will be reorganized into a new system on the mansion worlds. A morontia form will replace your physical body, and you'll wake up as a functioning personality with memories, identity, and continuity of selfhood.

Understanding this system-based view of reality helps clarify what survives death and what doesn't. It's not that "you" survive as some vague spiritual essence. Rather, specific components of the system are preserved, reorganized, and integrated into a new form of existence. Your personality, that unique quality that makes you "*you*", serves as the unifying principle that holds it all together.

The Cosmic Importance of Sharing Knowledge

One insight that emerged during our group discussion deserves special attention. When you learn something and keep it to yourself, that knowledge becomes stagnant. It takes up space in your mind but doesn't grow, doesn't multiply, doesn't serve any purpose beyond your own intellectual satisfaction. It becomes, in a sense, dead matter, stored information with no life, no movement, no impact.

But when you share what you've learned, something remarkable happens. That knowledge multiplies exponentially. The person you teach shares it with others, who share it with still others, and what began as a single insight ripples outward through the cosmos. You've taken something that was static and made it dynamic, something isolated and made it communal.

This is why I've spent so many years putting study materials online, even when people thought I was wasting my time. "Why go to all that trouble?" they'd ask. "Why spend countless hours creating websites and uploading documents?"

Because we're not just sharing information, we're expanding a system. Every person who reads these materials and shares them with someone else becomes part of an ever-growing network of truth-seekers and truth-sharers.

Think of it like a snowball. If you hold a snowball in your hand, what happens? It melts. You lose it. But if you set that snowball at the top of a hill and give it a push, it rolls down, gathering more snow, growing larger, building momentum. That's what happens when we share spiritual truth. It grows, builds, and eventually becomes something far larger than what we started with.

The revelators tell us that in a cosmic system, individuals are connected to the whole. When you share spiritual insight, you're not just helping another individual, you're contributing to the growth of the Supreme Being itself. Your small act of teaching or sharing becomes part of the vast experiential growth of the evolving Deity of time and space. Nothing is wasted. Nothing is lost. Every act of genuine spiritual sharing has cosmic significance.

The Four Aspects of Selfhood

The revelators organize human selfhood into four distinct aspects, and understanding this organization clarifies how personality functions as a unifying principle. Let me break these down one at a time.

First, physical systems are subordinate. Your body, your brain, the material mechanisms that allow you to function in this world, these are subordinate to higher realities. They're important, certainly. You need them right now. But they're servants, not masters. Your personality can exercise control over your physical body, directing it, training it, using it as an instrument for achieving higher purposes. When you discipline yourself to exercise, to eat properly, to maintain your physical health, you're exercising personality control over subordinate physical systems.

Second, intellectual systems are coordinate. Here's where it gets interesting. Your brain is a physical organ; it's part of the subordinate physical system I just mentioned. But your mind is not your brain. They're two separate realities that work together in an integrated way. Your mind connects you to the universal mind circuits maintained by the Master Spirits and the Divine Minister of your local universe. This cosmic mind circuit coordinates with your physical brain. They work together, they're integrated, but they're not the same thing.

When you die, your brain dies with your body. But your intellect, your capacity for thought, understanding, and reason, continues because it's part of a circuit that transcends physical reality. On the mansion worlds, you'll have a new brain (morontia, not material), but your intellectual capacity will continue and expand because you'll still be connected to mind circuits, just more advanced ones. Eventually, you'll transition from the adjutant mind circuits to the cosmic mind circuits, and your intellectual capacity will expand dramatically.

Third, personality is superordinate. This means your personality supervises, coordinates, and unifies everything else. It's the executive function, if you will, of your entire being. Your personality decides how to use your physical body, how to employ your intellectual capacities, how to respond to your environment. It's the "you" that makes decisions, that chooses, that acts with intention and purpose.

Personality comes directly from the Universal Father. It's a gift, unique and unrepeatable. No other personality in all of creation is exactly like yours. And it's eternal, once bestowed, never withdrawn. Your personality is what provides continuity from your mortal life through all the stages of universe ascension to Paradise and beyond. It's the constant in an existence of constant change.

Fourth, the indwelling spiritual force is potentially directive. Notice that word *potentially*. Your Thought Adjuster doesn't control you. God doesn't force His will upon you. The indwelling spirit is only potentially directive because you must *choose* to actualize that potential. You have to make the conscious decision to align your will with God's will.

This is what Jesus demonstrated throughout his mortal life. Over and over, we hear him say, "Not my will, but Thy will be done." He wasn't denying having a will of his own. He was choosing to align his personal will with the Father's will. That's the pattern we're meant to follow. It's not automatic. It's not something that happens to you. You have to consciously, repeatedly, consistently choose to do the Father's will.

When you make that choice, the potential directive becomes actually directive. The Thought Adjuster gains increasing influence over your thoughts, decisions, and actions. Your personality begins to reflect divine qualities. Your soul grows. And you move steadily toward that distant day when your will and the Father's will become perfectly unified, when there's no longer any distinction between what you want and what God wants for you.

Living First, Thinking Later: The Development of Cosmic Insight

Here's something that struck me when I first read it: "In all concepts of selfhood, it should be recognized that the fact of life comes first, its evaluation and interpretation later. The human child first lives and subsequently thinks about his living."

You can go through your entire mortal life on autopilot. Seriously. You can be born, grow up, get a job, get married, have kids, pay bills, retire, and die, all without ever really thinking deeply about what you're doing or why you're doing it. Millions of people live exactly that way. They're not bad people. They're not doing anything wrong. They're just... going through the motions. Living but not evaluating. Experiencing but not interpreting.

I remember when I was about fifteen or sixteen years old, and this question started burning in my mind: What happens when I die? Is that it? Do I just cease to exist? The question wouldn't leave me alone. I couldn't rest until I found an answer. I spent four or five years studying, searching, reading everything I could find. At that point, I didn't know about *The Urantia Book*. I had access to the Bible and various Christian teachings, but even that was enough to start me on the path.

That's when life changes from mere existence to examined existence. That's when cosmic insight begins to develop. You start asking the big questions: Why am I here? What's my purpose? Where am I going? Is there a God? What does He want from me?

The revelators tell us that in the cosmic economy, insight precedes foresight. You have to gain insight into the nature of reality, into the purpose of existence, into the plan of God, before you can develop foresight about your own future. And that foresight, the understanding that you have an eternal future, that your choices matter, that you're building something that will last forever, that's what motivates the development of a salvageable soul.

Not everyone makes this transition. Some people live their entire lives on the surface level, never questioning, never evaluating, never developing cosmic insight. They may be kind people, good neighbors, loving parents, but if they never make that crucial decision to seek God, to believe in survival, to choose the Father's will, then what exactly is salvageable? What has been built that can survive the dissolution of the physical body?

This is why Jesus constantly said, "Let's go save some souls." He recognized that many people walking around, some of them religious leaders, people who claimed to know God, had built nothing of eternal value. They were going through religious motions, performing rituals, following rules, but they hadn't made the inner choice to actually seek God and do His will. Their souls were empty or nearly so. Nothing salvageable remained.

By contrast, when you begin to evaluate and interpret your life, when you start making conscious choices based on cosmic insight, when you choose to seek God and do His will, that's when your soul begins to grow in earnest. That's when you're building something that will survive.

The Role of Personality in Unification

Let me address something that often confuses students: the relationship between personality, soul, and survival. The revelators state clearly that "in the human organism, the summation of its parts constitutes selfhood, individuality, but such a process has nothing whatever to do with personality, which is the unifier of all these factors as related to cosmic realities."

Your body, your brain, your experiences, your memories, all of these constitute your selfhood, your individuality. But personality is something different. Personality is the unifier, the organizing principle that takes all these disparate elements and creates a coherent, functioning, continuous identity.

Think of it this way: your personality is like the thread that holds a pearl necklace together. The pearls are your experiences, your memories, your learned skills and knowledge. Each pearl is valuable in itself, but without the thread, they're just loose beads scattered on the floor. Personality provides continuity, unity, coherence.

When you die, your body dies. Many of your memories (the purely material ones, the trivial ones, the ones with no spiritual value) die with your brain. But your personality, that gift from the Universal Father, persists. It returns to the Father momentarily and then, at the resurrection, comes back to unify your surviving elements into a new, morontia form of existence.

Your soul awakens with your personality and your Thought Adjuster reunited. The soul, which has been growing throughout your mortal life, contains all the spiritually meaningful experiences you've had. It's been co-created by your personality and your Thought Adjuster, built memory by memory, choice by choice, experience by experience. When the three come together on the mansion worlds, personality, soul, and Thought Adjuster, you wake up as *"you"*, with consciousness, with identity, with memories of your mortal life.

But notice the crucial role personality plays. Without personality, the soul has no identity. It's just accumulated experience with no "I" to claim those experiences as its own. Without personality, the Thought Adjuster has recordings but no person to share them with. Personality is what makes you a unique, volitional, self-aware being rather than just a collection of experiences or a repository of data.

This is why personality is superordinate, it's the organizing principle, the unifying factor, the element that holds everything together and gives it meaning. And this is why personality is indestructible. Once the Father bestows a personality, it exists forever. It may remain dormant (as in the case of someone who chooses not to survive), but it cannot be destroyed.

What Makes a Soul Salvageable?

During one of our discussions, someone asked about people like Hitler. Would someone who committed such atrocities survive? Could someone with that much hatred and evil in their life build a salvageable soul? I'll be honest, I don't want to judge anyone's eternal destiny, and I'm grateful I'm not the one who has to make those decisions. But the question helps us understand what makes a soul salvageable.

The minimum requirement for survival appears to be belief, faith in God, trust in survival, a genuine desire for eternal life. But belief alone isn't enough to build a rich, developed soul. You have to *do* something. You have to live a life that generates spiritual value, that creates experiences worth preserving, that builds character of eternal quality.

Jesus said, "By their fruits you will know them." That applies not just to how we judge others but to how the universe adjudicates survival. What fruit has your life produced? What have you built? What choices have you made? What kind of person have you become?

Someone could go through life claiming to be religious, attending services, performing rituals, saying all the right things, and yet build no real soul. If there's no genuine love, no sincere desire to know God, no authentic choice to do His will, then what exactly is salvageable? You can't fake soul growth. You can't pretend your way into eternity.

On the other hand, someone who's never heard of *The Urantia Book*, who knows nothing of Thought Adjusters or mansion worlds or universe circuits, but who genuinely loves God and tries to live according to truth and goodness, that person is building a salvageable soul. It's not about having the right information or belonging to the right religion. It's about authentic spiritual growth, real choices for goodness, genuine love for God and neighbor.

This is why the Brotherhood of Man teaching is so crucial. When you truly love your fellow humans, when you serve them, help them, forgive them, work with them, you're building soul. When you share spiritual truth, when you help someone understand God better, when you comfort the suffering or encourage the discouraged, you're building soul. These aren't just good deeds that make you feel better about yourself. They're the actual substance of eternal survival.

Conclusion: Preparing for Cosmic Citizenship

As we close this chapter, I want you to think about what we've covered. Your mind mediates your experience of reality, making meaningful contact between your inner self and the outer environment. You are innately social, designed for relationship, destined for an eternity of expanding connections. You function as a system, body, mind, and soul integrated by personality, and that system will be reorganized and continued in morontia form after death.

Your personality, given by the Universal Father, serves as the unifying principle of your entire existence. It supervises the physical, coordinates with the intellectual, and chooses whether to actualize the spiritual potential within you. Every choice you make, every experience you have, every relationship you build contributes to the growth of your soul, or fails to.

The question isn't whether God loves you enough to save you. The question is whether you're building something worth saving. Are you living an examined life? Have you developed cosmic insight? Are you making conscious choices to seek God and do His will? Are you sharing spiritual truth with others? Are you building relationships of eternal value?

These aren't abstract theological questions. They're practical matters that determine your eternal future. You're building your soul right now, in this moment, with every choice you make. The mansion worlds await, with opportunities for growth and service beyond anything we can imagine. But you have to get there first, and that requires building a salvageable soul here and now.

In our next chapter, we'll explore the mechanics of survival in more detail, what happens at death, how the resurrection works, and what you can expect when you wake up on the mansion worlds. But for now, reflect on what we've covered here. Look at your own life. Evaluate your choices. Are you building something eternal? Are you growing a soul that will survive?

The Father has given you everything you need: a unique personality, a perfect indwelling spirit, a mind connected to cosmic circuits, opportunities for relationship and growth. What you do with these gifts determines not just the quality of your mortal life but the reality of your eternal future. Choose wisely. Build well. Your cosmic career has already begun.

In the next chapter, we'll examine the actual mechanics of death and resurrection, demystifying what happens in that transition and what awaits you on the first mansion world. Until then, live consciously, love generously, and seek God with your whole heart.

Chapter 30: The Soul's Reality - Understanding Personality Survival and Spiritual Growth

Introduction

Over the years of teaching *The Urantia Book*, I've found that few topics generate as much curiosity, and confusion, as the nature of the human soul. What is it, exactly? Where does it come from? How do we know it even exists? These questions aren't new, of course. They've echoed through human consciousness since we first became aware of ourselves as something more than mere animals struggling for survival.

Tonight, as we continue our study of Paper 112 on personality survival, I want to share something I discovered while preparing materials on Paper 133. Sometimes, you know, you can read these papers dozens of times, and then suddenly, there it is. A passage you've seen before takes on new meaning; connects dots you didn't even know needed connecting. That happened to me recently, and what I found ties so beautifully into what we've been studying that I couldn't let it pass without bringing it to your attention.

The universe fact of God becoming man, Michael's incarnation as Jesus, has forever changed all meanings and altered all values of human personality. This isn't just poetic language. It represents a fundamental shift in cosmic reality. When Jesus walked this earth, when he lived a complete human life from infancy to death, he demonstrated something that reverberates through all time and space: how a material creature can build something of eternal significance.

The Nature of Personality and Soul

Let me start with something we need to understand clearly: our mortal mind comes from the Infinite Spirit, channeled through our local Universe Mother Spirit. It's part of the Trinity's gift to us. Our personality, that unique, unchanging pattern that makes you "*you*", comes directly from God the Father, just as the Thought Adjuster does. These elements converge to do something remarkable: they build the soul.

Now here's what many people miss. The soul doesn't exist from birth. According to *The Urantia Book*, the soul begins to form when the Thought Adjuster arrives, which happens around five and a half to six years of age, whenever a child makes their first truly moral decision. Before that moment, we have mind and personality, but the soul hasn't been born yet.

Think about what this means. For the first few years of life, we're gathering experiences, developing consciousness, learning to navigate the material world. But that spiritual entity that will carry us beyond this life? It doesn't begin forming until we demonstrate the capacity for moral choice.

Jesus and the Greek Philosopher: A Pivotal Teaching

During Jesus' journey to Rome with Ganid and Gonod, a trip we often overlook in favor of his public ministry, he had a series of profound conversations with a Greek philosopher connected to the local school. This learned Greek, steeped in the philosophical traditions of his culture, finally asked Jesus directly: "What do you mean by 'soul'?"

Jesus' response deserves our careful attention:

"The soul is the self-reflective, truth-discerning, and spirit-perceiving part of man which forever elevates the human being above the level of the animal world. Self-consciousness, in and of itself, is not the soul. Moral self-consciousness is true human self-realization and constitutes the foundation of the human soul, and the soul is that part of man which represents the potential survival value of human experience".

Let me break this down, because it's crucial. Self-consciousness, simply being aware that you exist, doesn't make you spiritually significant. Animals appear to have a form of awareness, a recognition of their environment and perhaps even their pack members. But they don't have moral self-consciousness. They can't step outside themselves and ask, "Was that the right thing to do? Should I have acted differently? What does this mean for who I want to become?"

That capacity for moral reflection, that's the game changer. When you can look at your own behavior and judge it against some standard of right and wrong, when you can feel genuine remorse or satisfaction based on ethical considerations rather than mere survival instinct, you've crossed a threshold. You've demonstrated the foundation upon which a soul can be built.

Jesus continued:

"Moral choice and spiritual attainment, the ability to know God and the urge to be like him, are the characteristics of the soul. The soul of man cannot exist apart from moral thinking and spiritual activity. A stagnant soul is a dying soul, but the soul of man is distinct from the divine spirit which dwells within the mind."

That phrase, "a stagnant soul is a dying soul", should give us pause. It suggests something sobering: survival isn't automatic. If we do nothing to increase our spiritual attainment, if we make no moral choices that have survival value, we're essentially letting our souls atrophy. It's like having a muscle that withers from lack of use.

The Moment of Soul Birth

The divine spirit, the Thought Adjuster, arrives simultaneously with the first moral activity of the human mind. That moment represents the birth of the soul. Before that, we have potential. After that, we have a growing spiritual reality that can, if we cooperate, become our eternal identity.

I find it fascinating that animals, despite their sometimes-remarkable intelligence and even what appears to be affection, don't undergo this transformation. I remember Jesus explaining to young Ganid about his dog. The boy was troubled, wondering if his beloved pet would be with him in the afterlife. Jesus had to explain that since the dog had no concept of deity, no moral consciousness, it didn't have a soul in the human sense.

Now, does that mean nothing of the animal survives? The book suggests that these essences may be reconstituted in some way, perhaps as other beings in the universe, perhaps back into similar creatures. Nothing in God's universe appears to be wasted. But it's different from human survival, fundamentally different.

Here's the key distinction: when a human being fails to survive, when the soul doesn't achieve survival status, that personality ceases to exist. It's gone. Finished. The book is quite clear about this. But animals? They're not under that same survival system. They're not on the ascension plan to Paradise. They exist, they experience, and then... something else happens with their essence. We don't know exactly what, and I'd love to sit down with Jesus on the mansion worlds someday and get the full explanation.

Survival Value and Moral Consciousness

Jesus explained to the Greek philosopher that the saving or losing of a soul has to do with whether or not the moral consciousness attains survival status through eternal alliance with the associated immortal spirit endowment. Let me put that in simpler terms: Do you cooperate with your Thought Adjuster in building something that can survive death?

Salvation, and I know that word carries a lot of baggage from traditional Christianity, is really the spiritualization of self-realization. Your moral consciousness becomes possessed of survival value. All forms of soul conflict, Jesus taught, consist in the lack of harmony between the moral or spiritual self-consciousness and the purely intellectual self-consciousness.

You can be brilliant intellectually, you know. You can be a genius at organizing information, solving complex problems, creating innovative solutions. But if you're doing it all for your own aggrandizement, for personal glory without any spiritual dimension, without any moral foundation that seeks to align with divine will, what survival value does it have?

On the other hand, someone with modest intellectual gifts who consistently chooses to act in ways that reflect love, mercy, and service is building tremendous survival value. The Thought Adjuster can work with that. The soul grows from that.

The Nature of Relationships and Soul Growth

Here's something that might surprise you: every relationship you have with another person has divine significance. Every true relationship with other persons, human or divine, is an end in itself. Not a means to an end, but valuable in its own right.

This is why, when you reach the mansion worlds, you'll remember every relationship you've had with every individual human being. Nothing is lost. Even if the other person didn't survive, even if they made choices that led to their extinction, the value of your interaction with them still exists. It's recorded in the Supreme Being.

Let me give you an example that often comes up. Al Capone, the notorious gangster, ran soup kitchens during the Great Depression. He funded them out of his own pocket and fed thousands of hungry people. Now, assuming that act was genuinely altruistic, and that's a big assumption, I'll grant you, it still had positive value. Every person who was fed, who felt cared for in that moment, was affected. That experience is real and eternal, regardless of whether Al Capone himself achieved survival.

You see, this is the genius of the Supreme Being. Nothing of true value is ever lost. Every act of kindness, every moment of genuine love, every moral choice that elevates the human condition becomes part of the experiential deity that is the Supreme. So even if someone who did good doesn't survive, the good they did continues to reverberate through the universe.

This should change how we think about our daily interactions. Every conversation, every act of service, every moment of patience or understanding, these aren't just nice gestures. They're building blocks of eternity. They add to your soul, they contribute to the Supreme, and they affect everyone you touch.

The Cosmic Gulf and the Reality of Love

The book makes a striking statement: there exists a great cosmic gulf between matter and thought, and this gulf becomes immeasurably greater between material mind and spiritual love. Consciousness, especially self-consciousness, cannot be explained by any theory of mechanistic electronic association or materialistic energy phenomena.

When I read that passage decades ago, it didn't have quite the impact it does today. Back then, neuroscience was in its infancy. Today, researchers can map brain activity, trace neural pathways, even predict certain behaviors based on brain chemistry. Yet with all that sophisticated technology, with all those electrodes and imaging devices, they still can't measure love. They especially can't measure spiritual love.

They can see what parts of the brain light up when someone says they're experiencing love. They can track hormones like oxytocin. But the thing itself, that capacity to genuinely wish good for another being, to sacrifice your own comfort for someone else's welfare, to feel connected to the divine through service to others, that remains stubbornly resistant to material analysis.

Interestingly, this validates something I've always maintained about *The Urantia Book*. When it was published in 1955, much of what it said about the limitations of material science in explaining consciousness wasn't as obvious as it is today. We didn't have the advanced neuroscience we have now. The book made claims about what material investigation could and couldn't demonstrate, and those claims have held up remarkably well.

You either believe this book by faith, or you don't. Just like Jesus, you either accept by faith that he was the Son of God, or you don't. You can't prove it scientifically. That's not a weakness; it's the nature of spiritual reality.

The Progressive Nature of Reality

As mind pursues reality to its ultimate analysis, matter vanishes to the material senses but may still remain real to mind. When spiritual insight pursues that reality which remains after the disappearance of matter, it vanishes to mind, but the insight of spirit can still perceive cosmic realities and supreme values of a spiritual nature.

This reminds me of Plato's cave allegory, though with a twist. Plato suggested that material life is just the shadow of reality, that true reality exists in the realm of perfect forms. In a sense, he was onto something. Once you pass from this material existence to the morontia realm, your material memories become shadowy. They're still there, but they've faded in importance compared to your new reality.

Then, as you progress from morontia life to spiritual life, your morontia experiences become the shadow. And this happens seven times in our existence, seven stages of reality. Material is just the first. Morontia is the second, though it has several levels. Then comes spirit, then the superuniverse experience, then the billion worlds of Havona, and finally Paradise itself.

Here's something that might blow your mind: when you reach Paradise and become a finaliter, standing in the presence of God the Father himself, you're still only a sixth-stage spirit. Not seventh. We don't become seventh-stage spirits until all seven superuniverses reach light and life, when the Supreme Being comes into full fruition.

Why is that? Probably because at that moment, we'll all need to be ready for the next stage of cosmic evolution, the outer space levels. The first evolutionary age will be complete, and something transcendent will begin.

The Morontia Self Within

When Jesus spoke of the soul approaching heavenly status, he described it as an entity intervening between the material self and the divine spirit. That intervening entity is our morontia being. Right now, while we live in these material bodies, we're building our future morontia self. The soul is that morontia identity taking form.

Think of it like this: these material bodies are cocoons. The morontia body is like the larva or chrysalis stage. The spiritual body is the butterfly. We're in the cocoon stage right now, but inside, transformation is happening. Every moral choice, every spiritual decision, every act of worship or service adds to that developing morontia self.

Someone mentioned that our material bodies are like cocoons, and that's exactly right. We're not meant to stay in this form. We're transitioning, even now, into something more.

The evolving soul is difficult to describe and more difficult to demonstrate, Jesus told the Greek philosopher, because it's not discoverable by the methods of either material investigation or spiritual proving. Material science can't demonstrate the existence of a soul. Pure spiritual testing can't either. Yet every morally conscious mortal knows of the existence of their soul as a real and actual personal experience.

How do we know? Because we experience it. We experience that ability to step back from ourselves and evaluate our own actions. We experience moments of moral clarity, times when we know, we just know, what the right thing to do is, even if it costs us. We experience the growth that comes from choosing spirit over self.

That's the soul speaking. That's the morontia self-emerging.

Science, Philosophy, and Religion: An Integration

Science gives way to philosophy, the book tells us, while philosophy must surrender to the conclusions inherent in genuine spiritual experience. Thinking surrenders to wisdom, and wisdom is lost in enlightened and reflective worship.

You can't separate these elements. True reality includes science, religion, material and non-material, all integrated into a coherent whole. When students ask me what I teach, sometimes I say I teach the truth. That's not arrogance; it's just the simplest way to describe what *The Urantia Book* offers, an integration of everything we can know about reality.

There's a website out there called truthbook.com. It's not affiliated with our group, but I appreciate the name. That's what this revelation is, a book of truth. You read it, you either believe it and let it improve your life, or you don't. As the old saying goes, you can lead a horse to water, but you can't make it drink.

Some people ask, "Is *The Urantia Book* religion? Is it philosophy? Is it science?" The answer is yes. It's all of those things woven together. It's religion in that it teaches us about God and our relationship to deity. It's philosophy in that it grapples with questions of meaning, value, and purpose. It's science in that it describes the physical universe, its origins, and its mechanisms. But more than any of these individually, it's an integration of universal reality.

That's why I sometimes call my teaching series "The Ultimate Integration of Reality." When we go back through that series, and we will, I'm including many of Jesus' teachings that I didn't emphasize the first time through. I've grown over the past fifty years of study and fourteen years of teaching this book. My understanding has deepened. Just like yours will deepen if you let it. New connections have emerged.

That's how revelation works, I think. It meets you where you are, but it also has depths you haven't plumbed yet. You can spend a lifetime with these papers and still find new insights.

The Supreme and the Preservation of Value

Let me address something that came up in our discussion tonight. When all seven superuniverses reach light and life, the Supreme Being comes into full actualization. Some people interpret this as meaning the seven superuniverses somehow merge into one. That's not quite right.

The seven superuniverses will remain distinct because each reflects a different combination of the Paradise Trinity. The seven Master Spirits, positioned at the periphery of the Isle of Paradise, send out circuits that define each superuniverse. These circuits carry spiritual gravity, mind gravity, personality gravity, all the ways that Paradise influences and connects with creation.

Those circuits can't merge. They have to stay separate because each represents a unique expression of deity. What changes when we reach light and life is that the Supreme becomes fully actualized as God the Supreme, the experiential manifestation of the Trinity in time and space.

Then, as we move out into the four outer space levels, we'll be serving in a new capacity. The Supreme will begin functioning as God the Ultimate, and we finaliters will likely be involved in ministering to entirely new orders of beings who will themselves be ascending toward Paradise.

The point is, nothing is lost. Every experience, every relationship, every moral choice made by every creature throughout all time becomes part of the Supreme. Even if individuals don't survive, the value they created does. That's profound when you think about it. It means your life matters, not just for your own survival but for the entire cosmos.

Personality: The Divine Gift

Before we close this chapter, I want to emphasize something about personality that we sometimes take for granted. Your personality comes directly from God the Father. It's a gift that makes you unique in all of creation. No one else, in all the vast universe, past, present, or future, has exactly your personality pattern.

This divine gift is what allows you to make the connection between material and spiritual reality. Without personality, the Thought Adjuster couldn't work with you. Without personality, you couldn't form relationships that have eternal significance. Without personality, there would be no "you" to survive.

The book tells us that all non-spiritual things in human experience, except personality, are means to an end. But every true relationship, every genuine connection with other persons, human or divine, is an end in itself. That's because personality is sacred. It's a direct link to the First Source and Center (God The Father).

When people ask me why relationships are so important in the teachings of *The Urantia Book*, this is why. The Fatherhood of God and the Brotherhood of Man aren't just nice religious concepts. They're cosmic realities. God is literally our Father, in the sense that our personalities come from him. All humans are literally our brothers and sisters, sharing this same divine gift.

And here's the kicker: when you reach the mansion worlds, you'll remember every relationship. You'll have the opportunity to reconnect, to understand more fully how each person affected you and how you affected them. Those who survived will be there to greet you. Those who didn't survive, well, their good influence on you still remains, recorded in your soul and in the Supreme.

Practical Implications for Daily Life

So, what does all this mean for how we live right now, today?

First, it means every choice matters. Every decision you make that has moral or spiritual significance is being recorded by your Thought Adjuster and woven into your soul. You're literally building your future self with each choice.

Second, it means stagnation is dangerous. A stagnant soul is a dying soul, Jesus said. You can't coast spiritually. You can't just maintain your current level of spiritual development and expect that to be enough. Growth is the watchword of the universe. If you're not growing, you're declining.

Third, it means relationships are sacred. Every interaction with another person is an opportunity to create eternal value. Whether it's your spouse, your children, your friends, or even strangers you encounter briefly, each connection matters. Treat them accordingly.

Fourth, it means you need to cooperate with your Thought Adjuster. This fragment of God within you is working constantly to spiritualize your thinking, to present divine alternatives to purely selfish motivations. Listen to that still, small voice. Pay attention to those prompts toward mercy, patience, and love.

Finally, it means that worship matters more than we often realize. In time, thinking leads to wisdom, and wisdom leads to worship. But in eternity, worship leads to wisdom, and wisdom eventuates in the finality of thought. Worship isn't just a religious duty or a nice practice. It's how we connect most directly with deity. It's how we align our souls with the divine pattern.

Conclusion: The Journey Ahead

As we close this chapter, I want you to appreciate what we've covered. We've explored the very nature of the soul, what it is, when it begins, how it grows. We've looked at Jesus' direct teachings on this subject, teachings that integrate perfectly with everything else *The Urantia Book* reveals about personality, mind, spirit, and survival.

We've seen that our soul is our morontia self, forming even now as we live these material lives. We've understood that moral consciousness is the foundation of this soul, and that stagnation leads to spiritual death. We've grasped the cosmic significance of every relationship and every moral choice.

Most importantly, perhaps, we've begun to see how it all fits together, personality from the Father, mind from the Spirit, the Thought Adjuster as the Father's gift, and the soul as the co-creation of the mortal and the divine.

In our next chapter, we'll continue exploring Paper 112 and delve deeper into the mechanisms of personality survival. We'll look at what happens at death, how the resurrection works on the mansion worlds, and what it means to "sleep" between this life and the next. We'll examine the role of the seraphic guardians and the destiny guardians in preserving everything of survival value.

But for now, reflect on this: you have a soul. It's real. It's growing or dying with every choice you make. The question isn't whether you have a soul, every morally conscious human does. The question is, what are you doing with it?

Are you feeding it with spiritual nourishment? Are you exercising it through moral choices? Are you allowing the Thought Adjuster to help it grow toward its divine potential?

These aren't abstract theological questions. They're intensely practical. They affect how you spend your time, how you treat people, what you think about, what you value.

The soul's reality is the most important reality of human existence. Everything else, wealth, fame, achievement, pleasure, is temporary. Only the soul, only those meanings and values that have spiritual significance, survive beyond this life.

Choose wisely. Build well. Your eternal future depends on it.

In our next chapter, we'll explore the fascinating process of death and resurrection, examining what The Urantia Book teaches about survival, the sleep of death, and awakening on the mansion worlds of morontia life.

Chapter 31: Personality Survival and the Three Types of Death

Introduction

In my years of studying The Urantia Book, few topics have generated as much curiosity, and, frankly, as much anxiety, as the question of what happens when we die. It's the fundamental human question, isn't it? We all wonder whether something of us continues beyond this mortal existence, and if so, what that continuation looks like. Paper 112 addresses these concerns with remarkable clarity and depth, offering a cosmic perspective on personality survival that both challenges and comforts our conventional understanding of death.

Tonight's study takes us into section two, paragraph fifteen, where we encounter one of the most significant revelations in the entire text: the existence of three distinct types of death. Most of us on Urantia recognize only one kind, the physical cessation of life energies. But concerning personality survival, the reality appears far more nuanced. Before we examine these three types of death, though, we need to understand the broader context of cosmic evolution and the role our choices play in determining our eternal destiny.

The Cosmic Evolution Toward Spirit Dominance

The purpose of cosmic evolution, as The Urantia Book explains, is to achieve unity of personality through increasing spirit dominance. This represents a volitional response, a willing choice, to the teaching and leading of the Thought Adjuster. Both human and superhuman personalities are characterized by what the text calls "an inherent cosmic quality," which may be described as the evolution of dominance.

What does this mean in practical terms? Simply put, the normal course of cosmic evolution involves us increasingly, over time, giving dominance of our personality from ourselves to the Thought Adjuster. The more we surrender our will to the Adjuster's guidance, the closer we move toward Divinity itself. If you want to become more Godlike in your life, and I suspect that's why you're reading this, what you need to do is give your personality over to the Thought Adjuster and consistently allow the Adjuster's will to become your will.

This evolution of dominance represents the expanding control of God the Father throughout all seven superuniverses. As this happens, we experience not only greater self-control but also an expansion of God the Father's dominance through the Supreme, through the collective experience of all of us. The more we surrender to the Adjuster's guidance, the more Divine we become, each and every one of us.

I want you to think about that for a moment. This isn't some distant theological concept, it's happening right now, in your daily decisions, in how you respond to challenges, in how you treat the people around you.

The Two Great Phases of Mortal Experience

An ascending, one-time human personality passes through two great phases of increased volitional dominance over the self and the universe. Understanding these phases helps us see the big picture of where we're headed.

The Prefinaliter Experience: God-Seeking

The first phase is what's called the prefinaliter or God-seeking experience. This involves augmenting our self-realization through a technique of identity expansion and actualization, together with cosmic problem-solving and what the text describes as "consequent universe mastery."

During this entire journey, from our first moral decision on Earth all the way through the mansion worlds, the constellation spheres, the superuniverse sectors, and finally to Havona and Paradise, we are engaged in a God-seeking experience. Our goal throughout this immense journey is simple: to grow, to become more Divine. By identifying ourselves with the cosmos and mastering the various tasks we're given through this experience, we develop mastery of the universe and the Divinity that God the Father bestows within our lives.

This is our prefinaliter experience, our self-realizing phase. Every challenge we face, every relationship we navigate, every moral decision we make contributes to this cosmic education.

The Postfinaliter Experience: God-Revealing

Once we've found God and stood before Him as finaliters, everything changes. We transition from ascending personalities to descending ones. The second phase begins: the postfinaliter or God-revealing experience. This involves the creative expansion of self-realization through revealing the Supreme Being of experience to God-seeking intelligences who haven't yet attained the Divine levels of Godlikeness.

In simpler terms, once we've completed the journey to Paradise and become finaliters, we go out in groups to help other individuals who are on the same path we just completed. Through the Supreme, through the experiential God of time and space, we share our accumulated experience with all the intelligences climbing the ladder we've just finished. This includes not only beings in the seven superuniverses or the grand universe, but also those in the master universe and all the outer space levels.

One question I'm often asked is: How can spiritual beings like postfinaliters help material beings? That's a fair question, and honestly, it's something of a mystery at our current level of understanding. We haven't experienced it yet, so I can't give you a definitive answer. It's similar to the secret of the bestowals, you remember when Jesus went through his seven bestowals and became seven different types of beings? How he did that remains a secret known only to the Paradise Sons. Similarly, this communication from finaliters to material beings may be something we won't fully understand until we experience it ourselves.

But here's what we do know: there are finaliters stationed on every planet coming up through the ascension plan, and they're doing something to benefit material beings in their process of reaching Paradise. Finaliters are helping us right now, I just don't know exactly how.

Let me offer a suggestion, though I'm just speculating here. Guardian angels communicate with us constantly in this life, don't they? Yet we don't consciously hear them. They're constantly at work, placing things in our pathway to help us grow. Maybe finaliters do something similar. Perhaps while you're asleep, they're whispering in your ear about what you need to do tomorrow because it's important. Your subconscious mind might pick it up, and your conscious mind might think, "I'm just talking to myself again." Who knows? There are many mysteries in the universe, but when we become finaliters, it will be revealed to us, just as the mystery of the bestowal is revealed only through experience.

Descending Personalities and Their Mission

It's worth noting that descending personalities, those created in the local universe, such as the Lanonandeks, Vorondadeks, and Material Sons and Daughters, attain analogous experience through their various universe adventures. They seek enlarged capacity for ascertaining and executing the Divine wills of the Supreme, Ultimate, and Absolute Deities.

Local universe created Sons start out as descending Sons. When they descend down to planets as Adams and Eves, for instance, and their planet reaches light and life, they're released to do what? To go on the ascension journey. They swap from being descending Sons to ascending Sons of God. The same applies to the midwayers, who stay on a planet for hundreds of thousands of years. When we reach light and life, the midwayers are released to become ascending sons of God.

There's a plan for everyone. You know, it's interesting, I always bring this up because people don't realize it, Lucifer rebelled because he was jealous of mortals ascending through the ascension plan. That's right there in the Lucifer papers. He was jealous of all the people going on the ascension journey and all the time spent on ascenders learning administration. He claimed all this was wasted because they came back as finaliters with jobs no more glorious than what they'd done as ascenders. He completely missed the point of the whole process.

Even Lucifer, a System Sovereign, would have eventually had the opportunity to ascend, just like we do. That's the whole process.

The Foundation of Survival: Transferring Identity

The material self, what we might call the ego-entity of human identity, depends during physical life on the continuing function of the material life vehicle. On Urantia, this has been given the name "life," which the text describes somewhat humorously as "the unbalanced equilibrium of energies and intellect." I appreciate that description, it captures something essential about our human condition, doesn't it? We're all a little unbalanced down here.

But selfhood of survival value, selfhood that can transcend the experience of death, is only evolved by establishing a potential transfer. This transfer moves the seat of identity of the evolving personality from the transient life vehicle (the material body) to the more enduring and immortal nature of the morontia soul, and then beyond to those levels where the soul becomes infused with and eventually attains the status of spirit reality.

This actual transfer from material association to morontia identification is affected by three critical qualities: the sincerity, persistence, and steadfastness of the God-seeking decisions of the human creature.

Let me repeat that because it's the secret of the universe: **sincerity, persistence, and steadfastness of God-seeking decisions**. That's the roadmap they've given us.

If you don't seek God, what happens? You die. That's correct, you cease to exist. Now, there's no requirement for constant, uninterrupted focus. You could theoretically take a thousand-year break and go to the carnival, forgetting about spiritual growth for that time. But if you don't eventually retake that pathway, you will die. As they say in the text: if you don't grow, you die. There's no way around it. You have to have spiritual growth.

The sooner we realize this, that spiritual growth is the only thing that truly matters, the easier it becomes to do the will of God in our lives.

The Three Types of Death

Now we come to the heart of tonight's study. Urantians generally recognize only one kind of death: the physical cessation of life energies. But concerning personality survival, there are really three kinds. Understanding these distinctions changes everything about how we view mortality, survival, and our daily choices.

Type One: Spiritual (Soul) Death

The first type is spiritual or soul death. This occurs if and when a mortal has finally rejected survival, when that person has been pronounced spiritually insolvent and morally bankrupt in the joint opinion of the Adjuster and the surviving seraphim. When such coordinated advice has been recorded on Uversa, and after the Censors and their reflective associates have verified these findings, the rulers of Orvonton order the immediate release of the indwelling monitor (the Thought Adjuster).

Here's what's critical to understand: this release of the Adjuster in no way affects the duties of the personal or group seraphim concerned with that individual. The person may continue living, going through the motions of existence. This kind of death is final in its significance, regardless of the temporary continuation of the living energies of the physical and mental mechanisms.

From the cosmic standpoint, the mortal is already dead. The continuing life merely indicates the persistence of the material momentum of cosmic energies.

This is what you might call "the walking dead."

I know that sounds harsh but let me explain what this looks like. These are usually individuals who have no care for other people, no interest in God, religion, or anything having to do with their survival or their soul. It's pretty easy to identify this type of person, they're often mean as a snake, impossible to get along with, and don't care about anybody else. They've made a permanent and final rejection of their own survival. That's what they've chosen: non-survival.

That's why the text describes them as "spiritually insolvent" and "morally bankrupt." They have nothing of spiritual value for the Adjuster to continue building a soul with them.

Can this happen on Earth? Absolutely. Can it happen in the morontia worlds? Yes, it can happen there too.

I can tell you from my experience as a one-time Baptist, I used to go out and try to convert everybody I ran into, you will meet many, many people in life who have no interest whatsoever in God or spirituality. They're out there. There are a lot of people on Earth right now who won't make it to the next level. That's why Jesus constantly told the apostles, "Let's go save some souls."

The matriculation rate from here to the mansion worlds isn't as high as some people think. You can't believe Lucifer's lie that everybody makes it, because they don't.

Now, here's the flip side: there can be significant salvation for tons of individuals you might think don't have a chance. Why? Because their relationship with God the Father and their personality is personal, only they know for sure. We can judge from the outside, but we're not in any position to make final determinations. That's between them and the Father.

Let me give you an example from Jesus's life. Remember when he went to the Sanhedrin and tried to explain who he was? Many of those religious people rejected him. Even when he talked to Nicodemus, Nicodemus asked him, "Rabbi, how do I go on?" And Jesus said, "You must be reborn."

"Reborn of what?" Nicodemus asked.

"Born of spirit," Jesus replied. "It's a spiritual rebirth."

When you decide you believe in God the Father and that you're going to survive, you become a new entity. You're no longer the walking dead, wandering around waiting to keel over. You become a faith son of God. As far as the Adjuster is concerned, you're already a son of God, he's just waiting for you to get to the point where he can fuse with you. It's called betrothal, just like a marriage.

When you make that final decision, "Yes, I want to survive. I love God. I want God in my life", that's a rebirth to a new being. You're not just flesh and blood anymore. You become a faith son of God who's going to survive this mortal existence.

That's what Jesus was explaining to Nicodemus, a spiritual rebirth. And Nicodemus was a scholar in the Sanhedrin, a man who'd studied religion his whole life, yet he'd never made that connection. Just because you study religious texts doesn't mean you've made the personal commitment.

But here's the beautiful part of the story: Jesus told Nicodemus, "You are not far from the kingdom." His curiosity and his questions showed Jesus that he was seeking. And who went and retrieved Jesus's body after the crucifixion? Nicodemus did, along with Joseph of Arimathea. In whose tomb did they place Jesus's body? Nicodemus's. He became a believer.

That's spiritual rebirth, the opposite of spiritual death.

Type Two: Intellectual (Mind) Death

The second type is intellectual or mind death. This occurs when the vital circuits of higher adjutant ministry are disrupted through aberrations of intellect or because of the partial destruction of the mechanism of the brain. If these conditions pass a certain critical point of irreparability, the indwelling Adjuster is immediately released to depart for Divinington. On the universe records, a mortal personality is considered to have met with death whenever the essential mind circuits of human will-action have been destroyed.

Again, this is death irrespective of the continuing function of the living mechanism of the physical body. The body, minus the volitional mind, is no longer human. But, and this is crucial, according to the prior choosing of the human will, the soul of such an individual may survive.

People constantly ask, "What happens if I get in an accident and my mind is destroyed?" This is what the text is addressing. This is intellectual mind death. The physical mechanism of your brain can no longer function as the vehicle for a spiritual being. Your soul can't grow anymore. So, what happens? The Thought Adjuster is released. Your records go with your Guardian Seraphim for judgment. Whatever decisions you made before that point will determine whether you survive or not.

Let me give you a practical example. If you make a decision tonight, you sit down and say, "God the Father, I love you. I want to be one of your sons", it's just like when people say, "I accept Jesus as my savior." It works the same way. If you acknowledge God and say, "I want to be a son of God," what is that? That's your seed of faith. And that's all it takes for survival from that point on.

When you die, your soul will go on, because you made that one crucial decision: you believed in God, you had faith in God, and you committed to survival.

Now, someone asked me a good question about this. They said, "What if I talked to a man who made that decision to follow God when he was ten years old, but now he's in his eighties and his mind has become diseased or damaged through dementia? Does that early decision still count?"

The answer is yes, but with an important caveat. It has to have been sincere and acted upon up until the point of the disease. If you made that decision at ten, sixteen, thirty, or whenever, and you didn't lead a particularly Godly life afterward, you'll at least survive. You made the crucial decision. But you'll likely find yourself in what amounts to a remedial class when you arrive on the mansion worlds, because your soul and personality didn't grow much while you were alive.

Does that mean you can go out and party from now on? Well, technically yes, you can go out and party, but it's not going to benefit you. In fact, it works just the opposite. If you try to live a holy life, if you repent of your sins, if you live a life that benefits other personalities, you're walking in the kingdom of God. That's what Jesus meant when he told people, "The kingdom is within you." You're in the kingdom because you're trying to walk a holy life, trying to do what your Thought Adjuster wants you to do, trying to build your soul.

You don't want to wake up on the mansion world and have the technician say, "Oh my goodness, here's another one. Better call the guys. This person doesn't know anything." You'd be like a dunce waking up on the mansion world. That's basically what happens when they put you in remedial classes, you didn't learn anything spiritually in your life.

Do you want to start out that way? I certainly don't.

Now, I'll be honest with you: that probably describes a lot of people. The majority of people, in fact. Most people follow traditional religion, Christianity, Buddhism, Islam, whatever it might be, and while there's truth in all of them, they're also human institutions. You know what happens when you get human beings involved in administering and propagating spiritual truth? You need only one human being to mess it up.

But here's the thing: because you're seeking truth and the will of God in your life, you're going to find seeds of truth in every single relationship and every single religion. That's our goal, to discover truth. The Urantia Book reveals truth, but you can find that truth everywhere because it's based on the fatherhood of God and the brotherhood of man. Every interaction with another human being gives you the opportunity to grow your soul.

Let me share a personal story that illustrates this. This morning I was talking to my wife about a neighbor in our community. Nine years ago, I had words with this man, harsh words. I'd witnessed him torturing animals, so I intervened, made sure the animals were safe, and told him if I ever saw him do that again, it would not be pretty. I don't normally say things like that, but I was that indignant.

I haven't spoken to this man in nine years. Not once. Not a single time.

This morning, I was hobbling out to the mailbox, I'd had heart surgery the day before and just wanted to walk a little. There he was, walking up the street with a puppy. He called out, "Roger, how are you doing? I heard you had surgery yesterday."

We started talking. He'd gotten this rescue dog, and he said to me, "You know, this dog has made me so happy. I didn't realize how much I was missing in my life."

This is a man I'd confronted nine years ago for torturing animals, and here he was having an epiphany about love and life. We had a wonderful conversation of a spiritual nature. I told him I'd heard his mother had died, and I was sorry for his loss but sure she was in a better place. He agreed.

Walking back down the driveway, I thought to myself: I love another human being now. And I missed out on nine years of loving that human being because of my own stubbornness. It wasn't his stupidity, it was mine. I didn't forgive him.

That reminds me of Christ's words: "Your goodness should know no bounds." Love your enemies. We all have room for improvement, every single one of us. Even Pope John XXIII, during his reign, went to prisons and talked to prisoners. He knew he still had growing to do.

Here's what struck me most: if I'd passed during my surgery yesterday, I would have never had the opportunity to love this individual, because I had a problem with forgiveness. I almost missed my chance to not only love another human being but to improve both his life and mine.

We have to be careful how we live. We pay for our sins one way or another.

Type Three: Physical (Body and Mind) Death

The third type is physical body and mind death. When death overtakes a human being, the Adjuster remains in the citadel of the mind until it ceases to function as an intelligent mechanism, about the time that measurable brain energies cease their rhythmic vital pulsations. Following this dissolution, the Adjuster takes leave of the vanishing mind as unceremoniously as entry was made years before and proceeds to Divinington by way of Uversa.

This is what we typically think of as death, when both the physical body and the mind shut down. The Adjuster leaves when the brain energy ceases to exist, when the brain waves stop their rhythm. We would call this "brain dead." The human brain has stopped functioning entirely.

This is different from the second type of death. In intellectual death, it's just the brain that's damaged beyond repair. In this third type, the body and mind shut down together. This is what most people consider "death," and it's what happens to all of us eventually if we don't die in one of the other two ways first.

What Happens After Death

After death, the material body returns to the elemental world from which it was derived. Whether you're buried or cremated, everything physical goes back to the Earth, dust to dust. But two nonmaterial factors of surviving personality persist.

First, the preexistent Thought Adjuster, carrying the memory transcription of your mortal career, proceeds to Divinington. Second, there remains in the custody of the destiny guardian the immortal morontia soul of the deceased human. These phases and forms of soul, these once kinetic but now static formulas of identity, are essential to repersonalization on the morontia worlds.

Here's how it works: Your Thought Adjuster takes your memory transcriptions, your personality record, to Divinington, then returns and waits for you on the mansion world. The Guardian of Destiny takes your soul itself, which also contains all your memories and experiences. So you effectively have two copies, the personality with the Adjuster and the soul with the guardian seraphim.

But there's more. There's an exact copy of your entire life that's held in trust by the Archangel corps. So really, everything exists in triplicate.

When you wake up on the mansion worlds, the Adjuster returns, the guardian angel brings back your soul, and your personality is reconnected with your soul. The Archangel is there to make sure the person who wakes up in that morontia body is the exact same being whose records he holds. He guarantees you are who you are when you wake up, no other being is put in your place.

It's the reunion of the Adjuster and the soul that reassembles the surviving personality, that re-consciousnesses you at the time of morontia awakening.

For those who don't have personal seraphic guardians, those who haven't yet reached the third psychic circle, a group guardians faithfully and efficiently performs the same service of identity safekeeping and personality resurrection. The seraphim are indispensable to the reassembly of your personality.

It's just that simple, and just that profound.

Conclusion

As we close this chapter, I want you to reflect on what we've covered. We've examined the cosmic purpose of spiritual evolution, the gradual transfer of dominance from our material self to our spiritual self, guided by the Thought Adjuster. We've explored the two great phases of our eternal career: the God-seeking experience that takes us to Paradise and the God-revealing experience that follows as we serve throughout eternity.

Most significantly, we've discovered that death is not the simple, single event we once imagined. Three types of death exist, each with profound implications for survival. Spiritual death can occur while we're still physically alive, when we finally reject survival through persistent refusal to seek God. Intellectual death happens when our brain is irreparably damaged, releasing the Adjuster but allowing our soul to survive based on choices made before the injury. Physical death, the kind we all face, is simply the transition point where our personality and soul separate temporarily before reassembling on the mansion worlds.

The common thread through all of this? Our choices matter. Our sincerity, persistence, and steadfastness in seeking God determine everything. This isn't about perfection, it's about direction. It's about making that fundamental decision to be a faith son or daughter of God and then living in alignment with that choice, even imperfectly, even with setbacks.

In our next chapter, we'll continue our exploration of Paper 112, looking more closely at the mechanics of survival and what factors contribute to successful repersonalization on the mansion worlds. We'll examine the role of various celestial personalities in preserving our identity and preparing us for the next stage of existence.

Until then, I encourage you to sit with these concepts. Think about your own spiritual journey. Have you made that crucial decision for survival? Are you growing spiritually, or are you stagnant? Remember: if you don't grow, you die. But the beautiful truth is that growth doesn't require perfection, it requires willingness, sincerity, and the daily choice to align your will with the Father's will.

That's all he asks of us. And that, my friends, is enough.

This chapter is based on a study session of Paper 112, Section 2 of The Urantia Book, focusing on personality survival and the phenomena of death. The insights shared reflect years of contemplation, teaching, and personal experience with these profound concepts.

Chapter 32: The Reality of Death and Personality Survival

When I first began studying Paper 112 of *The Urantia Book*, I thought I understood death. Like most people raised in Western religious traditions, I carried certain assumptions, some comforting, others troubling, about what happens when we die. But as I moved deeper into this revelation, I realized how much confusion surrounds this most fundamental human experience. Tonight, as we continue our exploration of personality survival, I want to address some of the most persistent misconceptions that keep us from grasping the profound truth of our eternal destiny.

Let me be direct: there are no ghosts. I know that statement may startle some of you, especially if you've had experiences you believe were encounters with departed loved ones. But, Dr. Paul, I know what I saw! No, you know what you thought you saw, or what you wished you saw, maybe what the human mind conjured up from that meal you just ate. Or maybe you have been watching to much Ghosts hunters on TV, (very convincing). But, if we're going to be honest students of this revelation, we need to face what it actually teaches, not what we wish it taught or what popular culture has led us to believe.

The Moment of Death: What Actually Happens

Paper 112, Section 3, Paragraph 7 states something that should forever change how we think about death: "Upon death, the Thought Adjuster temporarily loses personality but not identity; the human subject temporarily loses identity but not personality. On the mansion worlds both reunite in eternal manifestation."

Let me break this down, because it's crucial. When you die, and I mean the very instant your last breath leaves your body or your heart stops beating, several things happen simultaneously. I am not talking about near death experiences where you think you have died and your brain retains experiences of going to heaven or traveling toward a light or meeting Jesus, I could write a whole other book on this subject. Your Thought Adjuster, that fragment of God that has been building your soul throughout your lifetime, departs. It loses access to your personality, which was a gift from the Universal Father to you, not to the Adjuster. But the Adjuster retains its identity, it knows who it is, what it has experienced, and what it has been doing.

You, on the other hand, temporarily lose your identity. Why? Because your identity has been so intimately tied to your Thought Adjuster and the soul you've been building together. Your personality, however, remains intact. It stays with your soul, which is now being transported by your Guardian Angel to the mansion worlds. It is not transported there and then brought back to your body this process takes three days,

I've had people ask me, "But Roger, what about the three-day waiting period? Surely during those three days, people can reach out to their loved ones, can't they?" The answer is no. Absolutely not. Never.

The book uses that word, "never", repeatedly in this section, and it does so for a reason. "Never does a departed Thought Adjuster return to Earth as the being of former indwelling; never is personality manifested without the human will; and never does a disadjusted human being after death manifest active identity or in any manner establish communication with the living beings of Earth."

That's three "Nevers" in one paragraph. The authors of this revelation wanted to make this point unmistakably clear.

Why Communication with the Dead Is Impossible

Now, I know this teaching challenges deeply held beliefs. Some of you may have attended séances or consulted mediums. You may have had experiences that seemed to provide evidence of communication with departed loved ones. I'm not questioning your sincerity or dismissing your experiences. What I'm saying is that whatever happened, it wasn't communication with the dead.

Let me tell you a bit of history. William Sadler, the psychiatrist who facilitated the transmission of *The Urantia Book*, spent years working with Harry Houdini and Howard Thurston, two of the most famous magicians of their era, to expose fraudulent mediums. Houdini was obsessed with trying to contact his deceased mother. He and his wife made a pact: whoever died first would try to communicate with the one who remained. They never succeeded. Not once.

Why? Because it's not possible. It's not allowed. It violates universal policy.

The book states clearly: "Such disadjusted souls are wholly **unconscious** during the long or short sleep of death. There can be **no** exhibition of any sort of personality or ability to engage in communications with other personalities until after completion of survival. Those who go to the mansion worlds are **not** permitted to send messages back to their loved ones. It is the policy throughout the universes to forbid such communication during the period of a current dispensation."

Notice that phrase: "throughout the universes." This isn't just a local rule for Earth. This policy applies across all 700,000 local universes. Not one allows this kind of communication.

Even after you're repersonalized on the mansion worlds, even after you wake up in your new morontia body with all your memories intact, you still can't send messages back to Earth. Not for an entire dispensation, which typically lasts about a thousand years. And even then, if you need to return to Earth for some celestial purpose, you must be supervised the entire time you're here.

The Problem with Reincarnation

This teaching also demolishes the concept of reincarnation, which has become increasingly popular in Western spiritual circles. People often claim to remember past lives, and they attribute these memories to having lived before in another body.

But here's what the book teaches: when a Thought Adjuster is released from service, either because the person died without surviving or because they've been adjudicated as non-salvageable by the Ancients of Days, that Adjuster returns to Divinington to be reassigned. However, it is *never* reassigned to another mortal on the same planet.

Never. That word again.

Why is this significant? Because people who believe in reincarnation often explain their "past life memories" by suggesting that their Thought Adjuster carries memories from a previous indwelling. But that's impossible. Your Thought Adjuster has never been on this planet before, unless you're dealing with the personalized Thought Adjuster of a Creator Son or someone of that magnitude, and I doubt any of us fall into that category.

So where do these "memories" come from? I think there are several possibilities. Some may be products of imagination or wishful thinking. Others may be dimensional echoes, what I call "time loops", where significant events leave imprints in the fabric of space-time that sensitive people occasionally perceive. Still others may involve Midwayer beings or other celestial personalities who, for reasons we don't fully understand, occasionally allow glimpses of information from the past.

But they're not memories of your past lives, because you haven't had any.

What About Those "Ghost" Experiences?

I have been asked about this multiple times, especially by people who have had experiences they can't easily explain. "Roger, I saw my mother at the foot of my bed three nights after she died. I know I did. Are you telling me I am crazy?"

No, I am not telling you are crazy. What I am telling you is that what you saw was not your mother's spirit.

Over the years, I have studied materials on paranormal experiences, I have studied hypnosis, wake and suggestion and many other mind controlling subjects. Because I did not believe in ghosts, but because I wanted to understand what people are actually experiencing. One pattern that emerges repeatedly is what I call "dimensional loops." There seems to be something in our physical universe that occasionally creates what amounts to a recording of significant moments in time. These recordings can replay, sometimes repeatedly, under certain conditions.

This phenomenon appears most often in cases of violent death, particularly suicide. People report seeing the same figure at the same window or hearing the same sounds at the same time of night, over and over again. These are not conscious spirits trying to communicate. They are more like echoes in the fabric of reality.

I suspect this has something to do with the mechanical controllers and other beings who maintain the physical and morontia structures of our planet. Certain events may be so significant that they are recorded, intentionally or not, by Guardian Angels or other celestial beings who think the information may be needed later for some purpose. I can't say for certain, but it's the best explanation I have found for these phenomena that does not contradict what the book teaches.

As for objects moving across rooms or doors opening by themselves, assuming those experiences are genuine and not tricks or fabrications, I think we're looking at the activity of Midwayer beings or other morontia personalities who occasionally interact with physical reality. Before Pentecost, many of these activities could be attributed to rebel midwayers who remained on the planet. But Paper 53 makes clear that all rebel beings have been removed from Earth and confined to prison worlds. So, if genuine physical phenomena are occurring today, they're likely the work of loyal celestial beings carrying out some purpose we don't understand.

But again, not ghosts. There are no disembodied human spirits wandering around haunting houses or trying to finish unfinished business.

The Three Types of Death

The book mentions three types of death, and it's worth understanding the distinction.

First, there's material death, what we typically think of when we use the word "death." Your body ceases to function. Your heart stops, your brain stops, and the physical organism that housed you throughout your mortal life shuts down permanently.

Second, there's intellectual death. This occurs when the mind or brain dies, perhaps through severe dementia, brain injury, or similar conditions. Sometimes intellectual death precedes material death, though not always.

Third, and most sobering, is spiritual death. This happens when a person makes that final, irrevocable decision to reject God the Father. It is the moment when someone says, in effect, "I want nothing to do with this. I choose annihilation over eternity."

Every human being must eventually make this choice. It's our birthright, the exercise of free will at its most fundamental level. And the universe respects that choice absolutely. If you choose non-survival, your wish will be granted. Your personality will be dissolved, your identity will cease, and the portion of reality you occupied will return to the cosmic whole as if you had never been.

I don't say this to frighten anyone. The vast majority of people who've ever lived have chosen survival, even if they didn't articulate it in religious terms. But it's important to understand that spiritual death is a real possibility, and it's the only death that's truly final.

What Survives and What Doesn't

Here's something that troubles people when they first encounter it: when you die, everything that makes you physically who you are, your body, your brain, all the material structures that housed your consciousness, perishes completely. It dies. It returns to dust.

Some people find this disturbing. "But Dr. Paul," they say, "doesn't that mean I'm not really me anymore?"

No, because you were never primarily your body. You were always much more than that.

Think about it this way: the book describes your soul as a "morontia transcript" of your life, a spiritual material recording of everything you've experienced, thought, felt, and become. Your soul contains your identity in its truest form. It's the real you, stripped of all the temporary, decaying, limited physical structures that were necessary for your mortal experience but aren't needed anymore.

Your personality, that unique pattern of being that makes you distinctly you and not someone else, survives intact. The Universal Father gave you that personality, and it doesn't depend on your physical body or brain to exist.

Your identity, your sense of who you are, your memories, your character, these are preserved in the soul that your Thought Adjuster has been building throughout your lifetime.

When these three elements, soul, personality, and Thought Adjuster, come back together on the mansion worlds, you wake up and you're "you." Fully you. More you than you've ever been, actually, because you're no longer limited by a deteriorating physical body and a brain that was never designed to fully comprehend spiritual reality.

That's why the manner of your death doesn't matter. Whether you die peacefully in your sleep or you're vaporized in a nuclear explosion, it makes absolutely no difference to your survival. The physical body was always temporary. It was a vehicle, not the passenger.

The Process of Adjudication

So, what happens after death? Let me walk you through the process as the book describes it.

When you die, your Thought Adjuster departs immediately for Divinington, the home of all Thought Adjusters. It doesn't need to travel in the way we think of travel, it simply is there, instantaneously. Upon arrival, it's registered back in using the same identification number it was registered out with when it came to indwell you.

Meanwhile, through the process of reflectivity, a universal mechanism that allows instantaneous communication and observation across vast distances, that Thought Adjuster can observe what's happening in two places at once: the local universe headquarters, where your Guardian Angel is presenting the records of your life to the Universal Censors, and the superuniverse capital, where the Ancients of Days are reviewing your case.

The Universal Censors in your local universe make the initial determination of your salvageability. They examine three sets of records: the transcript from your Thought Adjuster, the transcript from your Guardian Angel, and the records maintained by the archangels. These three sources provide a complete picture of your spiritual life and character.

If they determine that you're a survivor, if they find that you've made sufficient spiritual progress and that you genuinely desire to continue, several things happen quickly. Your Thought Adjuster is immediately dispatched to the mansion worlds. Your Guardian Angel, who has been carrying your soul, transports it to the resurrection halls. Your personality is reunited with your soul and your Adjuster, and you're given a new morontia body suited for life on the mansion worlds.

Then you wake up. You're conscious again, fully aware, fully yourself, though you're now in a body you've never had before on a world you've never seen before.

The book says this can happen as quickly as three days after death. For some people, those who've reached the third psychic circle or higher during their mortal lives, it happens almost immediately.

For others, though, those who never reached the third psychic circle, there's a longer wait. They sleep until the next dispensational resurrection, which typically occurs about every thousand years. Why the difference? Because those who reached the third circle demonstrated sufficient spiritual awareness and commitment that they can begin their morontia education right away. Those who didn't reach that level need more extensive training, and it's more efficient to handle them in groups during dispensational resurrections.

The Third Psychic Circle: What It Really Means

People often ask me what it means to reach the third psychic circle. They want to know if they've achieved it, or how they can tell if they have.

The psychic circles aren't well defined in the book, which I think is intentional. But here's my understanding: the third psychic circle represents the point at which you consciously choose to make God's will your will. It's when you stop living primarily for yourself and start living for something larger, when you genuinely want what God wants for you more than you want what you want for yourself.

Some people call this "being called to ministry," though that phrase can be misleading. You don't have to become a preacher or a minister in the traditional sense. Jesus himself didn't establish churches or require religious institutions. What he taught was simple: the Fatherhood of God and the brotherhood of man. He was a teacher, not a preacher.

The calling isn't to a profession or a role. It's to a way of being. It's recognizing that the most important thing in your life is your relationship with God and your service to your fellow human beings.

You can reach the third psychic circle without ever reading *The Urantia Book*. Millions of people throughout history have done exactly that. Spiritual awareness doesn't require this revelation, though this revelation certainly helps us understand what's happening as we grow.

What matters is the reality of your spiritual commitment, not your theological sophistication.

What Happens to Non-Survivors?

I need to address something that troubles people, though the book is quite clear about it. What happens to people who don't survive, who reject God finally and completely?

The Ancients of Days, the highest authorities in the superuniverse, make the final determination. The Universal Censors in the local universe can recommend survival or non-survival, but they can't make the ultimate decision. That responsibility rests with the Ancients of Days, and their judgment is final. There is no appeal.

The book tells us that the Ancients of Days are so perfect in their judgment that they've never once made an error. When they declare that someone has chosen non-survival, that's exactly what has happened, that person has genuinely, finally, completely rejected continued existence.

When that happens, the person's personality is dissolved. Their identity ceases to exist. It's as if they never were. The Thought Adjuster that indwelled them is released and reassigned, always to a different planet, never to this one again.

This sounds harsh, doesn't it? But think about the alternative. What would it mean for God to force someone to continue existing against their will? That would be the ultimate violation of free will, the ultimate act of cosmic tyranny. God loves us too much to do that.

Everyone gets to make their choice. The universe respects that choice absolutely.

The Indestructibility of the World of the Cross

Before we close this chapter, I want to address one more topic that comes up frequently: the fear that humanity might destroy itself and this planet through nuclear war or some other catastrophe.

Let me be absolutely clear: this planet is not going to be destroyed. Not by nuclear war, not by environmental collapse, not by any human foolishness, no matter how profound.

Why? Because this is the world of the cross. This is the planet where Michael of Nebadon, our Creator Son, completed his seventh and final bestowal. This is, in a very real sense, the crown jewel of the local universe.

Do you really think the celestial beings who oversee this universe are going to let a handful of stupid, short-sighted politicians push some buttons and destroy it?

Here's what would happen if we somehow managed to set off enough nuclear weapons to make this planet uninhabitable: every salvageable being on Earth would be immediately transported off planet. The celestial authorities would install mechanisms all over the world that could instantly convert physical beings into morontia form and relocate them to another planet, probably one, very similar to this one.

You would complete your mortal life there, just as you would have here. You might not even remember that anything unusual had happened. Because every individual who has the capacity to survive has the absolute right to complete their mortal experience. That's your birthright as a child of God.

Even the Creator Sons go through it. That's how important the mortal experience is.

So no, a few idiots with nuclear weapons aren't going to destroy this planet or cheat you out of your cosmic destiny. The universe doesn't work that way.

And after we're all safely relocated, do you know what would happen to Earth? It would be recycled. The Life Carriers would return and restart the evolutionary process from scratch. It would take millions of years, but eventually this planet would be repopulated with life, and eventually new human beings would appear, and eventually this world would once again become what it was always meant to be: the planet where God became man, where the eternal touched the temporal, where the universe learned what divine love looks like when it walks among mortals.

That destiny cannot be thwarted. It can be delayed, perhaps, by our foolishness. But it cannot be destroyed.

Looking Forward

As we prepare to move into the next chapter of our study, I want you to hold onto this central truth: death is not the end, and it's not the enemy. Death is simply a transition, a doorway through which we pass from one phase of our eternal career to the next.

When you understand what actually happens at death, when you grasp the reality that your personality survives, that your soul is being carefully preserved, that your identity will be restored on the mansion worlds, the fear that surrounds death in our culture begins to dissolve.

We don't need to believe in ghosts or reincarnation or any of these comforting fictions we've created to cope with our fear of annihilation. The truth is far better than any fiction: we are eternal beings having a temporary physical experience, and when that experience ends, we don't cease to be. We simply move on to the next phase of an adventure that will continue literally forever.

In our next chapter, we'll explore what happens after you wake up on the mansion worlds. What does that first morning feel like? Who greets you? What do you learn? How do you adjust to having a morontia body instead of a physical one? These questions and many more await us as we continue our journey through Paper 112 and beyond.

But for now, rest in this knowledge: you are a child of God, indwelt by a fragment of the Father himself, and you are destined for eternity if you choose it. Nothing in all the universe can take that away from you, not death, not disaster, not even your own doubts.

The only thing that can stop your eternal career is your own final, irrevocable rejection of it. And I suspect most of you reading this have already made a very different choice.

Chapter 33: The Survival Journey - Understanding Thought Adjusters and Resurrection

Introduction: The Mystery of Divine Fragments

Throughout my years of studying *The Urantia Book*, few sections have captured my imagination quite like Paper 112, Section 4. Tonight, as I continue this series on personality survival, I find myself returning to questions that have puzzled me since I first encountered these revelations. What happens to our Thought Adjusters, those perfect fragments of God dwelling within us, during the waiting period between our death and resurrection? Why would a perfect fragment of divinity need training or observation? And perhaps most importantly, what determines whether we wake up on the third day or must await a dispensational resurrection that occurs roughly every thousand years?

These aren't merely academic questions. They strike at the heart of our spiritual destiny and reveal the intricate choreography of survival that involves not just ourselves, but Guardian Angels, Thought Adjusters, Universal Censors, and even the Ancients of Days on Uversa. Understanding this process helps us grasp why our spiritual choices during mortal life carry such profound weight, not just for our own futures, but for the entire cosmic organism of the evolving universes.

The Context: Death and Dispensational Resurrection

Let me set the stage by reviewing the foundational concept we've been exploring. According to *The Urantia Book*, subsequent to physical death, except in cases where an individual translates directly from among the living, the released Adjuster goes immediately to Divinington, the home sphere of Thought Adjusters. What transpires on that world during the waiting period depends almost entirely on whether the human being ascends to the mansion worlds on their own individual merit (typically within three days) or awaits a dispensational summoning of the sleeping survivors of a planetary age.

This distinction matters enormously. A dispensational resurrection occurs approximately every thousand years on most evolutionary worlds. During that millennium, Thought Adjusters whose human partners did not qualify for immediate resurrection must occupy themselves somehow. They don't simply hover around the mansion worlds waiting. That wouldn't make sense, would it? These are fragments of the Universal Father, perfect, divine, and purposeful. Even in waiting, they remain active.

The Seven Assignments: A Persistent Mystery

The Urantia Book outlines seven possible temporary assignments that an Adjuster may undertake while awaiting their human partner's dispensational resurrection. When I first read this list years ago, I'll admit it stopped me cold. I've returned to it countless times, and honestly, it still presents something of a mystery. Let me share these assignments with you:

1. **Be mustered into the ranks of vanished monitors for undisclosed service.** The very phrase "undisclosed service" suggests activities we're not privy to understanding at our current level of cosmic awareness.
2. **Be assigned for a period to the observation of the Paradise regime.** This one particularly puzzled me. Why would a perfect fragment of God need to observe Paradise?
3. **Be enrolled in one of the many training schools of Divinington.** Again, training? For a fragment of divine perfection?
4. **Be stationed for a time as a student observer on one of the other six sacred spheres which constitute the Father's circuit of Paradise worlds.** Student observer, the language is unmistakable.
5. **Be assigned to the messenger service of the personalized Adjusters.** This makes more sense as a service role, yet it still implies the Adjuster is gaining something from the experience.
6. **Become an associate instructor in the Divinington schools devoted to the training of monitors belonging to the virgin group.** Here, at least, we can see how an Adjuster with human experience might teach those who haven't yet indwelt a mortal.
7. **Be assigned to select a group of possible worlds on which to serve in the event that there is reasonable cause for believing that the human partner may have rejected survival.** This final option addresses the heartbreaking possibility that the mortal may ultimately choose non-survival.

Now, here's what has always intrigued me about this list: We're talking about Thought Adjusters, perfect fragments of God the Father. These are expressions of absolute divinity. So why would they need observation, training, or student status?

The Experiential Nature of Divine Fragments

Over the years, I've come to what I believe may be a reasonable explanation, though I acknowledge it remains somewhat speculative. The key appears to lie in understanding that Thought Adjusters, despite their divine perfection, are *experiential* beings from the moment of their creation and assignment.

Think about it this way: When God the Father creates and dispatches a Thought Adjuster to indwell a mortal being, that fragment embarks on an experiential journey. Before that moment, the Adjuster possessed divine perfection but lacked something crucial, human experience. From the instant of assignment, the Adjuster begins accumulating experiences that are entirely unique to that particular mortal partnership. The Adjuster experiences what you experience, learns what you learn, and even encounters what you encounter, including, significantly, the reality of good and evil.

This experiential dimension changes everything. While the Adjuster remains perfect in nature, it is no longer experientially identical to its pre-assignment state. It has gained something profound: firsthand knowledge of evolutionary existence, of time and space, of struggle and choice, and yes, even of the distinction between good and evil.

Here's where it gets even more interesting. These experiences must eventually flow into the Supreme Being, the evolving God of the finite universes. But the Adjuster carries this experiential knowledge forward. When assigned to a new mortal (in cases where the previous human partner chose non-survival), the Adjuster brings that accumulated wisdom along. It cannot simply erase or abandon what it has learned.

This may explain the mystery I've wrestled with for so long. Perhaps Thought Adjusters engage in observation, training, and study not because they lack divine perfection, but because they're integrating and processing the experiential reality they've gained. They're becoming something more than they were, not *more* divine, but more experientially complete.

The Question of Evil and Reintegration

This leads me to a somewhat sobering reflection that I want to share carefully. Good and evil are not equivalent forces in the universe. Good can exist in the presence of evil, but absolute perfection and evil cannot coexist in the same space. God the Father contains no evil, this is definitional to divine perfection.

We human beings, on the other hand, deal with the reality of good and evil every single day. It's woven into the fabric of our evolutionary existence on this world. We make choices between better and worse, between selfishness and service, between material gratification and spiritual growth. Our Thought Adjusters, dwelling within us, witness all of this. They're exposed to our struggles with these very real moral dynamics.

This raises a question I've pondered deeply: Can a Thought Adjuster, once it has been exposed to the human experience of good and evil, ever fully reintegrate back into God the Father, back into the I AM from which it came?

My sense is that perhaps it cannot. Once separated and assigned, once experientially enriched through mortal partnership, the Adjuster becomes forever a distinct entity. It remains *of* God the Father, communicates directly with God the Father, and functions as a perfect fragment of divinity. Yet it may never merge back into the undifferentiated reality of the Universal Father. Its consciousness now includes something the original I AM did not possess: the experiential knowledge of evolutionary imperfection.

This isn't a diminishment of the Adjuster. If anything, it's an enhancement, a fulfillment of the Father's purpose in fragmentizing himself in the first place. The Father seeks to know experientially what it means to evolve, to struggle, to choose. Through Thought Adjusters, he gains that knowledge.

Guardian Angels and the Psychic Circles

We cannot discuss survival and resurrection without addressing the critical role of Guardian Angels and our progression through what *The Urantia Book* calls the psychic circles. These circles represent stages of spiritual and intellectual achievement, ranging from the seventh (most primitive) to the first (most advanced short of fusion).

Let me paint a picture for you. When human beings function at the seventh psychic circle, they're assigned what I can only describe as minimal angelic supervision. One pair of Guardian Angels is responsible for a *thousand* individuals at this level. That's one very busy angel trying to watch over a thousand spiritually undeveloped mortals. Additionally, there are 144 pairs of cherubim and sanobim to assist, but still, the ratio tells you something important.

Why such minimal coverage? The text suggests it's because individuals at the seventh circle are, to put it bluntly, rather barbaric in their spiritual development. They're not making significant spiritual decisions. They're barely aware of their spiritual nature. There simply isn't that much for guardian angels to do when someone isn't actively engaging with spiritual reality.

But everything changes when you reach the third psychic circle. At this crucial threshold, you're assigned your own personal pair of Guardian Angels, along with dedicated cherubim and sanobim. This isn't honorary, it's functional. You've demonstrated enough spiritual progress that you now warrant full-time angelic attention because your choices and growth have real spiritual consequence.

More significantly, reaching the third circle essentially guarantees your resurrection on the third day following death. This is the "narrow door" that Jesus spoke about in a different context, but the metaphor fits beautifully. Not everyone makes it through. Those who don't must wait for the dispensational resurrection, which could be centuries away.

The Certification Process: Checks and Double Checks

The process by which someone qualifies for immediate resurrection is extraordinarily thorough. It involves multiple levels of verification and agreement, each serving as a check on the others. Let me walk you through it step by step, because understanding this process reveals just how seriously the universe takes the matter of survival.

First, when death overtakes you, assuming you've reached the third circle or higher and have been assigned a personal Guardian of Destiny, your Adjuster prepares what amounts to a final transcript. This is a summary of your survival character, a comprehensive record of who you became during your mortal life. The Guardian Angel prepares a similar record from their perspective.

Now here's the crucial part: These two records must match. The Adjuster and the Guardian must "essentially agree in every item of their life records and recommendations." Every item. If there's significant disagreement, the process stalls right there.

But it doesn't stop with agreement between Adjuster and Guardian. The records are then submitted to the Universal Censors stationed on the constellation headquarters, along with their reflective associates on Uversa (the capital of our superuniverse). These Censors possess the unique ability to determine spiritual status with absolute accuracy. They review everything, and they too must agree without equivocation or reservation.

Only after all these levels of confirmation, Adjuster, Guardian Angel, Universal Censors on the constellation, and their reflective counterparts on Uversa, does the matter go before the Ancients of Days. These are the supreme rulers of the superuniverse, and they issue the final mandate. If approved, this mandate flashes forth over the communication circuits back to Salvington (our local universe capital), and the tribunals of the Sovereign of Nebadon decree the immediate passage of your surviving soul to the resurrection halls of the mansion worlds.

Think about the implications of this multi-layered process. The universe wants you to survive. But it also operates with absolute integrity. Every safeguard exists to ensure that only those who truly choose survival and demonstrate readiness for morontia life actually proceed. There are no shortcuts, no favoritism, no oversights.

What the Adjuster Does Upon Approval

When final approval comes through, something profound happens with your Thought Adjuster. The sequence described in *The Urantia Book* moves me every time I contemplate it.

First, the Adjuster, upon learning of your approval for immediate resurrection, registers at Divinington. Then, and this is significant, the Adjuster proceeds directly to the Paradise presence of the Universal Father. Imagine that for a moment. Your Adjuster, who has been your constant companion through all your mortal struggles and triumphs, goes before God the Father himself.

What happens in that moment, we're not told explicitly. But I believe it represents a farewell of sorts, a checkout, if you will. The Adjuster is acknowledging that this particular phase of service, the service that involves returning periodically to Divinington, is ending. After fusion (which is now virtually certain, barring your free will rejection), that Adjuster will never return to Divinington again. The journey has become one-way. The Adjuster's destiny is now permanently linked with yours.

After this Paradise audience, the Adjuster returns immediately to the local universe and superuniverse of assignment, where it's embraced by the chief personalized Adjusters, those Adjusters who have already achieved permanent union with ascending mortals. This embrace represents recognition and welcome into a new phase of eternal service.

Then the Adjuster proceeds to the resurrection halls of the mansion world, where your new morontia form is waiting. This form has been carefully constructed by your Guardian of Destiny based on the soul you and your Adjuster built together during your mortal life. The Adjuster enters this new form, and on the third period, the third day, you awaken.

You wake up as *you*. Same identity, same personality, same memories. But now you're clothed in a morontia body, and your Adjuster is prepared to continue the journey that will eventually lead to fusion.

The Inevitability and the Exception

Here's something crucial to understand: Once you've been approved for resurrection and your Adjuster has been through this checkout process, fusion has become virtually inevitable from the Adjuster's perspective. The Adjuster knows you're going to make it. The universe has certified your survival. All that remains is your continued growth and eventual spiritual readiness for fusion itself.

But, and this is a significant "but", you still retain free will. Even on the mansion worlds, even after resurrection, even as you progress through morontia training, you can still choose to reject survival. You can still say, "I don't want to continue this journey."

I have difficulty imagining why anyone would make that choice after experiencing the mansion worlds and beginning to understand the magnificent destiny that awaits. But *The Urantia Book* makes clear that it does happen. Some individuals, even after resurrection, choose non-survival.

When this happens, it's devastating for the Adjuster. Remember, the Adjuster has already checked out of Divinington. It has already appeared before the Universal Father. It has already been embraced by the personalized monitors as one whose mortal partner is destined for fusion. And now it must start over. The Adjuster must return to Divinington, register again, and await assignment to another mortal.

This possibility highlights why free will is so sacred in the universe. God the Father himself will not override your choice, even when that choice leads to your extinction. Even when it means disappointment for a perfect fragment of himself.

The Uniqueness of Personality and Adjuster

I want to take a moment to emphasize something that's easy to overlook in all this technical detail about resurrections and assignments: the stunning uniqueness of both personality and Thought Adjuster.

When God the Father bestows personality upon you, he creates something that has never existed before and will never exist again. Your personality is absolutely unique. There is no one else in all of infinity like you. This isn't poetic exaggeration, it's cosmic fact. The personality the Father gives you is yours alone, and it's eternal.

But here's what I find even more remarkable: Thought Adjusters are equally unique. Each fragment of the Father is distinct. When people think about Thought Adjusters, they sometimes imagine them as identical pieces of divinity, like drops of water from the same ocean, indistinguishable from one another. But that's not accurate. Each Adjuster is individual, possessing unique characteristics and eventually unique experiential histories.

Now imagine what happens at fusion. You take a unique personality, one that has never existed before. You combine it with a unique Thought Adjuster, another singular expression of divinity. The result is a doubly unique being, a brand-new son or daughter of God who combines human experiential wisdom with divine perfection. That being is unprecedented. The universe has never seen another like it and never will again.

And this happens billions upon billions of times across the seven superuniverses. Each fusion creates a new, eternally unique finaliter who will eventually engage in services we can barely imagine.

Yet all of these unique individuals together form the cosmic organism, the living, evolving reality of the Supreme Being and the grand universe. Each person matters. Each choice matters. Each spiritual decision you make affects not just your own destiny but the destiny of the whole.

The Weight of Choice

This brings us to perhaps the most sobering aspect of everything we've discussed: the cosmic responsibility inherent in human choice.

The text from Paper 112 states this with remarkable directness: "Upon the integrity of the human free will choice depends the eternal destiny of the future finaliter; upon the sincerity of mortal free will the Divine Adjuster depends for eternal personality; upon the faithfulness of mortal choice the Universal Father depends for the realization of a new ascending son; upon the steadfastness and wisdom of decision-action the Supreme Being depends for the actuality of experiential evolution."

Read that again slowly. Your choices affect your own destiny, yes, of course. But they also affect your Thought Adjuster's destiny. They affect the Universal Father's purposes. They affect the very evolution of God the Supreme.

When you choose survival, you're not just saving yourself. You're enabling your Adjuster to achieve eternal personality through fusion with you. You're allowing the Father to gain one more ascending son or daughter. You're contributing to the experiential evolution of deity itself.

When you choose non-survival, or more accurately, when you fail to choose survival, you let down yourself, yes. But you also let down your Adjuster, who has invested everything in your success. You let down the Supreme Being, who depends on your experiential contribution. You let down the cosmic community, which loses the unique perspective and service only you could have provided.

I don't say this to generate fear or guilt. That's not the point. The point is to recognize the profound significance of our lives. We're not cosmic accidents stumbling through a meaningless existence. We're essential participants in the grandest adventure imaginable, the evolution of God in time and space.

Probation and Second Chances

Now, I don't want to leave you with the impression that the universe is harsh or unforgiving. Quite the opposite. *The Urantia Book* makes clear that if, "through no fault of your own, the accidents of time and the handicaps of material existence prevent your mastering these levels on your native planet, if your intentions and desires are of survival value, there are issued the decrees of probation extension."

In other words, you'll be given additional time on the mansion worlds to prove yourself. You'll enter what amounts to remedial spiritual education. The universe isn't looking for reasons to reject you, it's looking for reasons to advance you.

This is particularly relevant for those who awaken in the dispensational resurrections. Many of these individuals had little or no spiritual foundation during their mortal lives. Maybe they went to church for social reasons but never really engaged with spiritual reality. Maybe they lived in cultures or circumstances that provided minimal spiritual guidance. Maybe they were simply too young when death overtook them.

None of this disqualifies them from eventual survival. But it does mean they'll need intensive training upon resurrection. They can't be turned loose in the morontia realm without understanding spiritual principles, without developing cosmic perspective, without learning to make wise choices. That wouldn't be fair to them or to the broader universe community.

So, they receive probation, education, and time. The universe is patient. But it does require that eventually, you must choose. Eventually, you must demonstrate that your intentions and desires align with survival values.

Conclusion: The Narrow Door and the Broad Mercy

As we close this chapter, I'm struck by the tension between what Jesus called the "narrow door" and what I see as the broad mercy of the universe.

Yes, the door is narrow in the sense that not everyone makes it through. Spiritual growth requires effort, decision, and dedication. Reaching the third psychic circle, that threshold that qualifies you for immediate resurrection, demands real spiritual work. You cannot coast into it. You cannot inherit it. You must choose it and live it.

The checks and balances built into the certification process are rigorous precisely because survival is taken seriously. The universe doesn't hand out resurrections carelessly.

And yet, look at the provisions made for those who struggle. Look at the patience extended to those who need more time. Look at the willingness to offer probation, remedial training, and additional opportunities. Look at the fact that Thought Adjusters will patiently wait a thousand years for their mortal partners to awaken, then continue guiding them through the mansion worlds toward eventual fusion.

The door may be narrow, but the mercy is broad.

In our next chapter, we'll explore what happens after resurrection, the actual experience of awakening on the mansion worlds, the reunion with loved ones, the beginning of morontia education, and the long journey toward Paradise. But for now, I hope you can sit with the profound implications of what we've discussed.

Your life matters. Your choices matter. Your spiritual growth matters, not just for you, but for the entire cosmos. The fragment of God dwelling within you right now is counting on you. The universe is counting on you. And perhaps most importantly, you're being given every possible opportunity to succeed. The question is: Will you choose the journey?

Chapter 34: The Survival of the Soul and Journey to the Mansion Worlds

Introduction

Throughout my years of teaching *The Urantia Book*, I've discovered that few topics generate more questions, or more confusion, than what actually happens when we die. We've all wondered about it. Some of us fear it. Others approach it with curiosity tinged with uncertainty. During one particularly memorable study session, a student asked me point-blank: "Dr. Paul, if I die tomorrow, what exactly happens to *me*?" It's the most human question imaginable, and *The Urantia Book* offers answers that are both surprising and deeply comforting.

In this chapter, we continue our examination of Paper 112, focusing specifically on Section 5, which addresses the survival of the human personality and the initial stages of our ascension career. What I've found particularly striking about this material is how it dismantles many of our cherished assumptions while simultaneously offering a vision of divine mercy that exceeds anything we might have imagined.

The revelators are careful here, almost cautious, as they navigate topics that sit at the boundary between our material existence and the morontia reality that awaits us. They acknowledge their own limitations in conveying these truths, restricted both by our capacity to understand and by mandates from the celestial governing authorities of Urantia. Yet what they do reveal transforms our understanding of death, judgment, and the continuation of personal identity.

We'll explore three critical concepts in this chapter: first, the merciful provisions made for those whose spiritual development remains incomplete at death; second, the nature of that final, undoubted choice each of us must make; and third, the mysterious entity we call the soul, that "conjoint child of human and divine parentage" that actually survives the dissolution of our physical bodies.

The Mercy of Transitional Classification

Let me start with something that often surprises students when they first encounter it. The universe administrators, beings of extraordinary wisdom and experience, operate under a principle that might seem almost reckless to our cautious human sensibilities: when in doubt, advance the soul.

The Urantia Book tells us plainly: "If ever there is doubt as to the advisability of advancing a human identity to the mansion worlds, the universe governments invariably rule in the personal interest of that individual." Think about that for a moment. These aren't careless bureaucrats rubber-stamping applications. These are the Ancients of Days, universal censors, and guardian seraphim who see us with perfect clarity. Yet they choose mercy over caution.

What happens to these borderline cases? They're classified as "transitional beings" and placed in what we might call remedial classes on the first mansion world. I sometimes think of it as a probationary period, though that term carries unfortunate connotations from our earthly legal systems. These individuals haven't quite demonstrated the spiritual qualifications for guaranteed progression, but the universe gives them every opportunity to prove themselves.

During one of our study groups, a participant, I'll call her Margaret, shared her concern about a brother who had lived what she described as a "completely secular life" until his final days, when he experienced what some might call a deathbed conversion. "Does that count?" she asked. "Can he really be saved if he only believed at the very end?"

It's a fair question, and it touches on something Christians have debated for centuries, going back to the thief on the cross who received Jesus's promise: "This day will you sit with me in Paradise." But we need to understand what Jesus meant, and what he didn't mean. Paradise, in the cosmic sense, sits at the center of all creation, and reaching it requires millions of years of ascension. Jesus was speaking in terms his listener could understand, using the man's own conception of heaven.

The real issue isn't the *timing* of belief but its *authenticity* and *spiritual content*. Someone who makes a genuine decision to align with God's will at the last moment will indeed survive. But if their faith lacks any spiritual foundation, if they possess no understanding of God as Father or humanity as brothers and sisters, they'll wake on the mansion worlds essentially starting from scratch. Hence the remedial classes.

What strikes me most about this arrangement is its profound optimism about human potential. The universe would rather risk the complications of rehabilitating marginal cases than deny even one sincere soul the opportunity for eternal progression. As the text puts it, the administrators "had rather assume the risk of a system rebellion than to court the hazard of depriving one struggling mortal from any evolutionary world of the eternal joy of pursuing the ascending career."

The Gift of Mercy Credits

Here's something I rarely hear discussed in Urantia study groups, though it deserves more attention: each of us is issued what might be called "mercy credits" during our lifetime. These aren't literal credits in some cosmic ledger, but they represent the merciful allowances made for our impatience, intolerance, mistakes, and spiritual immaturity.

Your guardian seraphim keeps track of these provisions throughout your life. They're not punitive, quite the opposite. The system is designed with the understanding that mortals on evolutionary worlds like ours will stumble, will fail, will sometimes make terrible choices despite our best intentions. The mercy credits ensure that these all-too-human failures don't automatically disqualify us from survival.

I want to be clear about something, though, because students sometimes misunderstand this concept. The mercy credits aren't a license for deliberate wrongdoing. They're not "get out of jail free" cards you can spend frivolously. Rather, they represent the difference between the perfection God knows we'll eventually achieve and the imperfection we currently embody. They're the grace period in which we learn and grow.

The revelators tell us that sufficient mercy credits are issued for every individual on this planet to reach the mansion worlds if they genuinely choose to do so. Read that again: *every individual*. If you ever doubt whether you're "good enough" for survival, let that sink in. The universe has already allocated the mercy necessary for your success. The only question is whether you'll accept it.

The Final Choice: Conscious and Undoubted

Now we come to what I consider one of the most significant concepts in all of *The Urantia Book*: the requirement for "one true opportunity to make one undoubted, self-conscious, and final choice."

Notice the precision of that language. Not just any choice, but an *undoubted* choice. Not made in confusion or fear, but in clear *self-consciousness*. And not tentative or provisional, but genuinely *final*.

The text emphasizes this point: "The Sovereign judges of the universe will not deprive any being of personality status who has not finally and fully made the eternal choice. The soul of man must and will be given full and ample opportunity to reveal its true intent and real purpose."

What does this mean practically? It means that not everyone makes this final choice before physical death. Some people, through no fault of their own, die before reaching sufficient spiritual maturity to make an informed decision. Maybe they were children. Maybe they lived in circumstances of extreme deprivation with no exposure to spiritual concepts. Maybe they died suddenly in war or accident before their spiritual nature had awakened.

The universe doesn't hold these circumstances against anyone. If you haven't had the opportunity to make that clear, conscious, final choice during your earthly life, you'll be given the opportunity after your resurrection. This is why the concept of "transitional beings" matters so much. They're individuals still working toward that decisive moment of spiritual commitment.

During a study session several years ago, a military veteran in our group raised a troubling scenario. "I enlisted at eighteen," he said. "Raised in a non-religious household, thinking mostly about serving my country and maybe getting money for college. If I'd been killed in combat, where would that have left me spiritually?"

It's a penetrating question. Young people rarely contemplate eternal destinies, they're focused on the immediate challenges of growing up, finding their place, maybe starting families. Yet they can find themselves in life-or-death situations before their spiritual nature has fully emerged.

The answer, I believe, lies in understanding that the choice we're discussing isn't primarily about intellectual beliefs or religious affiliation. It's about fundamental orientation toward reality. At its core, the choice is this: Do you accept God as your Father? Do you accept all human beings as your brothers and sisters? Are you willing to align your will with the divine will?

These questions can be answered by someone with no theological training whatsoever. In fact, some of the most spiritually attuned people I've known would have struggled to articulate a single doctrine of formal religion. But they lived the brotherhood of man daily, treating others with compassion and dignity, sensing some larger purpose to existence even if they couldn't name it.

The universe judges intent, not vocabulary. It evaluates the direction of your soul's growth, not your ability to pass a theology exam.

Three Pathways to Resurrection

The revelators describe three distinct pathways by which mortals can reach the mansion worlds, and understanding these helps clarify the flexibility built into the divine plan.

The Third-Day Resurrection: This is the express route, if you will. Those who have achieved the third psychic circle during their mortal lives proceed immediately to the mansion worlds, typically awakening on the third day after death. Reaching the third psychic circle represents a significant spiritual milestone, it indicates cosmic awareness, recognition of your place in the universe, and commitment to the ascending path. When you achieve this level, you're assigned a personal seraphic guardian, and upon death, this guardian accompanies your soul directly to the mansion world resurrection halls.

I aspire to this pathway, as I hope we all do. It represents spiritual preparedness, the fruit of a life spent cultivating awareness of God and commitment to his will. If you're participating in serious study of *The Urantia Book*, engaging in sincere worship, and genuinely trying to live by spiritual principles, there's every reason to believe you're progressing toward this circle.

Adjudication Pathway: Here's something that rarely gets discussed but deserves our attention. Some individuals, after death, require a period of adjudication before proceeding to the mansion worlds. The text states: "Other mortals may be detained until such time as the adjudication of their affairs has been completed, after which they may proceed to the mansion worlds."

What does adjudication involve? Essentially, it's a thorough review conducted by your guardian seraphim, universal censors, and other relevant authorities. Through the mechanism of reflectivity, which allows the Ancients of Days to observe events anywhere in their superuniverse, your case is evaluated. The question being decided is straightforward: Does this individual qualify for continued existence?

This process could take time, perhaps years, perhaps much longer. But here's what's crucial to understand: you remain completely unconscious during this period. Whether adjudication takes a century or a millennium makes no subjective difference to you. When you awaken, it will seem as though no time has passed at all.

I sometimes imagine it like this: you close your eyes in death on Urantia, and in what seems like the very next instant, you open them on the mansion world. Whatever happened in between, three days, three centuries, or three millennia, simply doesn't exist in your experience. Time, after all, is largely a product of material existence. Once you've left that existence behind, time loses its hold on your consciousness.

Dispensational Resurrection: The third pathway involves waiting for what's called a dispensational resurrection, a mass awakening of sleeping survivors that occurs roughly every thousand years on Urantia. These are individuals who have qualified for survival but haven't quite reached the spiritual development necessary for immediate progression.

Here's what I find reassuring about this category: if you're assigned to a dispensational resurrection, the adjudication has already occurred. The decision has been made, you're approved for continued existence. You're simply waiting to be awakened along with others in your cohort so you can be placed in appropriate classes and begin your mansion world education.

Again, you experience no passage of time. You die, and an instant later (from your perspective), you awaken in a resurrection hall surrounded by others who died over the preceding millennium. You're grouped with companions of similar spiritual development, which actually facilitates the educational process.

One student once asked me, "But Dr. Paul, what if I die and have to wait a thousand years, and my wife dies later but wakes up in three days? Will she have to wait around for me all that time?"

It's a sweet question, and it reveals our human attachment to our earthly relationships. The honest answer is yes, if your spouse progresses faster than you, she could potentially be far ahead in her mansion world career by the time you awaken. This is why I encourage couples to pursue spiritual development together. It's not just about your individual progression; it's about maintaining connection with those you love as you all move forward.

That said, the mansion worlds aren't rigidly hierarchical in a way that prevents interaction between different levels. Reunion with loved ones remains possible, even if you're at different stages. But there's something appealing about walking the path together from the beginning, don't you think?

The Central Question: What About Jesus?

I need to address something that often creates discomfort in our study groups, but we can't avoid it because *The Urantia Book* itself doesn't avoid it. The question of Jesus, who he is, what role he plays, and whether belief in him is necessary for survival, sits at the heart of any serious discussion of eternal life.

Let me state this as clearly as I know how: Jesus is not optional in the universe career. He is the Creator Son of our local universe, the being through whom all of us came into existence. As he himself taught, "I am the way, the truth, and the life." And he said explicitly, "No one comes to the Father but by me."

Now, before anyone misunderstands, let me clarify what this does and doesn't mean. It doesn't mean that everyone must have heard the name "Jesus" or be able to recite Christian doctrine to survive. The universe judges hearts, not theological vocabulary. Someone who lives in genuine fellowship with God, even if they know him by another name or through another tradition, may well be honoring Jesus without realizing it.

But here's the reality we need to face at some point in your universe career, you must acknowledge Jesus Christ Michael as your Creator and sovereign. You cannot progress indefinitely while rejecting the very being who gave you existence and maintains your reality moment by moment.

This sometimes troubles students who worry about people of other faiths, Muslims, Jews, Buddhists, Hindus, those who followed sincere spiritual paths but never encountered Christianity. What happens to them?

The answer appears to be this: they'll have the opportunity to learn the truth about Jesus on the mansion worlds. If they have genuine faith in God and live according to their best understanding of truth, they can certainly survive. But their education on the mansion worlds will necessarily include coming to understand who Jesus really is, not as a sacrifice for sins (that's Pauline theology, not Jesus's own teaching), but as the Creator Son, the living expression of God's love, the path by which we progress toward Paradise.

Some will accept this truth readily once it's presented clearly. Others may struggle with it, perhaps for a long time. But ultimately, progression past the local universe level requires acknowledgment of the Creator Son. You cannot enter the superuniverse career while rejecting Michael of Nebadon. It's not a punitive rule; it's simply the structure of reality.

During one particularly intense study session, someone challenged me on this point. "So, you're saying all those good Buddhists and Muslims are going to hell?" he demanded.

No. I'm not saying that at all. I'm saying they may wake up on the mansion worlds, if they have genuine faith and moral character, and there begin learning truths that weren't available to them on Urantia. Whether they continue to progress depends on how they respond to those truths once presented.

The universe is neither narrow nor arbitrary. But it does have structure. Michael is the creator of our local universe and recognizing that fact isn't optional for those who would traverse his creation.

The Gospel Jesus Actually Taught

I want to take a moment here to distinguish between the gospel Jesus himself proclaimed and what later got built up around him. This matters because confusion on this point causes unnecessary anxiety about salvation.

Jesus came to teach one essential message: the Fatherhood of God and the brotherhood of man. That's it. That's the gospel. Not complex atonement theories. Not sacrificial theologies. Not elaborate doctrines about blood redemption. Simply this: God is your Father, and every human being is your brother or sister.

If you grasp that truth, really grasp it, and begin living accordingly, you're on the path Jesus laid out. You're doing what he asked. Everything else, all the theological superstructure that got added later, obscures rather than illuminates his actual teaching.

The early Christian church, shaped primarily by Paul's theology, transformed Jesus's simple gospel into something quite different. Paul created a religion *about* Jesus rather than the religion *of* Jesus. The difference matters enormously.

There was, for a brief time, a church in Philadelphia led by Abner that remained true to Jesus's actual teaching. It lasted about a century before Paul's version won out institutionally. So, the Christianity we inherited is largely Pauline Christianity, not the faith Jesus himself practiced and taught.

This doesn't make Christianity worthless, far from it. The church has done immense good and preserved the memory of Jesus through centuries when it might otherwise have been lost. But we need to distinguish between Jesus's own message and later interpretations of his mission.

When I talk about the necessity of accepting Jesus, I'm talking about accepting him as your Creator Son, your sovereign, your lord, and following his teaching about the Fatherhood of God and brotherhood of man. That's the essence. Everything else is commentary.

The Nature of the Soul

Now we come to perhaps the most mysterious concept in this entire chapter: the soul itself. What is it? Where is it? How does it function?

The Urantia Book describes the soul as "the conjoint child of the combined life and efforts of the human you in liaison with the divine you, the Adjuster." Let that image sink in. Your soul is not some pre-existing immortal essence trapped in a mortal body. Rather, it's something genuinely new, created through the partnership between your human will and your indwelling Thought Adjuster.

Every time you make a moral choice, every time you respond to beauty or truth or goodness, every time you reach out in love or service, you're building this soul. The Thought Adjuster, that fragment of God residing within you, takes these spiritually significant experiences and weaves them into an imperishable identity. Your decisions provide the material; the Adjuster provides the preservation and spiritual transformation.

The soul is therefore neither purely human nor purely divine. It partakes of both natures. It's mortal enough to be *"you"* carrying your personality, your memories, your essential character. Yet it's divine enough to be eternal, capable of surviving the dissolution of your physical brain and body.

During your earthly life, this soul remains largely in the background. It's there, growing quietly, but your conscious experience is dominated by your material mind and its electrochemical processes. The soul is like an embryo developing in the womb, present but not yet active in its own right.

Death changes everything. At death, your material body ceases to function. Your electrochemical brain patterns dissolve. Your material mind, dependent as it is on that physical substrate, terminates. What survives is the soul, carefully preserved by your guardian seraphim.

Your Thought Adjuster, meanwhile, returns to Divinington, carrying a transcript of everything spiritually valuable from your life. When you're ready for resurrection, whether on the third day or later, the Adjuster returns, your soul is revitalized, your personality is reinstated, and you awaken as a morontia being.

Here's what fascinates me: when you awaken, you *are* the soul. It's not that you *have* a soul somewhere inside you. Rather, the soul becomes your new identity. All those spiritual realities the Thought Adjuster was building during your life, they now constitute the conscious you.

This means you wake up on the mansion worlds already transformed. You're not the same finite, limited creature you were before. You've been spiritually upgraded. You carry all your significant memories, your personality remains intact, but you now exist on a different plane of reality.

And here's something remarkable: for the first time in your existence, you can consciously communicate with your Thought Adjuster. During mortal life, this communion was largely unconscious, mediated through feelings, intuitions, and subtle spiritual leadings. But as a morontia being, you can engage in actual dialogue with the divine presence within you. You can directly access God's guidance and participate consciously in the partnership that will eventually lead to fusion.

The Borderland of Life and Death

The revelators acknowledge significant limitations in describing what happens at death. As one of them admits, there are "two difficulties that hamper my efforts to explain just what happens to you in death." First, it's nearly impossible to convey to our material minds an adequate description of transactions occurring at the boundary between physical and morontia realms. Second, celestial authorities impose restrictions on what can be revealed.

But within these constraints, they tell us this much: something real, something of human evolution beyond the Thought Adjuster alone, survives death. This entity, the soul, "is wholly unconscious during the period from death to repersonalization and is in the keeping of the seraphic destiny guardian throughout this season of waiting."

Let me emphasize that word: *unconscious*. You are completely, totally unconscious from the moment of death until resurrection. There is no awareness, no experience, no passage of time. You don't float around in some ethereal state observing your funeral. You don't linger near loved ones, trying to communicate. You don't gradually "crossover" to some intermediate realm.

This deserves special attention because it contradicts so many popular ideas about death and the afterlife. Ghost stories, near-death experiences interpreted as actual death, mediums claiming to channel the dead, all of these rest on a fundamental misunderstanding of what happens when we die.

As the text puts it: "At death the functional identity associated with the human personality is disrupted through the cessation of vital motion. Human personality, while transcending its constituent parts, is dependent on them for functional identity. The stoppage of life destroys the physical brain patterns for mind endowment, and the disruption of mind terminates mortal consciousness."

In other words, when your brain stops, you stop, at least as a conscious being. Your personality and soul survive, but they're preserved in a state of suspended animation. There's no "you" capable of experiencing anything until that consciousness "can subsequently reappear" when "a cosmic situation has been arranged which will permit the same human personality again to function in relationship with living energy."

That "cosmic situation" is resurrection. That "living energy" is your new morontia body.

This means, and I want to be absolutely clear about this, there are no ghosts. There cannot be ghosts, not in any traditional sense. When someone claims to see a departed loved one or experience a haunting, they're either experiencing psychological phenomena, encountering an entirely different type of being (perhaps midwayers or visiting morontia beings), or in rare cases, dealing with outright deception.

The human personality cannot function without a body of some kind to serve as its vehicle. Until you're given a morontia body on the mansion world, you simply cannot be conscious. There's no intermediate state where you exist as a disembodied presence.

I sometimes think of it this way: energy can neither be created nor destroyed, but it can change forms. At death, everything that constitutes your spiritual identity, your personality, your soul, your relationships with the Adjuster, all of this is preserved, like data stored in a cloud. Then, at resurrection, this preserved pattern is downloaded into a new operating system (your morontia form), and you boot back up as a conscious being.

The gap between these two events, regardless of its actual duration, is subjectively instantaneous to you.

The One Exception: Adjuster Fusion

There is one exception to everything I've just described, and it's worth mentioning even though it applies to relatively few individuals. In rare cases, someone achieves fusion with their Thought Adjuster during mortal life.

When this occurs, the usual pattern doesn't apply. The fused individual doesn't die in the normal sense. Instead, at the natural end of life (or sometimes even before), they simply disappear. The Thought Adjuster, now permanently united with the human soul and personality, transports the entire being directly to the mansion worlds, or sometimes beyond.

These fusion candidates don't experience unconsciousness, don't require resurrection, and don't wait for adjudication. They transition directly and consciously from material to morontia existence.

But let me be honest: this is exceptionally rare. I don't personally know anyone I would confidently identify as having achieved fusion during earthly life. It represents such an advanced level of spiritual attainment that it's essentially beyond the reach of most mortals on a world like ours.

So, while it's theoretically possible, I wouldn't spend much time worrying about whether you'll achieve it. For nearly all of us, the normal pathway, death, sleep, resurrection, is what awaits. And that's perfectly fine. It's the plan designed for evolutionary mortals, and it works beautifully.

Practical Implications for Life Now

Understanding these truths about death and survival should change how we live today. Let me suggest several practical implications.

First, we can release our fear of death. If we're sincerely committed to doing God's will and living according to our best understanding of truth, survival is essentially assured. The universe wants you to succeed. Mercy credits have been allocated.

Every provision has been made. Death is not an ending but a transition, and not even a subjectively long one.

Second, we should focus our spiritual efforts on reaching that third psychic circle. This isn't about earning salvation, that's already secured if we choose it. Rather, it's about being prepared for what comes next. The more spiritual progress we make here, the better positioned we'll be to begin our mansion world career with confidence and competence.

Third, we might want to think about those we love and encourage their spiritual development. It would be wonderful to wake up on the mansion worlds alongside your spouse, your children, your close friends, all of you ready to begin the adventure together. That requires helping each other grow spiritually now.

Fourth, we should accept that some mysteries remain mysteries. The revelators have told us as much as they're permitted to share, but gaps remain. We don't know everything about how resurrection works, what the adjudication process involves in detail, or what those first moments on the mansion world will feel like. That's okay. We don't need to know everything; we need to trust the process and the beings administering it.

Fifth, we might want to examine our beliefs about Jesus. If I'm right that acknowledging Michael is eventually non-negotiable for universe progression, it is better to settle that question now than to struggle with it later. The good news is that recognizing Jesus as Creator Son and sovereign doesn't require accepting all the theological baggage that's been added to Christianity. It simply means acknowledging reality: the being who created you loves you and has provided a path for your eternal career.

Conclusion

We stand at the threshold of understanding something profound, the mechanism by which mortal creatures like ourselves can become eternal beings, progressing from material existence through morontia realities toward eventual Paradise destiny.

The system is elegant in its simplicity and profound in its mercy. Every provision has been made for our success. Transitional classifications give borderline cases every opportunity. Mercy credits cover our inevitable failures. Multiple pathways to resurrection ensure no one is arbitrarily excluded. And at the heart of it all, the soul, that remarkable partnership between human will and divine presence, survives to carry our identity forward into eternity.

I find this vision deeply reassuring. We're not abandoned to figure everything out on our own. We're not judged by impossible standards. We're not cast aside for failing to achieve perfection in seventy or eighty short years on a confused and isolated planet.

Instead, we're given chance after chance, provided with help at every stage, and assured that if we genuinely want to continue, if we make that one undoubted, self-conscious, final choice, the universe will move heaven and earth (sometimes literally) to support our progression.

The question isn't whether God wants us to survive. The question is whether we want to survive and are willing to align ourselves with the divine purpose: the Fatherhood of God and the brotherhood of man.

In our next chapter, we'll continue examining Paper 112, moving deeper into the mechanics of personality survival and exploring what those early mansion world experiences might actually involve. We'll look at the educational systems waiting for us, the relationships we'll form with beings of other orders, and the gradual process by which we'll be transformed from material mortals into spiritual beings.

But for now, let these truths settle into your consciousness. You have a soul. It's growing even now as you read these words. It will survive your death. And it will carry you, "*you*," unmistakably yourself, into realms of experience we can barely imagine from our present vantage point.

The universe has bet on your success. The only question remaining is whether you'll bet on it too.

In the name of Michael, Jesus of Nazareth, our Creator Son and sovereign, may we all find the courage to make that final, undoubted choice and embark on the eternal adventure that awaits us.

Chapter 35: The Mystery of Personality Survival and Resurrection

When I first began studying Paper 112 of *The Urantia Book*, I thought I understood what happened at death. I was wrong. What I discovered instead was something far more complex, beautiful, and mysterious than I could have imagined, a process so intricate that even celestial beings don't fully comprehend all its mechanics.

Tonight, as we continue our exploration of personality survival, we're going to confront one of the most profound mysteries in the entire revelation: What happens to your personality between the moment of death and your awakening on the mansion worlds? The answer, frankly, surprises even those who compiled this information for us.

The Disruption of Consciousness

Let me start with something that might seem obvious but has deeper implications than we typically consider. At death, something specific happens to personality that doesn't happen to other aspects of our being. The functional identity associated with human personality is disrupted through the cessation of vital motion. In simpler terms, when your body stops working, your personality stops functioning.

This seems straightforward until you realize what it means. Your personality, that unique pattern of being that makes you *"you"*, is different from your Thought Adjuster, different from your soul, and different from the mind transcripts that record your life experiences. While these other elements can be preserved or transported independently, your personality requires something specific to function: it needs to be connected to a living, functioning form.

Human personality, while transcending its constituent parts, depends on them for functional identity. The stoppage of life destroys the physical brain patterns for mind endowment. The disruption of mind terminates mortal consciousness. Once that happens, consciousness cannot reappear until a cosmic situation has been arranged that permits the same human personality to function again in relationship with living energy.

Think about what this means. When you die, you don't drift off to some ethereal waiting room, conscious and aware. You lose consciousness because personality itself loses consciousness. Without a functioning mind and body, there's simply no way for the human personality to maintain awareness.

The Safeguarding of Identity

This raises an immediate question: If personality loses consciousness at death, how is it preserved? Who keeps track of who you are?

The answer involves multiple layers of cosmic insurance, if you will. During the transit of surviving mortals from the world of origin to the mansion worlds, whether they experience personality reassembly on the third period or ascend at the time of a group resurrection, the record of personality constitution is faithfully preserved by the archangels on their worlds of special activities.

Let me be clear about something important here: These beings are not the custodians of personality itself, as the guardian seraphim are of the soul. What the archangels maintain is the *record* of your personality, a complete transcript, a backup system for the entire universe. If something goes wrong during the resurrection process, if some aspect of your personality pattern fails to transmit correctly, the archangels have a perfect copy that can reconstruct your personality from the ground up.

The guardian seraphim, by contrast, are the custodians of your soul. When you wake up in the mansion world, it's actually the guardian seraphim who brings your soul back to you. Your soul, that morontia entity that has been growing throughout your mortal life, is carried by your celestial guardian through the transition.

But here's where it gets interesting, and where even the revelators admit their knowledge has limits.

The Mystery They Don't Fully Understand

As to the exact whereabouts of mortal personality during the time intervening between death and survival, they do not know.

I've read that sentence dozens of times, and it still stops me cold. The celestial beings who provided us with this revelation, beings with knowledge and perspective far beyond anything we can imagine, openly admit they don't know where personality goes between death and resurrection.

This isn't a failure of the revelation. It's actually one of its most honest moments. Rather than inventing an explanation or glossing over the mystery, they simply tell us: We preserve the records, we safeguard the soul, we maintain all the systems necessary for resurrection, but the personality itself? Its exact location or state during this interval? That remains a mystery.

Over the years, I've developed a theory about this, though I want to emphasize it's just that, a theory based on careful reading of the text and logical extrapolation. I believe the Thought Adjuster takes possession of the personality during this interval. Let me explain why this seems probable.

The Adjuster as Custodian

Later in this same paper, we're told something crucial: "The Adjuster is the eternal custodian of your ascending identity." Not just a guide, not just a spiritual presence, but the *custodian*, the keeper, the guardian of your ascending identity.

What is your ascending identity? It's your personality expressed through your universe career. It's the continuity of *you* as you progress from one level of existence to another.

The text goes even further: "Your monitor is the absolute assurance that you yourself and not another will occupy the morontia form created for your personality awakening." The Adjuster guarantees that the right personality gets reconnected to the right form. How could the Adjuster make such a guarantee unless it maintained some direct connection to or possession of that personality?

Think about it from another angle. The Adjuster has a profound interest in preserving your personality intact because it's this personality that the Adjuster will eventually fuse with. The entire purpose of the Adjuster's mission in your life is to achieve eternal union with your personality. Of course, the Adjuster would take charge of safeguarding it during the vulnerable transition period.

This also explains why the text emphasizes that "the Adjuster will be present at your personality reassembly to take up once more the role of Paradise guide to your surviving self." The Adjuster is there, actively participating in the reassembly process, not just showing up afterward.

So, while I can't prove it definitively, the pattern suggests that during that mysterious interval between death and resurrection, your personality rests in the keeping of your Thought Adjuster, the one being in all the universe with the most invested in your eternal survival.

The Three Prerequisites for Resurrection

When the time comes for your repersonalization, three essential elements must come together. Understanding these helps us appreciate just how complex and carefully orchestrated the resurrection process really is.

The Morontia Energy Pattern

First, they must fabricate a suitable form, a morontia energy pattern in which you, the new survivor, can make contact with non-spiritual reality and within which the morontia variant of the cosmic mind can be encircuited.

Let me break this down because it's easy to gloss over the significance. This isn't just building you a new body. It's creating an entirely new kind of energy pattern that can interface with a different order of reality. You're not returning to material existence, but you're not yet a full spiritual being either. You're morontia, something in between.

This new form has to be compatible with what they call "non-spiritual reality." The mansion worlds, while far more advanced than our material world, still have a kind of semi-material substance. There are lakes, mountains, structures, things you can interact with physically, even though they're made of morontia matter rather than the kind of matter we know here.

Your new form also needs to be connected to the cosmic mind, specifically, the morontia variant of it. On Earth, you're connected to the mortal mind circuit. When you wake up on the mansion worlds, you'll be connected to a higher circuit, one that gives you access to greater understanding and cosmic awareness. But that connection has to be established; it doesn't happen automatically.

The energy controllers on the morontia worlds are the ones who create these forms. Think of them as blank patterns, waiting to be activated and individualized. They're preparing the vessel that will house your returning consciousness.

The Return of the Adjuster

Second, your Thought Adjuster must return to the waiting morontia creature. The Adjuster brings with it your personality, or at least this is what I believe happens, for the reasons I've already explained.

The Adjuster's presence is absolutely crucial. Without the Adjuster, there's no continuity of identity. The Adjuster has been the witness to your entire mortal life, the keeper of your spiritual memories, the preserver of everything worth keeping from your earthly experience.

When the Adjuster returns and reconnects with your new morontia form, it brings not just your personality but also the capacity for that personality to recognize itself and others. This is why you'll know who you are when you wake up, why you'll recognize people from your past life, why there's continuity of consciousness even though your physical brain has long since returned to dust.

The Delivery of the Soul

Third, the seraphic custodian of the potentialities of the slumbering immortal soul must deliver that soul to the waiting morontia mind-body form.

Your soul has been sleeping, unconscious, unaware, held in sacred trust by your guardian angel. Throughout your entire mortal life, you were never consciously aware of your soul. It was being built by the Adjuster, growing through every spiritually significant choice you made, but it remained beneath the threshold of your material consciousness.

Now, at resurrection, your soul becomes your primary identity. When these numerous cosmic personalities bestow this morontia entity upon and in the awaiting morontia mind-body form, they're essentially transplanting your soul into its new home. Your soul, which was embryonic and unconscious during your earthly life, suddenly becomes fully active and aware.

This is the moment of repersonalization, the reassembly of memory, insight, and consciousness-identity. The energy manipulators provide the electrical charge that activates the system, and you're alive again. Just like that. All three elements come together in an instant, and suddenly you're awake in an entirely new order of existence.

A Special Case: Fusion on Earth

Now let me throw in a complication that I find fascinating. What happens if you fuse with your Adjuster before you die? Not everyone does this, but it's possible. Some individuals achieve such spiritual harmony with their indwelling spirit that fusion occurs while they're still alive on their home planet.

If you've already fused, then when you die, your personality, your soul, and the Adjuster are already one unified entity. You don't need the same kind of three-part reassembly. Instead, you're already integrated. What happens then is that this fused entity simply needs to be invested in a morontia form, and the energy controllers activate it. It's a simpler process in one sense, though still utterly beyond anything we can fully comprehend from our current perspective.

The biblical figures Enoch and Elijah apparently achieved this kind of fusion. They didn't experience death in the normal sense. Their fusion with their Adjusters allowed them to transition directly to the morontia state. They're perfect examples of what can happen when a mortal achieves complete harmony with the divine spirit within.

Jesus, of course, represents something entirely different. He resurrected himself. He needed no celestial assistance to transition from his material death to morontia existence, and later from morontia to full spiritual form. Only a Creator Son possesses this ability, and the mechanics of how it works remain a mystery known only to the Creator Sons themselves.

The Seizure of Consciousness

There's a particular phrase in the text that caught my attention and held it: "The fact of repersonalization consists in the seizure of the encircuited morontia phase of the newly segregated cosmic mind by the awakening human self."

Seizure. It's an interesting word choice, isn't it? When we hear "seizure," we might think of an epileptic seizure, something that happens suddenly and affects the entire brain simultaneously. I don't think that comparison is accidental.

The repersonalization of your being happens like a wave of awareness sweeping through your entire consciousness at once. It's not gradual. You don't slowly wake up, piece by piece. The personality, reconnected to its new morontia form and to the cosmic mind circuit, springs into awareness all at once, a sudden, complete restoration of consciousness.

This is important for understanding something else the text tells us: There are some individuals who don't immediately recognize themselves when they wake up on the mansion worlds. These are people who, for various reasons, don't achieve fusion with their Adjusters during their entire mansion world career. They're sometimes called "seizure" beings or "spirit seizure" beings.

When these individuals are resurrected, something different happens. The personality seizure, that sudden wave of awareness, doesn't trigger the same kind of immediate memory recognition. They wake up feeling like blank slates, with no immediate memory of who they were or what they experienced in their previous life.

This doesn't mean their memories are lost. The guardian seraphim has to work with them, rehearsing their life experiences, helping them gradually recover their sense of identity. Over time, as their guardian angel relates events from their mortal life, they begin to remember. It's like déjà vu, "Oh yes, I remember that now." But it's not the immediate, complete recognition that most survivors experience.

This makes the guardian seraphim's job considerably more difficult in these cases. How do you verify that the right personality is in the right body if that personality can't tell you who it is? The backup system maintained by the archangels becomes especially important in such situations.

The Unchanging Foundation

One of the most important concepts to grasp about personality is this: Human life consists of endless change in the factors of life, unified by the stability of unchanging personality.

Your personality never changes in its essential nature. The tendencies, the preferences, the fundamental pattern of how you respond to reality, these remain constant. If you loved chocolate before you died (to use a somewhat silly example), that preference would still be part of your personality pattern when you wake up. Not because you'd necessarily remember chocolate or want chocolate in the mansion worlds, but because the personality tendency that led you to prefer certain flavors would still be there, perhaps expressed in some new way.

This unchanging nature of personality is crucial because it provides continuity. Your soul is new, newly awakened to consciousness. Your body is entirely different. Your mind is connected to a higher circuit. Everything has changed except your personality, and that's what holds it all together.

At the same time, personality must be able to grow and develop, or it would stagnate and die. The text makes this clear: "The true reality of all selfhood (personality) is able to function responsively to universe conditions by virtue of the unceasing changing of its constituent parts; stagnation terminates in inevitable death."

This seems paradoxical at first. How can personality be unchanging and yet constantly changing? The answer lies in understanding the difference between the pattern and its expression. The fundamental pattern remains the same, but how that pattern responds, grows, and develops is constantly evolving. You're always recognizably yourself, yet you're also always becoming more than you were.

What Survives and What Doesn't

Not everything from your mortal life makes the transition to mansion world existence. The Thought Adjuster recalls and rehearses for you only those memories and experiences that are part of and essential to your universe career.

Much of your past life and its memories, having neither spiritual meaning nor morontia value, will perish with the material brain. The text calls this "one-time scaffolding", temporary structures that helped you bridge from one level to another but no longer serve any purpose once you've made the crossing.

I've thought a lot about what constitutes scaffolding versus what survives. Physical skills you learned that have no application in morontia existence, those are scaffolding. Memories of trauma or abuse that served no spiritual purpose, those might be scaffolding that mercifully falls away. Mundane details of daily life that held no cosmic significance, scaffolding.

But here's what never becomes scaffolding: personality relationships. The text is emphatic about this: "Personality and the relationships between personalities are never scaffolding; mortal memory of personality relationships has cosmic value and will persist."

On the mansion worlds, you will know and be known. More than that, you will remember and be remembered by your one-time associates in the short but intriguing life on Earth. Every meaningful connection you made, every relationship that had spiritual significance, every bond of love or friendship or family, these survive intact.

This is why it's so important to focus on relationships in this life. They're not temporary. They're not scaffolding. They're eternal realities that you're building now and will continue to develop throughout your universe career.

The Transformation Beyond Recognition

When you wake up on the mansion worlds of Jerusem, you will be so changed, the spiritual transformation will be so great, that if it weren't for your Thought Adjuster and your destiny guardian connecting your new life with your old life in the first world, you would at first have difficulty connecting the new morontia consciousness with the reviving memory of your previous identity.

Let me emphasize this: Even with the continuity provided by the Adjuster and the seraphim, there's still a period of adjustment. Your soul, that entity you never consciously experienced in your mortal life, is now awake and forms your primary identity. You have to learn to integrate this new aspect of yourself with the memories and personality patterns from your mortal existence.

Much of mortal life would at first seem like a vague and hazy dream. This is natural. You're looking back at material existence from a morontia perspective, and the difference in viewpoint is substantial. But time will clarify many mortal associations. The Adjuster will help you sort through what's important. The seraphim will provide context and detail. Gradually, the past and present will knit together into a coherent whole.

This is probably why someone who knew you in your mortal life will be present when you wake up. Having a familiar face there, a spouse, a friend, a family member, someone you loved and who loved you, helps anchor your personality. They can call you by name. They can remind you of who you were and help you understand who you're becoming.

And yes, they'll use your old name, the one you had on Earth. You won't receive your new, eternal soul name until you fuse with your Adjuster. Until then, you're still, well, you're still Gary or Jane or whoever you were. I joke about this sometimes, but it's actually a beautiful continuity. Your earth name carries forward until you achieve that final union that marks you as a perfected ascending mortal.

The Emerging Butterfly

There's an image used in the text that I find particularly beautiful: "Just as a butterfly emerges from the caterpillar stage, so will the true personalities of human beings emerge on the mansion worlds, flitting about on the planets of ascendant progression, for the first time revealed apart from their onetime enshroudment in the material flesh."

This is resurrection. Not a return to what you were, but an emergence into what you're becoming. The caterpillar doesn't become a better caterpillar. It becomes something entirely different while remaining, in some essential way, itself.

Your personality emerges on the mansion worlds for the first time revealed apart from the limitations of material flesh. What you truly are, what you've always been becoming, finally has a form adequate to express it. You're no longer limited by the heavy, slow-moving material body that could barely keep up with your spiritual aspirations.

The transition involves what they call "the continued evolution-elevation of the personality mechanism from the beginning mortal and material level of soul existence up to the final morontia level of spirit-soul liaison." This isn't a single transformation but a journey through 570 different levels of morontia existence. You'll continue to change, to grow, to become more yourself all the way up through the local universe and beyond.

Beauty Reflecting Reality

Here's something intriguing: In the morontia state, your outward form increasingly reflects your inner spiritual nature. Physical bodies here on Earth are somewhat responsive to personality character, but only to a limited degree. A good person might have an outwardly beautiful appearance, or they might not. There's only a loose connection between inner character and outer appearance.

In morontia life, that connection grows stronger. The more spiritually advanced you become, the more your form varies directly in accordance with the nature of your inner personality. On the spirit levels, those realms beyond even the morontia state, outward form and inner nature begin to approximate complete identification, growing more perfect with each higher spiritual level.

This means, quite literally, that the more beautiful you are inside, the more beautiful you become outside. Goodness, love, truth, these qualities don't just affect your character; they actually transform your appearance.

I sometimes wonder if there are mirrors on the mansion worlds. Maybe not at first, because such comparisons might still trigger the old material ego responses we're trying to transcend. But eventually, being able to see your own spiritual progress reflected in your form would be a powerful reminder of how far you've come.

The Undifferentiated Mind

There's one section from this paper that I deliberately saved for our next session because it deserves its own detailed treatment. It deals with what happens to the mortal intellect and how mind continuity is maintained through the resurrection process. The concepts there are complex enough that I don't want to rush through them tonight.

But I'll give you a preview: The mortal intellect as such perishes, it ceases to exist as a focalized universe entity. Yet the meanings and values of the mortal mind do not perish. Certain phases of mind continue in the surviving soul. Certain experiential values of the former human mind are held by the Adjuster. And there persist in the local universe the records of the human life as it was lived in the flesh.

How all these different aspects of mind preservation work together, how they contribute to your resurrected consciousness, that's what we'll explore next time.

Closing Reflections

I want to end this chapter by emphasizing something that might get lost in all the technical details about energy patterns, cosmic mind circuits, and seraphic custodianship: The resurrection process is an act of profound love and respect for your individuality.

Think about the sheer cosmic expense involved in preserving your identity through death. Multiple orders of beings, archangels, seraphim, Adjusters, energy manipulators, and countless others, coordinate their efforts to ensure that you, specifically and uniquely you, continue to exist. Nothing is left to chance. Every possible safeguard is in place. Backup systems have backup systems.

This isn't assembly-line production of generic souls. This is the careful, intentional, loving preservation of each individual personality, with all its quirks and tendencies and unique ways of responding to reality. The universe goes to extraordinary lengths to make sure that when you wake up on the mansion worlds, you're still yourself, changed, yes, but recognizably, authentically the same person who fell asleep in death.

The mystery of where personality goes during that interval between death and survival? Maybe we're not meant to know everything. Maybe some mysteries are better left as mysteries, at least for now. What we do know is enough: that we're held securely, that nothing essential is lost, that we will wake up and recognize ourselves and be recognized by those who love us.

That's more than enough to give us courage when facing our own mortality or grieving the death of loved ones. Death is not the end. It's not even really a pause. It's a transition, carefully managed and lovingly guided, from one form of existence to another.

In our next chapter, we'll explore those complex questions about mind continuity, how the mortal intellect relates to the morontia mind, what actually carries forward, and how all these different streams of consciousness merge into the unified being you'll become. Until then, I encourage you to sit with these concepts, to let them settle into your understanding, and perhaps to look at death, yours or anyone's, with new eyes.

In the next chapter, we'll examine the fate of the mortal intellect and explore how the Nebadon modification of the cosmic mind endowment transforms ascending mortals into beings capable of comprehending increasingly complex universal realities. We'll also discuss what happens to those experiential values that seem to exist in multiple places simultaneously, in the surviving soul, in the custody of the Adjuster, and in the records maintained throughout the local universe.

Chapter 36: The Morontia Mind and Soul Survival

Introduction: Understanding the Transition Beyond Mortal Life

As we continue our exploration of Paper 112 on personality survival, we arrive at what I consider one of the most important, and initially unsettling, revelations in *The Urantia Book*. This chapter addresses a question that has haunted humanity since consciousness first awakened: What happens to *us* when we die? Not just our bodies, but our minds, our memories, our very sense of self?

The answer the book provides may challenge your assumptions. It certainly challenged mine when I first encountered it back in 1973. Yet understanding this transition from mortal mind to morontia consciousness opens a window into the cosmic architecture of survival itself. More importantly, it reveals why the choices we make *now*, in this present moment of earthly existence, carry weight far beyond what most of us realize.

We're going to take our time with this material because it's dense, layered, and requires careful unpacking. I've hesitated many times over the years before presenting some of these concepts to study groups, knowing they can initially seem harsh or even frightening. But I've learned that truth, however challenging, ultimately liberates rather than constrains us.

The Morontia Mind: A Modified Cosmic Awareness

Let me start with a foundational concept that shapes everything else we'll discuss. When we awaken on the mansion worlds as morontia beings, we're endowed with what the book calls "a Nebadon modification of the cosmic-mind endowment of the Master Spirit of Orvonton."

Now, that's quite a mouthful, so let's break it down.

You may recall that there are seven Master Spirits, one for each of the seven superuniverses. Our Master Spirit is number seven, representing the combined influence of God the Father, God the Son, and God the Infinite Spirit. Each of these seven Master Spirits provides a unique version of the cosmic mind, a modification, if you will, of the universal mind emanating from the Infinite Spirit.

But here's where it gets interesting. Our local universe, Nebadon, governed by Christ Michael and our Creative Mother Spirit, has further modified this cosmic mind to suit the particular needs and developmental plan of beings created within this local universe. Think of it as a specialized operating system designed specifically for Nebadon's ascending mortals.

This matters because during our earthly lives, we function under the influence of the seven-adjutant mind-spirits. These are the thought currents of our local universe Mother Spirit, reaching down to animate and guide material beings. The first five, intuition, understanding, courage, knowledge, and counsel, we share with the higher animals. The sixth and seventh, worship and wisdom, make us distinctly human, capable of recognizing divinity and making moral choices.

But these adjutant circuits are superimposed upon us. We can't separate ourselves from them any more than animals can disconnect from the first five adjutants and remain alive. They're essentially the scaffolding of mortal consciousness.

The morontia mind is different. When we awaken on the first mansion world, we establish *direct contact* with the cosmic mind as modified by our Creative Mother Spirit. It's no longer a superimposition but an integrated connection. We've graduated, in a sense, from adjutant mind-ministry to cosmic mind-ministry, though still filtered through the Nebadon version of that cosmic awareness.

This direct connection remains our mental framework throughout all our morontia experiences, through all 570 progressive morontia bodies we'll inhabit across the seven mansion worlds, the constellation spheres, and the Salvington circuits. Only when we complete our local universe progression and transition from morontia being to first-stage spirit being do we plug directly into the cosmic mind of the Infinite Spirit, channeled through our superuniverse Master Spirit.

Jesus referred to this phenomenon in an interesting way. He spoke of the "seven dimensions of the universe," meaning that each superuniverse, influenced by its unique Master Spirit, represents a genuinely different dimension of experiential reality. We're experiencing one of those seven dimensions. No wonder we can't perceive everything, we haven't even fully grasped our own dimensional framework yet.

The Shocking Truth About Mortal Intellect

Now we come to the part I always approach with some trepidation. The book states it plainly: "The mortal intellect... has perished, has ceased to exist as a focalized universe entity."

Let me say that again, because it's important. Your mortal intellect, the thinking, reasoning, analyzing mind you're using right now to read these words, does not survive death. It perishes. It ceases to exist.

I remember the first time I truly absorbed that statement. It shook me. Everything I thought of as "me", my patterns of thought, my mental habits, my way of processing the world, all of that disappears when I die?

Yes. And no.

The resolution of this apparent paradox lies in understanding what *does* survive. The book is careful to specify: "The meanings and values of the mortal mind have not perished." Your mind as a *mechanism* dies, but the *content* of spiritual value within that mind continues. And it continues in a very specific place: your soul.

Think of it this way. Your material mind is like scaffolding around a building under construction. The scaffolding isn't the building itself, it's a temporary structure that allows the real structure to be built. When the building is complete (or complete enough for the next phase), the scaffolding comes down. It served its purpose.

Your soul is the building. Throughout your entire mortal life, your Thought Adjuster has been working with you to construct this soul out of every decision you make that has spiritual value, every moment you choose to align with truth, beauty, or goodness, every relationship that reflects divine love, every sacrifice made for higher purposes. All of this becomes incorporated into your soul as meanings and values.

The book puts it beautifully: "Certain phases of mind are continued in the surviving soul; certain experiential values of the former human mind are held by the Adjuster." So, you have a two-fold preservation system. Your soul contains the meaning-patterns of your mortal experience, and your Adjuster preserves experiential values. Additionally, there are records, living registrations maintained by various celestial beings, from your guardian seraphim to the Universal Censors who will eventually judge your worthiness for continued survival.

These records apparently persist even beyond the Supreme Being, which suggests that your experiential contribution feeds into the evolving deity of the Supreme itself. Your life *matters* cosmically, not just personally.

The Birth and Awakening of the Soul

Understanding what happens when you awaken on the mansion worlds requires grasping what your soul actually is. I've come to think of the soul as a vessel of storage during mortal life, a growing repository of spiritual experience, that becomes a *living entity* at resurrection.

When you die, if you're deemed worthy of survival, your Thought Adjuster departs with the essence-pattern of your personality and the transcript of your soul. Your guardian seraphim carries the soul itself, carefully preserved. And then comes the journey to the first mansion world.

What happens upon arrival depends significantly on your spiritual status.

For many of us, perhaps most, we'll awaken on the first mansion world *without* having yet fused with our Thought Adjuster. In this case, the resurrection process involves a delicate reassembly. The seraphim provides your soul, the physical controllers construct your new morontia body, and the Adjuster returns to reunite with this new configuration.

And here's where it gets fascinating. When your soul awakens in that new morontia body, you're essentially starting with what appears to be a blank slate. Remember, your old mind is gone. Your new consciousness is your *soul*, which has all the memories and values of your previous life encoded within it, but lacks the mental mechanism that previously interpreted those memories.

So, the first task of your celestial helpers, your seraphim, your Adjuster, your assigned guides, is to help kickstart your memory. They need to help you remember *who you were*. As you begin to recognize familiar faces, perhaps family members or friends who died before you, the memory patterns stored in your soul activate. It's like watching someone wake from amnesia as familiar contexts trigger cascading recognition.

The book says your soul "becomes active memory when the patterns thereof are energized by the returning Adjuster." Your Adjuster is essentially the ignition key that brings your soul memories online.

But you are, in a very real sense, a new being. You have continuity of identity through your personality and your soul, but you're operating on an entirely different mental platform. You're no longer limited by adjutant mind-circuits.

You're now functioning with morontia consciousness, plugged directly into the cosmic mind of Nebadon.

The Exception: Pre-Fusion During Transit

There's an exception to this process that I should mention, and it's a beautiful one. Sometimes, more often than you might expect, individuals earn fusion with their Thought Adjuster *during* the transit to the mansion worlds, between death and resurrection.

If this happens to you, your awakening experience is completely different. You don't need the memory-reactivation process because your Adjuster is already fused with your soul. The Adjuster *knows* everything about your previous life, and upon fusion, you have immediate access to that complete record. There's no adjustment period, no gradual rekindling of memory. You awaken fully conscious, fully yourself, ready to begin.

This is particularly common for individuals who achieved high levels of spiritual attainment during mortal life. If you've genuinely lived in close partnership with your Adjuster, consistently chosen to do the Father's will, and built substantial morontia mota (we'll discuss that shortly), you may very well fuse during transit.

I find this possibility deeply encouraging. It suggests that our spiritual work here and now directly impacts the nature of our resurrection experience. The closer we draw to our Adjuster now, the more seamless our transition becomes.

The Challenge of Spirit-Fused and Son-Fused Mortals

Not all ascending mortals are destined to fuse with their Thought Adjusters. Some will fuse instead with a fragment of the Infinite Spirit (Spirit-fusion) or the Eternal Son (Son-fusion). These individuals face a more challenging resurrection process.

You might wonder how someone can have a soul if they're not going to fuse with their Adjuster. The answer is that Adjusters are assigned to these individuals *on loan* during their mortal lives. The Adjuster still builds a soul with them, still preserves meanings and values. But because these individuals cannot achieve permanent fusion with the Adjuster, perhaps due to inherent intellectual limitations or other factors beyond their control, the Adjuster must eventually depart.

These are often individuals from earlier evolutionary periods, perhaps single-brained beings or those with severe cognitive limitations. On our planet, since the bestowal of the Spirit of Truth, such cases are probably rare. But they do exist, and the universe makes full provision for them.

When Spirit-fused or Son-fused mortals awaken on the mansion worlds, they face the challenge of memory reconstruction without their Thought Adjuster to activate those memories. Their seraphim must painstakingly review their entire life history, using the soul-records and transcripts, essentially teaching them who they were. It can take considerable time for these individuals to "re-explore and relearn, to recapture the memory consciousness of the meanings and values of a former existence."

Some people worry that this represents a disadvantage that will hamper them eternally. It doesn't. Once you're past the initial adjustment and your morontia education begins in earnest, these differences fade. Spirit-fused and Son-fused mortals go through the same training, develop the same capacities, and eventually reach the same spiritual heights as Adjuster-fused mortals. The path may start differently, but the destination remains glorious for all.

What does happen, though, is that Spirit-fused mortals typically remain in the superuniverse of their origin, while Son-fused mortals serve the local universe. Neither becomes a finaliter in the Corps of Mortal Finaliters, which is reserved for Adjuster-fused beings. But they have their own noble destinies of eternal service.

Building Morontia Mota Now

This brings us to a concept that has profound practical implications for our current lives: morontia mota.

Morontia mota is essentially cosmic wisdom, insight that transcends purely material or intellectual understanding and approaches spiritual comprehension. It's the currency of morontia existence, the mode of understanding we'll use throughout our morontia career. And here's the key point: *we can begin developing it now*.

The book tells us that when we awaken on the mansion worlds, our early conduct and progress will be guided largely by "the character patterns inherited from the human life and by the newly appearing action of morontia mota." In other words, who you are when you arrive on the first mansion world depends substantially on the morontia mota you've already cultivated during your earthly existence.

Think about the implications of this. Someone who has spent decades studying spiritual truth, making decisions aligned with the Father's will, choosing to see life from an increasingly cosmic perspective, that person has been building morontia mota. When they awaken on the mansion worlds, they have something to build from. They have a foundation.

Now contrast that with someone who has "muddled through life," as I sometimes put it, rarely making conscious spiritual decisions, living almost entirely for material concerns, never developing their inner life. When that person awakens on the first mansion world, they're nearly starting from scratch. They have minimal morontia mota to work with.

The book mentions "probationary nurseries" and "transitional spheres" for individuals who arrive with insufficient development. These aren't punishments, they're remedial programs, if you will. Special rehabilitation is designed to bring these individuals up to the minimum level needed to even begin mansion world progression.

I don't say this to frighten anyone or to suggest that only the spiritually elite make it through. Far from it. The universe is extraordinarily patient and generous with its ascending children. But I do want to emphasize the practical advantage of spiritual development *now*. Every truth you embrace, every act of love you perform, every moral decision you make is building your morontia foundation.

And this doesn't require perfection. It requires sincerity and effort. I've been studying this revelation since 1973, over fifty years now, and I still discover new insights almost daily. If you stick yourself in spiritual truth for decades, you absorb it. You can't help but change. As I sometimes joke with my students, if you stick yourself in mud for twenty years, you're going to look like mud when you get out. Stick yourself in spirituality for twenty years, and you're going to look like spirituality.

The Role of Relationships and Communication

One aspect of building morontia mota that doesn't get enough attention, in my view, concerns our earthly relationships. The book indicates that when we awaken on the mansion worlds, we may recognize loved ones who've preceded us. But the *quality* of that recognition, the depth of continued relationship, depends on what we built together during mortal life.

If your marriage consisted primarily of practical arrangements, coordinating schedules, managing finances, raising children, but rarely if ever touched on spiritual realities, then what do you have to build on when you meet again on the mansion worlds? You'll recognize each other, certainly. You'll remember the relationship. But the foundation for continued spiritual partnership may be thin.

On the other hand, if you and your spouse have spent years discussing spiritual truths, sharing your inner lives, exploring cosmic meanings together, you've built something substantial. When you reunite on the mansion worlds, you have a rich tapestry of shared spiritual experience to continue weaving.

This applies equally to friendships, parent-child relationships, siblings, any meaningful connection in our lives. I often encourage people not to be afraid of discussing spiritual matters with those close to them. Yes, it requires vulnerability. Yes, it can feel awkward at first if you're not accustomed to it. But the rewards, both now and eternally, are immeasurable.

Think of it in terms of Jesus and his apostles. There was nothing the apostles couldn't ask Jesus about. He created an atmosphere of complete openness, where questions were welcomed and discussions flowed freely. The limitation wasn't Jesus's willingness to share, it was the apostles' capacity to understand. He worked right at the edge of their comprehension, always inviting them deeper.

We can create that same atmosphere in our relationships. We can choose to share our spiritual journey, our struggles and insights, our questions and discoveries. In doing so, we're not only enriching our present lives but building eternal bonds.

The Seven Psychic Circles

The book mentions "the seven circles of pre-morontia attainment," referring to levels of spiritual-intellectual achievement that ascending mortals ideally complete before physical death. These psychic circles represent progressive mastery of the relationship between your material mind, your evolving soul, and your indwelling Adjuster.

The seventh circle is achieved when you first make a moral decision and receive your Thought Adjuster, usually around age five or six. From there, progress through the circles represents increasingly effective cooperation with your Adjuster, growing dominance of spirit over matter, and expanding cosmic awareness.

Reaching the first circle doesn't guarantee Adjuster fusion during mortal life, that's rare, but it does indicate a high level of spiritual attainment. More importantly for most of us, consistent progress through these circles means we're building the morontia mota that will serve us so well upon resurrection.

The book encourages us to complete all seven circles before we die, if possible. Each circle traversed makes our transition smoother and our early mansion world experience more productive. Those who reach the third circle or higher often move rapidly through the early mansion worlds, being promoted to higher levels every ten days until they reach the sphere appropriate to their development.

Here's how that works. Even if you're advanced enough to start on, say, the fifth mansion world, you still begin on the first. But after ten days, you're transported (by seraphim, naturally) to the second world. Another ten days, you move to the third. And so on, until you reach your actual level.

Each time you're promoted, the physical controllers adjust your morontia body to match the requirements of the new sphere. Think of it as a "spa treatment," as one of my students jokingly called it. You'd become quite the veteran of seraphic transport.

But even advanced souls who rapidly progress through the initial worlds must eventually return to experience each level as a teacher. This ensures you gain the full experiential value of every mansion world. The universe wastes nothing; every experience serves a purpose.

Creature Volition and the Will of God

Before we move forward, I want to clarify a concept that runs throughout this entire discussion: creature volition.

When I first encountered this term decades ago, I had to look it up. Volition simply means *will*, the capacity to make choices. Creature volition is our will, our choosing capacity as created beings.

The book makes a profound statement early on: the volition of God initiates everything. The entire universe exists because God *wills* it to exist. If the Father's volition were withdrawn for even an instant, all reality would cease. We truly do live and move and have our being within the divine will.

But within that overarching divine volition, we have our own volition. And here's the mystery: God's will cannot operate in our lives without our willingness. Our volition must align with divine volition for the Father's purposes to unfold through us.

This is why I constantly emphasize the importance of choosing to do God's will. It's not that God can't act without us, but that the Father has chosen to work *through* willing cooperation rather than by override. When we volitionally decide to seek and do the Father's will, we become channels for divine action in the world.

Think of it as a step-down transformer. The full force of divine will would overwhelm finite creatures. But when we willingly align our volition with God's volition, we become appropriate vessels for precisely calibrated expressions of that will in our sphere of influence.

This has direct bearing on our soul development. Every time we choose God's way over our own preferences, we're not only doing the Father's will, we're building soul substance. We're creating meanings and values that will survive death. Conversely, when we persistently choose our own will in opposition to divine leading, we're essentially wasting time. We're not building anything of eternal value.

The universe is extraordinarily patient with us in this learning process. But the reality remains: we're here to learn to align our will with God's will. The sooner we embrace that purpose, the more productive our mortal life becomes.

The Continuity of Character

One of the more comforting aspects of the survival plan appears in this statement: "The surviving personality is in great measure guided by the character patterns inherited from the human life and by the newly appearing action of morontia mota."

Notice that word *character*. Not beliefs, not accomplishments, not status or wealth or even intelligence. Character, the settled patterns of how you respond to life, how you treat others, how you face challenges, what you value.

Character is what you've become through countless choices over time. It's the accumulated weight of your decisions, crystallized into relatively stable patterns. And this character *persists*. It provides continuity between who you were and who you're becoming.

This makes sense when you think about it. If everything about you disappeared at death except some abstract list of "spiritual values," you wouldn't really be *you* anymore. But character, that's the essence of your unique personhood, the distinctive flavor of your being.

Of course, character continues to evolve on the mansion worlds. Many of us arrive with character flaws that need extensive work. That's precisely what much of mansion world training addresses. But your character provides the starting point, the raw material that morontia education will refine and transform.

I find this reassuring. It means we don't have to achieve perfection before death to be "acceptable." We need to have developed enough character, enough genuine goodness, enough truth-seeking, enough love, to provide a foundation. The universe will work with whatever we've authentically built, however imperfect.

The Adjustment Period

For those of us who awaken on the mansion worlds without having achieved fusion during transit, there's an adjustment period that deserves attention. The book mentions that our new morontia soul "does not retain self-consciousness without the Adjuster."

This is a sobering thought. Your soul, separated from your Thought Adjuster, has no consciousness of its own. It's like a computer without power, all the data is there, perfectly preserved, but nothing is active. Only when the Adjuster returns and reunites with your soul does consciousness reboot.

This creates the interesting situation I described earlier, where you awaken in what feels like a blank state. You're conscious, but you don't immediately know *who* you are. You possess all the memories, but they're not yet accessible. It takes the combined efforts of your Adjuster, your seraphim, and your other helpers to reactivate those memory patterns.

The book describes this process beautifully: your soul's character "becomes active memory when the patterns thereof are energized by the returning Adjuster." It's not instantaneous, though from your subjective experience it might feel rapid. As soon as you begin recognizing familiar faces or places, the memory cascade begins.

I imagine it's something like the experience of waking from a deep sleep in an unfamiliar place. For a moment, you don't know where you are. Then context clues trigger recognition, and everything snaps into focus. Except in this case, you're reconstructing not just your location but your entire identity.

The text notes that for Spirit-fused and Son-fused mortals, this reconstruction takes "considerable time" because they don't have their Thought Adjuster to catalyze the process. For Adjuster-fused mortals (or those fusing during transit), the restoration of memory consciousness happens much more quickly.

The Persistence of Memory

A question that naturally arises: If my mortal mind perishes, and if my consciousness requires reconstruction, what guarantees I'm really "me" and not just a copy?

The book's answer centers on memory. "The persistence of memory is proof of the retention of the identity of original selfhood; it is essential to complete self-consciousness of personality continuity and expansion."

Your memories, not all of them, but those with spiritual significance, are meticulously preserved. They persist in three places: in your soul, in your Adjuster's keeping, and in the records maintained by celestial beings. When these memory patterns are reactivated in your new morontia consciousness, you have direct experiential continuity with your mortal life.

This isn't theoretical to you when it happens. You don't wake up thinking, "I wonder if I'm really Roger Paul (myself), or just a copy of him." You wake up *knowing* you're "you" because you remember being you. The memories are yours, not implanted. They carry the subjective quality of lived experience.

The book makes an important distinction, though. Without the Adjuster, "it requires considerable time for the mortal survivor to re-explore and relearn, to recapture the memory consciousness of the meanings and values of a former existence." This suggests memory reconstruction isn't perfect or instantaneous. It's a process of gradual recovery and integration.

But the essence of your identity, your selfhood, your personality, never wavers. Your personality, that unique pattern bestowed by the Universal Father himself, provides unbroken continuity. It's the changeless constant that unifies all your changing experiences, from mortal birth through eternal destiny.

Practical Implications for Our Lives Today

Let me bring all this cosmic philosophy back to earth for a moment. Understanding the survival mechanism has profound implications for how we live *now*.

First, it clarifies what truly matters. If your mortal intellect perishes but your spiritual values survive, then obviously developing those values should be your highest priority. Accumulating mere knowledge for its own sake, clever arguments, impressive credentials, none of that transfers. What transfers is wisdom, love, truth-seeking, moral courage, compassionate service, and genuine spiritual insight.

Second, it emphasizes the importance of relationships. The memories that survive are those with spiritual content. A relationship based purely on material conveniences will leave you with very little to carry forward. But a relationship enriched by shared spiritual journey, mutual growth, and genuine love becomes part of your eternal treasure.

Third, it should motivate us to cooperate consciously with our Thought Adjusters. Every moment we spend in genuine prayer, meditation, worship, or service provides the Adjuster with material for soul-building. We're literally constructing our future selves through our present choices.

Fourth, it removes any excuse for spiritual laziness. You can't coast through mortal life assuming everything will be sorted out on the mansion worlds. Yes, the universe provides remedial help for those who arrive unprepared. But why handicap yourself? Why not arrive on the first mansion world with a rich soul, developed morontia mota, and strong character patterns that will launch you immediately into productive growth?

Finally, it should liberate us from excessive concern about material matters. I'm not suggesting we become irresponsible about practical affairs. We live in a material world, and we have legitimate material obligations. But we can hold these concerns lightly, knowing they're temporary scaffolding, not the permanent structure.

The Completion of Local Universe Progression

Before we close this chapter, I want to touch briefly on what happens at the *end* of our morontia career, hundreds or thousands of years from now.

Throughout our journey through 570 progressive morontia stages, from the first mansion world through the constellation training spheres to the circuits of Salvington, our local universe headquarters, we remain plugged into the Nebadon modification of the cosmic mind, provided by our Creative Mother Spirit.

But when we finally complete our local universe training, when we've absorbed all the experiences and wisdom this sector of creation can provide, we undergo our final morontia transformation. We become first-stage spirit beings.

At that moment, our mental framework shifts dramatically. We're no longer connected to the local universe Mother Spirit's version of the cosmic mind. Instead, we connect directly to the cosmic mind of Orvonton, our superuniverse, channeled through our Master Spirit.

This must be an extraordinary transition, though the book doesn't describe the subjective experience. Suddenly, you're perceiving reality through a much wider lens. You're thinking with the mind-currents of an entire superuniverse rather than just a single local universe.

And your journey is just beginning. From there, you proceed inward through the superuniverse, eventually reaching Havona and ultimately Paradise itself. Each stage brings new revelations, new capacities, new depths of understanding.

But all of it, every single step, builds on the foundation you're laying right now, today, in this material life. The person you're becoming in this moment is the person who will awaken on the mansion worlds, who will progress through the morontia spheres, who will eventually stand before the Universal Father on Paradise itself.

Conclusion: The Privilege of Conscious Cooperation

As I reflect on everything we've covered in this chapter, I'm struck by the extraordinary privilege we've been given. We're not passive recipients of salvation. We're not simply "saved" and that's the end of it. Rather, we're invited into conscious, willing cooperation with the divine plan of progressive perfection-attainment.

Your Thought Adjuster is building your soul *with* you, not despite you. The quality of that soul depends significantly on your choices, your values, your willingness to seek and do the Father's will. This is both sobering and exhilarating.

Yes, your mortal mind will perish. That can sound frightening at first. But what it really means is that everything temporary falls away, and only what's eternally real remains. The scaffolding comes down, the building stands. And that building, your soul, your character, your morontia mota, is something you're constructing every day through ten thousand seemingly small decisions.

I began this chapter by acknowledging that I've hesitated over the years before presenting this material, knowing it can initially seem harsh. But I've come to see it as profoundly hopeful. It tells us that our lives have genuine significance, that our choices truly matter, and that the universe provides generous support for every sincere seeker.

In our next chapter, we'll explore the actual mechanism of Adjuster fusion, what it means, how it happens, and why it represents the most crucial transition in our entire eternal career. We'll discover why the fusion of human will with divine presence is the foundation of all that follows.

For now, I encourage you to sit with the material we've covered. Let it challenge you, perhaps even disturb you a bit. But also let it inspire you. You're not just marking time until death. You're building your eternal self, one choice at a time. And the more intentionally you approach that process, the richer your resurrection will be.

The mansion worlds await. What will you bring with you when you arrive?

Chapter 37: The Divine Partnership - Understanding Thought Adjuster Fusion

When I began teaching *The Urantia Book* decades ago, I quickly realized that no topic captures both the mystery and the promise of our eternal destiny quite like Thought Adjuster fusion. It's the moment, or perhaps more accurately, the *process*, where everything we've been studying comes together in the most literal sense imaginable. Two separate identities, one divine and one human, become eternally one.

Tonight, as we continue our study of Paper 112 on personality survival, we're diving into Section 7, which focuses specifically on what happens when a mortal creature fuses with their indwelling fragment of God. I've taught this material many times over the years, but I confess it never loses its capacity to inspire awe. We're talking about the universe's most intimate partnership, the blending of the highest and the lowest, the eternal and the temporal, Creator and creature.

If you're new to these concepts, don't worry. I'll walk you through this carefully. And if you've been studying with us for a while, I think you'll find that revisiting this material brings new insights each time. The beauty of *The Urantia Book* is that it reveals itself in layers, what seems clear on first reading often opens up into profound new territory when we come back to it with fresh eyes.

The Transformation: From Potential to Actual

Let me start by reading directly from the text, because the opening statement of Section 7 sets the stage for everything that follows:

"Thought Adjuster fusion imparts eternal actualities to personality which were previously only potential."

Now, that might sound abstract at first, so let me break it down. During your human life, the Thought Adjuster, that fragment of the Father dwelling within you, is constantly at work. Every experience you have that possesses spiritual value, every decision you make that aligns with divine truth, beauty, or goodness, the Adjuster takes and creates a spiritual counterpart. This spiritual counterpart becomes part of your soul.

I often describe the soul as a sleeping embryo. It's real, it's growing, but it's not yet *you* in the fullest sense. When you go to sleep in natural death and eventually awaken on the first mansion world, it's this soul that wakes up. Your old material body is gone forever, but you, the essential *"you"*, continues because the Thought Adjuster has been faithfully building your morontia identity all along.

Here's what's remarkable: all those spiritual experiences the Adjuster stored in your soul were *potentials*. They existed, yes, but they hadn't yet become the lived reality of your consciousness. When you awaken on the mansion world, those potentials transform into *actualities*. You don't just possess those spiritual experiences theoretically anymore, you *are* those experiences. Your soul becomes the active, conscious you, equipped with all the spiritual growth you achieved during your mortal life.

The text goes on to list several specific endowments that fusion brings. Let me walk through these one by one, because each deserves our attention.

The Endowments of Fusion, Fixation of Divinity Quality

First, fusion brings what the book calls "fixation of divinity quality." What does that mean? Simply put, when you fuse with your Thought Adjuster, the divine nature of that God fragment becomes permanently fixed within you. You become, in a very real sense, a divine being, a true son or daughter of God, not just by declaration but by actual transformation.

Think about what this means. The Thought Adjuster is a fragment of the Universal Father himself, a piece of absolute deity. When that fragment fuses with you, you don't just receive divine approval or blessing, you become infused with actual divinity. From that moment forward, you are part divine, part experiential creature. This is what makes you immortal, what qualifies you to stand eventually before the Paradise Father, what ensures you can never be separated from God again.

Past Eternity Experience and Memory

Second, fusion grants you access to "past eternity experience and memory." This fascinates me every time I think about it. Your Thought Adjuster didn't just spring into existence when you were born. That divine fragment has a history, an existence that stretches back into eternity past. And when you fuse, all that memory becomes potentially available to you.

Now, the Adjuster doesn't dump all of this on you at once, that would be overwhelming, to say the least. But as you progress through the mansion worlds and beyond, as you grow in capacity and understanding, the Adjuster gradually reveals more and more of this eternal memory to you. You begin to understand perspectives that no merely human mind could grasp. You gain wisdom that spans ages before your planet even existed.

Immortality

Third, and perhaps most obviously, fusion grants immortality. But let me be clear about something that many people misunderstand: surviving death and waking up on the mansion world does *not* make you immortal. You're still a morontia being at that point, still in a transitional state. You could theoretically still rebel, still choose to reject God's plan (though this becomes increasingly unlikely as you progress).

True immortality comes only with fusion. Once you fuse with your Thought Adjuster, you become genuinely immortal. Why? Because you've become inseparably one with a fragment of eternal deity. God cannot die, and once God is fused with you, neither can you. This is forever. This is absolute. No event in time or eternity can undo it.

I want you to really grasp this: there has never been a single recorded instance of a fused mortal rebelling against the celestial government. Not one. Not during the Lucifer Rebellion, not ever. Why? Because once you're fused, you're literally part God. And God doesn't rebel against himself, hat would be absurd, almost like spiritual suicide. The very nature of fusion makes rebellion impossible.

A Phase of Qualified Potential Absoluteness

Finally, the text mentions "a phase of qualified potential absoluteness." Now that's a mouthful, isn't it? Let me see if I can make this clearer.

We know from earlier studies that God has seven absolutes. There's the Universal Father, the Eternal Son, the Infinite Spirit, and Paradise, those are four. The other three are the Deity Absolute, the Universal Absolute, and the Unqualified Absolute. These last three are particularly involved in the creation and evolution of the physical universes, especially the outer space levels that are currently forming.

When you fuse with a fragment of the Father, you gain a connection, however remote and potential, to all seven of these absolutes. You become qualified to participate in the absolute levels of reality that will emerge in the distant future. Ages and ages from now, when we finaliters are serving in the outer space universes, we'll be part of the experiential unfoldment of absolute deity. That potential begins with fusion.

I know that sounds abstract, maybe even incomprehensible. But here's what I want you to take away: because you carry a fragment of the Father, you're qualified for *everything* God has planned, all the way out into eternity future. There's no limit to your potential growth, no ceiling on your cosmic career. Fusion opens literally infinite possibilities.

When Does Fusion Occur?

One of the most common questions I get is: "When exactly does fusion happen?" And the answer surprises many people: it varies. It can happen at several different points in your ascension career.

The text tells us that fusion "is usually effected while the ascender is resident within his local system." In most cases, that means somewhere around the fifth mansion world. By that point, you've typically removed what the book colorfully calls "the marks of the beast", the remnants of your animal origin, the lingering effects of barbarism and selfishness. You've made sufficient spiritual progress that fusion becomes possible.

But that's just the average. Fusion can actually occur much earlier or, in rare cases, much later.

Fusion at Death

Some people reach such an advanced spiritual state during their mortal lives that they're ready to fuse essentially at the moment of death. They've already progressed to at least the third psychic circle, meaning they're definitely going to survive and continue to the mansion worlds. But the Ancients of Days, who oversee these matters, can determine that nothing is really holding this person back from fusion except their physical body.

When such a person dies naturally and their soul awakens on the mansion world, they immediately fuse. They wake up not just as a surviving mortal, but as a fused son or daughter of God. They receive their new name right then and there, on the very first mansion world. Can you imagine that? Going to sleep in death and waking up already fused, already immortal, already a permanent citizen of the universe?

Delayed Fusion

On the other hand, fusion can sometimes be delayed far beyond the mansion worlds. The text mentions it might not occur until you reach the constellation level, or in special cases, not until you arrive at Salvington, the headquarters of our local universe.

Now, you might wonder: why would anyone go that long without fusing? What possible reason could there be?

I can think of a few scenarios. Consider the Caligastia One Hundred, those volunteers who came to Urantia hundreds of thousands of years ago to help develop civilization. They couldn't be fused beings because their mission required them to remain on Urantia for an extended period. Fused beings have different requirements and limitations.

Or imagine you're an Adam and Eve who successfully completes your mission on a planet, bringing it all the way to light and life. When your work is done, they give you a Thought Adjuster and you proceed to the mansion worlds. But because of your extensive experience and advanced standing, they might have special projects for you, responsibilities that require you to remain in an unfused state for a time. You'd have the option, presumably, to decline and fuse immediately, but you might also choose to delay fusion in order to serve in ways that would otherwise be impossible.

Here's the critical point, though: you *cannot* leave the local universe without being fused. You must be at least a first-stage spirit being to proceed to the superuniverse, and you cannot become a spirit being without fusing with your Adjuster. So fusion might be delayed, but it cannot be avoided if you want to continue your Paradise ascent.

The Mystery of Identity: Who Are We After Fusion?

One of the most profound passages in this section asks a direct question:

"Has the triumphant Adjuster won personality by the magnificent service to humanity, or has the valiant human acquired immortality through sincere efforts to achieve Adjuster likeness?"

In other words, who won? Did the Adjuster triumph over the human, molding you into a divine being? Or did the human triumph, ascending to become like God through persistent effort?

The answer is beautiful in its simplicity: *neither*. It's not a competition, not a conquest. It's a partnership, a true collaboration. Together, and only together, you and your Adjuster have achieved something neither could accomplish alone. You've created a new being, a unique order of ascending personality, one who combines finite experience with divine nature in a way that has never existed before.

I like to think of it as the ultimate marriage. When a man and woman truly become one in a successful marriage, you can't really separate their achievements anymore. They think together, decide together, work together. The boundaries between "mine" and "yours" fade away into "ours." That's what happens in fusion, but at an even more profound level. Your will and God's will become one will. Your mind and the Adjuster's mind become one mind. You still retain your unique personality, that gift from the Father that defines you, but the consciousness, the identity, the very being you are becomes unified.

The text puts it powerfully: "This extraordinary partnership is one of the most engrossing and amazing of all the cosmic phenomena of this universe age."

The Habit of God

Let me share something I've been teaching for years, a concept I call "the habit of God." It connects directly to how fusion becomes possible.

In our material lives, we're constantly reacting to our environment, aren't we? Something happens, and we respond. Someone treats us kindly, we feel gratitude. Someone wrongs us, we feel anger. Our days are filled with reactions based on our habitual patterns of thinking and responding.

What I've observed in studying these papers, and in trying to live them, is that spiritual growth involves developing a new kind of habit. Instead of reacting based on fear, pride, self-interest, or any of the other animal-origin impulses, we can train ourselves to pause and ask: "What is God's will in this situation? What would love do here? What choice aligns with truth, beauty, and goodness?"

At first, this requires real effort. It's not natural to us because we've spent years, maybe decades, reinforcing other patterns. But like any habit, the more you practice it, the more automatic it becomes. Eventually, and this is what I mean by the habit of God, choosing divine will becomes your default response. You don't have to wrestle with yourself anymore, don't have to fight against selfish impulses. God's will flows through you naturally because you've made it your will.

When you reach this point, fusion becomes inevitable. Your will and the Adjuster's will have already become one in practice. The formal fusion event simply confirms and eternalizes what has already happened spiritually. There's no more chaos, no more inner conflict. You've found that remarkable freedom that comes from complete alignment with divine purpose.

The Registry of Ascendington

Here's a fascinating detail that reveals how unique fused mortals are in the cosmic scheme: when you fuse with your Adjuster, your number is stricken from the records of the superuniverse and from Divinington.

Now, Divinington is the headquarters sphere for all Thought Adjusters. Every Adjuster has a registry there, a record of their existence and service. But when an Adjuster fuses with a mortal, something remarkable happens, that registry gets removed from Divinington.

Why? Because the fused being is no longer under Divinington's jurisdiction. You're now an ascending mortal, and your headquarters becomes Ascendington, that special sphere reserved for those who have achieved fusion. The Adjuster, for all practical purposes, is no longer a separate Adjuster. It's become part of you, or perhaps more accurately, you've become part of each other.

The text admits that nobody knows for sure what happens to the Adjuster's registry. The author surmises that it gets transferred to the secret circles of the inner courts of Grandfanda, the first ascender, who serves as the acting head of the Corps of the Finality. But that's speculation. What we know for certain is this: fusion creates something so new, so unique, that the old categories don't apply anymore.

You're not an Adjuster. You're not merely a mortal. You're a fused being, a cosmic original, a partnership of time and eternity that has never existed in quite that form before.

The Journey Ahead: Standing Before Christ Michael

The text makes clear that eventually, after you've progressed through all the mansion worlds and all the necessary training spheres, you'll stand before Christ Michael, the Creator Son of our local universe, whom we knew on Earth as Jesus of Nazareth.

Imagine that moment. You're no longer the struggling mortal who died on Earth. You've been transformed into a morontia being, you've fused with your Adjuster, you've grown in wisdom and spiritual stature. And now you stand before the very being who created this entire universe, the one who lived among us as a man, who showed us what God is like.

At the hand of this Creator Son, at the hand of Jesus himself, you'll be granted credentials. These aren't just symbolic. They're your official authorization to leave the local universe and proceed to the superuniverse. You've graduated, in a sense. You're ready for larger adventures, for the next stage of your eternal journey.

But this happens only after you've become a full-fledged first-stage spirit being. And you cannot become a spirit being without first fusing with your Adjuster. Everything builds on everything else. The sequence matters. The progression is real.

The At-onement Authorization

I love this term that appears in the text: "the at-onement authorization." Not *atonement* in the theological sense of paying for sin, but *at-onement*, being at one with your Adjuster, unified, inseparable.

When the mandates of the superuniverse pronounce that your human nature has made a final and irrevocable choice for the eternal career, when fusion has occurred, you receive this at-onement authorization. It's official recognition that you and your Adjuster are now eternally one, that nothing in time or eternity can ever separate you again.

This authorization serves as your clearance to eventually leave the local universe and proceed to Uversa, the headquarters of our superuniverse. From there, in the distant future, you'll begin the long flight to Havona and eventually Paradise itself. But it all starts with that at-onement, that cosmic marriage of mortal and divine.

Our Destiny: Administrators of Outer Space

The chapter concludes with a vision of the future that frankly takes my breath away every time I read it. After we finaliters complete our training and stand before the Universal Father on Paradise, after we've traversed all seven circuits of Havona and experienced everything the present universe has to offer, what then?

The text suggests that we're destined to serve as administrators in the outer space levels, those vast galaxies now being organized far beyond the periphery of the seven superuniverses. And this makes perfect sense when you think about it.

Consider what a fused mortal represents: we combine the lowest form of intelligent life capable of comprehending the Universal Father with the highest manifestation of the essence of the First Source and Center. We're simultaneously creatures and creators, finite and infinite, experiential and divine. We understand struggle because we've lived it. We understand perfection because we've fused with it.

Who better to administer future universes than beings who embody both extremes? Who better to understand and sympathize with evolving creatures than those who once were evolving creatures themselves? Who better to represent divine administration than those who carry actual fragments of God within their very beings?

The text describes us as future "superb rulers, matchless administrators, and understanding and sympathetic directors." That's not arrogance, it's simply acknowledging what we'll have become through this long process of experiential growth combined with divine transformation.

When I teach the History of Urantia papers, I'm always struck by the timescales involved. It takes hundreds of millions of years for a planet to evolve to the point where life can even be implanted. The outer space universes are vast almost beyond comprehension. We have, quite literally, eternity ahead of us. There's no rush. The adventure has only begun.

The Cosmic Significance: Children of the Supreme

Throughout this chapter, we're reminded that fused mortals are the experiential children of the Supreme Being. Now, that might sound abstract but let me connect it to what I've been teaching about God's growth.

The Universal Father is infinite, absolute, perfect, but in a sense, he's also experientially limited. God cannot personally experience what it's like to be imperfect, to struggle, to grow from ignorance to wisdom, from selfishness to love. That's where we come in.

Every experience you have, every choice you make, every bit of spiritual growth you achieve, all of this becomes part of the experiential growth of the Supreme Being. The Supreme is God-in-time, God-in-evolution, God-growing-through-his-creatures. And when you fuse with your Adjuster, your entire experiential history becomes permanently and eternally part of the Supreme's nature.

So we're not just individual beings pursuing our own salvation. We're participants in something vastly larger, the experiential growth of God himself. The Supreme cannot fully emerge, cannot complete his evolution, without us. Every fused mortal adds something unique and irreplaceable to the Supreme's nature.

This is why we're qualified to serve in the outer space levels. We're not just representatives of ourselves or even of humanity. We're representatives of the Supreme Being's experiential growth. We carry within us both divine nature (from our Adjuster) and evolutionary experience (from our mortal origins). We're living bridges between the perfect and the imperfect, between the infinite and the finite.

From Dust to Divinity

Let me conclude with what I think is one of the most moving passages in this entire section:

"It is true you mortals are of earthly, animal origin; your frame is indeed dust. But if you actually will, if you really desire, surely the heritage of the ages is yours, and you shall someday serve throughout the universes in all true capacity, Children of the Supreme God of experience and divine sons of the Paradise Father of all personalities."

Think about where we start: creatures of dust, evolved from animal origins on a small planet in a vast universe. We're born in ignorance, selfishness, and confusion. We spend our early years figuring out basic things like walking and talking. We struggle with pride, fear, anger, lust, all the marks of our animal heritage.

And yet, if we *will*, if we truly *desire*, we can become divine sons and daughters of the Paradise Father. Not symbolically, not metaphorically, actually, literally, eternally. The heritage of the ages becomes ours. Immortality becomes our possession. The entire universe becomes our home, our playground, our field of service.

That's the promise of Adjuster fusion. That's what this whole magnificent process is about. Two separate beings, one divine, one mortal, become eternally one. And in that fusion, something emerges that has never existed before: a new order of personality, qualified for eternal service, destined for Paradise, capable of representing both the heights of divinity and the depths of creature experience.

I've been teaching this material for decades now, and I confess it never gets old. Every time I walk through these concepts, I'm reminded of the astonishing privilege we've been given. We didn't earn this. We didn't deserve it. God simply chose to share himself with us, to give us fragments of his own nature, to invite us into eternal partnership.

All we have to do is say yes. All we have to do is choose to cooperate with the Adjuster's leading, to develop that habit of divine will, to persist in our spiritual growth no matter how long it takes. The outcome is absolutely guaranteed if we simply don't give up.

In our time to come, we'll shift gears somewhat and begin exploring the foundational universe structures that make all of this possible. Understanding how reality is organized, from Paradise down through the superuniverses to our local universe, gives us context for the journey we've been discussing. We'll look at those slides I've been preparing, the ones I call the "pre-Foreword" material, because they provide the conceptual framework you need to really grasp what *The Urantia Book* is teaching.

But for now, let what we've studied tonight sink in. You're not just a temporary creature living out a brief material existence. You're a potential partner with God, a future administrator of universes, a being destined for Paradise and beyond. The Thought Adjuster within you is patiently, lovingly, faithfully building your eternal soul, transforming your experiences into spiritual realities, preparing you for fusion and for everything that follows.

That's not religious fantasy. That's cosmic fact. And it's the most extraordinary truth you'll ever encounter.

This concludes our study of the Thought Adjuster for now!

Source Materials:

The key source materials can be found and downloaded at:

https://www.youtube.com/@rogerpauldc

Universe Reality Concepts to Understand The Urantia Book:

https://www.youtube.com/playlist?list=PLbPjbuLCH4aj7dpiOnq8rb3Kr, GJkm4pI

Links

Fifth Epochal Revelation http://www.fifthepochalrevelationfellowship.com

https://fifthepochalrevelationfellowship.com/b-i-urantia-book-standardized/papers/contents-book.htm

www.ingramcontent.com/pod-product-compliance
Lightning Source LLC
Chambersburg PA
CBHW080049190426
43201CB00035B/2140